The **Research Log** is your own password-protected workspace on the *Bedford Researcher* Web site. You can use it to complete activities from the text, store your research writing materials, and actively manage your project.

Activities help you link what you learn in the text to your own project. Activities in the text, such as "Generate Research Questions" and "Create Your Working Bibliography," can be completed in the Research Log.

Checklists such as "Avoiding Plagiarism" and "Revising Your Document," located in the Research Log, help you complete research writing tasks.

Tutorials such as "How to Search a Database" and "How to Integrate Quotations" are interactive how-to guides that walk you through research writing processes.

Manuals such as "Online Library Catalogs" and "Designing Web Sites" include information that extends discussions in the text.

On the CD-ROM:
Research Assistant HyperFolio

Manuals	Worksheets	Note Card and Bibliography Tools
	●	
●	●	●
	●	
●	●	●
●	●	●
●		●
		●
		●
	●	●
●		
	●	●
●		●
●		
		●

**Research Assistant HyperFolio
CD-ROM (included with the text)**

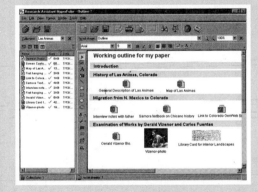

Tools within *Research Assistant,* such as the Note Card and the Bibliography Generator, allow you to collect, evaluate, and document your sources.

Worksheets allow you to organize sources in a format that will help you with your writing. Completing worksheets such as "Positions on an Issue," for example, can help you outline your project document.

The Bedford Researcher

The Bedford Researcher

An Integrated Text, CD-ROM, and Web Site

Mike Palmquist

Colorado State University

BEDFORD/ST. MARTIN'S   Boston ◆ New York

For Bedford/St. Martin's

Developmental Editor: Michelle M. Clark
Production Editor: Deborah Baker
Senior Production Supervisor: Catherine Hetmansky
Marketing Manager: Brian Wheel
Editorial Assistant: Karin Halbert, Erin Durkin
Copyeditor: Barbara G. Flanagan
Text Design: Claire Seng-Niemoeller
Cover Design: Donna Lee Dennison
Cover Art: Compact Disc: © Logan Seale/Photonica. Pen on Notebook: © IPS/
    Photonica. Internet, Globe, and City: © IPS/Photonica.
Composition: Stratford Publishing Services, Inc.
Printing and Binding: R.R. Donnelley & Sons Company

President: Joan E. Feinberg
Editor in Chief: Karen S. Henry
Director of Marketing: Karen Melton
Director of Editing, Design, and Production: Marcia Cohen
Managing Editor: Elizabeth M. Schaaf

Library of Congress Control Number: 2002102562

Manufactured in the United States of America.

6   5   4   3

f   e   d

For information, write: Bedford/St. Martin's, 75 Arlington Street,
Boston, MA 02116
(617-399-4000)

ISBN: 0–312–26013–X (paperback)
ISBN: 0–312–25100–9 (CD-ROM)
ISBN: 0–312–40430–1 (book and CD-ROM)

Acknowledgments

Jenna Alberter, "Images of Women in Seventeenth-Century Dutch Art and Literature."
    Reprinted by permission of the author.
Aaron Batty, "One China . . . ?" Reprinted by permission of the author.

*Acknowledgments and copyrights are continued at the back of the book on pages
417–18, which constitute an extension of the copyright page. It is a violation of
the law to reproduce these selections by any means whatsoever without the written permission of the copyright holder.*

Preface for Instructors

I began planning *The Bedford Researcher* with a single question in mind: What would a research writing textbook be like if it were written from scratch in the twenty-first century? As I began to write, however, I discovered that I needed to ask a more fundamental question: What significant new challenges face twenty-first-century research writers? I found the answer to this question in my own writing classes, where I've helped my students navigate the research writing process in the digital age:

- Because of the explosive growth of the Internet, the challenge for today's researchers has shifted from simply finding sources for a topic to finding sources relevant to a research writer's purpose.

- With the increased presence of electronic and media content in library collections, the line between "library source" and "Web source" has blurred. As a result, college researchers can no longer rely solely on traditional search strategies. In addition, documenting sources — always one of the most daunting parts of research writing — has become even more problematic.

- The ease with which virtually anyone can now publish on the Web means that evaluating sources is both more difficult and more critical.

- With an abundance of electronic, print, and field information available for any topic, collecting and managing sources is a more complex task, and recording bibliographic information accurately has become more essential.

- New technologies such as email, electronic discussion groups, newsgroups, and chatrooms have helped to change static research topics into dynamic conversations.

- Along with the usual rhetorical concerns — such as purpose, audience, and assignment — today's research writers need to consider the context and medium in which their project document will be read. Research writing in academic and professional settings is no longer limited to paper — and is often published electronically and distributed via the Web.

The Bedford Researcher: An Integrated Text, CD-ROM, and Web Site offers a three-part response to these challenges. The textbook combines the ease of use of a handbook with the sustained, example-driven discussions of a rhetoric. The companion software, *Research Assistant: HyperFolio for The Bedford Researcher,* provides a powerful tool for collecting and working with electronic sources. And the companion Web site (**http://www.bedfordresearcher.com**) is genuinely interactive, allowing students to create and save their work in their own database-supported research log.

My focus on the new challenges facing research writers has not meant a lack of attention to traditional hurdles. Today's research writers must still address fundamental concerns: understanding purpose and audience; reading sources critically and taking notes carefully and accurately; developing clear and appropriate thesis statements; integrating information from sources into a draft; and avoiding plagiarism and documenting sources.

The Bedford Researcher is designed to meet both sets of challenges—new and traditional. It does so with a comprehensive, process-oriented text that is supported by two powerful, accessible electronic tools. This integrated package of resources offers a promising means of meeting the new and continuing challenges of research writing in the twenty-first century.

Features

■ An Integrated System for Research and Writing

Three fully integrated learning tools, all cross-referenced to one another, the *Bedford Researcher* supports students as they plan, research, and write source-based documents—in print or online.

1. The Text. *The Bedford Researcher* is based on the premise that the decisions good research writers make are shaped primarily by rhetorical concerns—by the writer's purposes and interests, by the readers' needs and interests, by setting, and by course requirements, time limitations, and opportunities. To illustrate this premise, the book presents research writing as a process of choosing, learning about, joining, and contributing to a conversation of readers and writers.

A Familiar Organization. The text is divided into five parts. The first four parts correspond to the stages of an idealized research writing process, although the book stresses the recursive nature of research writing. The fifth part focuses on documentation systems. Part One, Joining the Conversation, introduces the concept of research writing as a social act. It helps students understand that research writing involves exploring conversations among writers and readers, narrowing their focus to a single conversation, and developing a research question to guide their inquiry into that conversation. Part Two, Collecting Information, helps students create a search plan based on their research question and then search for information using print resources, electronic resources, and field research methods. Part Three, Working with Sources, discusses critical reading strategies, evaluation criteria, note taking, and avoiding plagiarism. Part Four, Writing Your Document, helps students organize their information and ideas, integrate source material, develop an outline, plan and draft their document, revise and edit their drafts, and design their project document. Finally, Part Five, Documenting Sources, provides comprehensive chapters on MLA, APA, *Chicago*, CBE, and Columbia Online styles.

The text also includes three useful appendices. Appendix A presents three sample student research projects—one each in MLA format, APA format, and *Chicago* format. Appendix B presents an annotated list of print, database, and Web resources for more than forty disciplines. Finally, Appendix C is a user's guide for *Research Assistant: HyperFolio for The Bedford Researcher,* the CD-ROM that accompanies the text.

Detailed Case Studies of Student Researchers. Discussions throughout the text are illustrated by eight Featured Writers—students I worked with personally as they crafted a variety of research writing projects, including traditional research essays, Web sites, and feature articles. The emphasis in the text is on real-life examples that your student writers can understand and from which they can learn as they plan and conduct their own research, and draft and revise their own project documents.

Key Information Is Easy to Find. Each chapter is structured around a core set of Key Questions that allows students to find information quickly. In addition, the strategic design features clear and accessible illustrations, checklists, activities, and documentation guidelines—the parts of the text students will return to as they write. Finally, a thorough cross-referencing system directs students to the help they need—within the text, within *Research Assistant,* or on the Web site—when they need it.

Emphasis on Project Management. Managing a research project ranked first when we surveyed teachers to determine the part of the research process students find most difficult. To that end, numerous prompts throughout the text help keep researchers on track. In Chapter 1, students learn how to create and use a Project Timeline to plan and manage their project. Each of the first four parts of the book closes by prompting students to revisit their Project Timeline—in print or online—to monitor their progress.

Fifty Research Activities Promote Interactivity. Easy-to-find "Your Research Project" activities allow students to apply the concepts they learn to their own projects. Although the activities direct students to the Research Log on the Web site or to the *Research Assistant* CD-ROM, they can also be completed by hand in a notebook.

Useful across the Curriculum. Students need a research text suitable for various academic purposes, and *The Bedford Researcher* text, Web site, and CD-ROM feature examples and models from across the disciplines, providing research writing help for composition courses and beyond. Part Five provides guidelines for writing papers in MLA style, APA style, *Chicago* style, and CBE style — and each of these is supported by bibliography tools on the Web site and in the software. The text also includes a full chapter on documenting sources using Columbia Online Style.

2. The CD-ROM. *The Bedford Researcher*'s companion software, *Research Assistant: HyperFolio for The Bedford Researcher* (included free with the text), is a powerful new tool for collecting and managing sources. *Research Assistant* allows students to drag-and-drop sources — including Web pages, passages of text from Web pages, images or media files, database records, email messages, listserv posts, or word processing files — into a collection bin. Additional features allow students to organize the sources they've gathered.

Simplifies Documenting Sources. Automatically generated for every source, Note Cards prompt students not only to identify key ideas and information but also to record important bibliographic information.

Helps Students Evaluate Sources. Note Cards also guide students through evaluating each source, helping them to weigh its reliability and, even more important, its usefulness to their project.

Provides Tools for Analyzing and Organizing Sources. Built-in worksheets give students a flexible set of tools for organizing and presenting their research results. With *Research Assistant,* sources can be dragged from a collection into a worksheet and organized in ways that allow students to arrange their sources chronologically, by cause and effect, by sides of an argument, and so forth — letting them create a graphic outline for their document.

Moves Students into Writing. Since most research assignment writers use sources to write a document, *Research Assistant* allows students to export not only the content of the sources themselves but also a draft bibliography, completed note cards, and any worksheets they've created.

Built-in User's Guide. Students can either use the program's Help function to get them started or see page 403 of the text for a straightforward guide to using *Research Assistant.*

3. The Web Site. The *Bedford Researcher* Web site provides an extensive collection of online materials, including tools and content I designed specifically for an interactive environment.

Unique Interactive Research Log. In an innovative approach to online support for research writing, students create personal accounts on the Research Log and then use it to manage their portfolio of research materials—from planning notes and prewriting to outlines and full drafts. Within the Research Log, students also complete activities from the text, as well as other project-related tasks. The Research Log's Working Bibliography tool allows students to create a working bibliography and to view it in MLA, APA, *Chicago,* or CBE format. Students can print, save to disk, and email any work they've completed in the Research Log, and instructors can view student progress on Research Log activities individually or as a class. Password protection ensures student privacy.

Research Writing Manuals and Tutorials. These illustrate key research writing processes. Manuals, such as Online Library Catalogs, offer additional content. Tutorials, such as How to Integrate Quotations, offer step-by-step help.

Downloadable Checklists and Activities. These practical resources support "Your Research Project" activities found in every chapter of the text.

More on Featured Student Writers. The site provides detailed profiles of the eight student writers whose work is featured in the text. Students can view selected notes, completed activities, and rough and final drafts of research writing projects. They can also view edited transcripts of interviews in which the featured writers discuss their research writing processes.

Annotated Links for Research and Writing Help. From the site, students can access general writing resources, Web search engines and directories for more than sixty disciplines, and lists of print and database resources for those disciplines.

◼ A Thoroughly Cross-Referenced Package

Together, these three resources—the text, the *Research Assistant* CD-ROM, and the Web site—provide an integrated approach to research writing that helps today's students meet new challenges as they research and write. All three *Bedford Researcher* components are cross-referenced, taking students to just the right resources for their research writing needs. Throughout the book, you'll find references to *Research Assistant* and to resources on the Web site—and particularly to Research Log activities. Similarly, you'll find references within *Research Assistant* to the Web site, and on the Web site to the book and software.

Ancillary

■ *Teaching with The Bedford Researcher*

In addition to chapter overviews and specific teaching goals and tips, this practical instructor's manual includes a clear map of the system that directs you to specific resources for each skill that you'll teach (refining a thesis statement or integrating sources, for example) and that illustrates how the book's content aligns with content on the CD-ROM and on the Web site.

Acknowledgments

The work required to write this book, create its companion Web site, and participate in the development of *Research Assistant* has been rewarding, but demanding. Without the support of my family, I would have been unable to complete this project. I owe my wife Jessica, my daughter Ellen, and my son Reid a great deal of gratitude — and many hours of quality time.

I would have been unprepared for the intellectual challenges of this project had it not been for three scholars and friends who helped me start thinking about the relationships among rhetoric, pedagogy, and technology. David Kaufer, Chris Neuwirth, and Richard Young sparked my curiosity about those relationships while I was a graduate student in the mid-1980s and have continued to challenge me to explore them. I am particularly indebted to David and Chris for allowing me to teach with their textbook, *Arguing from Sources,* while it was still in manuscript form. The ideas they developed in that textbook — and in particular the conversation metaphor they used so skillfully — have strongly shaped my thinking about the rhetorical and disciplinary contexts in which student writers find themselves and have influenced not only the approach I've taken in this book but in all the writing courses I've subsequently taught.

I am indebted to my colleagues Kate Kiefer, Stephen Reid, Will Hochman, and Nick Carbone for their willingness to share ideas about research writing and about textbook writing in general. Collectively, their timely advice and encouragement strengthened this book far beyond what I could have accomplished alone. I appreciate the support provided by the reference librarians at Colorado State University's Morgan Library, and in particular the support of Doug Ernst and Tom Moothart. I also thank Paul Barribeau, lecturer at CSU, and Cathy Ackerson Rogers who annotated the lists of disciplinary and writing resources. I am also grateful for the opportunity to work with reviewers who provided thoughtful advice and honest reactions to drafts of this book. I was able to improve the text after reading reviews written by Michael Anzelone, Nassau Community College; Mary M. Balkun, Seton Hall University; Craig Branham, St. Louis University; Paul Cerda, Shoreline Community College; William Condon, Washington State University; Michael Day, Northern Illinois University; Loretta Henderson, Harford Community College; Will Hochman, Southern Connecticut State University; Andrew Jones, University of California at Davis; Michael Mackey, Community College of Denver; Virginia Montecino, George Mason University; Rich Rice, Ball State University; Dawn Rodrigues, University of Texas at Brownsville; Guy Shebat, Mount Union College; Barbara Sitko, Washington State University; Bill Stiffler, Harford Community College; James Stokes, University of Wisconsin at Stevens Point; Molly Tamarkin, Marlboro College; Todd Taylor, University of North Carolina at Chapel Hill; Kevin S. Wilson, Boise State University; and Troy T. Wolff, Shoreline Community College.

I'm also grateful to the following instructors who generously agreed to class test *Research Assistant:* Rick Branscomb, Salem State College; Jeffrey Cain, Sacred Heart University; Bill Church, Missouri Western State College; Gail Corso, Neumann College; Michael Day, Northern Illinois University; Kerri Eglin, Colorado State University; Jeanne Ekdahl, California State University at Hayward; Lorie Goodman, Pepperdine University; Ingrid Johnson, Modesto Junior College; Ellen Kaler, Northwest Missouri State; David LeMaster, San Jacinto College; Gloria Shearin, Savannah State University; Ralph Tufo, North Shore Community College; and Greg Van Belle, Edmonds Community College.

Perhaps the most rewarding part of working on this book has been the extraordinary support I've received from the editors I've worked with at Bedford/St. Martin's. I am fortunate to have worked with two outstanding development editors. Michelle Clark provided thoughtful and encouraging responses throughout this project and her suggestions inspired some of the book's strongest features. Shannon Leuma's well-considered questions and recommendations helped shape the final version of this book. I am grateful to Denise Wydra, director of new media, for her able leadership, wit, and good sense as we worked to integrate the book, the Web site, and *Research Assistant* into a cohesive package. Similarly, I appreciate the work of Katie Schooling, new media specialist, who took on the labyrinthine task of ensuring that *Research Assistant* made the difficult transition from promising beta software to finished product. Katie also served ably as development editor for the Web site.

Many others have contributed in significant ways to *The Bedford Researcher.* Editor in chief Karen Henry offered valuable insights into this project from its inception and provided thoughtful responses to several drafts of the text. New media specialist Nick Carbone made important contributions to the book, the companion Web site, and

Research Assistant. Kathy Retan provided detailed comments on a late draft of this book that resulted in meaningful changes to the opening chapters. I appreciate the good sense of production editor Deborah Baker, who guided a complex and at times unwieldy manuscript through production under the expert direction of managing editor Elizabeth Schaaf. Copyeditor Barbara Flanagan sharpened the prose and asked critical questions. Designer Claire Seng-Niemoeller imagined and executed a clean, attractive, and very practical design. Editorial assistant Erin Durkin helped to annotate the lists of disciplinary resources, and editorial assistant Karin Halbert handled permissions and completed other important tasks with grace. New media editor Harriet Wald conducted early reviews of *Research Assistant,* and new media assistant David Mogolov coordinated the class testing of the software.

This book would not exist without Rory Baruth, regional sales manager for Bedford, Freeman, and Worth Publishers, who introduced me to the editors at Bedford/St. Martin's many years ago. Rory's interest in the work I've done in technology-supported writing instruction and his encouragement as I worked on this project are appreciated. Most of all, I am grateful to Chuck Christensen and Joan Feinberg for their support and encouragement through the long process of moving this project from concept to finished product—and, most importantly, for entrusting a new author with a project of this scope.

Finally, I offer my sincere thanks to the eight student writers who shared their work, their time, and their insights into their research writing processes with the readers of this book: Jenna Alberter, Aaron Batty, Patrick Crossland, Kevin Fahey, Gaele Lopez, Holly Richmond, Maria Sanchez-Traynor, and Rianne Uilk. The many hours we spent discussing their research writing processes helped focus my exploration of the roles textbooks can play in teaching and learning. As I adapted their work for use in this book, their work served as a constant reminder that research writing is a process of continuous discovery and reflection.

Mike Palmquist
Colorado State University

Introduction for Writers

You live in the information age. You surf the Web, use email, carry a personal digital assistant, watch television, read magazines and newspapers, view advertisements, attend public events, and meet and talk with others. Understanding how to work with information is among the most important writing skills you can have. In fact, most of the writing that you'll do in your lifetime—in college courses or for a career or community project—requires this skill. Consider the following types of documents—all of which require a writer to use information from sources:

- college research papers
- informative Web sites
- letters of complaint about a product or service
- product brochures or promotional literature
- market research analysis to help start a new business or launch a new product
- feature articles in a newspaper or magazine
- proposals to a school board or community group
- slide presentations at fund-raising events
- restaurant reviews or travel guides

Given the wide range of documents that rely heavily on a writer's ability to work with information, *The Bedford Researcher* is not so much about research papers as research writing. What I hope you'll take from the text is a way of thinking about conducting research and writing a document based on the sources of information you find.

The primary goals of *The Bedford Researcher* are to help you learn how to:

- choose a topic on which you'll develop a research question and thesis statement
- collect information about your topic from electronic, print, and field sources
- read critically, evaluate, and take notes on the information you've collected

- plan, write, and design an effective document
- document your sources of information

Meeting these goals requires thinking about research writing in a new way. Instead of thinking of research writing as simply collecting and reporting information, think of it as a process of inquiry—of asking and responding to key questions. Instead of thinking of research writing as an isolated activity, think of it as a social act—a conversation in which writers and readers exchange information and ideas about a topic.

The research writing process you'll follow in this book consists of five main activities. These activities correspond to the five parts of this book:

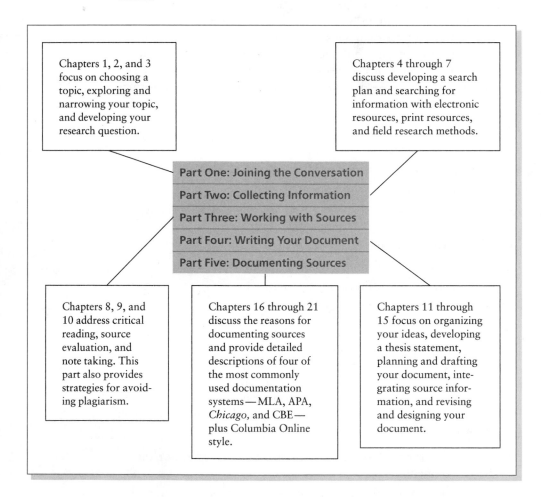

Chapters 1, 2, and 3 focus on choosing a topic, exploring and narrowing your topic, and developing your research question.

Chapters 4 through 7 discuss developing a search plan and searching for information with electronic resources, print resources, and field research methods.

Part One: Joining the Conversation

Part Two: Collecting Information

Part Three: Working with Sources

Part Four: Writing Your Document

Part Five: Documenting Sources

Chapters 8, 9, and 10 address critical reading, source evaluation, and note taking. This part also provides strategies for avoiding plagiarism.

Chapters 16 through 21 discuss the reasons for documenting sources and provide detailed descriptions of four of the most commonly used documentation systems—MLA, APA, *Chicago,* and CBE—plus Columbia Online style.

Chapters 11 through 15 focus on organizing your ideas, developing a thesis statement, planning and drafting your document, integrating source information, and revising and designing your document.

As you read about these activities and carry them out in your own research project, keep in mind that these reflect a typical writing process—not a step-by-step recipe. Whatever your process turns out to be, remember that the order in which you engage in these processes is far less important than adapting these processes to the needs of your particular project.

Three Resources Supporting Your Research Writing Process

The Bedford Researcher is really three resources that work together to help you complete a research project:

■ The Text

The textbook you are holding provides step-by-step guidance for writing research documents. It includes clear descriptions of research writing strategies, helpful examples, activities, documentation guidelines, and help with finding resources in over forty disciplines such as biology, history, marketing, and women's studies.

Key Questions begin each chapter and help you match your research writing needs to the material in the chapter.

Key Questions		
2a.	What strategies can I use to explore my topic?	20
2b.	What strategies can I use to narrow my topic?	34
2c.	How can I create my working bibliography?	44

◄ Your Research Project Activities connect what's in the text with your own research and writing.

Your Research Project

RECORD YOUR SEARCHES

One of the most important research strategies you can use as you collect information is keeping track of your searches. Note not only the keywords or phrases and the search strategies you used with them (wildcards, Boolean search, author search, and so on) but also how many sources the search turned up and whether those sources were relevant to your research project.

In your research log, record the following information for each source you search:

1. Resource that was searched
2. Search terms used (keywords, phrases, publication information)
3. Search strategies used (simple search, wildcard search, exact phrase search, Boolean search)
4. Date search was conducted
5. Number of results produced by the search
6. Relevance of the results
7. Notes about the search

If you'd like to complete this activity online, use the **Research Log** activity "Record Your Searches" at **http://www.bedford researcher.com**. If you have created a research log using a notebook or a word processor, you can print or download this activity.

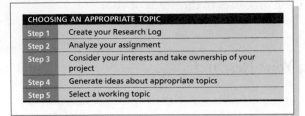

CHOOSING AN APPROPRIATE TOPIC	
Step 1	Create your Research Log
Step 2	Analyze your assignment
Step 3	Consider your interests and take ownership of your project
Step 4	Generate ideas about appropriate topics
Step 5	Select a working topic

Process Boxes offer a quick glance at a specific research or writing process.

Marginal References direct you to related material within the text, on the Web site, or on the *Research Assistant* CD-ROM.

IN THIS BOOK

Read more about searching online library catalogs on p. 81.

ON THE WEB SITE

Create your working bibliography in the **Research Log** on the *Bedford Researcher* Web site.

RESEARCH ASSISTANT

Use the worksheet Grouping Your Sources to place your sources into categories.

Project Timelines help you keep track of your progress from choosing a topic to submitting your final document.

PROJECT TIMELINE		
ACTIVITY	**START DATE**	**COMPLETION DATE**
Select your topic		
Explore your topic		
Narrow your topic to a single conversation		
Develop your research question		
Develop your plan to collect and manage information		
Collect information		
Read and evaluate information		
Take notes		
Organize your information		
Create your document outline		
Develop your thesis statement		
Write the first draft of your project document		
Review and revise your first draft		
Review and revise additional drafts		
Edit your draft		
Finalize in-text and end-of-text citations		
Design your document		
Publish and submit your project document		

Annotated Examples make it easier for you to learn from the many illustrations and screen shots throughout the text.

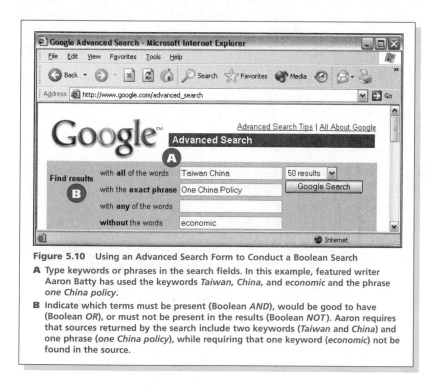

Figure 5.10   Using an Advanced Search Form to Conduct a Boolean Search

A Type keywords or phrases in the search fields. In this example, featured writer Aaron Batty has used the keywords *Taiwan, China,* and *economic* and the phrase *one China policy.*

B Indicate which terms must be present (Boolean *AND*), would be good to have (Boolean *OR*), or must not be present in the results (Boolean *NOT*). Aaron requires that sources returned by the search include two keywords (*Taiwan* and *China*) and one phrase (*one China policy*), while requiring that one keyword (*economic*) not be found in the source.

Color-coded Edging helps you find documentation guidelines quickly.

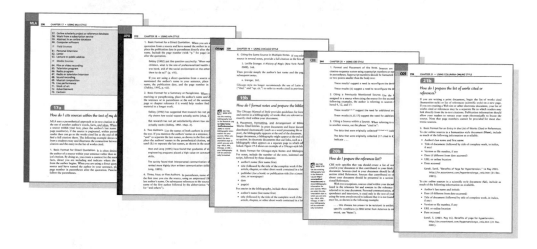

■ The CD-ROM

Research Assistant, a software application included in the back of the text, helps you do research by simplifying the most complex parts of the research process: collecting, evaluating, organizing, and documenting sources. A User's Guide (see page 403) is included in the text.

Note Cards, automatically created for each source you collect, prompt you to record important documentation information and help you to determine if a source is reliable and useful.

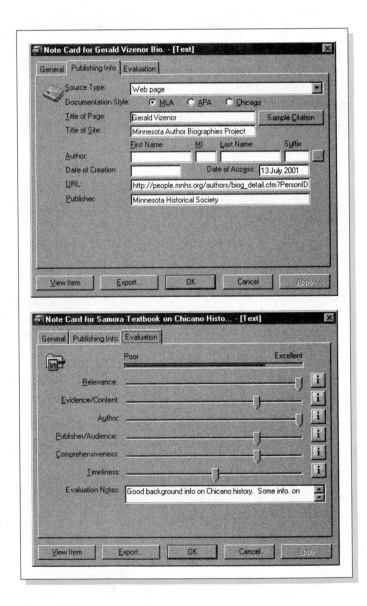

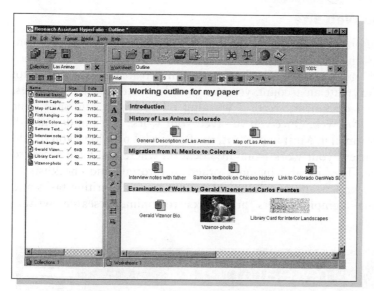

◄ **Built-in Work-sheets** help you organize your sources and plan your document.

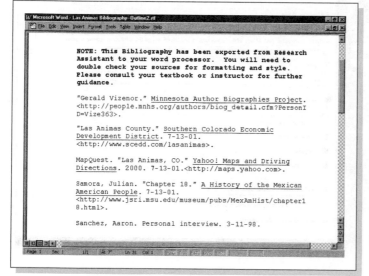

◄ **The Bibliography Tool** helps you generate a draft bibliography in MLA, APA, *Chicago,* or CBE documentation style.

■ The Web Site

The *Bedford Researcher* Web site at **http://www.bedfordresearcher.com** includes an innovative Research Log that helps you to manage your research project online. Think of it as your private research portfolio; once you create an account, you can complete activities, record notes, plan your document, create a working bibliography, and save your work on the Web. Once you've saved your work, you can download, print, or email it. Most important, the Research Log allows you to add to or retrieve your work from any location where you have access to the Web. The site also includes practical tutorials and checklists to help you understand and complete certain research writing tasks and additional sample papers and links to online research writing resources.

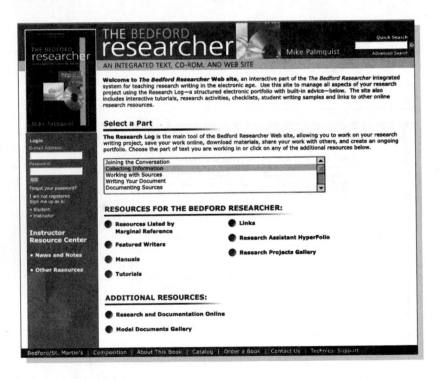

Brief Contents

Contents

Part I *Joining the Conversation*   1

1 Getting Started: Choosing an Appropriate Topic   3

2 Exploring and Narrowing Your Topic   20

Part II   *Collecting Information*   59

Part IV   *Writing Your Document*   181

11   Organizing and Outlining   183

12   Drafting Your Document   197

Part V   *Documenting Sources*   281

16   Understanding Why You Should Document Your Sources   283

17   Using MLA Style   288

21 **Using Columbia Online Style** 353

Part One

Joining the Conversation

1. **Getting Started: Choosing an Appropriate Topic**
2. **Exploring and Narrowing Your Topic**
3. **Developing Your Research Question**

Working on a research writing project is similar to joining a conversation. Before making your contribution to the discussion, listen carefully to what others are saying. By reading widely, talking with knowledgeable people, and observing firsthand, you can gain the knowledge you need to add your voice to the conversation.

In Part One of *The Bedford Researcher,* you'll read about how to choose an appropriate topic, how to explore and narrow your topic, and how to develop your research question.

CHAPTER 1

Getting Started: Choosing an Appropriate Topic

Getting started can be the hardest part of a research writing project. If you're like many research writers, you'll find yourself staring at a blank computer screen or twirling a pen in your fingers as you ask, "Is this project really necessary?" or "What in the world should I write about?" You might feel overwhelmed at first and not know exactly how to start.

This chapter helps you get started on your research writing project. It begins with a simple question with a surprisingly rich answer—How can I choose an appropriate topic?—and continues with a discussion of strategies you can use to select and prepare to explore a topic.

Key Questions

1a.	How can I choose an appropriate topic?	3
1b.	How can I prepare to explore my topic?	17

1a

How can I choose an appropriate topic?

In the most general sense, your topic is what you will research and write about—it is the foundation on which your research writing project is built. An *appropriate* topic, however, is much more than a simple subject heading in an almanac or encyclopedia. It is a subject of debate, discussion, and discovery. It is of interest not only to you but to your readers. It is, most importantly, a topic of conversation.

Thinking of your topic as a topic of conversation rather than as a static label for a particular set of ideas and information is critical to your success as a research writer. Research writing goes beyond merely locating and reporting information. Instead, research writing is an ongoing process of inquiry in which you must balance your purposes and interests with those of your readers as you explore and discuss ideas, issues, and information.

As you get started on your research writing project, you'll find that locating a topic is as easy as visiting your library, reading the newspaper, or browsing the World Wide Web. Choosing a topic that is well suited to your research writing project, however, requires additional work. It involves considering your assignment, your interests and experiences, and the needs and interests of your readers. To choose an appropriate topic, work through these five steps.

CHOOSING AN APPROPRIATE TOPIC	
Step 1	Create your Research Log
Step 2	Analyze your assignment
Step 3	Consider your interests and take ownership of your project
Step 4	Generate ideas about appropriate topics
Step 5	Select a working topic

■ Step 1: Create Your Research Log

If you've ever forgotten a phone number or misplaced tickets to a concert, you know how frustrating it can be to lose something. It can be just as frustrating to lose your interview notes or forget where you found a quotation or fact. When you're just starting to generate ideas and collect information, you can easily forget information that might prove useful later. As you begin your research writing project, decide how you'll keep track of ideas and information. A *research log*—a place where you can record your thoughts, observations, and progress—can help you keep track of what you find and think about as you work on a research project. A research log can take many forms:

- a simple notebook
- a word processing file
- a folder or binder
- a set of note cards
- notes taken on a personal digital assistant (such as a Palm handheld or the Handspring Visor)
- a tape recorder

Although it might seem like extra work now, creating a research log as you begin your project can save time in the long run.

Your Research Project

CREATE YOUR RESEARCH LOG ACCOUNT

The *Bedford Researcher* Web site at **http://www.bedfordresearcher .com** includes an electronic **Research Log** that helps you generate ideas, record information, and plan your research writing project. To use the **Research Log**, you'll need to create an account. (Directions for doing so are on the *Bedford Researcher* Web site.) After you create an account, you can log in using your email address and your password (which you'll choose when you set up your account).

The **Research Log** includes many resources you can use as you complete your research writing project. You can keep track of your progress with the Project Timeline tool, and you can create and maintain your working bibliography. You can generate ideas about your topic with brainstorming, freewriting, looping, and clustering activities, and you can plan your search for information. In addition, when you're ready, you can use the **Research Log** to download, print, or email your activities. Most important, the **Research Log** allows you to store your work on your research writing project on the Web — safely and privately. Only you — and your instructor, if you choose — can view your work.

If you decide that you'd rather create a research log using, for instance, a notebook or a word processor, you can still take advantage of the activities found in the **Research Log** on the Web site. Each activity can be printed or downloaded as a word processing file.

■ Step 2: Analyze Your Assignment

Once you've created your research log, you're ready to analyze your research writing assignment. Research writers in most academic and professional settings usually work in response to an assignment. In some cases, your assignment will carefully define your topic. More often, however, your assignment will provide general guidelines that help you select a topic — or leave the choice of topic completely up to you.

Analyzing an assignment requires careful thinking about your research writing situation: your purpose for starting the project, the needs and interests of your readers, the requirements and limitations of your project, and the opportunities you can take advantage of as you work on your project. Occasionally, you might start a research project strictly on your own. Although you won't need to formally analyze an assignment in this case, you'll still find it helpful to reflect on your research writing situation as it applies to potential topics.

To analyze your assignment, ask yourself a series of questions about your research writing situation.

What Is the Purpose of My Project?   Every writer has a purpose, or reason, for writing. In fact, most writers have multiple purposes. If you are a student writing a research project for a class, your purposes might include completing the assignment as required, learning something new, improving your writing skills, convincing others to adopt your point of view about an issue, and getting a good grade. If you are an employee working on a project status report, your purposes might include conveying key information to your superiors, performing well enough to earn a promotion, and gaining valuable experience in project management.

Whatever your purposes for conducting a research writing project, your topic should help you accomplish them. Patrick Crossland, a student writer whose work is featured in this book and on the *Bedford Researcher* Web site, was assigned in his introductory writing class to write an informative research paper on a topic of interest to college students. During the time that he worked on his research project, Patrick was considering transferring to another college or university, a common consideration for many college students. By focusing on the general topic of college admissions, Patrick was able to address both his personal reason for writing and the purposes defined by his assignment.

Who Are My Readers and What Are Their Needs and Interests?
Your research writing assignment may identify your readers, or audience, for you. If you are writing a research project for a class, one of your most important readers will be your instructor. However, you are likely to have additional readers, such as your classmates, people who have a professional or personal interest in your topic, or, should your

---

Featured Writer

Writing an Informative Research Paper about College Admissions Standards

Featured writer Patrick Crossland wrote a research essay about college admissions standards. Throughout the semester, Patrick worked in a group with four classmates. Although each student wrote his or her own essay, the students shared ideas and sources.

You can learn more about Patrick's research writing process by visiting the *Bedford Researcher* Web site at **http://www.bedfordresearcher.com** and clicking on Featured Writers. You can read excerpts of interviews in which Patrick discusses his work on his research project, view the notes he took as he worked on his project, and read drafts of his research essay.

project be published in print or online, the readers of a particular magazine, journal, or Web site. If you are writing in a business or professional setting, your readers might include supervisors, customers, or other people associated with the organization. In addition, your readers may be the writers of sources that you use in your research writing project—writers who share your interest in your topic and who might want to respond to what you will eventually write.

Kevin Fahey, a writer whose work is featured in this book, wrote a research essay for an introductory literature class. His assignment required him to address an audience of literary scholars—such as his instructor—who had an interest in his topic. As he considered various topics, he thought about the stories and poems he'd read so far in class, which included a number of Ernest Hemingway's short stories. He was intrigued by some of the apparent conflicts he'd seen between Nick Adams's reputation among literary scholars as a "man's man" and the manner in which Hemingway characterized his popular protagonist. Ultimately, he decided that an essay on Hemingway's work would be consistent with the needs, interests, and expectations of his readers.

In some cases, you might be asked to define your own audience. As you consider possible topics, ask yourself what these readers would be most interested in learning about. You would probably not write about the literature of Ernest Hemingway, for example, if your target audience was the reader of a magazine such as *PC World* or *Street Rod*.

Regardless of who your readers are, remember that they aren't empty vessels waiting to be filled with information. They will have their own purposes for reading your project document. If the topic you ultimately select doesn't address their needs and interests, they're

Writing an Analytic Research Essay about Ernest Hemingway's Characterization of Nick Adams

Featured writer Kevin Fahey wrote a research essay about Ernest Hemingway's characterization of Nick Adams, the character whom Hemingway scholars agree most closely resembles Hemingway himself.

You can learn more about Kevin's research writing process by visiting the *Bedford Researcher* Web site at **http://www .bedfordresearcher.com** and clicking on Featured Writers. You can read excerpts of interviews in which Kevin discusses his work on his research project, view the notes he took as he worked on his project, and read drafts of his research essay.

Featured Writer

likely to stop reading. As you examine potential topics, put yourself in the place of your readers and ask whether each topic is something you'd want to read more about.

What Are My Requirements and Limitations? Research writers — and the research writing situations in which they find themselves — are seldom free of requirements and limitations. If you are writing your research project for a class, you will have to examine the requirements of the assignment. As you analyze your assignment, consider the following factors:

- the required length or page count
- the project due date
- the number and/or type of sources you can use (electronic, print, and field)
- any suggested or required resources
- specific requirements about the organization and structure of your document (a title page, introduction, body, conclusion, works cited list, and so on)
- expected documentation format (such as MLA, APA, *Chicago*, or CBE)
- any intermediate reports or activities due before you turn in the final project document (such as thesis statements, notes, outlines, and rough drafts)

IN THIS BOOK
Read about organization on p. 183. Read about sections typically included in research writing documents on p. 197.

IN THIS BOOK
Read about MLA, APA, *Chicago,* and CBE styles in Part 5, on p. 281.

In addition to these requirements, you may face certain limitations, such as lack of access to information or lack of time to work on your project.

Considering your requirements and limitations will help you weigh the potential drawbacks of choosing a particular topic. Featured writer Patrick Crossland, for example, initially planned to research the broad topic of college admissions. He soon realized that he would need to narrow the scope of his topic significantly to meet the requirements of his assignment, which included a project due date and a page limit. He decided that an *appropriate* topic for his assignment — one that he could handle given his time and page limit — would be college admissions standards.

What Are My Opportunities? Sometimes writers get so wrapped up in the requirements and the limitations of the assignment that they overlook their opportunities. As you think about your topic, ask yourself whether you can take advantage of opportunities such as:

- access to a specialized or particularly good library
- personal experience with and knowledge about a topic
- access to people who are experts on a topic

Creating a Web Site about China-Taiwan Relations

Featured writer Aaron Batty created a Web site about relations between China and Taiwan and the impact of that relationship on the United States.

You can follow Aaron's research writing process by visiting the *Bedford Researcher* Web site at **http://www.bedfordresearcher.com** and clicking on Featured Writers. You can read excerpts of interviews in which Aaron discusses his work on his research project, view the notes he took as he worked on his project, and see drafts of his Web site.

You can also view pages from his Web site in Appendix A on p. 370.

Aaron Batty, a student writer whose work is featured in this book, was asked to create an informative Web site about a current event or issue. An English major with a minor in Japanese and Asian studies, Aaron had spent a year studying in Japan. During his year abroad, he had also spent a month in Hong Kong and mainland China. As he considered the topics he could write about, he thought about his knowledge of Asian affairs. Ultimately, he decided to focus on relations between China and Taiwan.

Your Research Project

ANALYZE YOUR RESEARCH WRITING ASSIGNMENT

In your research log, use the following questions to analyze your research writing assignment and to generate ideas about a potential topic:

1. Has a topic been assigned? If so, what is it? If not, what ideas do I have so far?

2. What are the purposes—both personal and as defined by the assignment—of my research writing project? What topics would help me accomplish that purpose?

3. Who are my primary readers and what topics are they interested in reading about? What topics do they need to read about?

4. What requirements or limitations in my assignment will affect my choice of topic? Are any of the topics I've considered too broad for my requirements?

   • What is the required length of the project?

   • When is the project due?

(continued)

- Are there requirements about the number and types of sources I should use?
- Have any resources been suggested or required?
- Is a specific type of organization and structure required?
- Is a particular documentation format expected?
- Are any rough drafts or other activities due before the final due date?

5. What opportunities can I take advantage of as I choose a topic?

If you'd like to complete this activity online, use the **Research Log** activity "Analyze Your Research Writing Assignment" at **http://www.bedfordresearcher.com**. If you have created a research log using a notebook or a word processor, you can print or download this activity.

■ Step 3: Consider Your Interests and Take Ownership of Your Project

Research writers aren't mindless robots who churn through sources and create documents without emotion or conviction—or at least they shouldn't be. Your topic should interest you. An interesting topic will keep you motivated as you carry out the work needed to complete your research writing project successfully. As you weigh alternative topics, ask yourself whether they intrigue you, whether they arouse strong feelings in you, or whether learning more about them might help you personally, academically, or professionally.

Your project should also be your own, even if it's been assigned to you. One of the most important things you can do as a research writer is to take ownership of your project, which means making a personal connection with the topic. Holly Richmond, a student writer whose work is featured in this book, was assigned to create an informative Web site. She chose her topic, the history of her family, because it fit one of the purposes of her assignment and because it was personally interesting to her. Similarly, featured writers Aaron Batty and Patrick Crossland considered their personal experiences as they decided what topics to pursue. For Aaron, the strong interest he had developed in China-Taiwan relations during his year studying abroad helped him choose his topic. For Patrick, the topic of college admissions was personally relevant to his research writing assignment because he was considering transferring to another college.

By examining their interests and choosing topics that reflected those interests, Holly, Aaron, and Patrick were each able to take ownership of their research writing projects. To take ownership of your project, look for ways in which your topic can help you pursue your personal, professional, and academic interests.

Creating a Family History Web Site

Holly Richmond created a family history Web site. Her project presented problems that she'd never encountered while writing a research paper, including difficulties locating sources and working with unpublished materials. "On the other hand," she said, "this project has been the most enjoyable and personally rewarding research I've done."

You can follow Holly's research writing process by visiting the *Bedford Researcher* Web site at **http://www.bedfordresearcher.com** and clicking on Featured Writers. You can read excerpts of interviews in which she discusses her work and view her Web site.

■ Step 4: Generate Ideas about Appropriate Topics

By now you should have some ideas of topics that interest you and that fit your research writing situation. Your next step in choosing an appropriate topic is to think more carefully about potential topics using prewriting activities such as brainstorming, freewriting, looping, and clustering. These activities will help you determine whether a topic is well suited to your research writing situation. You can also use these activities to generate possible topics and narrow your focus from broad, general topics to those that would be more appropriate for a research writing project. For instance, if you were interested in writing about the general topic of education, you might prewrite to focus on the role of religion in public education.

Brainstorming.   Brainstorming involves making a list of ideas as they occur to you. This list should not consist of complete sentences—in fact, brainstorming lists are meant to record the many ideas that come into your head as you think of them. Most often, brainstorming sessions are conducted in response to a specific question, such as "What do my readers need to know about this topic?" Brainstorming is most successful when you avoid censoring yourself. Typically, you'll end up using only a few of the ideas you generate during brainstorming, but don't worry about weeding out the useful ideas from the less promising ones until later.

Featured writer Aaron Batty thought that he wanted to write about China-Taiwan relations, but he wasn't sure how his topic would fit into his research writing situation. Aaron's brainstorming included the following responses to the question "What interests me academically about this project?"

Complexity of relationship between China and Taiwan
Taiwan as rightful property of China
Interesting history—different ethnic groups
Idea of Chinese unity
Impact on U.S./world
Use of force—a threat that goes beyond the two countries' borders

Brainstorming can also help you get started on your project by creating a list of potential topics. Whatever the focus of your brainstorming, you can use the ideas you generate as the basis for other activities, such as freewriting and looping.

Your Research Project
BRAINSTORMING A LIST OF POTENTIAL TOPICS
Use brainstorming to generate responses to the following questions:

- What do I want to accomplish with this project?
- What interests me personally about this project?
- What interests me academically about this project?
- Who are my readers?
- What topics do my readers need to read about?
- What topics would my readers like to read about?

If you'd like to complete this activity online, use the **Research Log** activity "Brainstorm about Potential Topics" at **http://www .bedfordresearcher.com**. If you have created a research log using a notebook or a word processor, you can print or download this activity.

Freewriting. Freewriting is another effective prewriting activity for generating topics or ideas for potential topics. Freewriting involves writing full sentences quickly, without stopping and—most important—without editing what you write. You might want to start with one of the ideas you generated in your brainstorming activity, or you can begin your freewriting session with a phrase such as "I am interested in my topic because . . ." Some writers set a timer and freewrite for five, ten, or fifteen minutes; others set a goal of a certain number of pages and keep writing until they have met that goal. (*Hint:* If you find it difficult to write without editing, try *blindwriting*—freewriting on a computer with the monitor turned off.)

After brainstorming about the general topic of college admissions, featured writer Patrick Crossland began to freewrite about his readers' needs and interests. The following is an excerpt from Patrick's freewriting:

People seem to love statistics. My readers may want to know about the statistics of who's getting into what colleges and why. My readers may want to use my information as a source for their own writing or thinking about the subject. They may also want to contest/agree with my stand and viewpoints about how students are admitted to college. They may even think they know how schools go about the process, like using SAT scores and activities and sometimes race.

Note that Patrick did not edit his work or worry about grammar or style as he wrote; his main goal was to generate ideas. By thinking about his readers' needs and interests, Patrick could begin thinking about specific aspects of his general topic of college admissions.

When you're done freewriting, identify the ideas you find most useful. You can use the results of your freewriting session as the basis for looping activities.

Your Research Project

FREEWRITE ABOUT POTENTIAL TOPICS
Begin freewriting by using one of the following prompts, replacing the *X*'s with the ideas for topics that you generated during your brainstorming session. Before you begin, set a goal of a certain number of minutes or a set amount of pages you will write.

- Writing about *X* will help me accomplish the following purposes:
- I am personally interested in *X* because . . .
- I am academically interested in *X* because . . .
- My readers need or would like to know about *X* because . . .

If you'd like to complete this activity online, use the **Research Log** activity "Freewrite about Potential Topics" at **http://www .bedfordresearcher.com**. If you have created a research log using a notebook or a word processor, you can print or download this activity.

Looping.   Looping is an alternative form of freewriting. During a looping session, you write for a set amount of time (say five minutes) and then go back and read what you've written. As you read, identify one key idea in what you've written and then write for five minutes with the new key idea as your starting point. By repeating this process, you can refine your thinking about a potential topic or come up with an entirely new topic.

Featured writer Patrick Crossland wrote the following sentence about his readers' interests in his freewriting activity:

My readers may want to know about the statistics of who's getting into what colleges and why.

In a looping exercise, Patrick might have taken this idea and written about it for another five minutes. In doing so, he might have generated a sentence such as this one:

> My readers will be both my professor, who has already gone through college, and my fellow students, who may be looking to transfer to other colleges or apply to graduate schools someday — what aspect of college admissions will all of these readers be interested in?

Patrick could then freewrite for another five minutes about this sentence, generating more and more ideas about his readers and helping him decide on a topic that suits his purpose and is consistent with his assignment.

Your Research Project

LOOPING TO GENERATE IDEAS ABOUT POTENTIAL TOPICS
In your research log, complete the following looping exercise.

1. Freewrite for five minutes about an aspect of your writing situation, such as your purposes, your interests, or your readers' needs and interests.
2. Identify the best idea in your freewriting session.
3. Copy and paste the idea at the bottom of your word processing file or write it at the bottom of a page in your notebook. Then freewrite for five more minutes about the idea.
4. Identify the best idea in this second freewriting session.
5. Freewrite for five more minutes about the idea you've identified.
6. Repeat the process until you've refined your idea into a clear definition of part of your research writing situation.

If you'd like to complete this activity online, use the **Research Log** activity "Looping to Generate Ideas about a Potential Topic" at **http://www.bedfordresearcher.com**. If you have created a research log using a notebook or a word processor, you can print or download this activity.

IN THIS BOOK
Read more about clustering on p. 185.

Clustering. Clustering involves presenting your ideas about a potential topic in graphical form. Clustering can help you gain a different and potentially useful perspective on a topic by helping you map out the relationships among your ideas about the topic. In addition, it can help you generate new ideas for a topic.

Featured writer Patrick Crossland used clustering to map out his ideas and further narrow his topic (see Figure 1.1). He began his clustering activity by writing a phrase he had generated while freewriting: "Who is getting into what colleges?" By reflecting on his research writ-

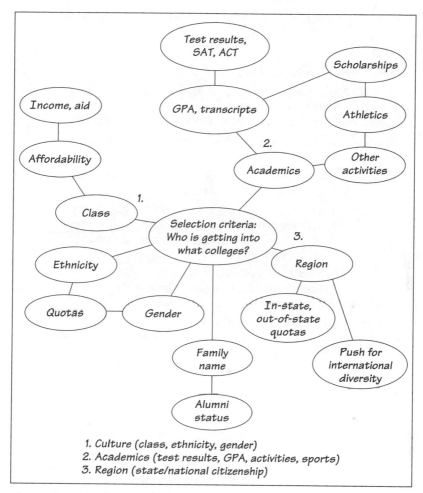

Test results, SAT, ACT

Scholarships

Income, aid

GPA, transcripts

Athletics

Affordability

2.

Other activities

Academics

1.

Class

Selection criteria: Who is getting into what colleges?

3.

Region

Ethnicity

Quotas — Gender

In-state, out-of-state quotas

Family name

Push for international diversity

Alumni status

1. Culture (class, ethnicity, gender)
2. Academics (test results, GPA, activities, sports)
3. Region (state/national citizenship)

Figure 1.1   A Cluster of Ideas Created by Patrick Crossland

Note how one of Patrick's bubbles, "Region," leads to a second bubble: "In-state, out-of-state quotas." By examining the relationships among ideas in this way, you can generate new and useful ideas about a potential topic. At the bottom of the page, Patrick noted the three key areas affecting admissions that emerged from his clustering activity.

ing situation, he identified three key areas that he wanted to explore: the cultural, academic, and regional factors that affect admissions decisions. He noted these ideas at the bottom of his cluster.

When you have completed your brainstorming, freewriting, looping, and clustering activities, review what you've written. You'll find that using these prewriting techniques to define your purpose, your interests, and your readers' needs and interests will help you select your topic.

> ## Your Research Project
> ### CLUSTERING TO VISUALIZE YOUR IDEAS
> ### ABOUT A POTENTIAL TOPIC
> In your research log, complete the following clustering exercise.
>
> 1. Review any brainstorming, freewriting, or looping exercises that you have done.
> 2. Write down the most important idea about the topic you are considering for your research writing project.
> 3. Identify ideas that are related to your central idea and write them near it. Think about the importance and relevance of each related idea, and draw lines and circles to show the relationships among your ideas.
> 4. Write additional ideas related to the ideas in Step 3. In turn, draw lines and circles to show their relationships to the other ideas in your cluster.
> 5. Repeat the process until you've created a cluster of ideas that represents your current understanding of the topic you are considering.

■ Step 5: Select a Working Topic

After you've spent time thinking and prewriting about potential topics for your research project, you should select the strongest candidate.

As you make your choice, think carefully again about the level of interest both you and your readers might have in the topic. Some topics, such as Patrick Crossland's, will appeal to a large number of people, including high school students applying to colleges, college students who might not have been accepted by their top choices, and the parents of these students. Other topics, such as Aaron Batty's (Taiwan-China relations), might appeal to a somewhat smaller group of readers, such as political science or foreign relations enthusiasts and China watchers. Still other topics, such as the ethical implications of drug-testing procedures in clinical studies, might appeal to a much smaller group of readers. The key is to identify which topics—whether they will interest many readers or only a handful of researchers—are compatible with your *purpose*, your *interests*, and your *readers' needs and interests*.

In addition, remember that your working topic is subject to change. It's a starting point, not necessarily a final destination. Remember as well that the topic you begin with is likely to be far broader than you expected. Most writers, as a result, find that they need to explore and narrow their topic.

📖 **IN THIS BOOK**
Read more about narrowing your topic on p. 34.

1b

How can I prepare to explore my topic?

You can learn about your topic by reading widely, observing, and talking with people who know about or have experiences related to your topic. At this early stage in your research writing process, your best strategy is to conduct a general exploration of your subject. Your goal is to find out what people are saying about the topic. That is, you want to map out the *conversations* taking place about the topic. Before you start exploring, however, you should take the time to create an informal plan and a project timeline that can guide your exploration.

■ Create an Informal Plan to Explore Your Topic

Think of your informal plan as a set of directions for locating, collecting, and managing information about your topic. The most common elements of a plan for exploring your topic include:

- a list of **people** with whom you can discuss your topic, such as people who know a great deal about the subject; people who can help you locate information about your topic, such as librarians; and people who have been affected in some way by your topic

- a list of **questions** to ask people who can help you explore your topic

- a list of **settings** you might observe to learn more about your topic

- a list of types of **resources** to search and browse, such as library catalogs, databases, Web search engines, and Web directories

- a **system** for keeping track of the information you collect

IN THIS BOOK

Read about interviewing on p. 124 and observing on p. 127.

IN THIS BOOK

Read more about electronic resources, such as library catalogs, databases, and Web search engines and directories, in Chapter 5 on p. 81. Read more about print resources in Chapter 6 on p. 112.

After you write your plan, use it to guide your exploration and to remind yourself of steps you might overlook in the midst of your exploration. A note such as "talk to Professor Garvey about recent clinical studies" can come in handy if you've become so engrossed in searching the Web or your library's catalog that you forget about your other plans for exploring your topic.

After you've drafted your plan, print it or photocopy it and share it with your instructor, your supervisor, or a librarian, who might suggest additional resources, shortcuts, and alternative strategies for exploring your topic. Then take notes on the feedback you receive and, if necessary, revise your plan.

Your Research Project

CREATE A PLAN TO EXPLORE YOUR TOPIC
In your research log, answer the following questions.

1. Who can help me learn more about my topic?
2. What questions should I ask people on my list?
3. What settings can I observe to learn more about my topic?
4. What resources can I search or browse to learn more about my topic?
5. How can I keep track of information I collect as I explore my topic?

Using your responses, write your plan as a series of steps and ask your instructor, your supervisor, or a librarian to review it.

If you'd like to complete this activity online, use the **Research Log** activity "Create a Plan to Explore Your Topic" at **http://www .bedfordresearcher.com**. If you have created a research log using a notebook or a word processor, you can print or download this activity.

■ Create a Project Timeline

As you complete your informal exploration plan, consider creating a project timeline. A project timeline can help you identify important milestones in your research writing project and determine when you need to meet them. At this point in your research writing process, you've completed your first milestone: selecting an appropriate topic. Next, you should make sure to plot the steps in your process and set start and completion dates for each one.

Your Research Project

CREATE A PROJECT TIMELINE
In your research log, create a project timeline like the one shown here. The steps in your process might be slightly different, but most research writing projects follow this general process. As you create your timeline, keep in mind any specific requirements of your assignment, such as handing in first drafts, revised first drafts, and so on.

PROJECT TIMELINE

ACTIVITY	START DATE	COMPLETION DATE
Select your topic		
Explore your topic		
Narrow your topic to a single conversation		

Develop your research question

Develop your plan to collect and manage information

Collect information

Read and evaluate information

Take notes

Organize your information

Create your document outline

Develop your thesis statement

Write the first draft of your project document

Review and revise your first draft

Write and revise additional drafts

Edit your draft

Finalize in-text and end-of-text citations

Design your document

Publish and submit your project document

If you'd like to complete this activity online, use the **Research Log** activity "Create a Project Timeline" at **http://www .bedfordresearcher.com**. If you have created a research log using a notebook or a word processor, you can print or download this activity.

In the long run, thinking carefully about potential topics and planning your topic exploration will save time and effort. It is far easier to research and write about your topic if you take the time to listen to and reflect on what is being said before you add your voice to the discussion. The next chapter discusses how to explore your topic and narrow it to a single conversation.

CHAPTER 2

Exploring and Narrowing Your Topic

Once you have selected a working topic, your next step is to further explore and narrow that topic. When you explore your topic, you conduct a wide-ranging search for conversations taking place about it. This search provides you with enough information so that you can begin narrowing in on a single, well-defined conversation about your topic. After you've narrowed your topic to a single conversation, you can develop a research question that will guide the remaining work on your project.

This chapter presents strategies for exploring and narrowing your topic and for keeping track of your sources. In this chapter, you will continue your research writing project by considering the following questions.

Key Questions

2a.	What strategies can I use to explore my topic?	20
2b.	What strategies can I use to narrow my topic?	34
2c.	How can I create my working bibliography?	44

2a

What strategies can I use to explore my topic?

Beginning to explore your topic is similar to attending a public meeting on a controversial issue. Imagine yourself at a meeting about a proposed development in your neighborhood. You're uncertain about whether to support or oppose the development, but it seems as though all the others at the meeting have made up their minds. After an hour of people shouting back and forth across the room, the moderator suggests a break to allow tempers to cool.

During the break, you wander from one group of people to another. Everyone is talking about the same topic, but the *conversations* are radically different. In one group, four people who bitterly oppose the development are talking about how to stop it. In another group, a developer is attempting to explain the steps that will be taken to minimize the development's impact on the neighborhood. Other groups discuss alternatives to the development, the impact on property values, and the increased traffic that will be generated by the development. As you wander around the room, you listen for information to help you decide which conversation you want to join. Eventually, you join the group discussing alternatives to development because it interests you most.

This process is similar to the strategies you'll use to explore and narrow your topic. At this early stage in your research writing project, you have a working topic, but you'll need to spend more time wandering around your topic, listening in on various conversations, before you'll know how to narrow it. At this early stage, you are not exploring any conversation in depth; rather, you are looking at what conversations are taking place about your topic so that you can narrow your focus to a particular conversation.

Exploring a topic involves five basic steps that build on the plan you created in Chapter 1.

EXPLORING YOUR TOPIC	
Step 1	Review your plan to explore your topic
Step 2	Discuss your topic with others
Step 3	Observe relevant settings
Step 4	Search and browse appropriate resources
Step 5	Record search results

■ Step 1: Review Your Plan to Explore Your Topic

As you'll recall from Chapter 1, the important elements of your plan to explore your topic include people who know about your topic, can help you locate information about your topic, or have been affected by your topic; questions you want to ask the people on your list; settings you might observe to learn more about your topic; and types of resources to search and browse. As you review your plan, identify items on your list that are likely to be most productive. Consider, as well, *how many sources* you should collect. If you are already familiar with your topic, you might need to collect as few as a half dozen sources. However, if you are unfamiliar with your topic, you might need to collect more sources in order to learn about the conversations taking place about it.

■ Step 2: Discuss Your Topic with Others

Discussing your topic with people who know about it or have been affected by it is an effective way to start exploring and can provide you with insights that are not available through other sources. In addition, discussing your plan for exploring a topic with an instructor, a supervisor, or a librarian can help you identify additional resources. Librarians, for instance, not only can help you locate print and electronic sources but also can suggest individuals on campus or in the local community who can help you learn more about your topic.

Rianne Uilk, a student writer whose work is featured in this book, explored her topic—education reform in Colorado—in part by talking with her mother, a public school teacher directly affected by the reforms. Rianne also talked with other teachers in Colorado, who shared their concerns about the impact of the reform legislation on their teaching practices, about the likelihood that teachers would focus more on test preparation than on general learning strategies, and about the potential loss of local control if schools fail to meet the new standards. By discussing her topic with people who were directly affected by it, Rianne was better able to see the complexities of the topic and the many different conversations she could join within it.

Exploring a topic by talking with people can involve the kinds of informal conversations Rianne had with her mother and other Colorado teachers. It can also involve more formal interviews in which you ask a series of prepared questions about your topic. In addition, you can discuss an issue through letters and email. If you are uncertain about how to find people you can interview about your topic, you might visit an Internet chat room. Although chat is often criticized, a number of chat rooms are devoted to discussion of serious issues. (For

IN THIS BOOK

Read about planning and conducting interviews on p. 124. Read about using chat and MOOs on p. 110.

Arguing about the Impact of Education Reform Laws on Public Schools and Students

First-year student Rianne Uilk wrote an argumentative research essay for her composition course. Her assignment required her to develop and support an argument with evidence from a range of sources.

 You can follow Rianne's research writing process by visiting the *Bedford Researcher* Web site at **http://www.bedfordresearcher.com** and clicking on Featured Writers. You can read excerpts of interviews in which Rianne discusses her work on her essay, read the assignment, view her notes, and read drafts of her essay.

 You can also read Rianne's completed essay on p. 373.

Featured Writer

examples of chat rooms that host substantive discussions, visit the chat rooms in the community section of CNN.com.)

ON THE WEB SITE
Learn more about chat in the research writing manual Chat and MOOs.

Your Research Project

DISCUSS YOUR TOPIC WITH OTHERS
Use the plan you created in the **Research Log** activity "Create a Plan to Explore Your Topic" (see p. 18) to identify likely candidates for interviews and review the questions you might ask them. If you haven't created a plan, make a list of people with whom you'd like to discuss your topic and generate questions you'd like to ask them. If you can, call ahead or send email to set up a time to meet. During your meeting, take notes or use a recorder to keep track of useful ideas and information.

■ Step 3: Observe Relevant Settings

Observation is a powerful tool, particularly when you are just getting started on a research project. Like discussing your topic with others, observing appropriate settings can provide you with valuable information that isn't available from other sources.

Maria Sanchez-Traynor, a student writer whose work is featured in this book, used observation to help explore her topic—the Intensive English Program at Colorado State University. At the beginning

IN THIS BOOK
Read more about planning an observation on p. 127. Read more about conducting an observation on p. 129.

Writing an Article about the Intensive English Program at Colorado State University

Maria Sanchez-Traynor wrote a feature article about the Intensive English Program (IEP) at Colorado State University. The IEP provides instruction in written and spoken English for students whose first language is not English. Maria explored her topic by observing classes, visiting the IEP Web site, reading promotional literature, and conducting interviews with the program's assistant director, two of its students, and a teacher.

 You can follow Maria's research writing process by visiting the *Bedford Researcher* Web site at **http://www.bedfordresearcher.com** and clicking on Featured Writers. You can read excerpts of interviews in which Maria discusses her work, view the notes she took as she worked on her project, and read drafts of her article.

Featured Writer

of her research writing project, Maria observed two classes in the program. Her observations helped her develop questions for interviews with teachers and students in the program. More important, they provided her with a different perspective than she could have gained through other information-gathering techniques. Observation, she said, helped her "learn from [her] own perspective rather than just second-hand."

Your Research Project

EXPLORE YOUR TOPIC THROUGH OBSERVATION
If your topic lends itself to observation, review the plan you created in the **Research Log** activity "Create a Plan to Explore Your Topic" (see p. 18) to identify likely settings to visit. If you haven't created a plan, consider how you might gain insights into your topic through observation. During your observations, take field notes to keep track of useful ideas and information.

■ Step 4: Search and Browse Appropriate Resources

After you've talked with others about your topic and observed relevant settings, take advantage of the work other writers have done on the topic by searching and browsing appropriate resources.

IN THIS BOOK
Read more about searching online library catalogs on p. 81.

RESEARCH ASSISTANT
Learn how to locate information using an online library catalog in the manual Library Catalogs and the tutorial How to Search an Online Library Catalog.

Search Your Library's Online Catalog. Online library catalogs allow you to search for sources by title, author, and subject words. Before you begin your search, generate a list of words and phrases that are associated with your topic. If you already know the names of authors or the titles of books or periodicals related to your topic, search for them. Usually, however, you'll conduct a subject search on your topic.

Jenna Alberter, a student writer whose work is featured in this book, wrote a research essay about images of women in seventeenth-century Dutch paintings. She began exploring her topic by conducting a word search in her library's online catalog on the broad topic of seventeenth-century Dutch art (see Figure 2.1).

As you search, keep track of the number of results that each search produces. You might want to try a particularly effective search again later or use the same terms to search a database or the Web.

Browse Your Library. Once you've located a relevant book or periodical through your library's online catalog, you can usually find other books or periodicals that discuss your topic on the same or nearby shelves (see Figure 2.2). Scan the titles of those works to locate additional sources you might not have found in your online catalog search.

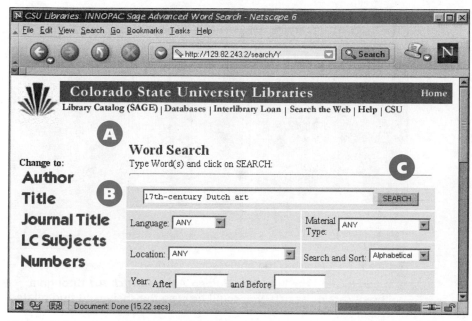

Figure 2.1   Jenna Alberter's Initial Search in Her Library's Online Catalog

A Jenna conducted a word search in her library's online catalog. She could also have chosen to conduct searches for authors, books, titles, journal titles, Library of Congress subject terms, and call numbers.

B Jenna typed the keywords *17th-century, Dutch,* and *art* in the search field.

C Jenna clicked on the SEARCH button to begin her search. Although your library's search page might not look just like this one, it will contain similar options.

Writing about Images of Women in Seventeenth-Century Dutch Art

Student writer Jenna Alberter wrote a research essay for an art history course. She explored the general topic of seventeenth-century Dutch art and then narrowed her topic to images of women in this art and the way these images "influenced and were influenced by the culture in which they were created."

You can follow Jenna's research writing process by visiting the *Bedford Researcher* Web site at **http://www.bedfordresearcher .com** and clicking on Featured Writers. You can read excerpts of interviews in which Jenna discusses her work on her research essay, read the assignment, view the notes she took as she worked on her project, and read drafts of her essay.

You can also read her research essay on p. 362.

Featured Writer

Figure 2.2   Browsing the Shelves in a Library

A If you located the book *The Golden Age of Dutch Art* through a library catalog search, you could browse the shelves to find related works . . .

B . . . including books such as *Flemish and Dutch Painting*.

RESEARCH ASSISTANT
Use the worksheet Search Library Catalogs, available for download from the *Bedford Researcher* Web site, to keep track of your searches of library catalogs.

As you browse, look for differences in the types of sources you might find in your library. Depending on your topic, some types of sources will be more appropriate than others. For example, if you are interested in a topic such as Rianne Uilk's (education reform in Colorado), which was only recently covered in the news and hadn't yet been addressed in books or scholarly journals, you might focus on magazine and newspaper articles. If you are interested in a topic such as Ernest Hemingway, as featured writer Kevin Fahey was, you would focus on books and articles in scholarly journals. Note the following characteristics of sources you might find as you browse your library:

IN THIS BOOK
Read about evaluating books and articles on p. 156.

- **Books** undergo a lengthy editorial process before they are published, and librarians evaluate them before adding them to the library collection.
- **Articles in scholarly journals** also undergo a lengthy editorial process before they are published. Most are reviewed by experts in the field before they are accepted for publication.
- **Articles in trade and other professional journals** may or may not go through a strict review process. You can find out whether articles are reviewed by looking at the submission policies printed in the journal.
- **Articles in magazines and newspapers** are usually reviewed only by the editors of the publication. Editorials typically represent an

editor's or editorial board's opinion on an issue and are not subject to review. Similarly, opinion columns and letters to the editor seldom go through a review process.

- **Theses and dissertations** are final projects for students in graduate programs. Theses and dissertations vary in quality and reliability, although they have been reviewed and approved by committees of professors.

- **Microfilm and microfiche** are methods of storing documents such as older issues of newspapers and magazines or government documents and reports.

- **Other sources** may include maps, videotapes, audiotapes, and multimedia items such as CD-ROMs and DVDs.

As you locate books, periodicals, and other sources, look for the sources writers cite to support their ideas and arguments. Many scholarly books and articles include a works cited list that provides publication information about related articles, books, and online sources. Other books and articles identify related sources in footnotes, endnotes, or the text itself. If you locate a source that seems particularly useful, its list of works cited or its notes can lead you to related sources.

Browse Newsstands and Bookstores. If your topic is a current one, consider searching out publications that might be found at a newsstand, such as specialty newspapers and magazines your library doesn't subscribe to. If your topic has a broad, popular appeal, you might look at the books and other reference works in a large bookstore or on a bookseller's Web site.

Search Available Databases. Databases organize information as records (or entries) on a particular topic. You can search these records using a search field, just as you search an online library catalog. Databases typically used by research writers, such as *MLA Online* or *Article First,* provide publication information about print and electronic documents. Many databases, such as *ERIC* and *PsycInfo,* also provide brief descriptions—or abstracts—of documents. Some databases, such as *Lexis-Nexis Academic Universe* and *Electric Library,* provide the complete text of documents. Many libraries provide access to databases through computers in the library or via their Web sites. If you have difficulty locating databases or aren't sure which databases are appropriate for your topic, ask a reference librarian for assistance.

Featured writer Patrick Crossland, who wrote an informative research essay about college admissions standards, found full-text databases particularly useful for his project (see Figure 2.3). "I was able to locate several articles through the *Electric Library,*" he said. "It helped me get a good start on my research."

 IN THIS BOOK

Read more about microfilm and microfiche on p. 120.

 RESEARCH ASSISTANT

Learn how to locate information using a database in the manual Databases and the tutorial How to Search a Database.

 IN THIS BOOK

Read more about searching databases on p. 88.

 ON THE WEB SITE

Use the worksheet Search Databases, available for download from the *Bedford Researcher* Web site, to keep track of the results of your database searches.

 IN THIS BOOK

Read about saving the results of your electronic searches on p. 69.

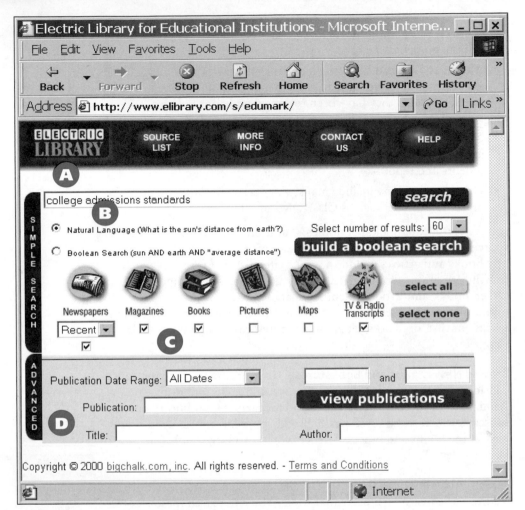

Figure 2.3   Patrick Crossland's Initial Search in the Electric Library Database

A Patrick typed the phrase *college admissions standards* in the SEARCH field.

B He chose the NATURAL LANGUAGE option instead of the BOOLEAN SEARCH option. BOOLEAN SEARCH provides a more powerful and specific type of search (see p. 101). At this point in his exploration, Patrick was not ready to start narrowing his searches.

C Patrick selected the types of sources he wanted to search.

D If Patrick had wanted a more advanced search, he would have selected additional options in the ADVANCED fields.

Conduct Web Searches.   You can search the World Wide Web for information about a topic in much the same way that you search a database. In fact, Web search engines *are* databases that constantly

ON THE WEB
DATABASE LINKS

You will find a list of more than 150 databases in the Research Links section of the *Bedford Researcher* Web site (**http://www.bedfordresearcher** **.com**). These databases are organized by discipline, such as art, biology, and economics. They also include general periodical and news databases. To locate a specific database, check your library Web site or ask a librarian whether your library subscribes to the database.

IN THIS BOOK

Read more about searching the Web on p. 88. Read more about using Bookmarks and Favorites on p. 70. Learn about strategies for evaluating sources found on the World Wide Web on p. 163.

explore and index Web sites. When they encounter a new or updated site, they enter the new information into their databases.

Conducting Web searches allows you to locate quickly a great deal of information about your topic—although not all of it will be reliable. To start searching the Web, visit one of the leading search engines, such as *AltaVista* (**http://www.altavista.com**), *Excite* (**http://www.excite.com**), or *Google* (**http://www.google.com**).

Gaele Lopez, a student writer whose work is featured in this book, wrote an informative research essay about voter turnout among 18-to-24-year-olds. Gaele used the Web to explore his topic (see Figure 2.4). "I used *AltaVista* and *MSN* to locate information on my topic," he said. "During my initial search, I found a report containing interviews with 18-to-24-year-olds about why they chose to vote or not."

ON THE WEB SITE

Learn how to locate information using a Web search site in the research writing manual The World Wide Web and the tutorial How to Use a Web Search Site.

Writing an Informative Research Essay about Voter Turnout among 18-to-24-Year-Olds

Student Gaele Lopez wrote an informative research essay about the low voter turnout among 18-to-24-year-olds for his first-year composition course. Gaele explored his topic by interviewing younger voters, searching the Web, and collecting sources from his university library.

You can follow Gaele's research writing process by visiting the *Bedford Researcher* Web site at **http://www.bedfordresearcher** **.com** and clicking on Featured Writers. You can read excerpts of interviews in which Gaele discusses his work on his informative research essay, read the assignment, view his outlines and working bibliography, and read drafts of his essay.

Featured Writer

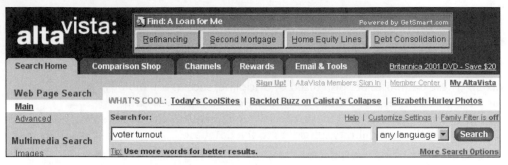

Figure 2.4 Gaele Lopez's Initial Search on *AltaVista*

To search *AltaVista,* Gaele entered the words *voter* and *turnout* in the SEARCH FOR field. He clicked on the SEARCH button to start the search. The site then produced a list of Web sites that matched the words Gaele entered in the SEARCH FOR field.

ON THE WEB SITE

Use the research writing manual The World Wide Web to learn how to search and browse the Web.

RESEARCH ASSISTANT

Use the worksheet Launch Pad to access leading Web search sites and directories and to keep track of promising sources.

ON THE WEB SITE

Use the tutorial Search a Web Directory to learn how to locate information using sites like *Yahoo!* and *Open Directory.*

When you search the Web using a search engine, it will produce a list of Web sites that match the keywords and phrases you entered in the site's SEARCH field. To visit a site in the list, simply click on the item. Once you visit a site, you can begin to browse the Web. Browsing the Web is similar to browsing the stacks in the library. Rather than placing Web pages on the same or similar topics in one part of the Internet, however, the Web uses *links* to help you locate similar sources. Once you've located a Web site that is relevant to your research question, you can usually follow links from that site to related sites. For instance, one of the Web sites Gaele Lopez visited as a result of his initial search on *AltaVista* was *Project Vote Smart,* which contains a list of Web sites related to voting and government (see Figure 2.5).

Like Gaele Lopez, featured writer Aaron Batty combined searching and browsing the Web as he explored his topic, China-Taiwan relations. "A useful Web site will often have a links page," said Aaron. "I'll bookmark that page separately so that I can follow the links. Not all will be useful, but browsing is sometimes better than searching with keywords."

Browse Web Directories. Unlike Web search engines, which automatically search the Web and enter each new site they find into large databases, Web directories, such as *Yahoo!* (**http://www.yahoo.com**), *Google Directory* (**http://directory.google.com**), and *Open Directory* (**http://www.dmoz.org**), use editors—real people—to organize their links to Web sites by categories. General categories, such as Education, are further divided into more focused subcategories, such as Colleges and Universities, which in turn are further subdivided into additional subcategories, such as Admissions, Financial Aid, and Distance Education. The result is that you can click on categories and subcategories of

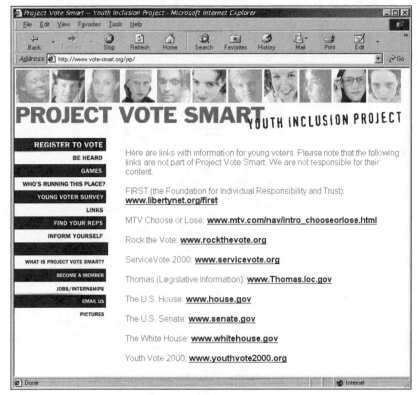

Figure 2.5   A Site Listed in Gaele Lopez's Initial Search Results
To browse other Web pages related to young voters, Gaele can click on items in the list of related links.

topics until you arrive at a list of Web sites that a human editor has decided are relevant to a topic (see Figure 2.6). When Gaele Lopez visited *Yahoo!*, he found information on his topic by clicking on the general category Government and then by clicking in succession on the subcategories Politics, Elections, and U.S. Elections.

ON THE WEB
LINKS TO WEB SEARCH ENGINES AND DIRECTORIES

If you are exploring a topic within a discipline, such as economics, nursing, or zoology, consult the list of Web search engines and directories available on the *Bedford Researcher* Web site at **http://www .bedfordresearcher.com**. You will find descriptions of and links to more than four hundred Web sites that focus on disciplines in the arts, humanities, sciences, social sciences, engineering, and business.

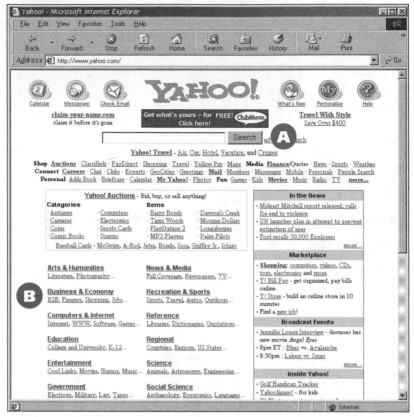

Figure 2.6   Searching the *Yahoo!* Directory

A Search for categories of information related to your topic using the SEARCH field.

B Click on categories in a Web directory to view a list of Web sites or subcategories related to your topic.

ON THE WEB SITE

To learn more about newsgroups and mailing lists, check out the research writing manual News-groups and Mailing Lists.

IN THIS BOOK

Read about evaluating messages posted to news-groups and electronic mailing lists on p. 107.

Browse Newsgroups and Electronic Mailing Lists.   Newsgroups and electronic mailing lists can be excellent sources of information as well as the source of some outrageous misinformation. Because most news-groups are unmoderated—that is, anything sent to them is published—you'll find everything from expert opinions to the musings of folks who know little or nothing about your topic. When read with a bit of skepticism, however, the messages posted to a newsgroup or mailing list can help you identify conversations within your topic and help you learn who on the list or newsgroup is well informed about them. If time permits, it's a good idea to subscribe to a newsgroup or mailing list and then *lurk* — read the messages without posting any yourself — until you have a good idea of what is regarded as appropriate behavior on the newsgroup or mailing list.

Your Research Project

EXPLORE YOUR TOPIC

As you work through the strategies discussed in this chapter, use the following activity to keep track of your topic exploration.

1. What is your working topic?

2. Have you reviewed your plan to explore your topic? Have you had others look at your plan? If so, what have you learned that could improve your plan?

3. Have you discussed your topic with others? If so, what have you learned about your topic?

4. Are there any settings you should observe? Have you observed them? If so, what have you learned?

5. Have you searched and browsed your library's online catalog and shelves; newsstands and bookstores; available databases; Web search engines, expert sites, and directories; and newsgroups and electronic mailing lists? If so, what have you learned about your topic?

If you'd like to complete this activity online, use the **Research Log** activity "Explore Your Topic" at **http://www.bedfordresearcher .com**. If you have created a research log using a notebook or a word processor, you can print or download this activity.

■ Step 5: Record Search Results

RESEARCH ASSISTANT

To learn more about *Research Assistant,* see p. 403, visit the Research Assistant section of the *Bedford Researcher* Web site at **http://www .bedfordresearcher .com,** or install it on your computer and try it out.

As you explore your topic, you should record your searches: Identify the sites you search, list the words and phrases you use in your searches, and note the quality and quantity of results produced by each search. Recording your searches will allow you to conduct searches again or conduct the same searches on different search sites or databases.

You can record your searches easily using *Research Assistant: HyperFolio for The Bedford Researcher. Research Assistant,* a software program found on the CD-ROM at the back of this book, allows you to save and work with information from online sources, including Web sites, databases, library catalogs, newsgroups, email messages, Chat and MOO transcripts, and word processing files.

RESEARCH ASSISTANT

Use the worksheet Keywords and Searches to keep track of your searches of online resources.

You can also record your searches using the **Research Log** activity "Record Your Searches," on the *Bedford Researcher* Web site. If you have created a research log using a notebook or a word processor, you can print or download this activity.

2b

What strategies can I use to narrow my topic?

Exploring allows you to listen in on several conversations about your topic, each of which will have a different focus. Now your most important goal is to narrow your topic by determining which of these focused conversations is the best fit for your project.

After exploring the working topic of seventeenth-century Dutch art and the conversations taking place about it, featured writer Jenna Alberter decided to narrow her topic by focusing on a single conversation. She chose *images of women* in seventeenth-century Dutch art.

Similarly, Aaron Batty's working topic—relations between China and Taiwan—has been addressed in numerous sources. Knowing this, Aaron narrowed his topic to the implications for the United States of efforts to establish Taiwan as an independent nation.

Like most research writers, Jenna and Aaron began to narrow their topics as soon as they began to explore them. As Jenna read each source, viewed reproductions of Dutch paintings, and talked with her professor about her topic, she kept a running list of ideas and information that interested her. As Aaron surfed the Web, reviewed the notes he had taken in his political science courses, and read back issues of newspapers such as the *New York Times,* he highlighted and made brief notes in the margins of print copies of his sources. At first, both writers found it challenging to see connections among the wide range of ideas and information they encountered. Those connections came into focus, however, as they explored their topics. Finally, after reflecting on their research writing situations—their respective purposes, interests, readers, limitations, and opportunities—they each narrowed their topic to a single conversation.

Table 2.1 shows the topics explored by the featured writers and the conversations they decided to enter.

Moving from seeing your topic as a disjointed collection of ideas and information to focusing on a single conversation about that topic involves three main steps.

NARROWING YOUR TOPIC	
Step 1	Locate conversations in your sources
Step 2	Identify important conversations about the topic
Step 3	Evaluate each of the important conversations

TABLE 2.1 THE PROGRESSION FROM TOPIC TO CONVERSATION

FEATURED WRITER	TOPIC	CONVERSATION
Jenna Alberter	Seventeenth-century Dutch art	Images of women in seventeenth-century Dutch art
Aaron Batty	China-Taiwan relations	Implications for the United States of efforts to establish Taiwan as an independent nation
Patrick Crossland	College admissions	Impact of college admissions standards on the makeup of U.S. colleges and universities
Kevin Fahey	Ernest Hemingway	Hemingway's characterization of Nick Adams
Gaele Lopez	Voter turnout	Factors influencing low turnout among voters under age 25
Holly Richmond	Richmond family history	The lives and times of previous generations of Holly Richmond's family
Maria Sanchez-Traynor	English as a Second Language (ESL) instruction	Effectiveness of the Intensive English Program (IEP) at Colorado State University
Rianne Uilk	Education reform	Impact of education legislation on Colorado public schools

■ Step 1: Locate Conversations in Your Sources

As you explore your topic, you begin to get a sense of the conversations that are taking place about it. Identifying conversations about your topic is the first step in determining which conversation is the best fit for your research writing project. At this stage, you are not reading through your sources closely; instead, you are locating conversations by skimming, marking, annotating, and taking brief notes.

Locate Conversations by Skimming Your Sources. Skimming—reading just enough to get a general idea of what a document is about—allows you to gather information quickly from the sources you've located as you've explored your topic. You can skim books, articles, Web pages, newsgroups, chat transcripts, interview notes, observation notes, or anything else in written form.

To skim books and periodicals effectively (see Figure 2.7):

- *Check the title.* The title is often, although not always, a good indicator of what the document is about.
- *Check the table of contents,* if one is provided. This provides a useful overview of the content and organization of the document.

Figure 2.7   **Skimming a Print Document**

Source: Mariët Westermann, *A Worldly Art: The Dutch Republic 1585–1718* (New York: Harry N. Abrams, 1996).

A The title may indicate the purpose and content of the document.

B Pull quotes or captions may contain information about key points.

C Headings may indicate content and organization.

D The first and last sentences of paragraphs often contain key information.

- *Check the index,* if one is provided, to learn more about the content of the document.
- *Check the glossary,* if one is provided. The terms that are defined can provide clues about the focus of the document.
- *Check the works cited list,* if one is provided, to learn about the types of evidence used in the document.
- *Check for information about the author.* Descriptions of the author can often tell you about the author's background, interests, and purposes for writing the document.
- *Check for headings or pull quotes* (quotations or brief passages pulled out of the text and set in larger type elsewhere on the page). Headings and pull quotes often call attention to important ideas in a document.
- *Scan the first sentences and last sentences of paragraphs.* Authors often put key information at the beginnings and ends of paragraphs.

- *Scan the captions for any photos and figures.* Like headings and pull quotes, captions often call attention to important ideas and information.

Figure 2.8   Skimming a Web Page

A The URL often indicates whether the page is part of a larger Web site. This page is an article in one issue of the organization's newsletter.

B Navigation headers and menus link to major sections of the Web site.

C Links to other pages on the site provide related content.

D The page title on the screen and in the title bar of the browser provide information about the purpose and content of the page.

E Scan images and captions for clues about the purpose and content of the Web page.

F The first and last sentences of text paragraphs can be a quick indication of the content of the page.

NOTE: Some pages contain information about and ways of contacting the author of the Web document. This page does not give that information.

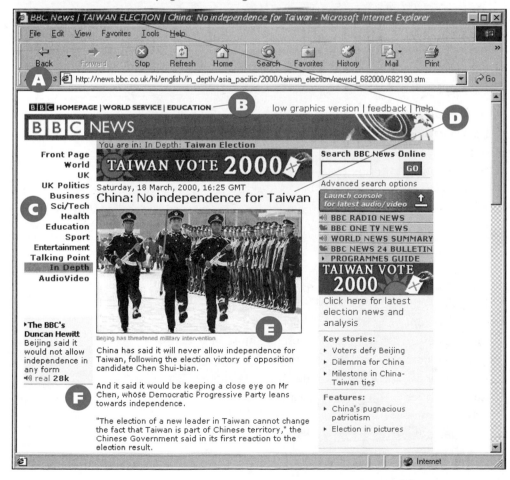

To skim a Web site effectively (see Figure 2.8):

- *Check the URL.* The URL itself can often tell you the purpose of a Web page; for instance, whether or not the page is part of a larger site, such as an article on the *Atlantic Monthly* Web site, or if it is the homepage for the site. Identifying extensions such as *.com,* for business, *.edu,* for education, and *.gov,* for government, will often, although not always, provide clues about the purpose of the site.

- *Check the navigation headers and menus,* which provide a useful overview of the content and organization of the site.

- *Check the page title on the screen.* Page titles are often used in the same way as an article title in a book or periodical.

- *Scan for boldface, colored, or italic text.* Important information is often highlighted in some way on the page.

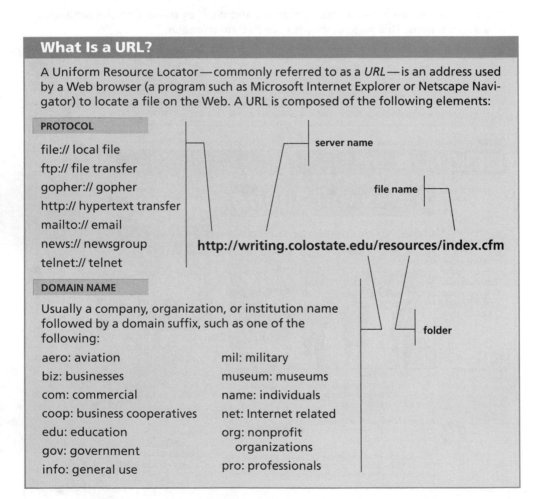

What Is a URL?

A Uniform Resource Locator—commonly referred to as a *URL*—is an address used by a Web browser (a program such as Microsoft Internet Explorer or Netscape Navigator) to locate a file on the Web. A URL is composed of the following elements:

PROTOCOL

file:// local file
ftp:// file transfer
gopher:// gopher
http:// hypertext transfer
mailto:// email
news:// newsgroup
telnet:// telnet

server name

file name

http://writing.colostate.edu/resources/index.cfm

DOMAIN NAME

Usually a company, organization, or institution name followed by a domain suffix, such as one of the following:

aero: aviation
biz: businesses
com: commercial
coop: business cooperatives
edu: education
gov: government
info: general use

mil: military
museum: museums
name: individuals
net: Internet related
org: nonprofit
  organizations
pro: professionals

folder

- *Check for information about the author,* if it is provided. Descriptions of the author can often tell you about the author's background, interests, and purposes for writing the document.
- *Skim the first and last sentences of paragraphs.* As in books and periodicals, Web site authors often put key information at the beginnings and ends of paragraphs.
- *Scan the captions for any photos and figures.* Like headings and pull quotes in print documents, captions often call attention to important ideas in a Web page.
- *Check for links to other sites,* if they are provided, to learn more about the conversations taking place about the topic.

Locate Conversations by Marking, Annotating, and Taking Brief Notes. As you skim your sources, do the following:

- mark them by highlighting or underlining important passages
- annotate them by writing brief comments in the margins
- take brief notes in your research log

Marking your sources allows you to easily locate key passages later in your research writing process (see Figure 2.9). Annotations

Figure 2.9 Aaron Batty's Annotations and Highlighting on a Printout of a Web Page

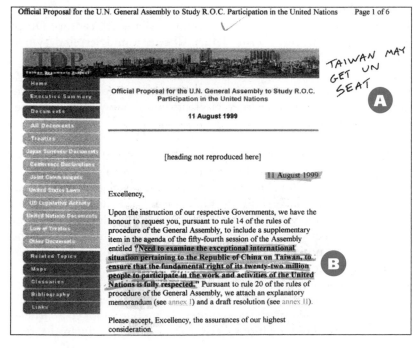

record your initial reactions to a source. Brief notes allow you to start to pull together ideas and information that several of your sources touch on. For example, you might note similarities or differences among your sources, such as different proposals for solving a problem or different interpretations of an issue.

■ Step 2: Identify Important Conversations about the Topic

ON THE WEB SITE

Use the worksheet Identify Conversations, available for download from the *Bedford Researcher* Web site, to identify and organize sources about important conversations.

After you have skimmed, marked, annotated, and taken brief notes about your sources, you are ready to identify important conversations about your topic. To identify conversations important to your research writing situation, consider your personal connection to your topic as well as the many repeated ideas, problems, similarities and dissimilarities, agreements and disagreements, recurring voices, and gaps that are present in the information you have collected. As you do this, make note of conversations you are drawn to repeatedly and find most interesting.

Consider Personal Connections to Your Topic. It is much easier to stay involved with a research writing project when you can create links between your project and your life. As you review your sources, identify what interests you most about your topic. By identifying personal connections between your sources and your own interests, you'll be able to make an informed decision about which conversation to focus on.

As she considered her sources about seventeenth-century Dutch art, for instance, featured writer Jenna Alberter found herself drawn to conversations about how Dutch art helped define women's roles. As a young woman, she was intrigued not only by the fact that paintings played a role in educating women about appropriate behaviors and attitudes in seventeenth-century Holland but also by what those behaviors and attitudes were.

Find Ideas Repeated in Your Sources. When several sources refer to or respond to the same idea, you can assume that this information is central to the topic. Some repeated ideas serve as background information that allow a conversation to take place. For example, several of the articles featured writer Patrick Crossland read addressed economic factors that affect students' abilities to gain admission to colleges and universities. By noting this information, Patrick gained a better understanding of the conversation he was planning to join.

Other repeated ideas indicate disagreements among people involved in the conversation—in a sense, they are the reason for the discussion. For instance, as featured writer Aaron Batty looked at articles and Web sites about relations between China and Taiwan, he read repeatedly that the United States might become involved in armed conflict should China attempt to take over Taiwan by force. By noting this repetition, Aaron was able to identify one of the important conversations about his topic.

Find Problems Discussed in Your Sources.   Looking for problems that are mentioned repeatedly can help you identify important conversations about your topic. For example, as featured writer Gaele Lopez looked for conversations about his topic of voter turnout, he found that many sources discussed the problem of low voter turnout among 18-to-24-year-olds.

Find Similarities and Differences among Sources.   Sources that discuss the same ideas and information are most likely involved in the same conversation. Among the sources that Jenna Alberter explored, she found that some focused on what images of women in seventeenth-century Dutch painting reveal about the status of women at the time, while others focused on the style and technique used to create portraits of women, and still others focused on the role these images played in helping women understand their place in society. By noting these similarities and differences, Jenna was able to identify some of the key conversations taking place about her topic.

Find Agreements and Disagreements among Your Sources.   Some sources will explicitly indicate that they agree or disagree with information, ideas, or arguments in other sources. For example, Aaron Batty found that some sources that favored Taiwanese independence directly referred to sources including statements made by those opposed to Taiwanese independence. Looking for such explicit statements of agreement and disagreement helped Aaron identify a group of sources that were engaged in conversation with one another.

Find Recurring Voices in Your Sources.   As you read sources about your topic, you might find that some authors speak more often than others or that some authors are referred to frequently by other writers. These authors might have significant experience or expertise related to the topic, or they might represent particular perspectives on the topic. Staying alert for recurring voices can help you identify important conversations about your topic.

Find Gaps in Your Sources.   As you learn more about your topic, you'll come up with ideas of your own. If you find that your sources aren't addressing these ideas, you might have the basis for starting a new conversation about the topic. Be cautious, however, about concluding that you've come up with a brand new idea. It might be that you need to continue exploring your topic.

> ## Your Research Project
> ### IDENTIFY IMPORTANT CONVERSATIONS ABOUT YOUR TOPIC
> It might be helpful to create a table to identify important conversations about your topic. For each source that you have consulted, record your personal connection to the information and to your topic as well as to any repeated ideas, problems, similarities and dissimilarities, agreements and disagreements, recurring voices, and gaps in information. As you fill out the table, identify the conversations and ideas that interest you most.
>
> If you'd like to complete this activity online, use the **Research Log** activity "Identify Important Conversations about Your Topic" at **http://www.bedfordresearcher.com**. If you have created a research log using a notebook or a word processor, you can print or download this activity.

◼ Step 3: Evaluate Each of the Important Conversations

IN THIS BOOK
Read more about elements of a research writing situation on p. 5.

RESEARCH ASSISTANT
Use the worksheet Evaluate Conversations to evaluate important conversations about your topic.

Once you've located important conversations about your topic, you are ready to narrow your topic further. To settle on one specific conversation, evaluate each of the important conversations with your research writing situation in mind. To do so, ask yourself a series of questions.

Will Joining This Conversation Help Me Achieve My Purposes as a Writer?   The most important consideration in deciding which of the conversations you should join is your purpose. If your purpose, or reason for writing, is clearly defined, examine how each of the important conversations you have identified will help you better accomplish it. For example, if your purpose is to win approval of a funding proposal for a student organization, it would be better to join a conversation about the benefits of funding the organization rather than one about the history of student organization funding.

Will Joining This Conversation Help Me Sustain Interest in This Project?
As you've explored your sources, you've been identifying conversations that interest you the most—personally, professionally, or academically. Featured writer Maria Sanchez-Traynor, for example, was interested in writing about the Intensive English Program at Colorado State University because of her strong personal interest in diversity and education.

As you evaluate each of the important conversations you've identified, determine which will allow you to best pursue your interests within the context of your writing situation.

Will My Readers Want or Need to Read about This Conversation?

Looking at your research writing project from your readers' point of view can help you decide which conversation you should join. For instance, as you think about a proposal to expand a local park, speculate on what your readers will want to know. If you're writing to an audience of municipal officials (for instance, a parks and recreation board or a zoning commission), you'll probably write your proposal much differently than you would if you were addressing the people who live in the neighborhood. The members of a parks and recreation board might be interested in whether the expansion will increase demands on the park's maintenance budget. The neighbors, in contrast, might want to know whether the expansion will include athletic fields that would increase noise and traffic in the neighborhood.

As you evaluate each of the important conversations, ask yourself which conversation your audience would be most interested in or need to know about most.

Is This Conversation Compatible with My Requirements and Limitations?

Requirements and limitations restrict your ability to achieve your purposes, while opportunities expand your options for achieving them. In looking at the requirements of your writing situation, ask yourself whether the conversations you are interested in are focused enough to be addressed adequately within the type of document you're expected to produce (such as a research essay, an article, or a Web site). For example, if your document's required length is ten pages, your conversation must be narrow enough to be adequately covered in that amount of space. If you have a short time before your project is due, ask yourself whether you can locate and analyze enough information to understand and contribute to a conversation before the due date.

Some limitations can be so formidable that they rule out your ability to focus on a specific conversation. For instance, if you want to write a research paper about the daily lives of Native Americans in northern New Mexico, you should consider your research techniques and available sources. If observation and other field techniques are beyond the scope of your research writing project, then you must turn to print and online sources. However, if your library has no sources about this conversation and you find only one Web site that appears to address it, then you should choose another conversation.

What Opportunities Do I Have if I Decide to Join This Conversation?

Opportunities can lead you in directions you might not have anticipated when you began exploring a topic. As featured writer Holly Richmond worked on her family history Web site project, she learned of a local Family History Center sponsored by the Church of Jesus Christ of Latter-day Saints. The Family History Center provided Holly with access to extensive, computerized listings of families throughout the world. Working with the staff at the center, said Holly, "I found a lot of information about one side of my family that I hadn't been able to find. I found names and dates going back to 1742." When you evaluate each of your conversations, take such special opportunities into account.

Your Research Project

NARROW YOUR TOPIC TO A SINGLE CONVERSATION

In your research log, complete the following activity to narrow your topic to a single conversation.

1. What are the three most important conversations I have identified so far?
2. Of these conversations, which one will best help me achieve my purposes as a writer?
3. Of these conversations, which one will best help me sustain my interest in this project?
4. Of these conversations, which one will best address my readers' needs and interests?
5. Of these conversations, which one best fits the requirements of my assignment?
6. Of these conversations, which one has the fewest limitations?
7. Of these conversations, which one presents the most opportunities for me to take advantage of?
8. Based on these answers, the single conversation that I will join is:

If you'd like to complete this activity online, use the **Research Log** activity "Narrow Your Topic to a Single Conversation" at **http://www.bedfordresearcher.com**. If you have created a research log using a notebook or a word processor, you can print or download this activity.

2c

How can I create my working bibliography?

RESEARCH ASSISTANT

The Bibliography tool helps you to maintain a working bibliography in MLA, APA, *Chicago*, or CBE style.

Once you've narrowed your topic to a single conversation, you are ready to create your working bibliography. No doubt you've already been keeping track of your sources in your research log or in *Research Assistant*. A working bibliography is a running list of the sources you've explored and plan to use in your research project—with publication information for each source.

By definition, your working bibliography will change frequently as you add potentially useful sources to your list or as you decide sources are no longer relevant. It's important to keep your working bibliography up-to-date. Because it lists your sources, your working bibliography helps ensure that you'll cite all the sources you use in your research document and decrease your risk of plagiarism.

IN THIS BOOK Read about strategies for avoiding plagiarism on p. 173.

The organization of your working bibliography can vary according to your needs and preferences. You can organize your sources in any of the following ways:

- alphabetically by author
- using categories developed while organizing your notes
- according to your outline
- according to the order in which you found and skimmed your sources

The entries in a working bibliography should include as much publication information about a source as you can gather (see Table 2.2).

You can create your working bibliography in paper or electronic form. If you're using a notebook to keep track of your research, set aside a few pages to record your working bibliography. Add new sources to the bottom of your list and draw a line through sources as

TABLE 2.2 INFORMATION YOU SHOULD LIST IN YOUR WORKING BIBLIOGRAPHY	
TYPE OF SOURCE	**INFORMATION YOU SHOULD LIST**
All Sources	• Author(s) • Title • Publication year • Editor(s) of book, if applicable
Book	• Publication city • Publisher • Series and series editor (if applicable) • Translator (if applicable) • Volume (if applicable) • Edition (if applicable)
Chapter in an Edited Book	• Publication city • Publisher • Editor(s) of book • Book title • Page numbers
Journal, Magazine, and Newspaper Article	• Journal title • Volume number or date • Issue number or date • Page numbers
Web Page, Newsgroup Post, Email Message, and Chat and MOO Transcript	• URL • Access date (the date you read the source) • Sponsoring organization, if listed

you decide not to keep them. If you're saving your bibliography in a word processing file, you can use the SORT tool to keep your list alphabetized assuming you list your sources using the author's last name first and use "anonymous" for sources without authors. (In Microsoft Word, for example, use the TABLE→SORT... menu command to sort the sources you select.) If you're listing your sources in the working bibliography tool in the **Research Log**, which is found on the *Bedford Researcher* Web site at **http://www.bedfordresearcher.com**, you'll have no need to keep a separate file containing your working bibliography. Once you create your account in the **Research Log**, you can record your bibliography online.

Your Research Project

CREATE YOUR WORKING BIBLIOGRAPHY

The Working Bibliography tool in the **Research Log** allows you to enter information about print, online, and field sources. You can

- display your working bibliography in MLA, APA, *Chicago*, or CBE style
- evaluate individual sources
- update or delete entries in your working bibliography
- print your working bibliography, save it as a downloadable file, or send it via email

To use the Working Bibliography tool, follow these steps:

1. Log in to your **Research Log** account and click on the Update Your Working Bibliography link.
2. Select Add New Sources to Your Working Bibliography.
3. Select the type of source you want to add, such as a book, a Web site, or an article in a newspaper.
4. Enter the publication information for your source, such as the author, publication date, and title, into the publication information form. Examples of complete citations are provided at the top of the form in MLA, APA, *Chicago*, and CBE styles.
5. Add notes about the source. If you prefer, you can leave this field blank—or decide to update it later.
6. Click on the ADD CITATION button. You will be returned to the main page of the Working Bibliography.

Exploring and narrowing your topic to a single conversation allows you to begin the process of developing your research question. The next chapter discusses how a research question helps you focus your attention on a particular aspect of the conversation you've decided to join.

Getting Started:
Choosing an
Appropriate
Topic

Exploring and
Narrowing Your
Topic

► Developing
Your Research
Question

CHAPTER 3

Developing Your Research Question

As a research writer, you join a conversation because you are interested in a certain aspect of a topic. You might want to learn something or share your ideas with others. You might want to help solve a problem or persuade others to adopt a point of view.

Whatever your reasons for joining a conversation, you should learn what has been said about it before sharing your ideas with others. Your research question provides a starting point for investigating a conversation. In this chapter, you'll learn how to develop and refine your research question by answering the following questions.

Key Questions

3a

What is a research question and how does it shape my research writing project?

A *research question* is a brief question that directs your efforts to collect, critically read, and evaluate your sources. Since your research question may change as you learn from your sources, it's best to think of your research question as a flexible guide as you work on your research writing project.

Research writers typically focus on a single research question. Most research questions begin with the word *what, why, when, where,*

🌐 **ON THE WEB SITE**

Read more about Patrick Crossland and the other student writers discussed in this chapter in Featured Writers on the *Bedford Researcher* Web site.

who, or *how.* Each of these question words focuses your attention on a single aspect of a conversation. Some research questions use the word *would* or *could* to ask whether something is possible. Still others use the word *should* to analyze the appropriateness of a particular action, policy, procedure, or decision. Consider the difference, for instance, between the following research questions. Each is based on the research writing project completed by featured writer Patrick Crossland on college admissions.

1. **What** cultural, academic, and regional factors affect college admissions decisions?

2. In what ways **could** state and federal laws affect standards for college admissions decisions?

3. **Should** the federal government take a more aggressive role in defining the standards used in college admissions decisions?

The first question asks for information that will help a reader understand the factors that affect college admissions decisions. The second question asks for information about the potential impact of state and federal laws on those decisions. The third question asks for information about whether the federal government should define those standards. These three questions, although all focusing on college admissions standards, will lead a researcher to collect different information from different sources.

Table 3.1 provides a list of research questions that the featured writers developed after they had narrowed their topics to single conversations. Notice how the question words the writers use in their research questions will lead them to collect different information from different types of sources. Note too that in writing a research question in a certain way, they have directed their attention to a particular aspect of their conversation.

3b

What is the difference between a research question and a thesis statement?

Research questions serve different functions at different points in your research writing process. At this early point in the process, when you have just completed your initial exploration and have narrowed your topic to a single conversation, research questions are a way to mark your current understanding of your conversation and direct your research efforts. As you continue to search for, collect, evaluate, and

TABLE 3.1	THE FEATURED WRITERS' RESEARCH QUESTIONS		
FEATURED WRITER	**TOPIC**	**CONVERSATION**	**RESEARCH QUESTION**
Jenna Alberter	Seventeenth-century Dutch art	Images of women in seventeenth-century Dutch art	What was the relationship between seventeenth-century Dutch paintings of women and the culture in which they were created?
Aaron Batty	China-Taiwan relations	Implications for the United States of efforts to establish Taiwan as an independent nation	What are the implications for the United States of differences in China's and Taiwan's interpretations of the "One China" policy?
Patrick Crossland	College admissions standards	Impact of college admissions standards on the makeup of U.S. colleges and universities	What cultural, academic, and regional factors affect college admissions decisions?
Kevin Fahey	Ernest Hemingway	Hemingway's characterization of Nick Adams	How is Nick Adams characterized by Ernest Hemingway?
Gaele Lopez	Voter turnout	Factors influencing low turnout among voters under age 25	Why is turnout low among 18-to-24-year-old voters?
Holly Richmond	Richmond family history	The lives and times of previous generations of Holly Richmond's family	Who are my ancestors and what did they do during their lifetimes?
Maria Sanchez-Traynor	English as a Second Language (ESL) instruction	Effectiveness of the Intensive English Program at Colorado State University	How is English taught to foreign-language speakers at the Intensive English Program?
Rianne Uilk	Education reform	Impact of education legislation on Colorado public schools	What are the likely effects of Colorado Senate Bill 186 on education reform in Colorado public schools?

take notes on your sources, your research question can help you decide how to use the information you've found. Naturally, you might rethink your research question as you collect more information.

Later, as you prepare to draft your document, your research question will play an important role in the development of your *thesis statement*—a statement designed to help your readers understand your view of the conversation. A thesis statement answers your research question. For example, featured writer Gaele Lopez's research question and potential thesis statement might sound something like this:

> **Research Question:** Why is turnout low among voters under age 25?
>
> **Thesis Statement:** Turnout is low among voters under age 25 because younger voters lack a sense of investment in American government.

You'll read about thesis statements in much more detail in Chapter 12 when you start drafting your paper. For now, you should focus on your research question because it will affect where and how you search for information, how you work with the information you find, and how you organize, draft, and revise your document.

3c

How can I draft my research question?

Writing a research question about a particular conversation involves following some of the same steps you took as you narrowed your topic. These steps include considering your readers' needs and interests, reflecting on your role as a writer, generating potential research questions, selecting a working research question, and refining that question.

DRAFTING YOUR RESEARCH QUESTION	
Step 1	Consider what your readers want or need to know about the conversation
Step 2	Select a role (or roles) consistent with your purpose
Step 3	Generate potential research questions
Step 4	Select a working research question
Step 5	Refine your working research question

Step 1: Consider What Your Readers Want or Need to Know about the Conversation

Keep your readers' needs and interests in mind as you begin to develop your research question. Ask yourself what they already know or would like to know about the conversation you have decided to join. Brainstorm or freewrite in response to the following questions:

- Why will my readers care about this conversation?
- What do my readers already know about this conversation?
- What will my readers want or need to know about this conversation?
- What do I want my readers to learn about the conversation?
- If I am trying to persuade them of something, how easily will they be persuaded?
- What will my readers use my writing for?

Featured writer Gaele Lopez knew his readers would be mostly 18-to-24-year-old students like himself. As a result, he wrote a research question that would appeal to younger readers: Why is turnout low among voters under age 25? Had Gaele been writing for an audience of senior citizens, he might have focused on how senior citizens can encourage young people to vote.

Step 2: Select a Role (or Roles) Consistent with Your Purpose

As you think about the conversation you've decided to join, ask yourself how you can accomplish your purpose as a writer while addressing your readers' needs and interests. The answer will tell you what role—or roles—you'll need to take on as you work on your project. A *role* is a way of relating to your readers. The role(s) you take on will greatly influence your research question. Depending on what they want to say, research writers typically adopt one or more of the following roles:

- **Advocates** present evidence in favor of their side of an argument and, in many cases, offer additional evidence that undermines opposing views. If you are making an argument in your research writing project, you'll most likely adopt the role of advocate. Acting as an advocate typically means that you have already decided which side of an argument you believe in, and your research question will be directed at locating information that supports your views.

- **Informants** often present themselves as experts on a topic. Their writing is authoritative and suggests that they are knowledgeable about the topic. You've probably read articles with titles such as

"The Best New Sport Utility Vehicles," which present detailed but neutral information about a topic. An informant might also write a document that provides an overview of competing ideas about a topic—a guide to the positions of candidates for public office, for instance. If you adopt the role of informant, your research question will often be directed at locating sources that provide information about a topic.

- **Interpreters** analyze and explain a topic to readers. Many of the news reports and articles you read are produced by writers whose primary purpose is to explain the significance of ideas or events. An interpreter acts in some ways like an informant. However, while informants tend to present the information they've found in their sources as factual, interpreters are more likely to speculate about or question the accuracy and meaning of the sources they cite. Consider the difference, for example, between an informative article about *how* to invest in the stock market and an interpretive article about the recent *causes* of a downturn or upturn in the market. Research writers who adopt the role of interpreter will often develop questions directed at understanding the significance or potential impact of a person, place, or event.

- **Inquirers** are likely to produce a research project that presents new information about a topic. For instance, a scientist interested in the effects of a new type of diet on diabetics might review related research and then conduct a study that tests the effects of the diet. The report that emerged from the study would present the results. If you adopt the role of inquirer, your research question might focus on an area of scholarly inquiry, such as the cultural achievements of a previously overlooked historical group, the effectiveness of a drug developed to treat an illness, or the latest findings from the Hubble telescope's studies of the galaxy.

- **Entertainers** attempt to amuse or divert their readers. Although entertainment is not a primary goal in academic or professional writing, it is often an important part of articles written for magazines and newspapers. Research writers often write informative articles in an entertaining way in an attempt to keep their readers interested. For examples, recall some of the articles you've read in magazines such as *Cosmopolitan, Wired, Sports Illustrated,* or *Salon.com.*

Note that these five roles—advocate, informant, interpreter, inquirer, and entertainer—are not mutually exclusive. You might find yourself adopting one role or another at different points in a project, as featured writer Gaele Lopez did as he worked on his project. His initial purpose was to inform his readers about the causes of low voter turnout among voters under age 25. As he learned more about his topic, however, he found that he also wanted to suggest strategies for increasing voter turnout. His roles as a research writer included both informing his readers about the problem and advocating a solution to the problem.

Your Research Project

SELECT ROLES CONSISTENT WITH YOUR PURPOSE

Think about your purpose for starting your research project and then about which role or roles are best suited to helping you achieve that purpose. The following activity can help you rank the relative importance of the potential roles you might adopt as you work on your project. Remember that you can adopt more than one role as a research writer.

	Not Important				*Important*
Advocate	○—	—○—	—○—	—○—	—○

Notes about how this role can help me achieve my purpose:

| **Informant** | ○—|—○—|—○—|—○—|—○ |

Notes about how this role can help me achieve my purpose:

| **Interpreter** | ○—|—○—|—○—|—○—|—○ |

Notes about how this role can help me achieve my purpose:

| **Inquirer** | ○—|—○—|—○—|—○—|—○ |

Notes about how this role can help me achieve my purpose:

| **Entertainer** | ○—|—○—|—○—|—○—|—○ |

Notes about how this role can help me achieve my purpose:

If you'd like to complete this activity online, use the **Research Log** activity "Select Roles Consistent with Your Purpose" at **http://www.bedfordresearcher.com**. If you have created a research log using a notebook or a word processor, you can print or download this activity.

■ Step 3: Generate Potential Research Questions

Your next step is to generate a list of questions about the conversation you've decided to join. Start by writing questions that begin with *what, why, when, where, who,* and *how.* If the conversation you've decided to join relates to whether something is possible, generate questions beginning with the word *would* or *could.* If the conversation you've decided to join relates to determining an appropriate course of action, generate questions beginning with the word *should.* Gaele Lopez wrote the following potential research questions about turnout among voters under age 25:

What is the cause of low voter turnout among voters under age 25?

Why are voters under age 25 deciding not to vote?

When do eligible voters typically start to participate in local, state, and federal elections?

Where are voters under age 25 most likely and least likely to vote?

Who among voters under age 25 are most likely to vote?

How can we increase voter turnout among voters under age 25?

Could advertising campaigns increase turnout among voters under age 25?

Would it be appropriate to raise the minimum voting age to 25?

Should we be concerned about low turnout among voters under age 25?

Although each of these questions is related to turnout among voters under age 25, each focuses attention on a single aspect of the conversation. Each question would lead to differences in how to search for sources of information, which sources to use in a project document, what role to adopt as a writer, and how to organize and draft the document.

Your Research Project

GENERATE POTENTIAL RESEARCH QUESTIONS
Complete the following activity in your research log to help you generate potential research questions.

Identify the conversation you are focusing on:

Write ten questions related to the conversation you have decided to join. Begin each question with one of the following words:

What	Where	Would
Why	Who	Could
When	How	Should

If you'd like to complete this activity online, use the **Research Log** activity "Generate Potential Research Questions" at **http://www.bedfordresearcher.com**. If you have created a research log using a notebook or a word processor, you can print or download this activity.

■ Step 4: Select a Working Research Question

With the information you have gathered so far, you're ready to select a working, or preliminary, research question. To do so, review the questions you generated in Step 3 and then select a question that interests you, addresses your readers' needs and interests, and is consistent with the role (or roles) you have adopted.

■ Step 5: Refine Your Working Research Question

You will most likely refine your research question throughout your work on your project, especially as you collect information, work with your sources, and plan and draft your project document. You can begin that process now by testing the scope of your research question and conducting preliminary searches.

Test the Scope of Your Research Question. Early research questions typically suffer from lack of focus. You can narrow the scope of your research question by looking for vague words and phrases and replacing them with more specific words or phrases. Then ask whether you can further narrow the scope of your question by adding additional limitations to it.

Imagine that you began your research project by exploring the broad topic of women's sports. Eventually, you might have focused on a conversation about the increasing popularity of women's sports and created the research question

What is behind the increased popularity in women's sports?

You may have suspected that this question is far too broad for a brief research essay. With this concern in mind, you could test the scope of the question by identifying vague words and phrases and replacing them with more specific words and phrases. The process of moving from a broad research question to one that might be addressed effectively in a research essay might produce the following sequence:

Original Research Question:

What is behind the increased popularity in women's sports?

Refined:

What has led to the increased popularity of women's sports in colleges and universities?

Further Refined:

How has Title IX increased opportunities for women athletes in American colleges and universities?

Your Research Project

TEST THE SCOPE OF YOUR RESEARCH QUESTION
Complete this activity in your research log to identify vague words and phrases in your research question and replace them with more specific ones.

(continued)

1. What is my preliminary research question?
2. Are there any vague words or phrases in my research question?
3. What more specific words can I use to replace them?
4. My revised research question is _____.

If you'd like to complete this activity online, use the **Research Log** activity "Test the Scope of Your Research Question" at **http://www.bedfordresearcher.com**. If you have created a research log using a notebook or a word processor, you can print or download this activity.

Conduct Preliminary Searches. Even when you're comfortable with your phrasing of your research question, you can still be surprised by something you hadn't expected. One of the best ways to test your research question is to conduct some preliminary searches in an online library catalog or database or on the Web using words and phrases found in or related to your research question. You might find that your question produces a number of relevant, focused sources. If you locate a vast amount of information in your searches, however, you might need to revise your question so that it focuses on a more manageable aspect of the conversation. In contrast, if you find almost nothing in your search, you might need to expand the scope of your research question.

Your Research Project

UPDATE YOUR PROJECT TIMELINE
As you move into the next stage of your research writing project—collecting information—review your project timeline. At this point, you've completed four project milestones.

PROJECT TIMELINE		
ACTIVITY	**START DATE**	**COMPLETION DATE**
Select your topic		
Explore your topic		
Narrow your topic to a single conversation		
Develop your research question		
Develop your plan to collect and manage information		
Collect information		
Read and evaluate information		
Take notes		

Organize your information	
Create your document outline	
Develop your thesis statement	
Write the first draft of your project document	
Review and revise your first draft	
Review and revise additional drafts	
Edit your draft	
Finalize in-text and end-of-text citations	
Design your document	
Publish and submit your project document	

If you'd like to complete this activity online, use the **Research Log** activity "Create a Project Timeline" at **http://www .bedfordresearcher.com**. If you have created a research log using a notebook or a word processor, you can print or download this activity.

Once you have completed these steps, you should have a refined research question that focuses your attention on a specific aspect of your conversation. It serves as a lens through which to search for and work with information. In the next part of this book, you'll learn how to locate, collect, and manage the sources you'll use to write your project document.

Part Two

Collecting Information

4. **Planning to Collect and Manage Information**

5. **Searching for Information with Electronic Resources**

6. **Searching for Information with Print Resources**

7. **Searching for Information with Field Research Methods**

Learning how to collect information provides the foundation for a successful research project. As you begin to answer your research question, you'll want to know more about how and where to look for useful sources of information. In this section of *The Bedford Researcher,* you'll learn how to plan a search; how to use electronic resources, print resources, and field research methods to search for information; and how to manage the information you find.

CHAPTER 4

Planning to Collect and Manage Information

Your research question focuses your attention on an aspect of the conversation you've decided to join. Even with a focused research question, however, it's likely that your search for information will produce a large number of relevant sources. To use those sources most effectively, you should create a plan to collect and manage your information.

Plans for collecting information range from informal *search plans* to *research proposals*. Plans for managing information help you decide how you'll save and organize the print and electronic sources you will collect during your search. In this chapter, you can use the answers to the following questions to create your plans.

Key Questions

4a

What is a search plan and what are its essential elements?

Your *search plan* builds on the plan you created in Chapter 1 to explore your topic. The goal of that plan was to gain a broad understanding of the conversations taking place about your topic. Your search plan is more focused and more detailed: It provides a set of directions for collecting information about the conversation you've decided to join. Search plans typically define

- the **types of sources** you will want to collect (such as books, periodicals, and interviews)
- the **types of resources** you will use to locate sources of information (such as library catalogs, the World Wide Web, and interviews)
- the **strategies** you will use as you work with specific resources (such as keyword searches and publication information searches)
- a **schedule** for conducting your research

Keep in mind that planning how you'll collect and manage information will make your search more effective. It will save you time and ensure that you don't overlook or lose track of important sources of information.

4b

What role does my research question play in my search plan?

ON THE WEB SITE

Read more about Maria Sanchez-Traynor and the other student writers discussed in this chapter in Featured Writers on the *Bedford Researcher* Web site.

Your research question helps focus your attention on a specific aspect of the conversation you've decided to join. Your search plan should reflect that focus. Table 4.1 shows variations on featured writer Maria Sanchez-Traynor's research question and the different search plans that result. Maria's research question asks how English is taught to foreign-language speakers at the Intensive English Program (IEP) at Colorado State University. Her search plan led her to collect information for her project through interviews, observation, analysis of promotional materials from the program, and Web research. As you can see from the alternative search plans in Table 4.1, if she had written an article that analyzed or critiqued the instructional practices of IEP instructors, or if she had written about how American universities and colleges can best meet the instructional needs of students who are foreign-language speakers, she would have created a different search plan.

As you develop your search plan, keep your research question in mind. Doing so will help you determine the types of sources, resources, and search strategies you need to investigate the conversation you've decided to join.

TABLE 4.1	THREE RESEARCH QUESTIONS AND THEIR RELATED SEARCH PLANS			
	RESEARCH QUESTION	TYPES OF RESOURCES	TYPES OF SOURCES	SEARCH STRATEGIES
Maria's Search Plan	How is English taught to foreign-language speakers at the Intensive English Program (IEP)?	• Interviews • Observation • Web search sites and directories	• Interviews with IEP teachers and students • Classroom observation • Printed promotional materials • The IEP Web site	• Interview strategies • Observation strategies • Keyword searches
Alternative Search Plan 1	In what ways could instructors in the IEP improve their teaching?	• Interviews • Observation • Web search sites and directories • Online library catalogs • Databases	• Interviews with teachers and students at the IEP and other programs • Classroom observation • Interviews with professors who study English as a Second Language (ESL) instruction • Web sites sponsored by similar programs • Analysis of ESL textbooks • Analysis of ESL journal articles	• Interview strategies • Observation strategies • Keyword searches • Publication information searches
Alternative Search Plan 2	How can American universities and colleges best meet the instructional needs of foreign-language speakers?	• Online library catalogs • Databases • Interviews • Web search sites and directories	• Print publications, such as books and journal articles • Web sites addressing ESL issues • Interviews with ESL teachers • Interviews with ESL students	• Publication information searches • Keyword searches • Interview strategies

4c

How can I create my search plan?

With a clear understanding of the basic elements of a search plan and the effect your research question has on that plan, you are ready to create your plan.

CREATING A SEARCH PLAN	
Step 1	Identify the types of sources that are most relevant to your conversation
Step 2	Identify the types of resources you will use to locate information
Step 3	Identify the search strategies you will use as you work with specific resources
Step 4	Create a schedule for carrying out your plan
Step 5	Get feedback on your plan

■ Step 1: Identify the Types of Sources That Are Most Relevant to Your Conversation

IN THIS BOOK

Read about searching for electronic sources on p. 81. Read about searching for print sources on p. 112. Read about conducting field research on p. 123.

Research writers use information found in a variety of sources—electronic, print, and field—to support the points they make in their project documents. As you begin to create your search plan, think carefully about which types of sources are most consistent with the conversation you plan to join. Some conversations, for example, rely heavily on articles found in magazines, newspapers, and Web sites, while others rely primarily on scholarly books and articles in scholarly and trade journals. Still other conversations make extensive use of field sources, such as interviews, observations, and surveys.

Featured writer Rianne Uilk, who wrote an argumentative research essay for her composition course, knew she wanted to focus on the impact of the recently passed Colorado Senate Bill 186, which mandates performance standards for public schools in Colorado. "I knew I wouldn't find anything in books because it was such a recent issue," she said, "so I decided to focus my search on newspapers, magazines, and the Web." Rianne also seized the opportunity to interview her mother, a high school teacher in Denver, and her mother's colleagues about the issue.

Featured writer Jenna Alberter, in contrast, knew that searching books and journal articles would be most productive. The conversation she had decided to join, images of women in seventeenth-century Dutch art, was not likely to be addressed in recent newspaper or magazine articles. Nor was it well suited to observation or other types of field research, although she might have interviewed professors who were familiar with seventeenth-century Dutch art.

■ Step 2: Identify the Types of Resources You Will Use to Locate Information

Once you've identified the types of sources being used in your conversation, identify the types of *resources* you might use to locate those sources. In general, you can use three sets of resources to locate sources:

- **Electronic resources,** such as online library catalogs, databases, and Web search sites and directories, allow you to search and browse for sources using a computer. Electronic resources provide access to publication information about—and in some cases to the complete text of—print, electronic, and multimedia sources.
- **Print resources,** such as bibliographies, indexes, encyclopedias, dictionaries, handbooks, almanacs, and atlases, can be found in library reference and periodical rooms. Unlike electronic resources, which typically cover recent publications, many print resources provide information about publications over several decades—and in some cases over more than a century.
- **Field research methods** allow you to collect information firsthand. These methods include conducting observations, interviews, and surveys; corresponding with experts; attending public events and performances; and viewing or listening to television and radio programs.

> **IN THIS BOOK**
> Read about resources you can use to locate information and strategies for locating information in Chapters 5, 6, and 7.

■ Step 3: Identify the Search Strategies You Will Use to Work with Specific Resources

Your search plan should identify the strategies you will use for each set of resources. Search strategies include keyword searches, publication information searches, interview techniques, observation techniques, and so on. If your topic lends itself to Web searches, for instance, your search plan should define the keyword searches you will use. If you need to interview people, your search plan should identify the questions you want to ask each person.

> **IN THIS BOOK**
> Read about conducting keyword searches on p. 99. Read about conducting publication information searches on p. 110.

Because featured writer Rianne Uilk was searching for recently published sources, such as newspaper articles and Web sites, her search plan included searches of the newspaper databases in her university's library and several Web search sites and directories. In addition, since she was interviewing teachers, she needed to develop interview questions. In contrast, because Jenna Alberter was searching primarily for books and journal articles, she based her search plan almost exclusively on publication information searches in library catalogs and databases.

Step 4: Create a Schedule for Carrying Out Your Plan

As you develop your plan, schedule time to carry out specific searches for information. Next to each activity—such as searching databases, searching the Web, searching a library catalog, conducting an interview, and so on—identify start dates and projected completion dates. Creating a schedule for carrying out your plan will help you budget and manage your time.

Your Research Project

CREATE YOUR SEARCH PLAN

In your research log, use the following questions to create your search plan:

1. What types of sources are most relevant to my conversation?
2. What types of resources should I use to locate information?
3. What search strategies should I use with each resource?
4. When should I start and finish each of my searches?

   If you'd like to complete this activity online, use the **Research Log** activity "Create Your Search Plan" at **http://www .bedfordresearcher.com**. If you have created a research log using a notebook or a word processor, you can print or download this activity.

Step 5: Get Feedback on Your Plan

As you might have done with your plan for exploring your topic, share your search plan with your instructor, your supervisor, or a librarian. Each might suggest additional resources, shortcuts, and alternative search strategies for your project. Take notes on the feedback you receive on your plan and, if the feedback warrants it, revise your plan.

4d

What is a research proposal and how can I create one?

In some cases, you might be asked to create a more formal version of a search plan: a *research project proposal*. A proposal—sometimes called a *prospectus*—provides an opportunity to test and formally present your plan for your research writing project. A research project proposal helps you pull together the planning you've done on your project and identify areas where you need additional planning.

Unlike a search plan, which is designed primarily to help *you* decide how to collect information, a research proposal is addressed to *someone else,* usually an instructor, supervisor, or funding agency. Because research proposals are directed to a specific audience, they are both more formal and more complex. Depending on your audience, a research proposal might include the following:

- **A title page** serves as a cover for your research proposal. It should include the working title of your research writing project, your name and contact information, and the date.

  IN THIS BOOK
  Read about formatting a title page on p. 263.

- **An abstract, or executive summary** is a brief summary — usually fifty to two hundred words — of your project. You should identify your topic, the conversation you've decided to join, and your research question and thesis statement. You should briefly list the types of sources you hope to collect, the resources you'll use to collect those sources, and the strategies you'll use in your searches. Finally, you should specify the duration of your project.

  IN THIS BOOK
  Read about creating a thesis statement on p. 200.

- **An introduction** should describe your topic and identify the conversation you've decided to join; state your research question and, if you have created one, your working thesis statement; describe your purpose; and identify your readers and describe their needs and interests.

  IN THIS BOOK
  Read about writing introductions on p. 205.

- **A review of literature** provides a brief overview of the key ideas and information in the sources you've collected so far. You should identify useful sources found during your exploration of your topic and explain why you've found them useful. After reading this section, your readers should have a general understanding of the conversation you've decided to join and the key voices — or sources — contributing to that conversation.

  IN THIS BOOK
  Read about working thesis statements on p. 143.

- **Your search plan** identifies the types of sources you hope to collect, the resources you'll use to locate those sources, the strategies you'll use to conduct your search, and a schedule for conducting your search.

  IN THIS BOOK
  Read about creating a search plan on p. 64.

- **A project timeline** will give your reader an indication of the range of days, weeks, or months over which you will be completing your research and writing your project document.

  IN THIS BOOK
  Read about creating a project timeline on p. 18.

- **An overview of key challenges** encourages you to think about potential problems you will need to address as you work on your project. This section of your research proposal might discuss difficulties locating or collecting specific types of sources, such as interviews or print materials not owned by your library, difficulties meeting a project due date, or difficulties creating a project

  IN THIS BOOK
  Read about addressing requirements and limitations on p. 8.

IN THIS BOOK

Read about the MLA, APA, *Chicago,* CBE, and COS documentation systems on p. 281.

ON THE WEB SITE

Create your working bibliography in the **Research Log** on the *Bedford Researcher* Web site.

document that has length requirements. It also provides an opportunity for your instructor, supervisor, or potential funder to suggest strategies for meeting specific challenges.

- **A funding request and rationale** provides a budget that identifies costs for key project activities, such as conducting your search, reviewing the sources you collect, writing and designing the project document, and publishing the document.

- **A working bibliography** lists the sources you've collected so far. Sometimes you will be asked to create an annotated working bibliography, which contains a brief description of each source. Your working bibliography should conform to the documentation system (MLA, APA, *Chicago,* CBE, COS) specified by your instructor, supervisor, or funding agency.

A formal research proposal allows you to consolidate the work you've done so far on your research project. It also allows you to get feedback on your plans to carry out your project from your writing teacher, supervisor, or potential funding agency.

Your Research Project

CREATE A FORMAL RESEARCH PROJECT PROPOSAL

Use the following activity to create a formal research project proposal.

1. Provide the working title for your project.
2. Describe your topic and the specific conversation you've decided to join.
3. State your research question.
4. Describe your purpose for working on this project.
5. Describe your readers' needs and interests.
6. Discuss the key challenges you face.
7. Provide your search plan.
8. Identify specific funding requests (optional).
9. Include your working bibliography.
10. Include your project timeline.

If you'd like to complete this activity online, use the **Research Log** activity "Create a Research Project Proposal" at **http://www.bedfordresearcher.com**. If you have created a research log using a notebook or a word processor, you can print or download this activity.

4e

How should I manage the information I collect?

Before you put your search plan into action, decide how you will save and keep track of the electronic and print information that you collect.

■ Saving Electronic Sources

Although it can be satisfying to know that you've found numerous electronic sources during your searches, you need to save those sources before you can begin working with them. The most useful techniques for saving electronic sources include printing, saving to disk, copying and pasting to a word processing file, using your email account to store materials, using Bookmarks or Favorites lists, and using *Research Assistant*.

Printing. If you're like most research writers, you like to print out articles or Web pages to read them. This allows you to highlight key passages, write comments in the margins, and circle text and graphics on a page. It also allows you to cut out a section of a page and tape it to another section.

When you print out a Web page, make sure the URL is readable. If it's not included on the printout or if it's incomplete (which can happen when URLs are too long to fit on the printout), write it down on the first page of the printout. Also check for the date on printed Web pages. If your browser doesn't print the date (most browsers do), write it on the first page of your printout.

IN THIS BOOK

Learn more about URLs in "What Is a URL?" on p. 38.

Printing Web pages and articles from full-text databases is one of the most convenient ways to collect information. Think about what you really need, however, before you send page after page to the printer.

Saving to Disk. Toward the end of your research writing project, particularly when you are drafting your project document, you might find yourself wishing that you'd saved all of your electronic sources to disk. In this case, *disk* refers to a storage medium such as a hard drive, a diskette, a Zip disk, a Super Disk, or a writable CD. Saving sources to disk allows you to open them in a Web browser or word processor at a later time.

ON THE WEB SITE

Use the tutorial How to Save Information to Disk to learn how to save different types of electronic information.

How you save your sources will vary according to the type of electronic source you're viewing. Web pages can be saved using the FILE→SAVE AS... or FILE→SAVE PAGE AS... menu command in your browser. Images and other media materials from the Web can be saved by right-clicking or Command-clicking on the item you want to save

IN THIS BOOK
Read more about databases on p. 88.

IN THIS BOOK
Read about creating your working bibliography on p. 44.

ON THE WEB SITE
Use the Working Bibliography tool in the **Research Log** to keep track of your sources.

ON THE WEB SITE
Use the research writing manual Using Your Word Processor to learn more about copying and pasting.

and selecting SAVE IMAGE AS… or SAVE PICTURE AS… or some variation of that command from the pop-up menu.

Databases on CD-ROM often allow you to save some or all of the results of your search. Depending on the database, you might be able to mark a record returned by your search. After you've marked all relevant records, you can save them to a disk. Databases viewed via the Web do not usually allow you to save directly to disk. However, they often allow you to mark and then either print or email the records.

Saving a source to disk does not automatically record the URL or the date on which you viewed the source for the first time. Be sure to record that information in your working bibliography.

Copying and Pasting. You can use the COPY and PASTE commands in your browser and word processor to save electronic documents, especially if you want to keep only parts of documents. You can usually copy and paste text and graphics from a browser into a word processor. Note that you also need to copy and paste the URL and record the date you accessed the page so that you can return to it if necessary and cite it appropriately.

Using Email. You can email yourself messages containing electronic documents you've found in your research. Some databases, such as *Dialog* and *OCLC/FirstSearch,* allow you to email the text of selected records directly from the database (see Figure 4.1). You also might be able to use your own email program to send the text of database records and Web pages to your email account. Using the COPY and PASTE commands, you can paste text from a Web page or database record into an email message.

Using Bookmarks and Favorites. Many of the Web pages you'll locate during your research will be linked to other pages. If you save a Web page to disk, some or all of the links on the page might stop working. If you need the links, you can use a Bookmarks or Favorites list to keep track of the sources. Bookmarks and Favorites lists contain links that you create in your Web browser. The links in the Netscape Navigator list are called Bookmarks; those in Microsoft Internet Explorer are called Favorites.

Bookmarks and Favorites lists appear on your computer screen as drop-down menus containing names of Web pages. When you click on an item in the Bookmarks or Favorites list, your Web browser goes directly to that page. Adding items to your Bookmarks or Favorites list is straightforward. Figure 4.2 shows how to add to a Bookmarks list in Netscape Navigator. This process is similar to that used in Microsoft Internet Explorer.

If you're not careful, your Bookmarks or Favorites list can become disorganized. To avoid this problem, use the built-in management tools provided in your Web browser:

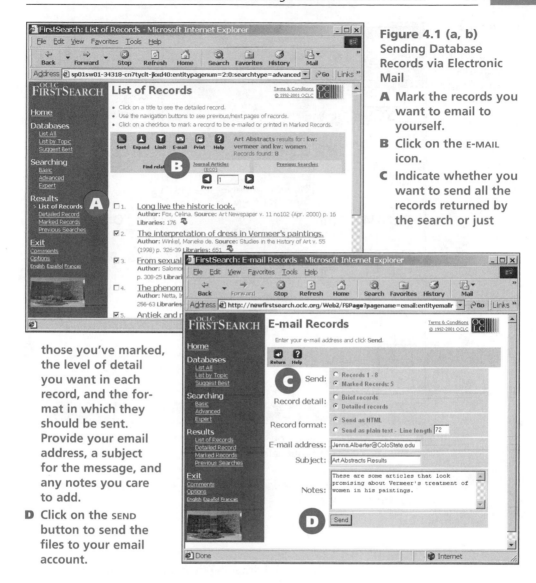

Figure 4.1 (a, b)
Sending Database
Records via Electronic
Mail

A Mark the records you
want to email to
yourself.

B Click on the E-MAIL
icon.

C Indicate whether you
want to send all the
records returned by
the search or just

those you've marked,
the level of detail
you want in each
record, and the for-
mat in which they
should be sent.
Provide your email
address, a subject
for the message, and
any notes you care
to add.

D Click on the SEND
button to send the
files to your email
account.

- **Use folders to manage your Bookmarks or Favorites lists.** Folders allow you to organize your Bookmarks or Favorites items into related groups. For example, you can place links to Web pages that support your argument in one folder and those that oppose your argument in another.

- **Organize your Bookmarks and Favorites lists.** You can use the MANAGE BOOKMARKS (EDIT BOOKMARKS on the Mac) and ORGANIZE FAVORITES dialog boxes to change the order of items in your lists, perhaps moving your most frequently used items and folders near the top of the lists. Microsoft Internet Explorer also allows you to change the order of Favorites items and folders

**Figure 4.2
Adding an
Item to Your
Bookmarks
List (Netscape
Navigator)**

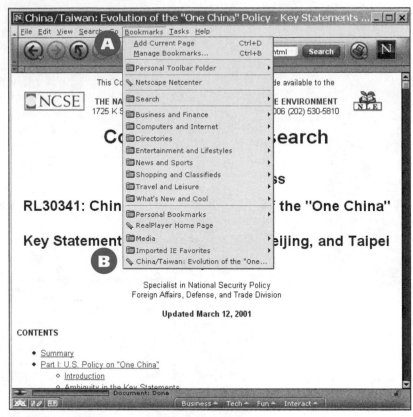

A Open the Web page you want to add to your Bookmarks list. In the BOOKMARKS menu, select ADD CURRENT PAGE. (On a Mac, select ADD BOOKMARK.)

B Netscape Navigator adds the link to the Web page at the bottom of the Bookmarks list.

by clicking on them and dragging them to a new location when the Favorites list is open.

- **Use descriptive names and annotations.** By default, items in Bookmarks and Favorites lists are named using the title of the Web page. Sometimes those names are descriptive, and sometimes they're not. Giving items on your list descriptive names will help you remember the content of the Web page you've added.

A Caution.　There are drawbacks to relying on a Bookmarks or Favorites list as a place to "store" your sources. First, pages on the Web can and do change. If you suspect that the page you want to mark might change before you complete your research project, save it to disk or print it so that you won't lose its content. Second, some Web pages are generated by database programs. In such cases, you might not be able to return to the page using a Bookmarks or Favorites list. A URL like the following usually indicates that a Web page is generated by a database program:

> http://firstsearch.oclc.org/FUNC/QUERY:%7Fnext=NEXTCMD%7F%
> 22/FUNC/SRCH_RESULTS%22%7FentityListType=0%7Fentitycntr=
> 1%7FentityItemCount=0%7F%3Asessionid=1265726%7F4%7F/
> fsres4.txt.

This long string of characters starts out looking like a normal URL. However, the majority of the characters are used by the database program to determine which records to display on a page. In many cases, the URL works only while you are conducting your search. If you add the URL to your Bookmarks or Favorites list, there's a good chance it won't work later.

IN THIS BOOK

Learn more about URLs in "What Is a URL?" on p. 38.

Using *Research Assistant*.   *Research Assistant: HyperFolio for The Bedford Researcher,* the information collection software that is found on the CD in the back of this book, allows you to save information from electronic sources, including Web pages, email messages, and word processing documents. Whatever you save—whether it's a complete Web page, a few sentences from a page, a graphic, a video or audio file, or all or part of a word processing file or email message—appears as an icon in an overall list called a *collection* (see Figure 4.3). From the collection, you can drag icons into *worksheets* that are designed to help you work with your sources and organize your project document (see p. 403).

   Research Assistant can be installed on your computer using the CD at the back of this book.

RESEARCH ASSISTANT

To learn more about the program, consult Appendix C on p. 403, or visit the Research Assistant section of the *Bedford Researcher* Web site at **http://www .bedfordresearcher .com**

◼ Keeping Track of Electronic Sources

As you work on your research writing project, you will accumulate a great deal of electronic information. You can manage this information by creating a *project workspace* on your computer using file folders or *Research Assistant*. You can also create a project workspace with a personal digital assistant such as a Palm handheld or Handspring Visor.

Creating a Project Workspace Using Folders.   The simplest project workspace is a single folder on your hard drive containing every file you've collected or created as you've worked on your project (see Figure 4.4). The single-folder approach can serve you well if you follow these guidelines:

A To add a source to a collection in *Research Assistant,* highlight the URL and then click and drag it onto the program's collection icon.

B The collection icon floats on top of your browser window so that it's visible while you are using *Research Assistant.* Note that you can also drag text, images, and other elements from a Web page into a *Research Assistant* collection.

C The source will show up in your collection. Double-clicking on an icon in a collection will open the Web site where the source can be found.

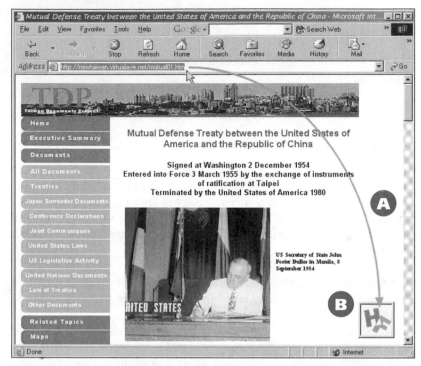

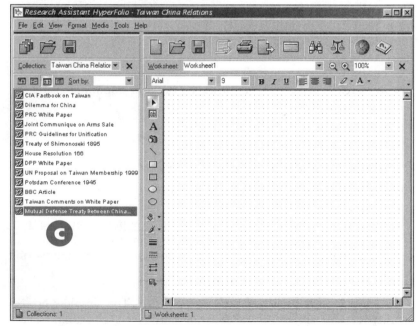

Figure 4.3 (a, b)   Collecting Materials from the Web with *Research Assistant*

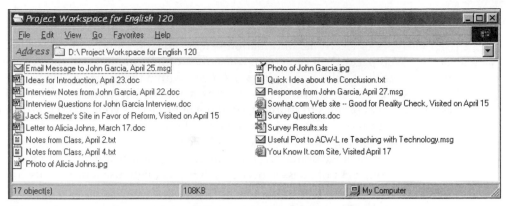

Figure 4.4 **A Project Workspace Using a Single Folder**

1. Save everything in the same place, including your Bookmarks or Favorites list, relevant email messages, newsgroup posts, Web pages, and *Research Assistant* collections and worksheets. It's not enough to save just your word processing documents in your project workspace. You need to have easy access to *all* of your materials.

2. Use descriptive file names that indicate what each file contains. Ideally, include the date you collected the information in your file name. Rather than naming a file *Notes 1.doc*, for instance, name it *Interview Notes from John Garcia, April 22.doc*.

3. Save relevant Bookmarks or Favorites items in your project workspace.

The single-folder project workspace might not work well for larger projects. At some point, the sheer number of files in the folder makes it difficult to find a single file easily. Rather than scrolling through several screens of files, you might find it more efficient to create multiple folders to hold related files (see Figure 4.5).

Figure 4.5 **A Project Workspace Using Multiple Folders**

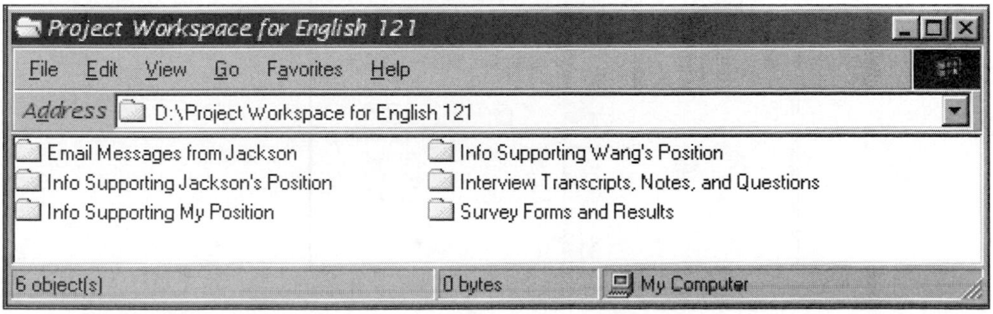

RESEARCH
ASSISTANT
To view the work-
sheets included
with *Research
Assistant,* open
the program and
select NEW WORK-
SHEET from the FILE
menu.

Creating a Project Workspace Using *Research Assistant.* As you've learned, *Research Assistant* allows you to collect and organize all types of electronic information—text, images, audio and video files, Web pages. You can create *collections* of information and then organize these collections using *worksheets* within the program. Think of a collection in *Research Assistant* as a folder that contains all of the sources or links to sources that you want to use in your project. Worksheets allow you to visually organize those sources to see the relationships among them (see Figure 4.6). For example, in a worksheet, you might arrange some of your sources chronologically, reflecting the development of an issue over time. Or you might use a pro versus con organizing principle. You can also display the same source on several worksheets.

Research Assistant has several built-in worksheets, including some that allow you to identify and organize sources that support or oppose your argument about a topic. You can also create custom worksheets, using your own organizing principle to arrange your sources.

A Click on a source in the collection and hold down the mouse as you drag the source into a worksheet.

B Release the mouse button, and the source appears in the worksheet. You can change the location of worksheet icons by clicking and dragging.

**Figure 4.6
Organizing
Sources on a
Worksheet in
*Research
Assistant***

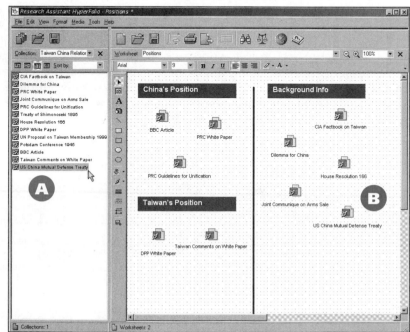

Finally, you can use the worksheets in *Research Assistant* to keep track of your ideas about your sources. You can type your ideas directly in a worksheet or annotate individual sources using a note card (see Figure 4.7). You can also indicate relationships among sources by drawing lines from one source to another or grouping related sources within a box or circle.

Working with a Personal Digital Assistant. The personal digital assistant (PDA) is quickly becoming a commonplace information appliance. Products such as Palm handhelds, Handspring Visors, and various versions of the Pocket PC make it easy to take notes on a device that can fit into a shirt pocket. One of the most appealing aspects

Figure 4.7 Using a Note Card in *Research Assistant* to Keep Track of Ideas about a Source

A Click on the icon of the source you want to annotate.

B Click on the SHOW NOTE CARD icon in the toolbar (or select NOTE CARD from the context-sensitive menu).

C The note card for that source appears. You can take notes, record publication information, and evaluate the source.

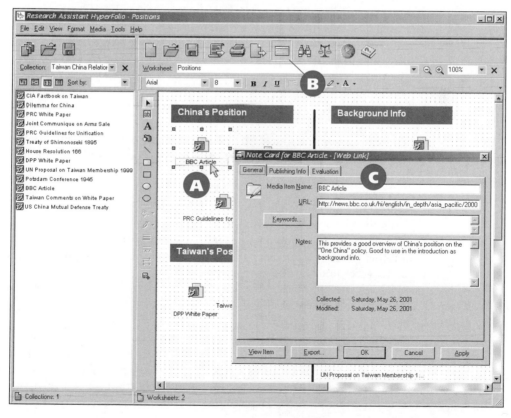

of PDAs for research writers is that you can take notes and easily transfer those notes to your primary computer. You can use a PDA to

- keep track of your ideas by jotting quick notes
- keep a copy of your research question
- list useful Web search sites and databases
- keep a running list of the keywords you've used in your electronic searches
- keep a list of useful contacts in the address book
- list interview questions
- keep your observation notes and download them onto your personal computer
- create a current outline of your project document
- use the "to do" list to remind yourself about important activities related to your research project

Backing Up Your Information.   The more time and energy you invest collecting and managing information, the more valuable that information becomes. Replacing lost information takes time and effort. Avoid the risk of lost information by taking the time to back up your electronic files, saved Web pages, email messages, Bookmarks or Favorites list, and *Research Assistant* collections and worksheets. You can back up your project workspace to removable media such as floppy disks, Zip disks, Super Disks, or writable compact discs (CD-R or CD-RW).

■ Saving Print Sources

You can save print sources by checking them out from your library, buying sources from a bookstore, making photocopies of sources, and using fax-on-demand services.

Checking Out Materials from the Library.   Checking out materials from the library allows you to have access to original sources, but this approach has its drawbacks. First, a source might be recalled by another library patron. Second, it's inappropriate to highlight passages or to write notes in the margin (even in pencil), so your options for marking and annotating are limited to devices such as Post-it Notes, bookmarks, and paper clips.

Purchasing Sources.   Purchasing sources from a bookstore allows you to have complete control over your sources, but it can be quite expensive. Most bookstores stock only recently published books and periodicals—and, in contrast to a library collection, only a relatively small number of those. Depending on your research topic, you might find that some of the most important sources for your project are out of print and available only through your library.

Photocopying.   Photocopying is the option chosen by most research writers to save print sources. When copying pages from a source, copy the title page of the book or periodical or jot down the publication information on the first page of the copies you've made. You'll need this information later, when you're documenting your sources.

Fax-on-Demand Services.   Fax-on-demand services allow you to receive a paper fax containing the text of a document—usually an article from a magazine, newspaper, or journal. In many cases, you can request a fax through the database that you used to locate the article. The *Dialog* database, for instance, which is available through many library Web sites, will fax the complete text of an article to your fax machine. The charge for this service varies according to the agreement your library has with the database company.

Some interlibrary loan departments also provide a fax service. Rather than sending a copy of an article to your library and notifying you when it arrives, a library can send the text of the document directly to your home fax machine. In some cases, this service is offered free of charge. Ask your librarian for information regarding your library's fax-on-demand services.

■ Keeping Track of Print Sources

During your research project, you'll accumulate a great deal of print information, including

- your written notes (in a notebook, on loose pieces of paper, on Post-it Notes, and so on)
- printouts from Web pages and databases
- printed word processing documents, such as your plan to explore your topic, your search plan, various drafts of your research question, and so on
- books, magazines, newspapers, brochures, pamphlets, government documents
- photocopies of articles, book chapters, and other documents
- letters, printed email messages, and printed newsgroup posts
- printed interview transcripts
- observation and interview notes
- completed survey forms and printouts of tabulated survey results

Rather than letting all of this information build up in piles on your desk or stuffing it into folders in your backpack or briefcase, create a filing system to keep track of your print documents. Filing systems can range from well-organized piles of paper labeled with Post-it Notes to portable file folders to file cabinets filled with neatly labeled files and folders.

Regardless of the approach you take, keep the following principles in mind:

- *Create an organizational scheme that allows you to locate your print materials.* Decide whether you want to group material by topic, by date, by pro versus con, by type of material (Web pages, photocopies, original documents, field sources, and so on), or by author.
- *Stick with your organizational scheme.* You'll find it difficult to locate materials if you use different approaches at different points in your research writing project.
- *Write a brief note on each of your print materials* indicating how it might contribute to your project.
- *Make sure printed documents provide complete publication information.* As you organize your print information, make sure that the source contains publication information, or write it on the source yourself.
- *Date your notes.* Indicating dates when you recorded information can help you reconstruct what you might have been doing while you took the note. It is also essential for documenting Web sources and other sources obtained online.

Effective plans for searching for and managing information will help you stay focused and organized as you collect information. In the next three chapters, we'll look at ways you can search for information using electronic resources, print resources, and field research methods.

CHAPTER 5

Searching for Information with Electronic Resources

Research writers are living in exciting times. Entire industries are devoting their efforts to making it easier to locate information. However, the rapidly growing collection of resources for finding information can be bewildering. This chapter provides an overview of the electronic resources you can use to put your search plan into action. It also provides a discussion of strategies for using these resources. In this chapter, you will continue your research writing project by answering the following questions.

Key Questions

5a

How can I use online library catalogs to locate sources?

One of the resources most commonly used by researchers is the library catalog, which provides information about the materials in a library's collection. Most libraries now allow access to their collections through online catalogs — usually via the Web. Online library catalogs store a record for each source owned by a library. Think of these records as electronic versions of the printed cards found in physical card catalogs. At a minimum, each record identifies author(s), title, publication date, subject, and call number. Many online library catalogs also indicate the location of the source in the library and whether the source is available for checkout.

Online library catalogs focus primarily on print publications in a library collection. However, they can also provide information about publications in nonprint media, such as audiotape and microfilm. Library catalogs typically help you locate

- books
- journals owned by the library (although not individual articles)
- newspapers and magazines owned by the library (although not individual articles)
- documents stored on microfilm or microfiche
- videotapes, audiotapes, and other multimedia items owned by the library
- maps
- theses and dissertations completed by college or university graduate students

Note that library catalogs are not well suited for locating journal, magazine, or newspaper articles or online sources such as Web pages. You can learn more about these types of sources later in this chapter and the next.

Although you can limit your use of online library catalogs to your college or university, you can benefit from searching other catalogs available on the Web. The Library of Congress online catalog, for example, presents a comprehensive list of publications on a particular subject or by a particular author (visit **http://catalog.loc.gov**). If your library doesn't have a publication in its collection, you can request it

📖 **IN THIS BOOK**

Read about the characteristics of these types of sources on p. 24. Read more about microfilm and microfiche on p. 120.

📖 **IN THIS BOOK**

Read about using databases to locate articles on p. 89. Read about using Web search sites to locate Web pages on p. 92.

🌐 **ON THE WEB SITE**

View the Research Links on the *Bedford Researcher* Web site for additional sites that list online library catalogs.

ON THE WEB
SELECTED WEB SITES LISTING ONLINE LIBRARY CATALOGS

Karlsruhe Virtual Catalog
http://www.ubka.uni-karlsruhe.de/hylib/en/kvk.html

Libweb
http://sunsite.berkeley.edu/Libweb

lib-web-cats
http://staffweb.library.vanderbilt.edu/Breeding/libwebcats.html

LibDex
http://www.libdex.com

Yahoo's Library Directory
http://dir.yahoo.com/Reference/Libraries

Open Directory Project Library Listings
http://dmoz.org/Reference/Libraries

through interlibrary loan. You can also search the online library catalogs at schools that are well known for their work in a specific area, such as the drama program at Carnegie Mellon University or the math program at St. Olaf College. Finally, some sites allow you to locate or search multiple online library catalogs, such as the *Karlsruhe Virtual Catalog* (**http://www.ubka.uni-karlsruhe.de/hylib/en/kvk.html**).

Most online library catalogs allow you to search for sources by author(s), title, words in source records, subject headings, publication date, and call number.

■ Author Searches

Author searches, as the name implies, are searches for sources written by a particular author or authors. Figure 5.1 shows a search Jenna Alberter conducted for sources written by Patricia Phagan, one of the writers she'd learned about as she explored her topic. Using the Library of Congress catalog, she found seven books written by Phagan, including some that appeared to be promising sources.

Most library catalogs assume that you will enter the last name of the author first, followed by a first name or initial. Some library catalogs and databases allow you to browse sources by entering all or part of the last name or by using wildcard symbols.

■ Title Searches

If you know the exact title of a source, such as *Six Subjects of Reformation Art: A Preface to Rembrandt,* you can enter the entire title. If you know only part of the title, such as *Rembrandt, Six Subjects,* or *Reformation Art,* you might have to sift through a list of books whose titles contain the phrase or word you enter.

■ Word Searches

Word searches are similar to keyword searches used in databases and on Web search sites. In many online library catalogs, however, you can decide whether to search some or all of the parts (or fields) of a catalog record. The Harvard University Library Union online catalog, for example, allows you to search for words in some or all of the different parts of its electronic records (see Figure 5.2).

■ Subject Searches

Subject searches allow you to search for sources that are cataloged under specific subject headings. Many college and university libraries use the Library of Congress classification system to organize their collections, while others use the Dewey decimal classification system.

IN THIS BOOK
Read more about using interlibrary loan on p. 122.

ON THE WEB SITE
Read more about Jenna Alberter and the other student writers discussed in this chapter in Featured Writers on the *Bedford Researcher* Web site at **http://www.bedfordresearcher.com**.

IN THIS BOOK
Read about using wildcard symbols on p. 100.

ON THE WEB SITE
View the tutorials How to Search an Online Library Catalog and How to Refine Searches with Publication Information to learn more about using online library catalogs to locate sources.

IN THIS BOOK
Read about keyword searches on p. 99.

Figure 5.1 Searching the Library of Congress Catalog On-line (http://catalog.loc.gov)

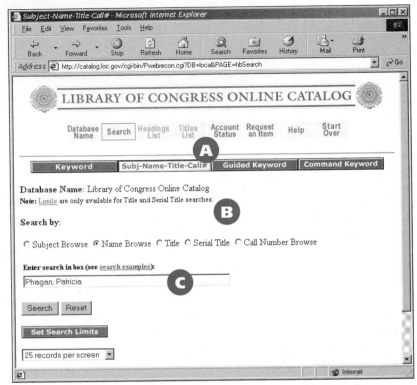

A The Library of Congress online catalog allows numerous types of searches (keyword, publication information, guided keyword, and command keyword). This search is a publication information search (SUBJ-NAME-TITLE-CALL#).

B The catalog allows you to place additional limits on your search, such as publication date.

C The SEARCH field is a text box. The SEARCH button is located immediately below it. Pressing the SEARCH button produces a list of sources, in this case written by Patricia Phagan.

These systems use subject headings to organize publications owned by a library. By searching your online library catalog for specific subject headings, you can identify sources that are relevant to your research writing project.

■ Publication Date Searches

If you're working on a subject that is time-sensitive—such as recent developments in gene therapy or information about an event or period of time—limit your search by *publication date*. Such a search reduces the number of sources to those published during a certain time period.

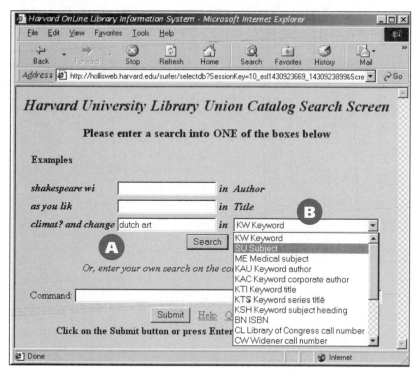

**Figure 5.2
Conducting a
Word Search
in an Online
Library
Catalog**

A In this library catalog, you can enter words and then choose where
you want the catalog to look for those words (in the author listings, the title listings, or in specific record fields).

B A drop-down list provides a list of record fields in which to conduct
your word search, from the keyword and subject fields to the
series title field.

■ Call Number Searches

Call number searches allow you to take a virtual stroll through your
library's stacks. If you are viewing the record for a book that you find
interesting, you can often click on the call number to browse a list of
sources with nearby call numbers. This technique is also useful if you
know the call numbers for specific subjects.

    If your library catalog allows searching for call numbers, you can
enter a call number from the Library of Congress classification system
or the Dewey decimal system (see p. 86). You will be taken to a page
listing publications owned by the library beginning with the call
number you entered. (Expanded, detailed versions of these lists can be
found in the research writing manual Library Classification Systems
on the *Bedford Researcher* Web site, at **http://www.bedfordresearcher
.com**.)

**RESEARCH
ASSISTANT**
Use the worksheet
Search Library Cat-
alogs to keep track
of your searches of
library catalogs.

🌐 **ON THE WEB SITE**

Expanded versions of these systems are available in the research writing manual Library Classification Systems.

Library of Congress Classification System

A General Works

B Philosophy, Psychology, Religion

C Auxiliary Sciences of History

D History: General and Old World

E History: United States

F History: United States Local and America

G Geography, Anthropology, Recreation

H Social Sciences

J Political Science

K Law

L Education

M Music and Books on Music

N Fine Arts

P Language and Literature

Q Science

R Medicine

S Agriculture

T Technology

U Military Science

V Naval Science

Z Library Science and Information Resources

Dewey Decimal Classification System

000 Computers, Internet, and Systems

100 Philosophy

200 Religion

300 Social Sciences, Sociology and Anthropology

400 Language

500 Science

600 Technology

700 Arts

800 Literature, Rhetoric and Criticism

900 History

■ Compound Searches

Library catalogs can help you locate sources quickly, especially when you conduct simple searches, such as an author search by last name. If the last name is a common one such as Smith or García or Chen, however, your search might produce far more results than you would like. In this case, a *compound search* might help. A compound search can involve searching for more than one type of information at the same time. It can also involve conducting a single search, such as an author search, followed by additional searches within the results produced by the first. You might, for example, conduct an author search in combination with a title or keyword search. Or you might conduct an author search and then conduct a subject or title search on the results of that search.

Jenna Alberter conducted a series of searches on the library catalog at her university. Her art history professor had suggested that she look at work by a scholar named Westermann. Jenna conducted an author search for Westermann, which produced forty-three possible sources. Rather than looking up each one, she conducted a second search to find out which of the forty-three sources were concerned with the subject of Dutch art (see Figure 5.3).

After narrowing her search, Jenna found two books written by Mariët Westermann about seventeenth-century Dutch art. After making a note of the results in her research log, she browsed by call number to see what other sources she might find.

Your Research Project

PREPARE TO SEARCH ONLINE LIBRARY CATALOGS

As you prepare to search online library catalogs, return to your search plan and make a list of names, keywords, and phrases. Examine your working bibliography to identify the authors, titles, and subjects of your best sources. Then answer the following questions:

1. What are the names of authors I can use for author searches?
2. What are the titles of works that have been referred to me or that I have found in works cited pages that I can use in title searches?
3. What keywords and phrases can I use in word searches?
4. What keywords and phrases can I use in subject searches?
5. Does my conversation lend itself to publication date searches? If so, what are the dates I should search within?
6. Would call numbers in the Library of Congress or Dewey decimal classification systems be useful for me to browse? If so, what are these call numbers?

If you'd like to complete this activity online, use the **Research Log** activity "Prepare to Search Online Library Catalogs" at **http://www.bedfordresearcher.com**. If you have created a research log using a notebook or a word processor, you can print or download this activity.

Figure 5.3
Narrowing
Search Re-
sults with a
Compound
Search

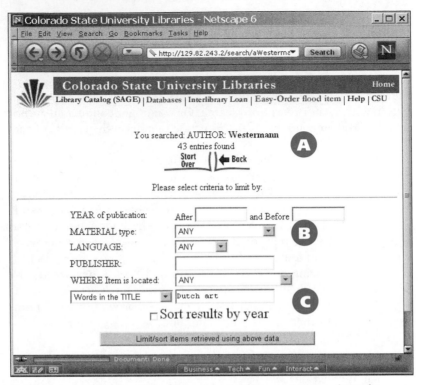

A Jenna's author search produced forty-three sources written by authors whose last name is Westermann.

B Jenna had the option of limiting her search in several ways: publication date, material type (including monographs, maps, videos, and newspapers), language, publisher, location, and words in the author, subject, or title fields.

C Jenna chose to reduce her results by searching for the subject words *Dutch art* in the titles of the publications found in her author search.

5b

How can I use databases and Web search sites to locate sources?

Databases and Web search sites operate much like library catalogs, although they focus on a different collection of sources. While a library catalog allows you to search for publications owned by the library, a *database* allows you to search for articles published in magazines, newspapers, and journals. Some databases provide information about theses and dissertations, multimedia materials, papers presented at professional conferences, and government documents. You can access the databases owned by your library from the library Web site or by using computers in the library.

Web search sites allow you to search for Web sites that might be relevant to your conversation. The most widely known Web search sites, such as *Google* (**http://www.google.com**), *AltaVista* (**http://www .altavista.com**), and *Lycos* (**http://www.lycos.com**), cover the entire Web. You can also find specialized Web search sites, such as *Fictionsearch .com* (**http://www.fictionsearch.com**), which focuses on resources for writers and readers of fiction. Some Web search sites also allow you to locate images, multimedia materials, messages sent to electronic mailing lists and newsgroups, and other texts available on the Internet (such as the large collection of books and poems on the *Project Gutenberg* site at **http://promo.net/pg**).

■ Types of Databases

Databases vary in the topics they cover and the information they provide. Some databases include publication information and brief descriptions of all articles published in a group of scholarly journals or in a field, such as microbiology or American history. Others provide access to the complete text of articles published in newspapers and magazines. The databases you're likely to find in a library or on the Web usually contain information about both print and electronic publications.

As a research writer, you will be most interested in four types of databases: subject databases, bibliographies, full-text databases, and citation indexes.

Subject Databases.   Subject databases provide information about a broad subject, such as education, business, or psychology. The *Art Abstracts* database, for instance, presents publication information (including author, title, publication date, and publisher) and abstracts, or summaries, of work published in the field of art. Subject databases usually don't give access to the full text of the articles and research reports they list (see Figure 5.4).

Bibliographies.   Bibliographies are specialized databases with information about publications in a subject area. They are similar to subject databases; however, they focus more narrowly on a particular field, and they typically provide only publication information. *The MLA Bibliography,* for example, includes bibliographic records about literature, language, linguistics, and folklore published since 1963 in nearly 4,000 journals, while *The International Bibliography of the Social Sciences* contains bibliographic information about publications

 ON THE WEB SITE

View the Research Links on the *Bedford Researcher* Web site at **http://www .bedfordresearcher .com** for an annotated list of databases, Web search sites and directories, and print resources organized by discipline.

 IN THIS BOOK

For a list of databases, Web search sites and directories, and print resources organized by discipline, see p. 381.

 RESEARCH ASSISTANT

Use the worksheet Search Databases to keep track of the results of your database searches.

**Figure 5.4
A Record
Retrieved
from the *Art
Abstracts* Sub-
ject Database**

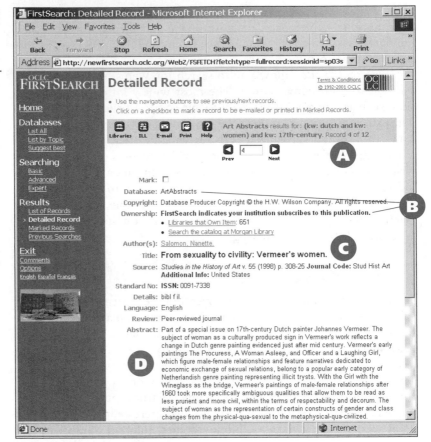

The record provides the following:

A The keywords that were used in the search: *Dutch, women,* and *17th-century.*

B Information about the database and whether the library that provided access to the database owns the journal in which the article
was published.

C Information about the author and title of the article as well as
about where and when the article was published.

D An abstract—or brief description—of the article.

**ON THE
WEB SITE**

View the tutorial
How to Search a
Database at
**http://www
.bedfordresearcher
.com** to learn more
about using data-
bases to locate
sources.

in economics, political science, sociology, and anthropology from over
2,600 journals published in more than one hundred countries.

Full-Text Databases. Full-text databases, such as *Lexis-Nexis Academic Universe,* the *ACM Digital Library,* and *Electric Library,* provide
the complete text of documents as well as their publication informa-

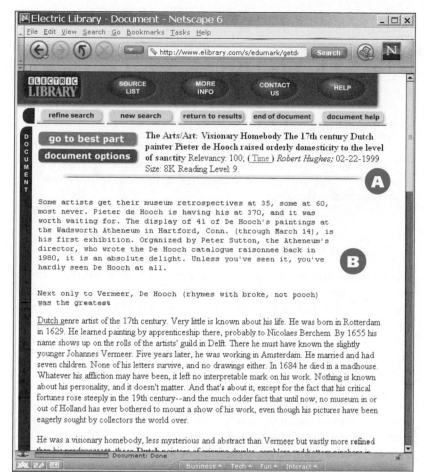

Figure 5.5
A Full-Text Article Retrieved from the *Electric Library* Database (http://www .elibrary .com)

A The *Electric Library* database record gives information about the author and title of the article as well as where and when the article was published.

B The record provides the complete text of the article.

tion (see Figure 5.5). These databases are becoming increasingly popular, as they provide access to a larger and larger number of publications.

Citation Indexes. Citation indexes are highly specialized but useful to researchers. A citation index can point the way to additional articles about a topic by identifying which publications have made reference to another publication. Such a resource can help you discover the many voices within the conversation you have joined.

Your Research Project

USE *RESEARCH ASSISTANT* TO COLLECT AND MANAGE YOUR ELECTRONIC SOURCES

As you work with databases, *Research Assistant* can help you keep track of useful citations, abstracts, and passages from full-text articles and books. *Research Assistant* allows you to save and work with all forms of electronic materials, including the text found on the results pages of Web-accessible databases.

Research Assistant is a computer program found on the CD-ROM at the back of this book. Read more about the program on p. 73 or visit the *Bedford Researcher* Web site at **http://www .bedfordresearcher.com**.

■ Types of Web Search Sites

The Web has become the largest and most accessible "library" in the world. In addition to content developed for online use, the Web is home to a great deal of material that was once available only in print. For example, many magazines and journals are placing their back issues on the Web, and others are moving completely to online publication. In addition, companies such as Bell & Howell are providing access to literature published long before the information age.

RESEARCH ASSISTANT

Use the worksheet Launch Pad to access leading Web search sites and directories and to keep track of promising sources.

Unfortunately, the Web is also the most disorganized library in the world, since it's being built by several million people without a common plan or much communication among them. Thus, to locate sources, researchers have turned to several types of Web search sites, including Web search engines, meta search sites, expert sites, alternative search sites, and specialized search sites.

Web Search Engines.   Like databases and online library catalogs, Web search engines typically display a field into which you can type keywords or phrases and a SEARCH button that you click on to start your search (see Figure 5.6). The primary difference between Web search engines and the databases and catalogs in a library is the *types of sources*. When you use a Web search engine, you'll obtain information about Web pages and other forms of information on the Internet, such as images, newsgroups, electronic mailing lists, telnet sites, FTP sites, Gopher sites, chat rooms, and MOOs. (You'll learn more about many of these sources later in this chapter.)

IN THIS BOOK

To learn more about keyword searches, see p. 99.

Web search engines are constantly searching for and adding new Web pages to their databases. The search engines also recheck the pages they already list to ensure that they are still active. This work takes time, and as a result the newest material on the Web might not be in a search engine's database. In addition, because Web pages can be changed or deleted, information found in the database might no longer

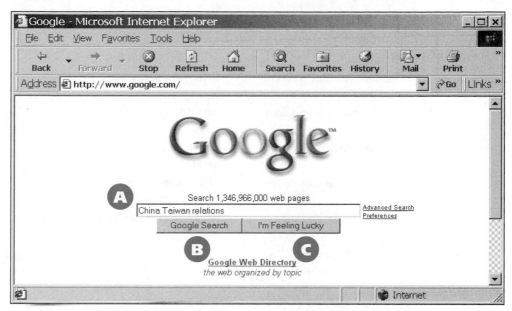

Figure 5.6 Searching the *Google* Web Site (**http://www.google.com**)

A To search, type a phrase or one or more keywords (in this case, *China Taiwan relations*) in the search field.

B To obtain a list of Web sites that match your search terms, click on the GOOGLE SEARCH button.

C To go directly to the Web site that *Google* judges to be most relevant to your search terms, click on the I'M FEELING LUCKY button.

be accurate at the time you conduct a search. Sometimes you won't find information that actually exists on the Web, and sometimes you'll find that a page located through a Web search engine no longer exists.

It's important to realize the limitations of Web search engines. Most search engines index only a portion of the Web—sometimes as much as 50 percent and sometimes as little as 5 percent. In practical terms, this means that you should use multiple search engines. If you don't find what you're looking for on one, it doesn't mean you won't find it on another.

Meta Search Sites. Meta search sites, such as *Metacrawler* (**http://www.metacrawler.com**), allow you to conduct a search on several search engines or directories at the same time. These sites typically search the major search engines and directories—such as *AltaVista, Google, Lycos,* and *Yahoo!*—and then present a limited number of results on a single page.

In some cases, you can customize the list of sites that are searched when you conduct a keyword search on a meta search site. *Dogpile*

ON THE WEB SITE
View the Research Links on the *Bedford Researcher* Web site at **http://www.bedfordresearcher.com** for a list of additional Web search engines.

ON THE WEB
SELECTED WEB SEARCH ENGINES

All The Web
http://www.alltheweb.com

Google
http://www.google.com

AltaVista
http://www.altavista.com

HotBot
http://hotbot.lycos.com

AOL Search
http://search.aol.com

Lycos
http://www.lycos.com

Direct Hit
http://www.directhit.com

MSN Search
http://search.msn.com

Excite
http://www.excite.com

Netscape Search
http://search.netscape.com

Go.com
http://www.go.com

(**http://www.dogpile.com**) and *ProFusion* (**http://www.profusion.com**), among others, allow you to specify which sites are searched and, in some cases, the order in which sites are searched.

Use a meta search site early in your search for information on the Web. A meta search site allows you to do a side-by-side comparison of various search sites and directories. When featured writer Aaron Batty searched for the phrase *one China policy* on *ProFusion,* for example, he found that the search sites *AltaVista, Excite,* and *MSN* produced more useful sets of results than the *LookSmart* and *Netscape* search sites. In subsequent searches, as a result, he was more likely to use *AltaVista, Excite,* and *MSN* than *LookSmart* and *Netscape.*

ON THE WEB SITE

View the Research Links on the *Bedford Researcher* Web site at **http://www.bedfordresearcher.com** for a list of additional meta search sites.

ON THE WEB
SELECTED META SEARCH SITES

Dogpile
http://www.dogpile.com

Query Server
http://queryserver.dataware.com

InfoZoid
http://www.infozoid.com

Search.com
http://www.search.com

Ixquick
http://www.ixquick.com

Supercrawler.com
http://www.supercrawler.com

Mamma.com
http://www.mamma.com

SurfWax
http://www.surfwax.com

MetaCrawler
http://www.metacrawler.com

Vivisimo
http://vivisimo.com

ProFusion
http://www.profusion.com

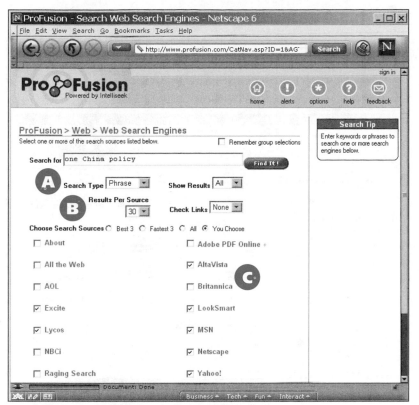

Figure 5.7 Customizing a Search on the *ProFusion* Meta Search Site (http:// www .profusion .com)

A The advanced search page on *ProFusion* lets you indicate the type of search you want to conduct. You can search for *all* of the terms listed in the search field or *any* of the terms listed in the search field. You can also search for a phrase, or you can conduct a Boolean search.

B *ProFusion* lets you specify the number of results returned by the search as well as the number of sources obtained from each search engine or directory. It also lets you determine whether you want it to check whether the links are still active.

C *ProFusion* lets you select which search engines and directories are searched.

Expert Sites.   Expert sites, such as *Abuzz* (**http://www.abuzz.com**) and *Askme.com* (**http://www.askme.com**), let you ask questions and then receive responses from real people who are knowledgeable about a subject, such as foreign policy or kayaking (see Figure 5.8). Typically, these sites also allow you to view answers to questions that other people have asked about the conversation you've decided to join.

Be wary of the quality of the answers you receive. Although you might receive useful advice, the "expert" replying to your question might actually know surprisingly little about the topic.

Figure 5.8 Getting an Answer from *Askme.com* (http://www .askme.com)

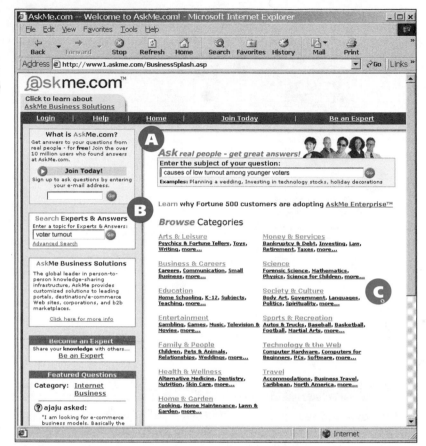

A Type a question or subject in the ASK box and click on the GO button to get an answer from an *Askme.com* expert. Featured writer Gaele Lopez typed *causes of low turnout among younger voters*.

B You can also conduct a keyword search to view answers previously provided by experts. Gaele typed the keywords *voter turnout*.

C You can also browse the *Askme.com* categories to view previously provided answers on specific topics. Gaele might have chosen to click on the Government subcategory of the Society & Culture category.

ON THE WEB SITE

View the Research Links on the *Bedford Researcher* Web site at **http://www .bedfordresearcher .com** for a list of additional expert sites.

ON THE WEB
SELECTED EXPERT SITES

Abuzz.com
http://www.abuzz.com

AllExperts
http://www.allexperts.com

Ask Jeeves Answer Point
http://answerpoint.ask.com

Askme.com
http://www.askme.com

Alternative Search Sites. Alternative search sites attempt to add value to your search with features not available on standard Web search sites and directories. Two sites—*Ask Jeeves* and *Oingo*—are examples of alternative search sites.

Ask Jeeves (**http://www.askjeeves.com**) combines the question-and-answer format of an expert site with the look and feel of a Web search engine. (In fact, *Ask Jeeves* has a companion expert site—*Ask Jeeves Answer Point* at **http://answerpoint.ask.com**.) *Ask Jeeves* presents a list of questions that are similar or identical to your question and asks you to select the one that most closely resembles your question (see Figure 5.9). If you select one of the suggested questions, you will be taken to a page created by the *Ask Jeeves* staff or directly to a Web site that *Ask Jeeves* judges relevant to your question. If *Ask Jeeves* can't answer your question, you can use its online help to refine your question.

Oingo (**http://www.oingo.com**) uses what it calls "meaning-based search" to search the Web. Rather than looking for occurrences of specific keywords or phrases, as most search engines do, *Oingo* attempts to look for relationships among the words and phrases you enter in the search field. For example, rather than looking for Web sites in which the search terms *one* and *China* and *policy* appear, *Oingo* would look for Web sites that addressed policy issues related to China and, in particular, for Web sites that addressed a "one China" policy.

Alternative search sites can help you navigate the often overwhelming amount of results you might obtain from a standard search site. *Ask Jeeves*'s suggested questions and *Oingo*'s meaning-based search aren't guaranteed to work, but in many cases they can save you time by focusing your search.

Specialized Search Sites. Specialized search sites allow you to search within a specific content area, such as microbiology, art history, or politics. One of the best strategies for locating specialized search sites is to visit *InvisibleWeb.com* (**http://www.invisibleweb.com**).

IN THIS BOOK
Read more about expert sites on p. 95. Read more about Web search engines on p. 92.

IN THIS BOOK
Read more about Web directories on p. 104. For an annotated list, organized by discipline, of databases, Web search sites and directories, and print resources, see p. 381.

ON THE WEB
SELECTED ALTERNATIVE SEARCH SITES

Aeiwi
http://www.aeiwi.com

Ask Jeeves
http://www.askjeeves.com

Disinformation
http://www.disinfo.com

Links2Go
http://www.links2go.com

Oingo
http://www.oingo.com

ON THE WEB SITE
View the Research Links on the *Bedford Researcher* Web site at **http://www.bedfordresearcher.com** for a list of additional alternative search sites.

Figure 5.9
Results of a
Search on
Ask Jeeves
(http://www
.askjeeves
.com)

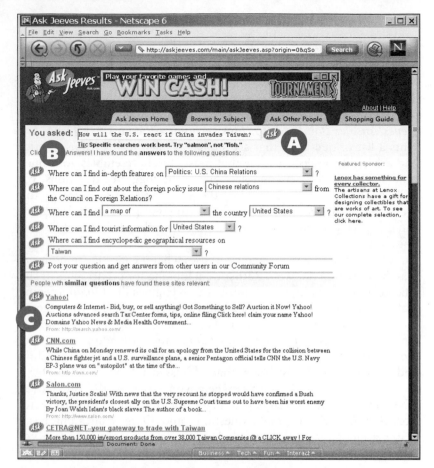

A You type your question in the search field, where you can revise it or ask another if the responses don't seem useful. Featured writer Aaron Batty asked the question "How will the U.S. react if China invades Taiwan?"

B *Ask Jeeves* presents a list of questions from its database that are similar to or identical to your question. If one of the questions is relevant to your conversation, check the ASK button next to that question.

C *Ask Jeeves* also conducts a search on selected search engines and Web directories. You can view the results of any search by clicking on the ASK button next to it.

> **Your Research Project**
>
> **USE *RESEARCH ASSISTANT* TO COLLECT AND MANAGE YOUR WEB SOURCES**
>
> As you prepare to collect information using Web search sites, consider the advantages of using *Research Assistant* to keep track of useful Web pages as well as the text, images, and media materials found on those pages. *Research Assistant* is well suited to working with Web sites.
>
> *Research Assistant* is a computer program found on the CD-ROM at the back of this book. Read more about the program on p. 73 or visit the *Bedford Researcher* Web site at **http://www .bedfordresearcher.com**.

■ Using Keywords to Search Databases and Web Search Sites

Keywords are the words and phrases you enter in the search field of a database or Web search site. Featured writer Gaele Lopez used the keywords *voter* and *turnout* in some of his searches for information about his research writing project, while Rianne Uilk used the phrases *Colorado Senate Bill 186* and *education reform*.

Keyword searches include

- **simple searches** that use one or more words, such as *voters* or *turnout*
- **wildcard searches** that use special characters, such as * or ?, to increase the scope of a search
- **searches for exact phrases** that find sources containing words in a specific order, such as *Colorado Senate Bill 186*
- **Boolean searches** that allow you to specify which keywords or phrases to include or exclude from a search

Simple Searches. Simple searches involve entering one or more keywords into a search field and clicking on the SEARCH button. In some databases, library catalogs, and Web search sites, adding keywords to a search *increases* the number of sources you find (as in "find all sources containing the keywords *research* **or** *writing*"). In other cases, adding keywords *decreases* the number of sources you find (as in "find only sources containing **both** the keywords *research* **and** *writing*"). You can find out how your database, library catalog, or Web search site treats multiple keywords by consulting online help—or by conducting some test searches and reviewing your results.

Test searches can also tell you whether the order in which you type your keywords matters in a database or Web search site. For example, changing the order of the keywords makes a difference in the results returned by *Google* but not *AltaVista*.

 ON THE WEB SITE
View the tutorials How to Use a Web Search Site and How to Refine Searches by Adding Keywords at **http://www .bedfordresearcher .com** to learn more about searching the Web.

Your Research Project

USE YOUR RESEARCH QUESTION TO GENERATE SEARCH TERMS
To generate keywords for your searches, write your research question on a piece of paper or in a word processor and then underline or boldface the most important words and phrases in the sentence. Brainstorm a list of related words and phrases:

Example:

What was the relationship between **seventeenth-century Dutch paintings** of **women** and the **culture** in which they were created?

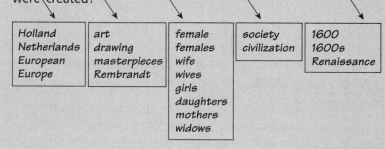

Holland Netherlands European Europe	art drawing masterpieces Rembrandt	female females wife wives girls daughters mothers widows	society civilization	1600 1600s Renaissance

If you'd like to complete this activity online, use the **Research Log** activity "Use Your Research Question to Generate Keywords" at **http://www.bedfordresearcher.com**. If you have created a research log using a notebook or a word processor, you can print or download this activity.

Wildcard Searches.   Sometimes you're not sure what form of a word is most likely to occur. Rather than conducting several searches for *paint, paints, painting, painted,* and *painters,* for example, you can combine your search into a single *wildcard search.* Wildcards are symbols that take the place of letters or strings of letters. By standing in for multiple letters, they allow you to expand the scope of your search.

The most commonly used wildcard symbols are

* usually takes the place of one or more characters
? usually takes the place of a single character

To search for sources containing the keywords *vote, voting, voter, voters,* and *voted* you can type *vot** in the search field of a Web search site or database that supports wildcard searches. The result will be sources that include any words that begin with the letters *vot.*

Remember that some databases, library catalogs, and search sites might not support wildcard symbols.

Searches for Exact Phrases.   Sometimes the best way to locate information in a keyword search is to search for an exact phrase. If you're interested in the economic impact of a damaging hurricane, such as

Hurricane Hugo, for instance, you might search for sources containing the exact phrase *Hurricane Hugo*. This would eliminate sources in which the word *hurricane* or *Hugo* appears by itself, such as general definitions of hurricanes and sites about scholar Hugo Bedau.

You can get even more specific and search for the phrase *economic impact of Hurricane Hugo*. However, you might find it more effective to create a search in which you look for the phrase *Hurricane Hugo* and the keyword *economic* (or, better yet, *econom**). Or you could search for two phrases: *Hurricane Hugo* and *economic impact*.

Most databases and Web search sites allow you to specify phrases using quotation marks. They'll treat any words placed within the quotation marks as a phrase, as in *"Hurricane Hugo"* or *"economic impact."* In addition, some databases and Web search sites provide a drop-down menu where you can indicate whether a string of words consists of separate keywords or is a phrase.

Boolean Searches. Keyword searches often result in lists of sources that are only somewhat related to the conversation you've decided to join. *Boolean searches* allow you to focus your search more precisely. The basic elements of a Boolean search involve specifying whether keywords or phrases *can* appear in the results of a search, *must* appear in the results, or *must not* appear in the results. Boolean operators (specific terms such as *AND, OR,* and *NOT*) allow you to search for keywords or phrases that appear next to, before or after, or within a certain distance from one another within a document. Table 5.1 lists commonly used Boolean operators and their functions.

ON THE
WEB SITE
View the tutorial
How to Conduct
Boolean Searches
at **http://www
.bedfordresearcher
.com/** to learn
more about using
Boolean searches
to locate sources.

TABLE 5.1 COMMONLY USED BOOLEAN OPERATORS		
BOOLEAN OPERATOR	**FUNCTION**	**EXAMPLE**
AND	Finds sources that include both terms	China AND Taiwan
OR	Finds sources that include either term	China OR Taiwan
NOT	Finds sources that include one term but not the other	China NOT Taiwan
ADJ (adjacent)	Finds sources in which the keywords appear next to each other	China ADJ Taiwan
NEAR	Finds sources in which the keywords appear within a certain number of words of each other (usually twenty-five; depending on the search engine, you may be able to change the default setting)	China NEAR Taiwan
BEFORE	Finds sources in which keywords appear in a particular order	China BEFORE Taiwan
Parentheses ( )	Although not strictly a Boolean search term, parentheses are used to group keywords and Boolean operators	(China AND Taiwan) NOT U.S.

Depending on the features of the database, library catalog, or Web search site you are using, you can conduct Boolean searches in one of three ways: using + (plus) or − (minus) signs in a search field, using advanced search forms, and using Boolean expressions.

- **Using + (plus) or − (minus) signs in a search field:** Most Web search sites and databases use + and − signs to require (+) and exclude (−) keywords or phrases. *AltaVista*'s approach is typical: place a + sign in front of words or phrases that *must* be present in a source and place a − sign in front of words or phrases that *must not* be present in a source. Featured Writers Rianne Uilk and Gaele Lopez might have conducted the following searches on databases and Web search sites that support the use of + and − signs to require and exclude keywords and phrases.

  +"Colorado" +"Senate Bill 186" −"congress" +"impact" +"voter turnout" +"younger voters" −"senior citizens" +"presidential elections"

- **Using advanced search forms:** Most databases, library catalogs, and Web search sites allow you to conduct an advanced search. Advanced search options let you specify exactly what you want to include and exclude from your search results and whether a particular set of words is a phrase or multiple keywords (see Figure 5.10).

- **Using Boolean expressions:** Depending on your comfort level with Boolean expressions, you can create highly complex searches. Combining keywords, phrases, Boolean operators, and parentheses, you can specify searches that would otherwise be impossible in even the most complex, advanced search forms. Featured writer Aaron Batty created a complex Boolean search that involved two keywords (*U.S., economic*), one phrase (*one China policy*), and one compound expression (*China AND Taiwan*) that uses parentheses to set off two required terms. This search required that the terms *China, Taiwan,* and *U.S.* and the phrase *one China policy* must be found in all sources returned in the search, while the term *economic* must *not* be found:

  (China AND Taiwan) AND U.S. AND "one China policy" NOT economic

Although the general principles underlying Boolean search are shared across databases, library catalogs, and Web search sites, it's important to remember that the specific commands for requiring or excluding keywords or phrases will vary. The online help on Boolean searches will tell you which commands to use.

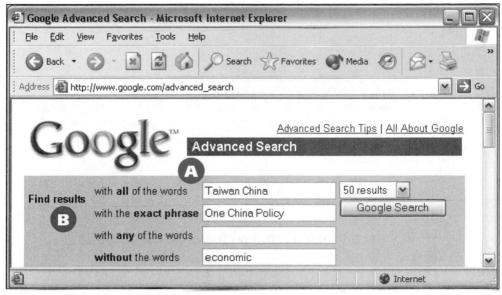

Figure 5.10 Using an Advanced Search Form to Conduct a Boolean Search

A Type keywords or phrases in the search fields. In this example, featured writer Aaron Batty has used the keywords *Taiwan, China,* and *economic* and the phrase *one China policy*.

B Indicate which terms must be present (Boolean *AND*), would be good to have (Boolean *OR*), or must not be present in the results (Boolean *NOT*). Aaron requires that sources returned by the search include two keywords (*Taiwan* and *China*) and one phrase (*one China policy*), while requiring that one keyword (*economic*) not be found in the source.

Your Research Project

RECORD YOUR SEARCHES

One of the most important research strategies you can use as you collect information is keeping track of your searches. Note not only the keywords or phrases and the search strategies you used with them (wildcards, Boolean search, author search, and so on) but also how many sources the search turned up and whether those sources were relevant to your research project.

In your research log, record the following information for each source you search:

1. Resource that was searched
2. Search terms used (keywords, phrases, publication information)
3. Search strategies used (simple search, wildcard search, exact phrase search, Boolean search)
4. Date search was conducted

RESEARCH ASSISTANT

Use the worksheet Keywords and Searches to keep track of your searches of online resources.

(continued)

5. Number of results produced by the search
6. Relevance of the results
7. Notes about the search

If you'd like to complete this activity online, use the **Research Log** activity "Record Your Searches" at **http://www.bedford researcher.com**. If you have created a research log using a notebook or a word processor, you can print or download this activity.

5c

How can I use Web directories to locate sources?

RESEARCH ASSISTANT
Use the worksheet Launch Pad to access leading Web search sites and directories and to keep track of promising sources.

ON THE WEB SITE
View the tutorial How to Search a Web Directory at **http://www .bedfordresearcher .com** to learn more about using Web directories to locate sources.

Unlike Web search sites, which automatically enter information about each Web page into a large database and then give tools to help you search that database, *Web directories* such as *Yahoo!* and the *Open Directory Project* employ human editors to organize information about Web pages into categories and subcategories.

Directories allow you to browse lists of Web sites by clicking on general topics, such as Health or Education, and then successively narrowing your search by clicking on subcategories of topics. In addition to browsing the categories on a directory, many directories permit you to conduct keyword searches within specific categories (see Figure 5.11). This enables you to search within a collection of Web sites that have already been judged to be relevant to your conversation by real people.

ON THE WEB SITE
View the Research Links on the *Bedford Researcher* Web site at **http://www .bedfordresearcher .com** for a list of additional Web directories.

ON THE WEB
SELECTED WEB DIRECTORIES

4anything.com
http://www.4anything.com

About.com
http://www.about.com

Galaxy
http://www.galaxy.com

FuzzyCrawler
http://fuzzycrawler.com

Google Directory
http://directory.google.com

Internet Public Library Reference Center
http://www.ipl.org/ref

LookSmart
http://www.looksmart.com

Open Directory Project
http://dmoz.org

Yahoo!
http://www.yahoo.com

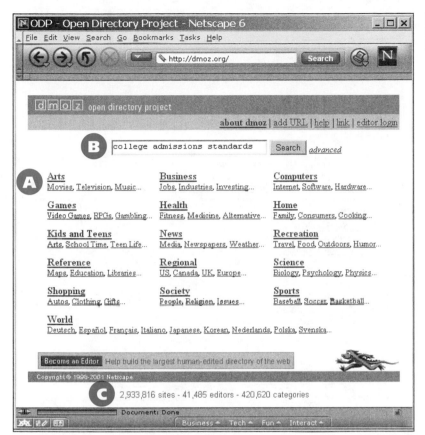

Figure 5.11a
Searching a
Web Directory

A The *Open Directory Project* home page (**http://dmoz.org**) contains
a list of categories, such as Reference and Health. Inside these
categories are subcategories, such as Maps and Fitness.

B The *Open Directory Project* also supports keyword searches, which
produce a list of categories and related Web sites in those categories.

C The *Open Directory Project* indicates the number of sites that are
listed in its directory, the number of categories on the site, and the
number of editors who have contributed to the project.

(continued)

For your project, you may want to try specialized directories that
focus narrowly on one topic, such as biology (*Biolinks* at **http://www**
.biolinks.com) or history (*Horus' Web Links to History Resources* at
http://www.ucr.edu/h-gig/horuslinks.html). Specialized directories are
often the product of one or a few individuals. As such, they vary in
quality and comprehensiveness.

📖 **IN THIS
BOOK**

For a list of data-
bases, Web search
sites and directo-
ries, and print
resources organ-
ized by discipline,
see p. 381.

**Figure 5.11b
Searching a
Web Directory**

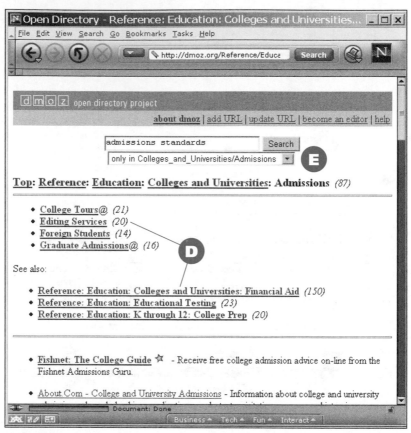

D Clicking on the Reference category on the *Open Directory Project*
home page results in a list of related categories. You can continue
your search by clicking on one of these categories.

E The most useful feature of keyword searches on Web directories
is the ability to restrict your search to sources within a particular
category. To restrict your search to a specific category in the *Open
Directory Project,* select the ONLY IN... option from the pull-down
menu.

5d

How can I use other online resources to locate sources?

You can locate useful information about your conversation by searching portals and vortals, electronic mailing lists, newsgroups, transcripts
of chat and MOO sessions, and government documents.

■ Portals and Vortals

Think of *portals* as the logical next step for a Web search site or directory that wants to be all things to all Web users. Many of the more successful Web search sites and directories, such as *Yahoo!, AltaVista, LookSmart, Lycos, MSN,* and *NBCi,* have shifted their focus from merely helping readers locate Web sites to providing a comprehensive set of Web-based services, such as email, stock quotes, weather reports, news, entertainment, sports information, telephone directories, and online shopping. Today these sites compete with one another to offer a one-stop gateway—or portal—to the Web.

Portals offer several advantages to research writers. Most portals allow you to customize the content and layout of the page you see when you visit their site. *My Yahoo!* (**http://my.yahoo.com**), for example, allows you to display the *Yahoo!* search field and directory listings, a list of saved searches, and information from a variety of news, sports, and entertainment sources, among many other options (see Figure 5.12). With a personalized site on *My Yahoo!,* you can save searches that were useful (*My Yahoo!* keeps track of your search terms and can rerun the search on request), take note of important sites and ideas as you search for information, and create your own customized directory of *Yahoo!* categories. Most important, regardless of whether you are searching for information from your home computer, a library computer, a classroom computer, or a work computer, you have access to all of the information on your personalized *My Yahoo!* site.

Vortals are portals for specific groups. (The name comes from combining the two words *vertical* and *portal.*) Some of the most popular vortals include *women.com* and *iVillage.com,* which are directed toward women, and *ZDnet.com* and *Cnet.com,* which are targeted at computer users.

Like portals, vortals offer opportunities for research writers. In addition to gaining an insider's view on a particular community, you can also use vortals to obtain specialized information about that community and to interact with its members through email, discussion forums, or chat.

■ Electronic Mailing Lists and Newsgroups

Electronic mailing lists enable an individual to distribute an email message to hundreds or even thousands of people who belong to the list. You read a message sent to a mailing list, sometimes referred to as a *listserv,* in the same way that you read other email messages. *Newsgroups,* in contrast, are places on the Internet where you can go to read messages on particular topics. Several Web sites allow you to search for mailing lists and newsgroups and in some cases individual messages sent to lists or groups.

ON THE WEB SITE
To learn more, view the research writing manual Newsgroups and Mailing Lists at **http://www .bedfordresearcher .com**.

**Figure 5.12
Customizing
the *My
Yahoo!* Portal
(http://my
.yahoo.com)**

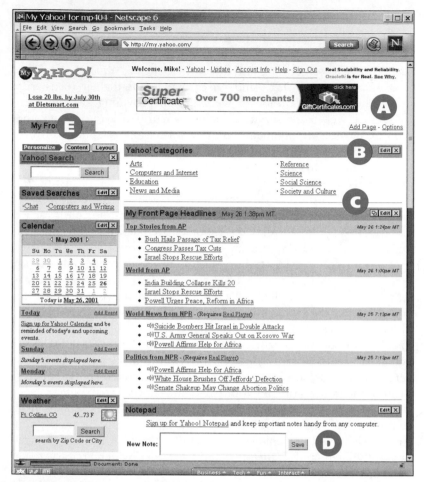

A Click on the OPTIONS link to access all customizable options (layout, colors, content) on *My Yahoo!*

B Click on the EDIT button to specify which *Yahoo!* categories appear on your *My Yahoo!* page.

C Click on the next EDIT button to select the type of news you want to see on your page as well as the news services that provide your news.

D Write a note and click on the SAVE button to save notes about your research project in the *My Yahoo!* Notepad.

E Click on the CONTENT button to specify a range of additional content and services for your *My Yahoo!* page, including local weather, a calendar, *Yahoo!* search, and your saved searches. Click on the LAYOUT button to set the location of information on that page.

ON THE WEB SITE

View Research Links on the *Bedford Researcher* Web site at **http://www .bedfordresearcher .com** for links to additional search sites for news-groups and mailing lists.

ON THE WEB

SELECTED MAILING LIST AND NEWSGROUP SEARCH SITES

CataList
http://www.lsoft.com/catalist.html
Google Groups
http://groups.google.com
Topica
http://www.topica.com

Electronic mailing lists and newsgroups can play an important role in this stage of your research writing project. Earlier, when you were exploring your topic, newsgroups and mailing lists allowed you to listen in on conversations without actually making your own contributions. As you begin to collect information in earnest, post questions of your own on relevant newsgroups and mailing lists. Although there is no guarantee that you'll receive helpful responses, experts in a particular area often belong to newsgroups and mailing lists. If you are fortunate enough to get into a discussion with one or more knowledgeable people, you can obtain useful information. Remember that one of the biggest advantages of newsgroups and mailing lists is that they are interactive. Unlike a Web page, you can ask questions and get answers from real people. If you read *posts,* messages posted to a newsgroup or mailing list, that are relevant to your research project, add those sources to your working bibliography.

IN THIS BOOK

For more information on adding electronic sources to your working bibliography, see p. 46.

▪ Transcripts of Chat and MOO/MUD/MUSH Sessions

Chat is a form of electronic communication in which the participants in a discussion are online at the same time (in a *chatroom*) and can view typed messages immediately. It's similar to the popular instant messaging services offered by companies such as Microsoft and America Online. Chatrooms are accessible through a Web browser or as standalone programs.

A number of chatrooms on the Internet host discussions in which knowledgeable people exchange views about a topic. *CNN.com,* for instance, frequently hosts chat sessions with leading authors, politicians, news reporters, and entertainers. If you learn of a scheduled public chat session that is relevant to your conversation, join it and record a transcript of the session. (If your browser or your chat program doesn't allow you to record a transcript, you can copy relevant passages during the session and paste them into a word processing file.)

If no relevant chats are scheduled, edited transcripts of chat sessions are available on the Web. The *CNN Chat* page provides links to

ON THE WEB SITE

To learn more, view the research writing manual Chat and MOOs on the *Bedford Researcher* Web site at **http://www .bedfordresearcher .com**.

ON THE WEB SITE

View Research Links on the *Bedford Researcher* Web site at **http://www .bedfordresearcher .com** for additional links to chatrooms and MOOs.

ON THE WEB
SELECTED SOURCES FOR CHATROOMS AND TRANSCRIPTS

ABC News Transcripts
http://www.abcnews.go .com/sections/us/DailyNews/ CHAT_INDEX.html

CNN Chat
http://www.cnn.com/ community/chat/transcripts

Lycos Chat Transcripts
http://clubs.lycos.com/live/ ChatRooms/ChatHome.asp

MSNBC Chat Transcripts
http://www.msnbc.com/chat

Open Directory Project Chat Transcripts
http://dmoz.org/Computers/ Internet/Chat/Transcripts

Yahoo! Chat
http://chat.yahoo.com

edited sessions at **http://www.cnn.com/community/chat/transcripts**. Other news organizations and Web search sites (such as *Yahoo!*) host chat sessions on various topics and provide access to transcripts.

MOOs, MUDs, and *MUSHes* serve a purpose similar to chat, although they allow for more control of the discussion environment. If you are working on a research project that focuses on the use of technology to support writing instruction, for example, you might visit some of the MOOs devoted to discussion of writing instruction, such as the *Connections MOO,* which can be accessed via telnet or MOO client at **connections.moo.mud.org:3333**.

ON THE WEB SITE

View Research Links on the *Bedford Researcher* Web site at **http://www .bedfordresearcher .com** for additional links to government document sites.

ON THE WEB
SELECTED SOURCES FOR LOCATING ONLINE GOVERNMENT DOCUMENTS

About.com's US Government Info Directory
http://usgovinfo.about.com

Catalog of U.S. Government Publications
http://www.access.gpo.gov/ su_docs/locators/cgp

FedStats
http://www.fedstats.gov/ search.html

FedWorld
http://www.fedworld.gov

FirstGov
http://www.firstgov.gov

Google Uncle Sam
http://www.google.com/ unclesam

Open Directory Project's Government Directory
http://dmoz.org/Society/ Government

SearchGov.com
http://www.searchgov.com

Yahoo's Government Directory
http://dir.yahoo.com/ Government

■ Government Publications on the Web

Many government agencies and institutions have turned to the Web as their primary means of distributing their publications. *FirstGov* (**http://www.firstgov.gov**), sponsored by the U.S. government, allows you to search the federal government's network of online resources. The *Catalog of U.S. Government Publications* (**http://www.access.gpo .gov/su_docs/locators/cgp**) provides publication information about print documents and links to those publications when they are available online. Sites such as *FedStats* (**http://www.fedstats.gov/search .html**) and *FedWorld* (**http://www.fedworld.gov**) give access to a wide range of government-related materials. In addition to these specialized government Web sites, you can locate government publications through many Web directories, such as *Open Directory Project* and *Yahoo!*

Your Research Project

DISCUSS YOUR RESEARCH PROJECT WITH OTHERS
As you collect information about the conversation you have decided to join, reconsider how the plan you created in the **Research Log** activity "Create Your Research Project Search Plan" capitalizes on available electronic resources. If you are uncertain about how you might use these resources, discuss your project with a reference librarian or your instructor. Given the wide range of electronic resources that are available, a few minutes of discussion could save you a great deal of time searching for useful sources.

If you'd like to update your search plan online, use the **Research Log** activity "Create Your Research Project Search Plan" at **http://www.bedfordresearcher.com**. If you have created a research log using a notebook or a word processor, you can print or download the search plan activity.

As you learn more about your conversation from the sources you collect, take time to review and, if necessary, to revise your research question. Ask yourself whether your search plan needs to be updated as well. In addition, as you collect sources, continue to add them to your working bibliography. At this point in your research writing process, you'll want to include any sources that have some relevance to your project. Don't start eliminating sources until later, when you begin to critically read and evaluate your sources. The next chapter focuses on searching for information with print resources.

 ON THE WEB SITE
Use the Working Bibliography tool in the **Research Log** at http://www .bedfordresearcher .com to keep track of your sources online.

CHAPTER 6

Searching for Information with Print Resources

Contrary to recent claims, there's life (and information) beyond the Internet. A wealth of print resources can help you locate information relevant to your research project. This chapter examines some of the most useful print resources you'll find in library reference rooms, library periodical rooms, and library stacks by asking the following key questions.

Key Questions

6a

How can I use a library reference room to locate sources?

IN THIS BOOK
Read more about databases on p. 88.

Library reference rooms house reference books that can help you locate information. Many of these reference books serve the same purposes as the electronic subject, bibliographic, and citation databases discussed in Chapter 5. Others provide information not available in databases, such as explanatory articles, short biographies, maps, and photographs of paintings and other works of art.

Locating sources using print resources in addition to electronic resources such as databases has several benefits:

- *Most databases have short memories.* Databases seldom index sources published before 1970, and typically index sources only as far back as the mid-1980s. Depending on the conversation you've decided to join, a database might not allow you to locate important sources. For this reason, many libraries own both the print and electronic versions of indexes such as the *Social Sciences Citation Index.* Although the electronic version owned by your library might include only listings that are less than a decade old, the older print versions usually go back much further than that.

- *Most databases focus on short works.* In contrast, many of the print resources in library reference rooms will refer you to related books and longer publications as well as to articles in periodicals.

- *Many library reference resources are unavailable in electronic form.* In some cases, these resources are so specialized that it would not be cost-effective to make them available in electronic form. For instance, the *Encyclopedia of Creativity,* which offers more than two hundred articles, is available only in print form.

- *Entries in print indexes are easier to browse.* Despite efforts to support browsing, databases support searching far better than they do browsing.

Reference rooms contain print resources on a range of topics, from government to finance to philosophy to science. Some of the most important print resources you'll find in a reference room include bibliographies, indexes, dictionaries, biographies, general and specialized encyclopedias, handbooks, almanacs, and atlases.

■ Bibliographies

Bibliographies list books, articles, monographs (which are typically longer than articles but shorter than books), and other publications that have been judged relevant to a topic. Although older bibliographies are more likely to focus on books and monographs, you'll find that those published more recently include important articles in their lists. Some bibliographies and subject indexes provide only bibliographic citations, while others provide *abstracts* — brief descriptions — of listed sources.

Complete bibliographies attempt to list all of the sources published about a topic, while *selective bibliographies* attempt to list only the best sources published about a topic. Some bibliographies limit their inclusion of sources by time period, often focusing on sources published during a given year.

You're likely to find several types of bibliographies in your library's reference room or stacks, including trade bibliographies, general bibliographies, and specialized bibliographies.

ON THE WEB SITE

View Links on the *Bedford Researcher* Web site at **http://www .bedfordresearcher .com** for an annotated list of databases, Web search sites and directories, and print resources organized by discipline.

IN THIS BOOK

For an annotated list, organized by discipline, of databases, Web search sites and directories, and print resources, see p. 381.

ON THE WEB SITE

Read more about Kevin Fahey and the other student writers discussed in this chapter in Featured Writers on the *Bedford Researcher* Web site at **http://www .bedfordresearcher .com**.

Trade Bibliographies. Trade bibliographies allow you to locate books published about a particular topic. Leading trade bibliographies include *The Subject Guide to Books in Print, Books in Print,* and *Cumulative Book Index.* Featured writer Kevin Fahey found a large number of books about Ernest Hemingway in *Books in Print* (see Figure 6.1).

General Bibliographies. General bibliographies cover a wide range of topics, usually in selective lists.

- For sources on humanities topics, consult *The Humanities: A Selective Guide to Information Sources.*

- For sources on social science topics, see *Social Science Reference Sources: A Practical Guide.*

- For sources on science topics, go to bibliographies such as *Information Sources in Science and Technology, Guide to Information*

Figure 6.1 An Entry from *Books in Print* on Ernest Hemingway

A The subject heading in *Books in Print*

B Recently published books are listed in bold print and set off with lines above and below, while older books are listed in normal print.

C Publication information includes the author's or editor's name(s), the title of the work, the Library of Congress number, the number of pages, the cover material (in this case, paper), the price, the International Standard Book Number (ISBN), and the publisher.

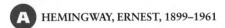

A HEMINGWAY, ERNEST, 1899–1961

B Astro, Richard & Beason, Jackson, J., eds.
Hemingway in Our Time: Published Record of a Literary Conference Devoted to a Study of the
C Work of Ernest Hemingway Held at Oregon State University on April 26–27, 1973. LC 73-18428. 222p. reprinted. Pap. 63.30 (0-317-28801-6.2020634) Bks Demand.

Baker, Carlos. Ernest Hemingway Life Story. 1976. 47.50 (0-685-45827-X, Scribners Ref) Mac Lib Ref.
—Hemingway, the Writer as Artist, 45h rev. ed. 440p. 1972, pap. Text 21.95 (0-691-01305-5, 86) Princeton U Pr.
Baldwan, Marc D. Reading "The Sun Also Rises" Hemingway's Political Unconscious. (Modern American Literature Ser.: Vol. 4). 168p. ©. 1997. 39.95 (0-8204-3033-1) P Lang Pubng.

Sources in the Botanical Sciences, and *Guide to Information Sources in the Physical Sciences.*

Specialized Bibliographies. Specialized bibliographies typically provide lists of sources—often annotated—about a topic. For example, *Art Books: A Basic Bibliography of Monographs on Artists,* edited by Wolfgang M. Freitag, focuses on sources about important artists.

Locating Bibliographies. Although you'll find most general and trade bibliographies in your library reference room, the majority of specialized bibliographies are in your library's stacks. To locate bibliographies about the conversation you've decided to join, use the following strategies:

- *Consult a cumulative bibliography.* Cumulative bibliographies provide an index of published bibliographies. *The Bibliographic Index: A Cumulative Bibliography of Bibliographies,* for instance, identifies bibliographies on a wide range of topics and is updated annually.

- *Consult your library's online catalog.* When you search your library's online catalog, use keywords related to your conversation plus the keyword *bibliography*. Featured writer Kevin Fahey searched his university's online catalog using the keywords *Hemingway* and *bibliography* (see Figure 6.2).

- *Seek advice from a reference librarian.* Reference librarians will help you locate bibliographies that are relevant to your conversation. Many college and university library Web sites also provide lists of reference materials, including bibliographies, for specific subject areas.

■ Indexes

While bibliographies focus on specific topics, *indexes* focus on sources found in a particular set of publications. Indexes provide citation information for the sources they list. In addition, many provide *abstracts*—brief descriptions—of sources. You can use abstracts to help determine whether a source is worth locating and reviewing. The most common type of indexes available in libraries are periodical indexes, indexes of materials in books, pamphlet indexes, government documents indexes, and citation indexes.

Periodical Indexes. Periodical indexes list sources published in magazines, trade journals, scholarly journals, and newspapers. Some periodical indexes cover a wide range of periodicals, others focus on periodicals that address a single subject, and still others focus on a small set or even an individual periodical.

IN THIS BOOK

Read about locating periodicals on p. 120.

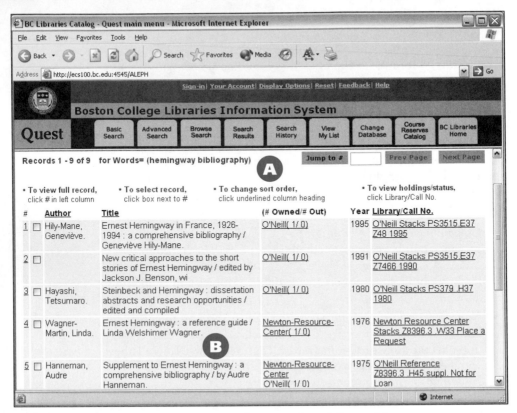

Figure 6.2   Searching an Online Library Catalog for Bibliographies

A Featured writer Kevin Fahey searched for bibliographies using the keywords
Hemingway and *bibliography*.

B The list of results contained several bibliographies.

- The *Readers' Guide to Periodical Literature* indexes roughly two hundred general-interest magazines. Updated monthly, the *Readers' Guide* organizes entries by author and subject.

- *Art Index* provides information about sources published only in art magazines and journals. Updated quarterly, *Art Index* orders entries by author and subject.

- The *New York Times Index* lists articles published only in that newspaper. Updated twice a month, the *Index* organizes entries by subject, geography, organization, and personal name.

Featured writer Patrick Crossland used the *Readers' Guide to Periodical Literature* to locate sources about college admissions (see Figure 6.3).

Significant differences exist between the print and electronic database versions of periodical indexes. Unlike the *Readers' Guide* data-

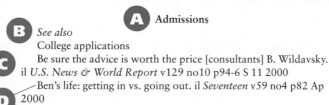

Figure 6.3   A Listing in the *Readers' Guide to Periodical Literature*

A The subject heading

B Other potentially relevant subject headings in the *Readers' Guide*

C Publication information for one article: title, author, the letters *il* for "illustrated," name of the periodical, volume, issue, page numbers, and date of publication

D Other articles related to the subject heading

base, which contains information on articles published since 1983, the printed *Readers' Guide to Periodical Literature* covers publications since 1900. Similarly, the *New York Times Index* database covers articles in the newspaper since 1969, while the print index covers articles since 1851.

Indexes of Materials in Books.   To locate articles in edited books, turn to indexes such as the *Essay and General Literature Index,* which indexes nearly five thousand book-length collections of articles and essays in the arts, humanities, and social sciences. You might also find subject-specific indexes of materials in books. *The Cumulative Bibliography of Asian Studies,* for example, covers articles in edited books.

Pamphlet Indexes.   Libraries frequently collect pamphlets of various kinds. To help patrons locate these materials, many libraries create a pamphlet index. Reference librarians will be able to tell you whether your library has a pamphlet index and where it is located. You can also consult the *Vertical File Index.* Updated monthly, this index lists roughly three thousand brief sources on ten to fifteen newsworthy topics each month. A reference librarian can help locate sources in the *Vertical File Index.*

Government Documents Indexes.   Government documents indexes list documents published by federal, state, and local governments. Many larger college and university libraries serve as depositories of government documents. As a result, you might be able to locate indexes to government documents in either the reference room or a

 ON THE WEB SITE

You will find an annotated list of periodical indexes, organized by academic discipline, on the Research Links page of the *Bedford Researcher* Web site at **http://www .bedfordresearcher .com.**

 IN THIS BOOK

Read about using the Web to search for government documents on p. 110.

separate government documents collection in your library. Ask a reference librarian for help. The following are some general strategies:

- To locate documents published by the federal government, consult the *Monthly Catalog of United States Government Publications*.
- To locate documents published by the U.S. Congress, consult the *CIS Index to Publications of the United States Congress*.
- To obtain information about the daily proceedings of the House of Representatives and the Senate, consult the *Congressional Record*.
- To locate documents published by the Supreme Court, consult *United States Reports*, the cumulative index of the *Official Reports of the Supreme Court*.
- To locate government documents containing statistical information, including census reports, consult the *Statistical Abstract of the United States*.

Libraries typically have state documents only for the state in which they are located. If you were conducting research in a library in Massachusetts, for example, you could locate documents published by the state of Massachusetts in the *Official Publications of the Commonwealth of Massachusetts*. Similarly, indexes of documents published by local (county, city) governments are seldom available in libraries outside the states in which those local governments are located.

IN THIS BOOK
Read about citation index databases on p. 91.

Citation Indexes. Citation indexes allow you to determine which publications have made reference to other publications, a useful strategy for finding sources that are engaged in the same conversation. To find out which sources had referred to an article published in a scientific journal, for example, you could consult the *Science Citation Index*, published by the Institute for Scientific Information.

■ Dictionaries

Dictionaries range from standard—such as *Merriam-Webster's Collegiate Dictionary*—to more specialized—such as *West's Tax Law Dictionary* or *Stedman's Medical Dictionary*. In addition, you may find specialized encyclopedias, handbooks, and bibliographies that include the word *dictionary* in their titles. These are more properly defined, however, as encyclopedias, handbooks, and bibliographies than as dictionaries.

■ Biographies

Biographies cover key figures in a field, time period, or geographic region. *Who's Who in America*, for instance, provides brief biographies of important figures in the United States during a given year, while *Great Lives from History* takes a broader view, offering biographies of key figures in world history.

■ General and Specialized Encyclopedias

General encyclopedias attempt to provide a little knowledge about a lot of things. In some ways they're like a friend who knows enough about everything to have an opinion but lacks the knowledge to be termed an expert. The idea behind a general encyclopedia, such as the *New Encyclopaedia Britannica* or the *Encyclopedia Americana,* is to present enough information about a topic to get you started on a more detailed search.

Specialized encyclopedias, as the name suggests, take a narrower focus than general encyclopedias, usually of a field of study or a narrow historical period. The *MIT Encyclopedia of the Cognitive Sciences,* for example, focuses on topics related to the study of the cognitive sciences. Depending on the encyclopedia, you might find articles that are written by leading scholars in a field, or you might find articles written by professional editors. In addition, articles in specialized encyclopedias are typically longer and offer more detailed coverage of topics than do articles in general encyclopedias.

■ Handbooks

Handbooks occupy a place between dictionaries and encyclopedias. Typically, their entries are longer than dictionary definitions but shorter than the articles found in encyclopedias. Most handbooks, such as *The Engineering Handbook* and the *International Handbook of Psychology,* cover a narrow topic area.

■ Almanacs

Almanacs contain lists, charts, and tables of information of various types. You're probably familiar with *The Old Farmer's Almanac,* which is known for its accuracy in predicting weather over the course of a year. Information can range from the average rainfall in Australia to the batting averages of the 1927 Yankees to the average income of Germans and Poles prior to World War II. Library reference rooms are likely to have many types of almanacs, some focusing on a single area of interest and others covering an array of topics.

■ Atlases

Atlases provide maps and related information about a region or country. Some atlases take a historical perspective, while others take various topical perspectives. The defining feature of an atlas is its attempt to define relationships between geography and the perspective it has adopted.

Your Research Project

DISCUSS YOUR RESEARCH PROJECT WITH OTHERS

As you collect information about the conversation you want to join, reconsider how the plan you created in the **Research Log** activity "Create Your Research Project Search Plan" capitalizes on the print resources available in your library reference room. If you are uncertain about how you might use these resources, discuss your project with a reference librarian. Given the wide range of specialized print resources that are available, a few minutes of discussion with a knowledgeable librarian could save you a great deal of time.

If you'd like to update your search plan online, use the **Research Log** activity "Create Your Research Project Search Plan" at **http://www.bedfordresearcher.com**. If you have created a research log using a notebook or a word processor, you can print or download the search plan activity.

6b

How can I use a library periodicals room to locate sources?

IN THIS BOOK
Learn more about browsing your library's stacks on p. 24.

Periodicals are publications that appear in sequential issues. They include newspapers, magazines, and academic and professional journals. A periodical room (sometimes called a *journals room*) allows you to browse recent issues of periodicals. Some libraries also have a separate newspaper room in which they keep newspapers published in the last few weeks or months.

To ensure everyone's access to recently published periodicals, most libraries don't allow you to check out journals or magazines that have been published within the last year, and they usually don't allow you to check out newspapers at all. In fact, some libraries don't allow you to take current periodicals into other parts of the library.

IN THIS BOOK
Read about using databases to locate articles in periodicals on p. 88. Learn about using print bibliographies and indexes on p. 112.

Depending on the space available in a library's periodicals room, older periodicals are sometimes placed in bound volumes in the stacks. Few libraries, however, keep back issues of newspapers in paper form. Instead, you can often find back issues of leading newspapers, such as the *New York Times* or the *Washington Post*, in full-text databases, or in *microform*. Microform is a generic name for *microfilm*, a strip of film containing greatly reduced images of printed pages, or *microfiche*, film roughly the shape and size of an index card containing the same kinds of miniaturized images. You can view these images using a micro-form reader, a projection unit that looks something like a large computer monitor. Many microform readers allow you to print full-size copies of the pages.

To help you locate articles in periodicals, most periodical rooms provide access to electronic databases, which are more likely than print indexes and bibliographies to contain listings of recent publications. Once you've identified articles you want to review, you'll need to locate the periodicals containing those articles. Most online library catalogs will allow you to conduct a title search for a periodical, in the same way you conduct a title search for a book. The online catalog will tell you the call number of the periodical, and most online catalogs will give information about its location in the library. In addition, some libraries provide a printed list that identifies the location of periodicals owned by the library. If you have difficulty locating a periodical or judging which publications are likely to contain articles relevant to your research project, ask a librarian for assistance.

6c

How can I use the library stacks to locate sources?

The library stacks—or shelves—house the library's collection of bound publications. One of the advantages of the classification systems used by most libraries—typically the Library of Congress or Dewey decimal classification system—is that they are subject based. As a result, you can *browse the stacks* to locate sources on a topic. That is, books on similar subjects are shelved together. For example, if your research takes you to the stacks for books about alcohol abuse, you're likely to find books on drug abuse, treatment and recovery programs, and codependency nearby.

When you find a book or article that seems useful, check the works cited page for related articles. You'll probably find one or two sources—and sometimes many more. The combination of browsing the stacks for sources and checking the works cited pages of those sources can help you find books that refer to one another—an ideal way to find books that are involved in the conversation you've decided to join.

■ Checking out Books and Periodicals

In some cases, you'll find that a book you want is not available because it has been checked out, reserved for a course, or placed in off-site storage. If a book is checked out, you may be able to recall it—that is, ask that it be returned to the library and held for you. If the

 ON THE WEB SITE
To learn how to use a database to locate sources, use the research writing manual Databases and the tutorial How to Search a Database, both located at http://www.bedfordresearcher.com.

 IN THIS BOOK
Read about conducting title searches in an online library catalog on p. 83.

ON THE WEB SITE
To learn more about online library catalogs, view the research writing manual Library Catalogs and the tutorials How to Search an Online Library Catalog at http://www.bedfordresearcher.com.

 IN THIS BOOK
Read about browsing the stacks on p. 24. Read about the Library of Congress and Dewey decimal classification systems on p. 86.

ON THE WEB SITE
To keep track of your sources online, use the Working Bibliography tool in the **Research Log** at **http://www .bedfordresearcher .com.**

book has been placed on reserve, you may be able to photocopy or take notes on relevant sections of the book. If the book has been placed in off-site storage, you can usually request the book at the circulation desk.

Using Interlibrary Loan

If you can't obtain the book or periodical you need from your library, use interlibrary loan to borrow materials from another library. Most libraries allow you to request materials in person or on the Web. Some libraries allow you to check the status of your interlibrary loan request or renew interlibrary loan materials through the Web. You can find out how to use interlibrary loan at your library by consulting its Web site or a librarian.

As you collect sources, continue to add them to your working bibliography. At this point in your research writing process, you'll want to include any sources that have some relevance to your project. Don't start eliminating sources until later, when you begin to critically read and evaluate your sources. In the next chapter, we'll focus on searching for information with field research methods.

Planning to Collect and Manage Information

Searching for Information with Electronic Resources

Searching for Information with Print Resources

► Searching for Information with Field Research Methods

CHAPTER 7

Searching for Information with Field Research Methods

Published documents aren't the only source of information for a research project. Nor are they always the best. Publications—such as books, articles, Web sites, or television reports—offer someone else's interpretation of an event or an issue. By relying on another person's interpretation, you're looking through that person's eyes rather than through your own.

Experienced research writers know that you don't have to use published reports to find out how an issue has affected people—you can ask the people yourself. You don't have to view television or radio coverage of an event—you can go to the event yourself. And you don't have to rely on someone else's survey of public opinion—you can conduct your own. This chapter discusses field research methods frequently used by research writers as they collect information about the conversation they've decided to join. To learn about field research, consider the following questions.

Key Questions

7a

How can I use interviews to collect information?

Interviews play an important role in research writing. Reporters use interviews to obtain firsthand accounts of an event, authoritative interpretations of events and issues, and reactions to an event or issue from the people who have been affected by it.

Most interviews follow a question-and-answer format, but some more closely resemble a free-flowing discussion. You can conduct interviews face to face, over the telephone, and even over the Internet in a chat or instant messaging program. No matter what format you use, however, the defining feature of an interview is that one person is seeking information from another.

◼ Deciding Whether to Conduct an Interview

The most important decision you'll make regarding an interview is whether to conduct it in the first place. Typically, interviews provide one or two types of information:

- background information that helps you understand the conversation you plan to join
- statements that you can use as evidence

If you don't need either type of information, don't conduct the interview. Thinking carefully about the role an interview might play in your research project can help you decide whether and how to conduct it.

Sometimes the decision to interview is a natural extension of the kind of work you're doing. For example, although featured writer Rianne Uilk was able to find plenty of information from other sources about the potential effects of Colorado's new school reform laws, she decided to interview teachers because she knew that firsthand reports from teachers would strengthen her argument.

 ON THE WEB SITE

Read more about Rianne Uilk and the other student writers discussed in this chapter in Featured Writers on the *Bedford Researcher* Web site at **http://www .bedfordresearcher .com**.

Sometimes the decision to conduct an interview isn't so much the result of careful planning as it is the recognition of an available opportunity. Featured writer Aaron Batty, who created an informative Web site about relations between Taiwan and China, learned that two of his coworkers—one from Taiwan and the other from mainland China—might be good interview candidates. His interviews produced background information and personal perspectives about the status of Taiwan's independence that he wouldn't have been able to find through print or electronic sources.

◼ Planning an Interview

Once you have decided that conducting an interview will help your research writing project, plan it carefully. The most important things to consider as you plan are whom to interview and what to ask.

Deciding Whom to Interview. Your decisions about whom to interview should be based on the kind of information you want for your research project.

- If you're trying to better understand a specific aspect of a conversation, interview an *expert in the field*.
- If you're trying to understand what people in general think about an issue, interview a number of *people who are affected by the issue*.
- If you're trying to collect quotations from people who are authorities on a subject, interview *someone who will be recognized as an authority*.

Once you've decided what sorts of people you want to interview, you'll need to identify interview candidates. First, use your network of contacts. If you're working on a research project for a class, ask your instructor and classmates for suggestions. Once you've assembled a list of potential candidates, contact the candidates or ask a mutual acquaintance to introduce you. If your instructor suggests that you interview a professor who has expertise relevant to your project, ask your instructor whether he or she knows the professor. If so, your instructor might agree to call the professor for you.

Second, prepare before you call to set up the interview.

- Write a script to help you remember what to say.
- Prepare a list of dates and times that work for you.
- Estimate how much time you'll need to complete the interview.
- Be ready to suggest a location for the interview.
- Leave your phone number or email address so that your interview candidate can get in touch with you in case a conflict arises.

Deciding What You Should Ask. Your interview questions should focus on the issues you want to address in your project. As you prepare your questions, keep the following principles in mind:

1. *Consider your research question, the role you are adopting, and the kind of information you want to collect.* Are you seeking background information or do you want someone's opinion? An answer to the question "How did this situation come about?" will be quite different from an answer to the question "What do you think about this situation?"

2. *Ask questions that require more than a yes or no answer.* You'll learn much more from an answer to a question such as "What factors will affect your vote on referendum X?" than from an answer to "Will you vote for referendum X?"

3. *Prepare a limited number of main questions and many follow-up questions.* Good interviews seldom involve more than eight to ten

IN THIS BOOK
Read about the roles you can adopt as a writer on p. 5.

**ON THE
WEB SITE**

View the Research Links on the *Bedford Researcher* Web site at **http://www .bedfordresearcher .com** for Web sites that address the use of interviews to collect information.

main questions, but experienced interviewers know that each question can lead to several follow-up questions.

4. *Be flexible.* Sometimes you'll learn things in an interview that are completely new. Be flexible enough to ask follow-up questions you didn't anticipate.

■ Conducting an Interview

Be sure that you arrive early to an interview so you have time to review your questions. If you are conducting your interview over the phone, set time aside before the call to review your questions and then call the person you are interviewing at the agreed-upon time. Before you begin, introduce yourself and explain why you are conducting the interview. Also ask for permission to record the interview and to quote the person you are interviewing in your document.

Ideally, use an audio or video recorder to make a complete record of your interview. At a later time, you can review what was said and carefully transcribe exact quotations from the tape. Even when you record an interview, however, take notes. A set of handwritten notes will serve as a backup in case of technical glitches and will help you remember ideas you had during the interview.

As you conduct your interview, allow the person you are interviewing a chance to answer your questions fully. Don't insist on strictly following your list of interview questions; if discussion naturally flows in another, useful direction, be prepared to shift your line of questioning. If you learn during the interview about specific sources

**ON THE
WEB SITE**

This checklist can be completed online in the **Research Log** on the *Bedford Researcher* Web site at **http://www .bedfordresearcher .com**. It can also be printed or downloaded for use in your word processor.

Interview Checklist

- Set up an interview with an appropriate person.
- Create a list of interview questions and follow-up questions.
- Arrive early for the interview.
- Review your questions and follow-up questions.
- Introduce yourself and ask for permission to record the interview.
- Set up and test your recording equipment.
- Ask your questions clearly and be ready to respond with follow-up questions.
- Take notes, even if you are using a video or audio recorder.
- Be alert for related sources mentioned in the interview—and, if appropriate, ask for copies of those sources.
- Leave your contact information when the interview is over.
- Send a thank-you note to the person you interviewed.

that might be relevant to your research writing project, ask for copies of those sources.

When the interview is over, leave your contact information so that the person you interview can reach you to change or add anything to his or her comments. Finally, send a thank-you note to the person you interviewed.

7b

How can I use observation to collect information?

Like interviewing, observing a setting can provide you with valuable information you would not be able to find in other sources. Some observations involve activities as simple as making a single visit to a setting and taking notes. Others are more complicated: You might decide to observe a specific setting over a period of time, collect your impressions on an observation form, and use recording equipment to gain a more complete record of the setting you've chosen to observe. Remember, however, that an observation need not be complicated to be useful.

■ Deciding Whether to Conduct an Observation

The most important decision you'll make regarding an observation is whether to conduct it in the first place. Some topics are more suited for observation than others. For example, before writing her article on the Intensive English Program at Colorado State University, featured writer Maria Sanchez-Traynor observed students and teachers in the program. She went to two classes, watched, listened, and took notes. Seeing the classes provided Maria with insights that she couldn't have gained simply by reading about the program or interviewing its students and teachers.

■ Planning an Observation

As you plan your observation, determine what you'll observe, how often you'll observe it, what you'll look for as you observe, and whether you'll need permission to observe.

Deciding What You Should Observe and How Often You Should Observe It. After deciding that you want to conduct an observation, you will need to decide *what* you'll observe and *how often* to observe it. Imagine, for example, that you are writing a feature article about day-care centers and you've decided to observe children in day care. You'll quickly learn that there are not only many day-care providers in your community but also several different kinds of providers. Clearly, observing a large day-care center won't tell you much about what happens in a small center operated out of a home. In addition, there's no guarantee that what you'll see in one day-care center on any given day will be typical. Should you conduct multiple observations? Should you observe multiple types of day-care providers?

The answers to these questions will depend largely on what role the information you collect during your observations will play in your research writing project. If you want to learn more about the topic but don't plan to use anything you observe as a source of evidence in your project, then you might want to conduct a fairly limited observation. If you decide to use evidence from your observations throughout your project, then you will need to conduct multiple observations, possibly in more than one setting.

Deciding What to Look For. You'll quickly find that one of the biggest limitations of observation is that you can see only one thing at a time. Experienced observers focus their observations on activities that are most relevant to their research projects. As a result, their observations are somewhat selective. A researcher observing teenagers in a suburban mall, for instance, might focus on groups of young men or groups of young women or on couples, but probably not on all three groups—there's simply too much to see, and spreading yourself too thin will result in fairly "thin" results.

Then again, sometimes you'll want to spread yourself thin. Experienced observers also know that they don't always know what they're looking for. Narrowing in too quickly can mean that you miss important aspects of the setting. As you consider what you should focus on—or whether to focus on anything at all—think about your research writing situation and what you hope to gain from an observation. Your reasons for conducting an observation are probably your best guide to what to focus on.

ON THE WEB SITE

View the Research Links on the *Bedford Researcher* Web site at **http://www .bedfordresearcher .com** for Web sites that address the use of observations to collect information.

Determining Whether You Need Permission to Observe. Many research writers overlook an important element of observation: asking for permission. Seeking permission to observe someone can be extremely complicated. On one hand, ethical considerations should not be ignored, particularly if you are observing minors. People have expectations about privacy. Although you might not expect the same degree of privacy in a restaurant that you would expect in your home, you don't expect every aspect of your behavior to be open to scrutiny— much less to be recorded on tape for analysis. On the other hand, when people know they are being observed, they can (and often do) change their behavior.

As you consider whether to ask for permission, try to place yourself in the position of someone who is being observed. If you are uncertain about whether to ask for permission or whether you need a consent form, ask your instructor for advice.

■ Conducting Your Observations

You'll find a number of similarities between collecting information in an interview and collecting information during an observation. These similarities include the following:

- *Arrive early.* Give yourself time to prepare for your observation session.
- *Review your planning notes.* Remind yourself about what you're looking for and how you will record your observations.
- *Introduce yourself.* If you have asked for permission to observe a setting (such as a class or a day-care center), introduce yourself before you begin your observation. Use your introduction as an opportunity to obtain signatures on consent forms if you need them.
- *Set up your recording equipment.* You'll certainly want to make sure you've got a notepad and pens or pencils. You might also have an audio or video recorder, a laptop computer, or a personal digital assistant. Test whatever you've brought with you to make sure it's working properly.
- *Take notes.* As with interviews, take notes during your observation even if you're using an audio or video recorder. Noting your impressions and ideas while conducting an interview can help you keep track of critical events. In addition, if your recorder doesn't work as expected, a set of notes can mean the difference between salvaging something from the observation and having to do it all over again.

Observation Checklist

- Decide what you will observe and when you will observe it.
- Obtain permission to observe the setting if appropriate.
- Arrive early.
- Review your planning notes and remind yourself what you are looking for or what you should focus on.
- Introduce yourself if appropriate.
- Set up and test your recording equipment.
- Take notes, even if you are using a video or audio recorder.
- Leave your contact information if appropriate.
- Send a thank-you note if appropriate.

 ON THE WEB SITE

This checklist can be completed online in the **Research Log** on the *Bedford Researcher* Web site at **http://www .bedfordresearcher .com**. It can also be printed or downloaded for use in your word processor.

Occasionally, you might find yourself in a situation where you can't take notes. (Observing a swimming lesson, for instance, when you're involved in the lesson.) In this situation, try to write down your thoughts about what you've observed immediately after the session.

- *Leave contact information and send thank-you notes.* If you have asked someone for permission to observe the setting, leave your contact information in case the person wishes to contact you, and send a thank-you note after you have completed the observation.

7c

How can I use surveys to collect information?

Surveys allow you to collect information about beliefs, attitudes, and behaviors from a targeted group or a wide range of people. Typically, surveys help you answer *what* or *who* questions, such as

- What do you think about prayer in schools?
- Who will you vote for in the next election?
- What do you think are the most important issues facing the country today?

Surveys are less useful in obtaining the answers to *why* questions. In an interview, for instance, you can ask, "Why did you vote the way you did in the last election?" and expect to get a reasonably well-thought-out answer. In a survey, however, people often neglect to write careful responses to *why* questions.

■ Deciding Whether to Conduct a Survey

IN THIS BOOK

Read about collecting information through interviews on p. 124. Read about collecting information through correspondence on p. 135.

The first question you should ask yourself about conducting a survey is what role it might play in your research writing project. In many cases, you'll find that other field research methods are more appropriate than surveys. For instance, if you simply want to sample attitudes about an issue (from five to ten people), you can gain that information through detailed responses provided in interviews or correspondence.

Surveys are useful, however, if you want to collect information about the attitudes and behaviors of a larger group of people (more than five or ten). If you need to survey much larger groups (more than one hundred), surveys are by far the better choice because of time restrictions. Your decision about whether to conduct a survey should be based on the amount of work required to do a good job and the kind of information you need for your project.

■ Planning Your Survey

As you plan your survey, consider whom to survey, what to ask and how to ask it, and whether you are asking your questions clearly.

Deciding Whom to Survey. Your survey will reflect not only the needs of your research writing project but also the people you choose to survey. You must decide whom and how many to survey. For instance, if you're interested in what students in a particular class think about an issue, survey all of them. Even if the class is fairly large (say, one hundred students), you probably won't have too much trouble tabulating the results of a brief survey.

ON THE WEB SITE

View the Research Links on the *Bedford Researcher* Web site at **http://www .bedfordresearcher .com** for Web sites that address the development, use, and analysis of surveys.

Most surveys aren't given to everyone in a group. National polls, for instance, seldom survey more than one thousand people. Yet they are used to assess the opinions of everyone in the country. To get a fairly accurate idea of what students are thinking at a university with more than twenty thousand undergraduates, you probably won't need to survey more than a few hundred students.

So how will you select your representative sample? One way is to choose people from the group at random. You could open your school's telephone book, start with the person whose name comes twentieth, say, and then pick every twentieth name after that. Another way to select a representative sample is to *stratify* your sample. To ensure that your sample of college students reflects the enrollment at your school, you could randomly select a specific number of first-year, second-year, third-year, and fourth-year students—and you could make sure that the number of men and women in each group is proportional to their enrollment at the school.

Deciding What to Ask and How to Ask It. Designing effective surveys can be challenging. Understanding the strengths and weakness of the kinds of questions that are frequently asked on surveys is a good way to get started. The following are popular types of survey items:

- *Yes/no items.* Yes/no items are useful for dividing respondents into groups. They are best used when there are only two possible responses to a question.

  Did you vote in the last presidential election? ❑ yes ❑ no

- *True/false items.* Items that ask for a true or false response are similar to yes/no questions. However, they more often deal with attitudes or beliefs than with behaviors or events.

  Voting is a civic duty: ❑ true ❑ false

- *Likert scale items.* Likert scales allow respondents to indicate their level of agreement with a statement, their assessment of something's importance or value, or how frequently they engage in a behavior.

	Strongly Agree	Agree	Not Sure	Disagree	Strongly Disagree
All eligible voters should participate in local, state, and national elections.	❏	❏	❏	❏	❏

Please rate the following reasons for voting on a 1-to-5 scale, in which 5 indicates very important and 1 indicates not at all important:

	1	2	3	4	5
To be a good citizen	❏	❏	❏	❏	❏
To have a say in how government affects my life	❏	❏	❏	❏	❏
To support a particular cause	❏	❏	❏	❏	❏
To vote against particular candidates	❏	❏	❏	❏	❏

	In Every Election	In Most Elections	In about Half of the Elections	Rarely	Never
I vote	❏	❏	❏	❏	❏

- *Multiple-choice items.* Multiple-choice items can help you determine whether a respondent knows something or engages in specific behaviors. The primary drawback of multiple-choice items is that they don't always include every possible answer. As a result, you must take great care when including these types of items on a survey.

  I have voted in the following types of elections (check all that apply):
  ❏ Regular local elections
  ❏ Special local elections
  ❏ Regular statewide elections
  ❏ National elections

- *Ranking items.* Ranking forces respondents to select the best and the worst (and everything in between) among a group of items.

  Please rank the following reasons for voting from most important (4) to least important (1):
  ___ To be a good citizen
  ___ To have a say in how government affects my life
  ___ To support a particular cause, such as environmentalism, the pro-life movement, or gun control
  ___ To vote against particular candidates

- *Short-answer items.* Short-answer items ask respondents to write a brief response to a question or statement. Although short-answer items allow greater freedom in the response, they are more difficult to tabulate than other types of survey items.

  Please tell us what influenced your decision to vote or not vote in the last election.

  In your opinion, what can be done to increase voter turnout among 18-to-24-year-old voters?

Determining Whether You Are Asking Your Questions Clearly.   Test your survey items before administering your survey by asking your classmates or family members to read your questions. A question that seems perfectly clear to you might cause confusion to someone else. If your "testers" get confused, ask them which questions cause the confusion and why they found the questions confusing. Try to rewrite confusing questions and then test them again. By testing your questions, you can improve the clarity of your survey.

Consider the evolution of the following question:

Original Question:

What can be done about voter turnout among younger voters?

Two elements of this question might cause confusion to a survey respondent. First, a reader might interpret "about voter turnout" in one of several ways: to increase voter turnout, to decrease voter turnout, or to encourage younger voters to be better informed about candidates. Second, the phrase "younger voters" isn't specific. A respondent may interpret "younger voters" to mean 18-year-olds or 30-year-olds, depending on the respondent's age.

Revised Question:

In your opinion, what can be done to increase turnout among 18-to-24-year-old voters?

■ Conducting Your Survey

The sheer number of surveys people are asked to complete these days has reduced the public's willingness to respond to them. In fact, a "good" response rate for a survey is 60 percent. The following strategies can help you achieve a high response rate:

- *Keep it short.* Surveys are most effective when they are brief. Don't exceed one page.

- *Format your survey appropriately.* If you are distributing your survey on paper, make sure the text is readable and the page isn't crowded with questions. If you are distributing your survey through email, you can either insert the survey questions into the body of your email message or attach the survey as a word processing file. If you are distributing your survey on the Web, you have several options:

  - You can code your survey so that survey responses are added to a database (if you can create Web pages of this kind or know someone who can).

  - You can ask respondents to copy the text on the page and paste it into an email message that they then send to you.

- You can link a word processing file containing your survey to a Web page and ask respondents to fill it out and return it to you as an email attachment.
- You can ask respondents to print the survey and fax or mail it back to you.

- *Explain the purpose of your survey.* Explaining who you are and how you will use the results of the survey in your research writing project can help increase a respondent's willingness to complete and return your survey.

- *Treat survey respondents with respect.* People respond more favorably when they think you are treating them as individuals rather than simply as part of a mailing list. Use first-class stamps on surveys sent through the mail and, when possible, address potential respondents by name in cover letters or email messages.

- *Make it easy to return the survey.* If you are conducting a survey through the mail, make sure to include a stamped, self-addressed envelope. If you are conducting your survey on the Web or via email, make sure to provide directions for returning completed surveys.

ON THE WEB SITE

To learn more about analyzing results from a survey, visit the Research Links on the *Bedford Researcher* Web site at **http://www .bedfordresearcher .com**.

■ Analyzing Your Results

Once you've collected your surveys, you must tabulate your responses. It's usually best to tabulate survey responses using a spreadsheet program, which provides flexibility when you want to analyze your results. You can also tabulate your survey results in a table in a word processing program.

ON THE WEB SITE

This checklist can be completed online in the **Research Log** on the *Bedford Researcher* Web site at **http://www .bedfordresearcher .com**. It can also be printed or downloaded for use in your word processor.

Survey Checklist

- Determine whom to survey.
- Create a list of survey questions.
- Test your survey questions on other people to make sure they are clear and focused.
- Keep your survey brief.
- Explain the purpose of your survey.
- Format your survey so that it is easy to read, complete, and return.
- Tabulate and analyze the results of your survey.
- Include a copy of your survey questions in an appendix within your project document.

7d

How can I use correspondence to collect information?

Correspondence includes any textual communication—letters, faxes, and email being most typical. Many research writers benefit from corresponding with experts in a field. Correspondence need not be sent only to experts, however. If you are writing an article about the effects of recent flooding in the Midwest, you might send letters or email messages to relatives, friends, or even strangers to ask them about their experiences with the floods. You can use their responses to your correspondence to illustrate the impact of the flood on average folks. You can also correspond with staff at government agencies, corporations, and organizations. Many of these institutions hire public relations and information personnel to respond to inquiries from the public.

Courtesy is essential when corresponding. Introduce yourself and explain the goals of your research writing project. Make sure that your letter is clear and asks specific questions. Tell your reader that you look forward to hearing from him or her. And make sure to say thanks. If you decide to send a letter via regular mail, include a self-addressed, stamped envelope with your letter to increase your chances of getting a response.

IN THIS BOOK
Read about organizing and managing the results of your research on p. 69.

7e

How can I use public events to collect information?

Public events—whether they are held in an arena or on the Web—often provide research writers with useful information. Public events include lectures, conferences, and public meetings and hearings. You can record public events in much the same way that you record observations. You can almost certainly take notes. In some cases, you can also bring an audio or video recorder. In addition, a number of communities broadcast public events on local access cable channels. Finally, if you attend a public event in person or on the Web, find out whether a transcript of the event will be available.

Your Research Project
DISCUSS FIELD RESEARCH METHODS WITH OTHERS
As you collect information about the conversation you've decided to join, reconsider how the plan you created in the **Research Log** activity "Create Your Research Project Search Plan" capitalizes on field research methods. As you decide whether to use observations,

(continued)

interviews, surveys, correspondence, or other forms of field research, seek advice from researchers who have used these methods. You can also seek advice about field research methods from your instructor or a librarian.

If you'd like to update your search plan online, use the **Research Log** activity "Create Your Research Project Search Plan" at **http://www.bedfordresearcher.com**. If you have created a research log using a notebook or a word processor, you can print or download this activity.

7f

How can I use broadcast media to collect information?

Radio and television are sources of information that research writers frequently overlook. National Public Radio, for example, offers a range of information and opinion programs that might be of use to research writers. News and information programs on television, such as the *News Hour with Jim Lehrer* and *60 Minutes*, might provide useful information about the conversation you plan to join. In addition, check the Web for radio programs and transcripts. National Public Radio's news information program *All Things Considered,* for instance, provides audio archives going back to January 1996 that you can listen to on the Web (visit **http://www.npr.org** and search the program's archives).

Your Research Project

UPDATE YOUR PROJECT TIMELINE
As you move into the next stage of your research writing project—working with sources—review your project timeline. At this point, you've completed six project milestones.

PROJECT TIMELINE		
ACTIVITY	START DATE	COMPLETION DATE
Select your topic		
Explore your topic		
Narrow your topic to a single conversation		
Develop your research question		
Develop your plan to collect and manage information		
Collect information		

Read and evaluate information

Take notes

Organize your information

Create your document outline

Develop your thesis statement

Write the first draft of your project document

Review and revise your first draft

Review and revise additional drafts

Edit your draft

Finalize in-text and end-of-text citations

Design your document

Publish and submit your project document

> If you'd like to complete this activity online, use the **Research Log** activity "Create a Project Timeline" at **http://www .bedfordresearcher.com**. If you have created a research log using a notebook or a word processor, you can print or download this activity.

Many research writing projects can benefit from field research. Revisit your search plan and consider the role field research might play in your project.

Once you've collected sources using field research methods, you'll be ready to consider how they can contribute to your project document. The next part of this book shifts your focus from collecting sources to reading critically, evaluating, and taking notes on your sources.

Part Three

Working with Sources

8. **Reading Critically**
9. **Evaluating Your Sources**
10. **Taking Notes and Avoiding Plagiarism**

After you've collected your information, you'll be ready to devote your complete attention to reading critically, evaluating, and taking notes on your sources. The next three chapters of *The Bedford Researcher* lead you through the process of deciding which information is most useful for your research writing project.

► Reading
Critically

Evaluating Your
Sources

Taking Notes
and Avoiding
Plagiarism

CHAPTER 8

Reading Critically

As you've collected your sources, you've no doubt begun to read and assess them—and perhaps even to mark and take notes on them. If so, you have a good idea of what your sources can tell you about your topic and the conversation you've chosen to join. To move yourself closer to your goal of contributing to that conversation, however, you must read your sources critically.

Critical readers read actively and with an attitude. *Reading actively* means working with a text as you read: skimming, reading for meaning, and rereading passages that leave you with questions. It means underlining and highlighting text, noting your reactions in the margins, and responding to ideas. *Reading with an attitude* means never taking what you read at face value. It means asking questions, looking for implications, making inferences, and making connections to other sources. Reading sources for a research project also involves considering your research writing situation. As you learn to read critically, ask several key questions:

Key Questions

8a

How does reading critically differ from evaluating?

At first glance, reading critically might seem to be the same as evaluating, which is discussed in detail in the next chapter. Although the two processes are related, they're not identical. Critically reading a

source — questioning what it says and thinking about what it means —
focuses on your attempts to *make meaning* out of the source. Evaluation, in contrast, involves determinbing *how reliably* a source presents
its information and *how well* it meets your needs as a research writer.
Although you can read a source critically without necessarily thinking
about how it fits into your research writing project, you can't evaluate
a source without having read it. Critical reading is the first step in evaluating a source.

8b

What role do my research question and working thesis statement play in critical reading?

As you learned in Chapter 3, your research question focuses your attention on one aspect of your topic. It provides the foundation for your
search plan and directs your attention to particular sources as you collect information. Your research question also plays an important role in
critical reading. It provides the basis for creating a working thesis statement about the conversation you've decided to join, and it's your working thesis statement that you will use to guide your critical reading.

A *working thesis statement* is your current answer to your research
question. At this point in your research writing process, your answer
to your research question is a preliminary one. It is neither as formal nor as complete as the thesis statement you'll use when you draft
your project document. However, a working thesis statement is an
important first step toward developing your thesis statement — your
statement of your main point. Figure 8.1 shows the progression from
research question to working thesis statement to thesis statement in
the context of the research writing process.

As a preliminary response to your research question, your working thesis statement can help you decide whether you agree or disagree
with an author — and thus whether you want to align yourself with his
or her position in the conversation. It will also help you judge whether
the evidence provided in a source is effective and how you might be
able to use the new ideas and information you read about.

Use your working thesis statement to test your ideas about the
conversation against the ideas and information you encounter in your

IN THIS BOOK
Read about drafting your document on p. 197.

Figure 8.1   Moving from a Research Question to a Working Thesis Statement to a Thesis Statement

| GETTING STARTED | COLLECTING INFORMATION | WORKING WITH SOURCES | WRITING YOUR DOCUMENT | DOCUMENTING SOURCES |

RESEARCH QUESTION ....> WORKING THESIS STATEMENT ....> THESIS STATEMENT

reading. As your ideas about the conversation change, revise your working thesis statement.

■ Drafting Your Working Thesis Statement

To draft your working thesis statement, brainstorm a list of responses to your research question. After collecting information for his research paper, which focused on low turnout among young voters, featured writer Gaele Lopez brainstormed responses to his research question:

My Research Question:

Why is turnout low among 18-to-24-year-old voters?

Responses:

Young voters lack political awareness. They don't understand the issues. They don't realize that voting is important, or maybe they are waiting for other people to tell them it's important. Maybe they don't care. They don't realize the downsides of not voting. They don't think there are any downsides to not voting.

After reviewing his brainstorming, Gaele settled on a working thesis statement he could use to guide his critical reading:

Working Thesis Statement:

Turnout among voters under age 25 is low because they don't understand why it's important to vote.

This statement was too vague to use as a thesis statement, but it proved to be an effective guide as he critically read his sources. For example, when Gaele read a source that tried to explain low turnout among younger voters, he could ask whether that explanation was consistent with his idea that they lack understanding of the importance of voting or whether it was arguing something else.

Table 8.1 presents the movement from research question to working thesis statement in the featured writers' projects. Note how the working thesis statement attempts to answer the question that the research question poses and thus lets readers know what the writer thinks an answer to the research question *might be*.

ON THE WEB SITE

Read more about Gaele Lopez and the other student writers discussed in this chapter in Featured Writers on the *Bedford Researcher* Web site at **http://www.bedfordresearcher.com**.

Your Research Project

DRAFT YOUR WORKING THESIS STATEMENT

In your research log, complete the following activity to draft your working thesis statement.

1. Write your current research question.
2. Brainstorm a list of responses to your research question.

(continued)

3. From these answers, select the response that best reflects your current understanding of the conversation you have decided to join. If appropriate, combine responses into one working thesis statement.

4. Write your working thesis statement.

If you'd like to complete this activity online, use the **Research Log** activity "Draft Your Working Thesis Statement" at **http://www.bedfordresearcher.com**. If you have created a research log using a notebook or a word processor, you can print or download this activity.

TABLE 8.1	THE FEATURED WRITERS' MOVEMENTS FROM RESEARCH QUESTION TO WORKING THESIS STATEMENT	
FEATURED WRITER	**RESEARCH QUESTION**	**WORKING THESIS STATEMENT**
Jenna Alberter	What was the relationship between seventeenth-century Dutch paintings of women and the culture in which they were created?	Seventeenth-century Dutch paintings reflected society's expectations of women and helped women understand their roles in society.
Aaron Batty	What are the implications for the United States of differences in China's and Taiwan's interpretations of the "one China" policy?	The United States might be drawn into a war over the "one China" policy.
Patrick Crossland	What cultural, academic, and regional factors affect college admissions decisions?	Factors affecting college admissions decisions include race, gender, and intellectual ability.
Kevin Fahey	How is Nick Adams characterized by Ernest Hemingway?	Nick Adams is a flawed character with whom readers can identify.
Gaele Lopez	Why is turnout low among 18-to-24-year-old voters?	Turnout among voters under age 25 is low because they don't understand why it's important to vote.
Holly Richmond	Who are my ancestors and what did they do during their lifetimes?	My parents, grandparents, and great-grandparents lived rich and varied lives.
Maria Sanchez-Traynor	How is English taught to foreign-language speakers at the Intensive English Program?	Teachers use immersion techniques and explain the theory of the English language to help students at the IEP learn to speak and write English.
Rianne Uilk	What are the likely effects of Colorado Senate Bill 186 on education reform in Colorado public schools?	Schools, teachers, and students will be negatively affected by Colorado Senate Bill 186.

8c

How can I read with an attitude?

Reading critically means reading with an attitude. Your attitude will change during your research writing process. As you begin to read your sources critically, your attitude might be one of curiosity. You'll note new information and mark key passages that provide you with insights into the conversation you're joining. You will adopt a more questioning attitude as you attempt to determine whether sources fit in your project or are reliable. Later, after you begin to draw conclusions about the conversation, you might adopt a more skeptical attitude, challenging arguments made in sources more aggressively than you did at first.

Regardless of where you are in your research writing process, you should always adopt a *critical* attitude. Accept nothing at face value; ask questions about your topic; look for similarities and differences in the sources you read; examine the implications of what you read for your research project; be on the alert for unusual information; and be ready to take note of relevant sources and information. Most important, be flexible. Be open to new ideas and information, even if you don't initially agree with what you've read. You can easily choose not to use something later, but give it a chance to affect how and what you think about the conversation you've decided to join.

■ Approaching a Source with Your Research Writing Situation in Mind

One way to get into the habit of reading critically is to approach a source with your research writing situation in mind. To do so, think about your research question and working thesis statement, your purpose, your readers' needs and interests, the context in which your project document will be read, your requirements and limitations, and your opportunities.

Your Research Question and Working Thesis Statement. Keep in mind your research question and working thesis statement as you critically read your sources. As you read, consider the following questions:

- Are the information and ideas in this source relevant to my research question and working thesis statement?
- Does this source present information that makes me reconsider my research question or working thesis statement?
- Does this source provide any new information?
- Does this source offer a new perspective on the conversation?

Your Purpose. Return to your research log and review your purpose. Keeping your purpose in mind as you read will make it easier to recognize useful information when you come across it. As you read, consider the following questions about your purpose:

- Will the information in this source help me accomplish my purpose? Can I use the information in this source as support for points I want to make? Can I use it to illustrate ideas that differ from mine?
- Is the information in this source more useful for my purpose than what I've found in other sources?
- Does the source provide a good model of a convincing argument or an effective presentation of information? Can I learn anything from the presentation of the points and evidence in this source?

Your Readers' Needs and Interests. Consider your readers' needs and interests as you work with sources. As you read, ask the following questions about your readers' needs and interests:

- Would my readers want to know about the information and ideas found in this source?
- Would my readers find the source information convincing or compelling?
- Would my readers benefit from a review of the points and evidence presented in this source?
- What are my readers likely to think about the points and evidence presented in this source? How will they respond to them?

Your Project Document and the Context in Which It Will Be Read. Research projects are presented in a variety of formats — simple printed texts, highly formatted printed texts, Web pages, word processing files attached to email messages, and posts to newsgroups and electronic mailing lists. They're also read in a wide range of settings: in an office by someone sitting at a desk, on a bus or train as someone commutes to or from work, on a computer with a large, high-resolution monitor, or on a laptop computer with a cramped screen. As you read your sources, be alert to what you can learn about organizing and formatting your project effectively. Answer the following questions about your project document and the context in which it will be read:

IN THIS BOOK
Read more about designing your document in Chapter 15.

- Does this source provide a useful model for organizing my project document?
- Does this source provide a useful model for formatting my project document?
- Can I learn anything from how figures, tables, or photos are used in the source?

Your Requirements and Limitations.   As you read, keep your requirements and limitations in mind:

- If I find useful information in a source, will I be able to follow up on it with additional research? Will I have enough time to follow up on that information?
- How much information can I include in my project document? Will my readers be looking for a general overview or a detailed report?

Your Opportunities.   On a more positive note, keep your opportunities in mind as you read. Ask yourself whether the source presents any possibilities or opportunities you had not found yet. Instead of limiting your options, take advantage of them.

8d

What strategies can I use to read actively?

Once you have drafted your working thesis statement and thought about your research writing situation, you are ready to start reading actively. Reading actively means interacting with sources and evaluating them in light of the conversation you've decided to join. When you read actively, you might do one or more of the following:

- identify key passages for later rereading
- underline key ideas
- write questions in the margins
- jot down reactions to an idea
- link one part of the source to another visually

Reading actively ensures that you're engaged in understanding and interacting with a source. As you read sources, use two active-reading strategies: marking a source and annotating a source. Although you might have begun to mark and annotate your text as you explored your topic, when you read actively you should be reading your texts more closely than before.

■ Marking a Source

Marking a source to identify key information is a simple yet powerful active-reading strategy. Common marking techniques include the following:

- Using a highlighter, a pen, or a pencil to identify key passages in a print source.

ON THE WEB SITE

To learn how to highlight text in your word processor, view the manual Using Your Word Processor on the *Bedford Researcher* Web site at **http://www .bedfordresearcher .com**.

- Attaching notes or flags to printed pages.
- Highlighting passages in electronic texts with your word processor.

Annotating a Source

Research writers engage with source texts by writing brief annotations, or notes, in the margins of print sources or by using commenting tools for electronic sources.

Many research writers use annotations in combination with marking (see Figure 8.2). If you have highlighted a passage (marking) with which you disagree, for instance, you can write a brief note about why you disagree with the passage (annotating). You might make note of another source you've read that could support your side of the argument, or you might leave yourself a note about the need to look for information that will help you argue against the passage.

8e

What should I pay attention to as I read?

What you should pay attention to as you read each source varies from project to project. In general, however, you should pay attention to the following:

- whether the source is a primary or secondary source
- the author's main point and other key points
- evidence offered to support points
- new information (information you haven't read before)
- ideas and information that you find difficult to understand
- ideas and information that are similar to or different from the information you have found in other sources

By noting these aspects of a source through active reading, you will better understand the source, which will help you better understand the conversation you've decided to join.

Using Primary and Secondary Sources

RESEARCH ASSISTANT

Use the worksheet Primary & Secondary Sources to keep track of primary sources and the secondary sources that comment on them.

One of the first things you should determine about a source is whether it is a primary source or a secondary source. *Primary sources* are either original works of art or literature or are evidence provided directly by an observer of an event. Primary sources typically include

- poems, short stories, novels, essays, paintings, musical scores and recordings, sculpture, and other works of art or literature
- diaries, journals, memoirs, and autobiographies

Getting to the ivy league: How family composition affects college choice

go to Web site

Author: Lillard, Dean; Gerner, Jennifer **Source:** Journal of Higher Education 706–730 70, no. 6 (Nov/Dec 1999): p. 706–730 **ISSN:** 0022-1546 **Number:** 46386576 **Copyright:** Copyright Ohio State University Press Nov/Dec 1999

Introduction

A primary tenet of American society revolves around access to positions of influence and equality of opportunity. Educational attainment provides the central vehicle through which upward mobility can occur. Consequently, educational researchers have long been concerned about the extent to which higher education has been accessible to all students regardless of socioeconomic and racial characteristics. This study examines patterns of attendance at four-year and selective four-year colleges across students from single- and two-parent families. In particular, we examine whether these students differ in their choice of colleges to which they apply, are admitted, and which they attend.

A student's home life has an impact on college apps.

The college-aged population is increasingly characterized by the experience of family disruption. Rising rates of divorce and illegitimate births imply that an increasing number of children either directly experience the breakup of their parents' marriage or never live in traditional two-parent families. Among those children born in 1950, 28% of whites and 60% of blacks had at some time lived with only one (or no) parent by age 17. Of children born twenty years later, 41% of whites and 75% of blacks can expect to live with fewer than two parents by age 17. These figures imply that, in contrast to earlier cohorts, the experience of living in a single-parent home is increasingly common among children growing up in the late 1970s and 1980s.

Children from dysfunctional families less likely to apply

As family disruption becomes more prevalent, questions of equity and access arise if children from disrupted families are less likely to apply to and attend four-year colleges and selective four-year colleges. Differences in access might arise from two possible sources. First, disrupted and intact families may differ in the resources they can bring to bear to prepare their children for college. Second, the impact of these resources on college choices of children from disrupted and intact families may differ. Our results suggest that although both influences are present, differences in the levels of resources account for the largest proportion of the difference in the college choices between children from disrupted and intact families.

Two reasons why access to college varies with family makeup

Review of the Literature

In a general review of the college choice literature, Hossler, Braxton, and Coopersmith (1989) identify several important correlates of college choice. These include family socioeconomic status, student academic ability and achievement, parental levels of education, parental encouragement and support, student educational aspirations about career plans, and quality of the high school. Although many of these factors vary with family composition, little attention is paid in this literature to the role family composition plays in college choices.

Figure 8.2 A Source That Featured Writer Patrick Crossland Highlighted and Annotated

A Patrick makes a note to investigate the Web site of the *Journal of Higher Education* to determine whether it can provide him with more information on college admissions standards.

B Patrick highlights and makes a note of interesting passages in the text.

C Patrick also highlights the main points he thinks are being made in the text and includes a note in the margin to alert himself that the highlighted text clearly states the authors' chief claims.

- interviews, speeches, government and business records, letters, and memos
- reports, drawings, photographs, films, or video and audio recordings of an event
- physical artifacts associated with an event, such as a weapon used in a crime or a piece of pottery found in an archaeological dig

Secondary sources comment on or interpret an event, often using primary sources as evidence.

Primary Sources	Secondary Sources
A short story by Ernest Hemingway	An article that presents a critic's analysis of the short story
A transcript of the speech given by President George Bush on September 11, 2001	A recording of an interview in which a historian discusses the significance of the speech
A laboratory study concerning the benefits of strength training for women with osteoporosis	A Web site that presents a review of recent research about prevention and treatment of osteoporosis

As a research writer, you should attempt to obtain as many primary sources as possible so that you can come to your own conclusions about the conversation you've decided to join. If you rely entirely or mostly on secondary sources, you'll be viewing the issue through the eyes of other researchers. As you critically read your sources, ask yourself whether you are reading a primary or a secondary source. If you are reading a secondary source, ask yourself what factors might have affected the author's comments, interpretation, or analysis.

■ Identifying Main Points

Most sources, whether they are informative or argumentative, make a main point:

- An editorial in a local newspaper urges voters to approve financing of a new school.
- An article reports a new advance in automobile emissions testing.
- A Web page provides information about the benefits of a new technique for treating a sports injury.

As you read a source critically, pay attention to the main point that is being made.

■ Identifying Supporting Points

Once you've identified a main point, be alert for key points that support the main point. If an author is arguing, for instance, that English should be the only language used for official government business in the United States, that author might support his or her argument with additional points, such as the following statements:

> Use of multiple languages erodes patriotism.

> Use of multiple languages keeps people apart—if they can't talk to each other they won't learn to respect each other.

> Use of multiple languages in government business costs tax-payers money because so many alternative forms need to be printed.

■ Identifying Evidence

A point is only as good as the evidence—information or reasoning—used to support it. Evidence can take many forms, including the following:

- *Appeals to authority.* Appeals to authority are often presented in the form of quotations by experts on the topic.
- *Appeals to logic.* Appeals to logic are often presented in the form of if-then reasoning, as in "if this is true, then we can expect such and such to happen."
- *Empirical evidence.* Empirical evidence is often presented in numerical or statistical form.

■ Identifying New Information

As you read, mark and annotate passages that contain new information about the conversation you've decided to join. You might devote several pages of your research log to "new information." You might enter new information in the form of a list or as a series of brief descriptions of what you've learned and where you learned it.

IN THIS BOOK

Read about how to deal with common knowledge—information you find in several sources—on p. 176.

■ Identifying Hard-to-Understand Information

As you read, you might be tempted to ignore information that's hard to understand. Sometimes hard-to-understand information is technical: You might be working on a report about recent developments in medicine, for instance, and come across the following:

> The basis of the phenomenal potency of botulinum toxin is enzymatic; the toxin is a zinc proteinase that cleaves 1 or more of the fusion proteins by which neuronal vesicles release acetylcholine into the neuromuscular junction.

> Source: Arnon, S. et al. "Botulinum Toxin as a Biological Weapon." *Journal of the American Medical Association*, 285.8 (2001): 1059–70.

If you ignore this information, you might miss something that is critical to the success of your research writing project. When you encounter information that's hard to understand, mark it and make a brief annotation telling yourself to check it out later.

Sometimes you'll learn enough from your reading of other sources that the passage won't seem as difficult when you come back to it later. And sometimes you'll still be faced with a passage that's impossible to figure out on your own. In this case, turn to someone else for advice.

- Ask a question about the passage on a newsgroup or electronic mailing list.
- Interview an expert in the area.
- Ask your instructor or a librarian for help.
- Search a database, library catalog, or the Web using words you didn't understand in the source.

■ Looking for Similarities and Differences

You can learn a lot by looking for similarities and differences among the sources you read. You can identify authors, for instance, who take one side of a debate, and you can contrast this group of authors with another group that takes a different side. When featured writer Aaron Batty was collecting information from the Web about Taiwan-China relations, he kept track of Web sites that were generally informative, Web sites that favored Taiwanese independence, and Web sites that favored ultimate reunification with China.

Similarly, you can make note of information in one source that agrees or disagrees with information in another. This can help you build your own argument or identify information that will allow you (and potentially your readers) to better understand the conversation you have decided to join.

RESEARCH ASSISTANT
Use the worksheet Similarities & Differences to identify similarities and differences among your sources.

Your Research Project

NOTE CONNECTIONS AMONG SOURCES
In your research log, identify connections among your sources. Ask whether information in one source, for example, agrees or disagrees with information in another. How might you handle these connections in your research project?

If you'd like to complete this activity online, use the **Research Log** activity "Note Connections among Sources" at **http://www .bedfordresearcher.com**. If you have created a research log using a notebook or a word processor, you can print or download this activity.

8f

How many times should I read a source?

As you work through the sources you've added to your working bibliography, you'll find that many are less relevant to your research project than you'd hoped when you collected them—or you might find that they offer information and ideas you've found elsewhere. When you come across such sources, move on to the next one.

Other sources are worth reading more carefully. When a source offers new information or ideas, use a three-pass approach:

1. Skim the source to get a general idea of its organization and content.

2. Read actively, marking and annotating relevant passages in the text.

3. Reread passages that are either particularly promising or difficult to understand.

■ First Pass: Skimming for Organization and Content

Before investing too much time in a source, skim it. Skimming—reading just enough words to get the general idea of what a source is about—can tell you a great deal in a minimal amount of time. Skimming is a useful strategy for exploring a topic. It takes on even more importance as your first step in reading a source critically.

IN THIS BOOK
Read more about skimming on p. 35.

Skimming helps you understand how a source is *organized*, which can help you more quickly assess its usefulness and relevance. If the source uses a familiar organizational pattern, you'll find it easier to locate key information. Scientific reports, for example, typically consist of a literature review, methods section, results and discussion section, and conclusion.

You can also learn a great deal about the *content* of a source through skimming. Some of the most useful skimming techniques include the following:

- checking the title
- checking the table of contents if one is provided
- reading the abstract, if one is provided, or the introduction
- checking major headings and subheadings
- reading the titles or captions of any figures and tables
- looking for pull quotes (quotations or brief passages pulled out into the margins or set somewhere on the page in larger type)

- scanning the first sentences and last sentences of paragraphs for key information
- checking the works cited list, if one is provided

Skimming is most effective when you approach your sources with your research writing situation and specific questions in mind. Before you read a source, write a list of questions about the source in your research log. As you read, add questions to your list. When you're finished reading, write answers to your questions. Your questions might include the following:

- What is the main point of this source?
- What additional points are offered to support the main point?
- What evidence is offered to support the points?
- Who is it written for?
- Why was it written?

Your Research Project

USE QUESTIONS TO GUIDE YOUR CRITICAL READING

Before you read a source, generate a list of questions about it. As you read, keep those questions in mind and ask additional questions. After you've read the source, use this activity to keep track of the answers to your questions.

In your research log, create a table like the one shown here. For each source, write the name of the source and questions you would like to have answered as you read the source. After you read the source, write your responses to your questions in the appropriate column.

SOURCE:	
Question 1:	Response:
Question 2:	Response:
Question 3:	Response:
Question 4:	Response:

If you'd like to complete this activity online, use the **Research Log** activity "Use Questions to Guide Your Critical Reading" at **http://www.bedfordresearcher.com**. If you have created a research log using a notebook or a word processor, you can print or download this activity.

■ Second Pass: Reading Actively

You can identify promising sections of a source as you skim and then read those sections actively—highlighting or underlining key passages, making notes in the margin, or recording observations in your research log. As you learn more about the source, turn to other sections. Eventually, you'll have read either the entire source or at least enough to know that you don't need to read any more.

■ Third Pass: Rereading Important Passages

If you decide that a source is valuable—or if you still have questions about the source—reread passages that you've identified as important. Again, read actively, continuing to note your reactions and ideas as you read. Rereading key passages in this way can help you gain a better understanding of the source, which can make a tremendous difference as you begin writing.

Defining your working thesis statement provides a basis not only for reading critically but also for evaluating your sources. The next chapter discusses how you can extend your critical reading of your sources to include evaluation.

Reading
Critically

▶ **Evaluating Your
Sources**

Taking Notes
and Avoiding
Plagiarism

CHAPTER 9

Evaluating Your Sources

At the beginning of a research writing project, you'll most likely make quick judgments about your sources. Skimming an article, book, or Web site might be enough to tell you that spending more time with the source would be wasted effort. At this point in your research writing process, however, you begin to *evaluate* each of your sources to determine how well they meet your needs as a research writer and how reliably they present their information. Evaluating sources involves asking two key questions.

Key Questions

9a

What factors should I use to evaluate a source?

Evaluating a source means examining several important factors: the source's relevance, use of evidence, author, publisher, timeliness, and comprehensiveness.

■ Relevance

Relevance is the extent to which a source provides information you can use in your research writing project. The most important questions you should ask about the relevance of a source are:

- **Will the information in a source help me accomplish my purpose?** Sometimes you'll find a source filled with information that will not help you accomplish your purpose. For example, an analysis of the printing features in word processing programs might contain accurate and up-to-date information. If you're writing about the best laser and inkjet printers for college students, however, it won't be of much use to you.

- **Will the information in a source help me address my readers' needs and interests?** The information in a source should be useful and relevant to your readers. You might be tempted to include a beautifully worded quotation, but if your readers won't see how it contributes to your document, don't use it. Your readers will expect information that meets their needs. If they want to read about printers for personal computers, for instance, pass up sources that focus only on high-capacity office printers.

■ Evidence

Evidence is information offered to support a point. An argument in favor of charging local sales tax on Internet-based purchases might use statistics as evidence: It could calculate the revenue a town of fifty thousand might lose if 5 percent of its citizens made fifteen online purchases in a given year. Statistics, facts, expert opinions, and anecdotal evidence (accounts of the experiences of people involved with or affected by an issue) are among the many types of evidence you'll find. As a research writer, you can evaluate not only the kind of information offered to support points made in a source but also the quality, amount, and appropriateness of evidence. Ask the following questions about the evidence offered in a source:

- **Is enough evidence offered?** A lack of evidence might indicate that the argument being advanced by the author is fundamentally flawed.
- **Is the right kind of evidence offered?** More evidence isn't always better evidence. As you evaluate a source, ask yourself whether the evidence is appropriate for the points being made. Also ask whether more than one type of evidence is being used. Many sources rely far too heavily on a single type, such as personal experience or anecdotal evidence.
- **Is the evidence used fairly?** If statistics are offered as evidence, ask yourself whether they are interpreted fairly or presented in a clear manner. If a quotation is used to support a point, try to determine whether the quote is being used appropriately.
- **Is the evidence convincing?** There are several signs that an argument isn't convincing. Among the most important are reasonable alternative interpretations of the evidence, questionable or inappropriate use of evidence, and evidence that seems to contradict points made elsewhere in the source. In addition, ask yourself whether the author mentions and attempts to refute opposing viewpoints or evidence. If the author hasn't done so, his or her argument might not be strong.

- **Is the source of the evidence provided?** Knowing the origins of evidence used in a source can make a significant difference in your evaluation of it. For example, if a source quotes a political poll but doesn't indicate which organization conducted the poll, you won't be able to determine the reliability of that evidence.

■ The Author

In addition to relevance and evidence, you can evaluate a source based on who wrote it. Take, for example, two editorials that make similar arguments and offer similar evidence. Both are published in your local newspaper. One is written by a 14-year-old middle school student; the other by a U.S. senator. You would certainly favor an editorial written by the senator if the subject was U.S. foreign policy. If the subject was student perceptions about drug abuse prevention in schools, however, you might value the middle school student's opinion more highly.

The importance of authorship as an evaluation criterion varies from source to source. In some cases, including many Web sites, you won't even know who an author is. In other cases, such as signed opinion columns in a newspaper or magazine, your evaluation could be affected by knowing that the author is politically conservative, liberal, or moderate. Similarly, you might find it useful to know that a message published on an Internet newsgroup was written by someone who is recognized as an expert in the field.

Ask the following questions about the author of a source:

- **Is the author knowledgeable about the topic of conversation?** It can be difficult to judge an author since expertise can be gained in many ways. An author might be an acknowledged expert in a field; he or she might be a reporter who has written extensively about a topic; or he or she might be recounting firsthand experiences. Then again, an author might have little or no experience with a topic beyond a desire to say something about it. How can you tell the difference? Look for a description of the author in the source. If none is provided, the source might give a URL for the author's home page, and you can check out the credentials there. Or perhaps you can locate information about the author on the Web or in a biography reference such as *Who's Who*.

IN THIS BOOK
Read about print biographies on p. 118.

- **What is the author's affiliation?** Knowing the institution, agency, or organization that employs the author or the political party or organizations to which the author belongs can help you evaluate the assumptions that inform a source.

- **How do the author's biases affect the information and ideas in the source?** We all have a bias — a set of interests that shapes our perceptions of a topic. As you evaluate a source, consider the extent to which the author's biases affect the presentation of information and ideas in the source. To learn about an author's biases, try to learn more about his or her affiliations. You might infer a bias, for instance, if you learn that an author writes frequently on gun control and works as a regional director for the National Handgun Manufacturers Association.

◼ The Publisher

A publisher is a person or group that prints or produces the documents written by authors. Publishers provide access to print or electronic sources, including books, newspapers, journals, Web sites, sound and video files, and databases. Some documents—such as messages posted to newsgroups or sources obtained through field research—have no publisher.

You can make informed judgments about publishers in much the same way that you can evaluate authors. Ask the following questions about the publisher of a source:

- **How can I locate information about the publisher?** If a publisher is listed in a print document, search for information about the publisher on the Web. You can often tell whether a publisher is reputable by looking at the types of material it publishes. If you are viewing a document on the Web, search for a link to the site's home page.
- **How do the publisher's biases affect the information and ideas in the source?** Like authors, publishers have biases. Unlike authors, they often advertise them. Many publishers have a mission statement on their Web sites, while others provide information on their Web pages that can help you figure out their bias. You might already know a fair amount about the biases of a publisher, particularly if the publisher is a major newspaper or magazine, such as the *New York Times* (regarded as liberal) or the *Wall Street Journal* (regarded as conservative). If the publisher is a scholarly or professional journal, you can often gain an understanding of its biases by looking over the contents of several issues or by reading a few of its articles.

◼ Timeliness

The importance of timeliness—when a source was published—varies according to your research writing situation. If your research project would benefit from sources that have recently been published, then evaluate recent sources more favorably than dated ones. If you're writing a feature article on the use of superconducting materials in new mass transportation projects, you probably won't want to spend a lot of time with articles published in 1968. However, if you're writing about the 1968 presidential contest between Hubert Humphrey and

Richard Nixon, then sources published during that time period will take on greater importance.

Print sources usually list a publication date. However, it can be more difficult to tell when Web sources were created. When in doubt, back up undated information found on the Web with a dated source.

■ Comprehensiveness

Comprehensiveness refers to the extent to which a source provides a complete and balanced view of a topic. Like timeliness, the importance of comprehensiveness varies according to the demands of your research writing situation. If you are working on a narrowly focused project, such as the role played by shifts in Pacific Ocean currents on decreased

 ON THE WEB SITE

You can complete this checklist online in the **Research Log** on the *Bedford Researcher* Web site at **http://www .bedfordresearcher .com**. It can also be printed or downloaded.

Evaluation Checklist

- Determine whether the source is relevant.
    - Will the information in the source help me achieve my purposes as a writer?
    - Will the information in the source help me address my readers' needs and interests?
- Determine whether the source provides evidence and uses it appropriately.
    - Is enough evidence offered?
    - Is the right kind of evidence offered?
    - Is the evidence used fairly?
    - Is the evidence convincing?
    - Is the source of the evidence provided?
- Learn about the author of the source.
    - Is the author knowledgeable about the topic of conversation?
    - What is the author's affiliation?
    - How do the author's biases affect the information and ideas in the source?
- Learn about the publisher of the source.
    - Have I located sufficient information about the publisher? What does this information indicate?
    - How do the publisher's biases affect the information and ideas in the source?
- Consider the timeliness of the source and its impact on and relevance to your project.
- Consider the comprehensiveness of the source and its impact on and relevance to your project.

precipitation in Utah in the winter of 1999, you might not find this evaluation criterion as useful as the others. However, comprehensiveness can be a guide if you need to provide a complete and balanced treatment of a general topic, such as the potential effects of global climate change, or if you are still learning as much as you can about the conversation you plan to join.

■ Use *Research Assistant* to Evaluate and Rank Your Sources

Use *Research Assistant*—a software tool located on the CD-ROM at the back of this book—to evaluate sources on the six criteria discussed in this chapter. As you work with a source in the program, open its note card and view the Evaluation tab. You can rate your source from poor to excellent on each criterion. You can also write notes to remind yourself why you evaluated a source in a particular way (see Figure 9.1).

RESEARCH ASSISTANT
To learn more about *Research Assistant,* see p. 403 or visit the Research Assistant section of the *Bedford Researcher* Web site.

A In *Research Assistant,* you can evaluate each source on the criteria discussed in this chapter. On each criterion, you can rate the source from poor to excellent.

B Click on the "i" icons for brief descriptions of the evaluation criteria.

C For future reference, you can write notes explaining your evaluation decisions.

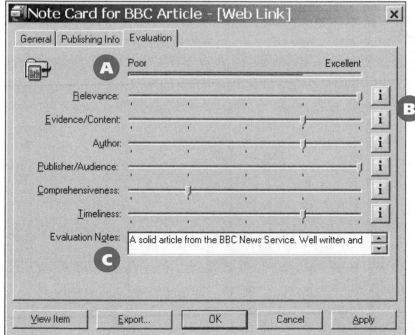

Figure 9.1 Evaluating a Source in *Research Assistant*

The importance of the criteria you use to evaluate your sources can vary from project to project. In some cases, you'll be concerned primarily with relevance and evidence. In other cases, authors and publishers might be most important. Using *Research Assistant,* you can assign different levels of importance to your evaluation criteria (rating author as twice as important as publisher, for example), or you can rank them all equally (see Figure 9.2).

9b

Should I evaluate all types of sources in the same way?

You can apply the general evaluative criteria discussed in section 9a to most types of sources. However, two sets of sources—electronic and field sources—can pose challenges during evaluation. The following

A You can evaluate each source in a collection or only those on a particular worksheet.

B You can choose which types of sources to include in your ranking.

C You can weight the criteria differently so that some criteria (in this case author, evidence, and relevance) are most important, while others (in this case timeliness and comprehensiveness) are irrelevant.

D You can choose to include notes and other information in the report generated when you rank your sources.

Figure 9.2 Ranking Sources in *Research Assistant*

discussion highlights additional factors to consider as you evaluate electronic and field sources.

■ Electronic Sources

Because anyone can create a Web site or post a message to a newsgroup, approach these sources with more caution than you would reserve for print sources such as books and journal articles, which are typically published only after a lengthy editorial review process.

Web Sites. To help assess the relevance and credibility of a Web site:

Check out the domain name. The three- or four-letter extension on the end of the first part of a URL, such as **http://www.bedfordresearcher.com** or **http://writing.colostate.edu,** can tell you whether the site is:

- in the aviation industry (.aero)
- commercial (.com and .biz)
- a business cooperative (.coop)
- educational (.edu)
- governmental (.gov)
- for general use (.info)
- related to the military (.mil)
- a museum (.museum)
- for personal use (.name)
- network related (.net)
- sponsored by a nonprofit organization (.org)
- for professionals, such as doctors (.pro)

Look for an "about this site" or a "site information" page. Consult this type of page to learn who sponsors the site, who developed it, and why it was developed. If you can't find a site information page, look for contact information and send an email message asking about it.

Messages Posted to Newsgroups and Electronic Mailing Lists. To help assess the relevance and credibility of a newsgroup or mailing list message:

Check for signature lines. Usually at the end of the message, a signature contains information about the sender, his or her home page, and additional contact information.

Locate the Frequently Asked Questions (FAQ) list. To learn whether the newsgroup or mailing list is moderated and whether it restricts its membership, find the FAQ page.

■ Field Sources

Field sources—such as interviews, correspondence, observations, and surveys—can pose challenges during source evaluation. With some

ON THE WEB SITE

For more information about evaluating different types of sources, view the tutorials on evaluating popular and academic books, newspaper and journal articles, and Web sites on the *Bedford Researcher* Web site, at **http://www.bedfordresearcher.com.**

IN THIS BOOK

Read more about URLs in "What Is a URL?" on p. 38.

ON THE WEB SITE

To learn more about newsgroups and mailing lists, view the research writing manual Newsgroups and Mailing Lists on the *Bedford Researcher* Web site at **http://www.bedfordresearcher.com.**

adjustment, most of the criteria discussed in this chapter can be applied to your field sources. Table 9.1 indicates how the criteria of relevance, evidence, and author can be used to evaluate field sources.

TABLE 9.1 SPECIAL CONSIDERATIONS FOR SOURCES OBTAINED THROUGH FIELD METHODS			
	RELEVANCE	EVIDENCE	AUTHOR
Interviews and Correspondence	• Determine whether the answers to your questions are related to the conversation you plan to join.	• Ask whether you learned anything new about the conversation you plan to join. • Ask whether the interview or correspondence confirmed your conclusions about the conversation. • Ask whether it provides potentially useful quotations.	• Consider whether the person who answered the questions was as qualified and knowledgeable as you expected. • Consider whether your questions were answered fully and honestly.
Observations	• Consider whether the information you collected relates to the conversation you plan to join.	• Consider the completeness and accuracy of your observation notes.	
Surveys	• Consider whether the questions asked in your survey are still relevant to your project.	• Consider the accuracy and completeness of the responses you collected. • Consider whether the questions asked what you wanted to know. • Ask whether the questions allowed for adequate responses. • Determine whether you received enough responses to make reasonable conclusions.	• Consider whether respondents honestly answered the questions. • Ask whether respondents had adequate time to fill out the surveys. • Ask whether respondents believed their privacy would be respected.

Your Research Project

USE EVALUATION TO TRIM YOUR WORKING BIBLIOGRAPHY

Use your evaluations to determine which sources should be added or removed from your working bibliography. Add any new sources you think will be useful. If you decide that a source is no longer relevant to your project, remove it. However, don't throw the information away. There's always a chance that you'll decide you need this information later. Rather than completely eliminating sources that don't meet your evaluation criteria, draw a line through them or move them into a new bibliography named "other sources" or "unused sources."

If you'd like to work on this activity online, use the Working Bibliography tool in the **Research Log** at **http://www .bedfordresearcher.com**. The Working Bibliography tool allows you to enter information at any time and use it later to generate a bibliography in MLA, APA, *Chicago,* or CBE format. It also allows you to evaluate your sources on the criteria defined in this chapter and to annotate your sources.

IN THIS BOOK
Read about planning an interview on p. 124. Read about sending correspondence on p. 130.

IN THIS BOOK
Read about planning and conducting observations on p. 129.

The sources that survive critical reading and evaluation will most likely play an important role in the document that emerges from your research writing project. In the next chapter, you can read about how to take notes on the ideas, information, and arguments in your remaining sources and in doing so avoid plagiarism.

Reading
Critically

Evaluating Your
Sources

▶ Taking Notes
and Avoiding
Plagiarism

CHAPTER 10

Taking Notes and Avoiding Plagiarism

Why take notes when you can easily make photocopies, borrow a source from the library, or print or save electronic sources? Taking notes allows you to focus more closely on what your sources tell you about your topic and how each source can help you answer your research question. By studying a source and noting the key points it makes, you'll gain a clearer understanding of it. You'll also lay the foundation for drafting the document that will contribute to the conversation you've decided to join. For these reasons, note taking is at the core of good research writing skills.

This chapter discusses how to take notes and how to avoid plagiarism. This chapter addresses three key questions.

Key Questions

10a

What form can notes take?

Some research writers take notes by hand, writing them on note cards, on photocopies of sources, in a notebook, on loose sheets of paper, on the transcript of an interview, on observation notes, or on correspondence. Other researchers choose to take notes electronically, writing them in a word processing program, in a database program; in a bibliographic citation program such as EndNote or Reference Manager, in email messages, in a personalized Web portal such as *My Yahoo!* (**http://my.yahoo.com**), or in a blog—a Web site that allows writers to write notes directly from a Web browser (visit *Open Directory* at **http://dmoz.org** and search for *blogs*).

As a research writer working with this book, you have access to two powerful tools for taking notes. You can use *Research Assistant* and you can use the Notes tool in the Research Log on the *Bedford Researcher* Web site. Each allows you to save, organize, and review your notes as you work on your research writing projects.

As you think about how you'll take notes, recall the techniques used by three of the featured writers. Jenna Alberter used note cards because they were easy to organize and carry around. Gaele Lopez took notes in a word processing program, a convenient place for organizing and drafting his project document. Maria Sanchez-Traynor took notes in a notebook that fit easily in her bag.

For more useful notes, take them systematically and consistently. For example, instead of taking some notes on Post-it Notes, some on note cards, and the rest in a word processing file, take all of your notes in one form. A consistent note-taking system will make it easier to find information later and reduce the time and effort you'll need during the later phases of your research writing project: organizing your ideas and planning and drafting your project document.

ON THE WEB SITE

You can save, organize, and review notes with the Notes tool in the **Research Log** on the *Bedford Researcher* Web site at **http://www .bedfordresearcher .com**.

RESEARCH ASSISTANT

For more on using the Note Card feature for taking notes within *Research Assistant*, see the User's Guide on p. 403.

10b

What types of notes can I take?

Notes provide you with a record of your reactions to your sources. Your notes will likely include a variety of information, such as direct quotations, paraphrases, and summaries of your sources. Notes can also include comparisons among sources and your thoughts about how to organize and write your document.

IN THIS BOOK

Read about marking and annotating on p. 147.

■ Direct-Quotation Notes

A direct quotation is an exact copy of words found in a source. When you create a direct quotation note, you should surround the passage you are quoting with quotation marks and identify the source and the page numbers (if any) on which the quotation can be found. Proofread what you have written to make sure it matches the original source exactly—including wording, punctuation, and spelling.

You should take direct-quotation notes when

- a passage in a source features an idea that you want to argue for or against
- a passage in a source provides a clear and concise statement that would enhance your project document

ON THE WEB SITE

View the tutorial How to Integrate Quotations into a Draft at http://www.bedfordresearcher.com for additional examples of quotations.

IN THIS BOOK

View additional examples of quotations on p. 208.

- you want to use an authority's or expert's exact words
- you want to use the exact words of someone who has firsthand experience with the issue you are researching

Avoid quoting passages that are more than a few sentences long; instead, use a summary note or a paraphrase note.

Featured writer Jenna Alberter took several direct-quotation notes. When she drafted her research paper, she used these quotations to support her argument about images of women in seventeenth-century Dutch paintings (see Figure 10.1). Here is an original passage from a source that Jenna Alberter read during her research. Following the passage is Jenna's note.

Original Passage:

In this sense, both art and literature present an exemplary image, a topos that does not necessarily reflect the actual situation of young women in seventeenth-century Dutch culture.

Wayne E. Franits, <u>Paragons of Virtue</u>, p. 25

A Jenna identified the author's last name, the title, and the page on which the quotation appears.

B Jenna used an ellipsis to indicate that she left out some words from the quoted sentence (the words "In this sense"). She quoted the rest of the passage exactly and enclosed the passage in quotation marks.

Figure 10.1 Direct-Quotation Note

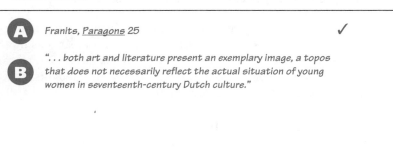

Modifying a Direct Quotation Using an Ellipsis.   Sometimes you'll want to quote only part of a passage in your notes. This might happen when only part of a passage relates directly to your research writing project. To indicate that you have changed a quotation by deleting words, use three spaced periods, or an ellipsis (. . .). Featured writer Rianne Uilk used an ellipsis in a note she took from a speech Colorado Governor Bill Owens made when he announced his plans to reform public education in the state. She found a transcript of his speech on the Web.

Original Passage:

I know there are wonderful and dedicated teachers in our public schools. And I know that hundreds of public schools provide a good education— including the three public schools my children attend. But I also know that illiteracy and high dropout rates plague too many children from low-income families.

When Rianne wrote the quotation on a note card, she indicated deleted material with an ellipsis (three spaced periods). Note that the first period marks the end of the sentence.

Quotation Modified Correctly Using an Ellipsis:

"I know there are wonderful and dedicated teachers in our public schools. And I know that hundreds of public schools provide a good education. . . . But I also know that illiteracy and high dropout rates plague too many children from low-income families."

If you don't use an ellipsis, your readers will assume that a quotation you are presenting is identical to the text found in the source. The following quotation does not use an ellipsis, so readers would not realize that the quotation differs from the original.

Quotation Modified Incorrectly:

"I know there are wonderful and dedicated teachers in our public schools. And I know that hundreds of public schools provide a good education. But I also know that illiteracy and high dropout rates plague too many children from low-income families."

IN THIS BOOK

See p. 170 for a note about using brackets around ellipses in MLA style.

Modifying a Direct Quotation Using Brackets.   To modify a direct quotation by changing or adding words, use brackets: [ ]. In the following quotation, a change material is correctly indicated with brackets. The original passage appears above.

Quotation Modified Correctly Using Brackets:

"I know there are wonderful and dedicated teachers in our public schools [and that] hundreds of public schools provide a good education."

If you don't use brackets when you change or add words, readers will assume the quotation you are presenting is identical to the text found in the source. In the following quotation, readers would not realize that the quotation differs from the original.

Quotation Modified Incorrectly:

"I know there are wonderful and dedicated teachers in our public schools and that hundreds of public schools provide a good education."

Modifying Quotations Responsibly. Remember that even if you use brackets and ellipses, you can substantially change the meaning of a text by adding, changing, or deleting words in a direct quotation. Check your notes against original passages to be sure you aren't misrepresenting the source. Because it can be difficult to tell whether an ellipsis was introduced by the writer of a research project or was present in the source being quoted, the Modern Language Association (MLA) recommends placing brackets around ellipses that you introduce when shortening a text, as has been done in the following quotation.

Using an Ellipsis in MLA Style:

"I know there are wonderful and dedicated teachers in our public schools. And I know that hundreds of public schools provide a good education [. . .]. But I also know that illiteracy and high dropout rates plague too many children from low-income families.

Modifying Quotations Using "Sic." Occasionally in a passage you are quoting a word is misspelled or a fact is incorrect. In such cases, use the word "sic" in brackets to indicate that the error occurred in the original passage. If you don't use "sic," your readers will think that the mistake is yours. The following quotation uses "sic" correctly.

IN THIS BOOK

Read about using your direct-quotation notes during drafting on p. 208.

Quotation Modified Correctly Using "Sic":

"Bill Clinten's [sic] last year in office was beset with nearly as many problems as any of his first seven years" (Richards 22).

■ **Paraphrase Notes**

If you restate a passage from a source in your own words, you are paraphrasing the source. Typically, a paraphrase is roughly as long as the original passage. To paraphrase, follow these guidelines:

1. Be sure that you understand the passage by reading it and the surrounding text carefully.

2. Restate the passage in your own words. Make sure that you do more than simply change key words.

ON THE WEB SITE

View the tutorial How to Integrate Paraphrases into a Draft at http://www .bedfordresearcher .com for additional examples of paraphrases.

3. Compare the original passage with your paraphrase. Make sure that you've conveyed the meaning of the passage but that the wording and sentence structure differ from those in the original passage.

4. Note the author, title, and the page on which the passage can be found.

You can use paraphrases to illustrate or support a point you make in your document or to refer to ideas with which you disagree. Even though you are using your own words when you paraphrase, you must cite the source because the paraphrase presents ideas and information that are not your own.

The following examples of paraphrasing are drawn from featured writer Patrick Crossland's research writing project.

IN THIS BOOK

Read more about documenting your sources in Chapters 16–20.

Original Passage:

"High school grades and test scores are not the only factors considered by colleges and universities in the admissions process. Other factors that influence college admissions decisions include high school rank, being an athlete, alumni connection, extracurricular activities, special talents, and other personal characteristics of applicants."

William H. Gray III, "In the Best Interest of America, Affirmative Action is a Must," p. 144.

The following note includes a paraphrase that preserves the meaning of the original passage while avoiding a replication of the sentence structure and wording.

Appropriate Paraphrase of the Original Passage:

William H. Gray III notes that, in addition to high school grades and test scores, factors affecting the admissions decisions made by most college and universities include an applicant's participation in sports, involvement in extracurricular activities, personal qualities, special talents, connections to alumni, and class rank (144).

The following inappropriate paraphrase uses the same sentence structure as in the original passage. It differs only through changes in some of the key words in the passage.

Paraphrase That Does Not Differ Sufficiently from the Original Passage:

William H. Gray III notes that high school grades and test scores are not the only issues weighed by colleges and universities during college admissions decisions. Other factors that influence those decisions are high school rank, participating in athletics, connections to alumni, out-of-school activities, unique talents, and other personal qualities of applicants (144).

The following inappropriate paraphrase does not accurately convey the meaning of the original passage.

Paraphrase That Distorts the Meaning of the Original Passage:

William H. Gray III notes that participation in sports and involvement in extracurricular activities are among the most important factors affecting college admissions decisions (144).

IN THIS BOOK

Read about using your paraphrase notes during drafting on p. 225.

■ Summary Notes

ON THE WEB SITE

View the tutorial How to Integrate Summaries into a Draft at **http://www .bedfordresearcher .com** for additional examples of summaries.

IN THIS BOOK

Read about using your summary notes during drafting on p. 226.

A summary is a concise statement of information in a source. Summaries can range from a brief statement — or nutshell — of the source's main points to brief descriptions of points made in the source. Research writers often summarize an entire source, but they can also summarize lengthy passages. Use summary notes when you want to capture the overall argument and information in a source. Keep in mind that summaries must include a citation of the source.

Here is an original passage from a source one might consult while researching television addiction. A note containing a summary of the passage, which appeared in *Scientific American* (February 2002), follows the original.

Original Passage:

What is more surprising is that the sense of relaxation ends when the set is turned off, but the feelings of passivity and lowered alertness continue. Survey participants commonly reflect that television has somehow absorbed or sucked out their energy, leaving them depleted. They say they have more difficulty concentrating after viewing than before. In contrast, they rarely indicate such difficulty after reading. After playing sports or engaging in hobbies, people report improvements in mood. After watching TV, people's moods are about the same or worse than before.

Robert Kubey and Mihaly Csikszentmihalyi, "Television Addiction," p. 76

Note That Includes an Appropriate Summary of the Original Passage:

Kubey and Csikszentmihalyi, "Television Addiction," p. 76

Although watching television may relax a viewer, studies have shown it does little to improve a viewer's alertness, energy level, or mood.

■ Source Comparison Notes

You can use notes to indicate connections among your sources. Identifying relationships among the ideas, information, and arguments in your sources can be useful when you begin planning and organizing your project document. Paying attention to your sources as a group — not just to individual sources — helps you gain a more complete understanding of the conversation you've decided to join.

Featured writer Maria Sanchez-Traynor used comparison notes when she was working on her feature article. After highlighting key passages from her observation notes of a class taught at the Intensive English Program, she reviewed all her notes and identified connections she saw between what she'd observed in the classroom and what she'd learned from her interviews with Marcos DaSilva, a student who had taken classes in the program, and Margaret Gough, the program's assistant director. In her observation notes, Maria identified a connection to her interview with Marcos, so she added a comparison note: *"This ties in with Marcos's quote."* This note became the basis for a key point Maria made in her feature article.

■ Planning Notes

Planning notes are directions to yourself about how you might use a source in your project document, how you might organize the document, or ideas you should remember later.

Maria Sanchez-Traynor used planning notes as she prepared to write her feature article. At the end of her observation of a class at the Intensive English Program, she talked to the teacher and looked at the course syllabus. She read a note attached to the syllabus reminding the teacher to "emphasize that you're here to help them—benefit comes from participation." She wrote down what she'd read and, later, as she reviewed her notes, wrote a planning note suggesting that she might use this comment as the lead for her feature article. Her note read, *"How will this tie in? Possible lead?"* The comment did, in fact, become the lead for her article.

Your Research Project

SAVE YOUR NOTES IN THE RESEARCH LOG
To save your notes in the Research Log:

- Login to your Research Log account, select your project, and click on the Notes tool.

- You can create as many notes as you'd like. In addition to including your notes about a source, each note card can contain a title, the name of the source, a label, and a number that corresponds to its order in your outline. You can save, edit, and delete notes; you can reorder your notes if you change your outline. To view your notes outside the Research Log, you can print, email, and download them.

You can find the Notes tool in the Research Log on the *Bedford Researcher* Web site at **http://www.bedfordresearcher.com**.

10c

What is plagiarism and how can I avoid it?

Plagiarism, a form of intellectual dishonesty, involves unintentionally using someone else's work without properly acknowledging where the ideas came from (the most common form of plagiarism) or intentionally

IN THIS BOOK

See the Checklist for Avoiding Plagiarism on p. 178.

copying someone else's work and passing it off as your own (the most serious form of plagiarism).

Plagiarism is based on the notion of "copyright," or ownership of a document or idea. Like a patent, which protects an invention, a copyright protects an author's investment of time and energy in the creation of a document. Essentially, it provides authors with an assurance that, if they create a document, someone else won't be able to steal ideas from it and profit from that theft without penalty.

In most cases, plagiarism is unintentional, and most cases of unintentional plagiarism result from taking poor notes or failing to use notes properly. You are plagiarizing if you

- quote a passage in a note but neglect to include quotation marks and then later insert the quotation into your document without remembering that it is a direct quotation.
- include a paraphrase that differs so slightly from the original passage that it might as well be a direct quotation.
- don't clearly distinguish between your ideas and ideas that come from your sources.
- neglect to list the source of a paraphrase, quotation, or summary in your text or in your works cited list.

■ Avoiding Problems with Quotations

IN THIS BOOK

Read more about quotations and taking notes on p. 167. Read more about using quotations in your document on p. 218.

In many unintentional cases of plagiarism, a writer quotes a source without using quotation marks in a note and then uses the information from the note in a document, forgetting that the material is a direct quotation. The solution to this problem is fairly simple: Take careful notes. If you are copying a direct quotation, be sure to include quotation marks around the quotation, use ellipses or brackets as necessary, and avoid distorting the meaning of the source. Sloppy note taking not only will waste time later but also might come back to haunt you.

■ Avoiding Problems with Paraphrasing

One of the most common problems with using source material is paraphrasing too closely—that is, making such minor changes to the words of a source that your paraphrase remains nearly identical to the original passage. To avoid paraphrasing too closely, focus on understanding the key ideas in the passage and then restate them in your own words. One useful strategy is to begin your notes with the phrase "In other words." This strategy reminds you that it's important to do more than simply rephrase the passage. You might also want to set the original source aside while you paraphrase so that you won't be tempted to copy sentences directly from it.

The key points to remember about paraphrasing are that you should be able to

- tell someone what the passage means in your own words
- phrase your explanation using a sentence structure that differs from the structure used in the original passage

Note that even when you paraphrase source information, you should cite the source.

IN THIS BOOK

Read more about paraphrases and taking notes on p. 170. Read more about using paraphrases in your document on p. 225.

Avoiding Problems with Summaries

Ideally, summaries are brief statements of the content contained in a source. Researchers often write notes that summarize key points in a source. Problems can arise, however, when a writer fails to summarize ideas and instead creates a patchwork paraphrase that is little more than a series of passages copied from the source. As with paraphrasing, you can remind yourself to summarize, rather than copying the original language and sentence structure of the source, by beginning your summary with the phrase "In other words." And you might want to set the original source aside while you write your summary so that you won't be tempted to copy sentences directly from it.

IN THIS BOOK

Read more about summaries and taking notes on p. 172. Read more about using summaries in your document on p. 226.

Distinguishing between Your Ideas and Ideas in Your Sources

Failing to distinguish between your ideas and ideas drawn from your sources can also result in plagiarism. Failing to identify the source of ideas and information can lead readers to think other writers' ideas are yours. The following passage is from featured writer Maria Sanchez-Traynor's article about the Intensive English Program (IEP) at Colorado State University. In her article, Maria draws on information she obtained through an interview with Heather Moffie, a teacher in the IEP.

> Moffie says she has turned to different resources, including texts and other teachers, to help her understand what may be difficult for her students. She also says that when she learns a different language at the same time as she teaches one, it helps her understand what her students are going through—or, as she puts it, "what it's like to be a learner."

Now read a passage that fails to distinguish between Maria's ideas and those she learned through her interview with Heather Moffie.

> Moffie has turned to different resources, including texts and other teachers, to help her understand what may be difficult for students. It is helpful to learn a different language at the same time as teaching one in order to understand what students are going through.

The second passage, because it fails to identify Heather Moffie as the person who told Maria about her strategies, implies that these ideas are Maria's rather than Heather Moffie's.

Fortunately, there is an easy solution to this problem. In your project document and in your notes, use the name of an author or the title of the source you're drawing from each time you introduce ideas from a source. This technique involves using *signal phrases*—phrases that alert your readers to the source of the ideas or information you are using.

Examples of Signal Phrases:

According to Scott McPherson . . .
Jill Bedard writes . . .
Tom Huckin reports . . .
Kate Kiefer observes . . .
Bob Phelps suggests . . .
In the words of Chris Napolitano . . .
As Ellen Page tells it . . .
Reid Vincent indicates . . .
Jessica Richards calls our attention to . . .

■ Identifying Sources in Your Document

IN THIS BOOK
Find out how to cite and document your sources in Chapters 17 (MLA), 18 (APA), 19 (*Chicago*), 20 (CBE), and 21 (Columbia Online Style).

Writers sometimes neglect to identify the sources from which they have drawn their information. Depending on the type of document you are writing, you should include a complete citation for each source you refer to in your document. The citation should be in the text of the document (in in-text citations, footnotes, or endnotes) or in a bibliography or references list.

Failing to cite sources is a common and serious problem. Your readers will not be able to determine which ideas and information in your text are your own or which are drawn from your sources. If they suspect you are failing to acknowledge your sources of information, they are likely to doubt your credibility, suspect your competence, and might even stop reading your document. Submitting academic work that does not include proper identification of sources might result in failure in the course or some other disciplinary action.

■ Understanding Common Knowledge and the Fair Use Provision

Much of the information you'll use in a research writing project falls under the category of *common knowledge*. Common knowledge is information that is widely known, such as the fact that smoking tobacco increases one's risk of developing lung cancer. Or it might be the kind of knowledge that people working in a particular field, such as petroleum engineering, use on a regular basis.

If you're relatively new to your topic, it can be difficult to determine whether information in a source is common knowledge. As you explore your topic, however, you'll begin to identify knowledge that is generally known. For instance, if three or more sources use the same information without citing its source, you can assume that the information is common knowledge. If those sources use the information and cite the source, however, then make sure you cite it as well.

It's also important that you know *how much* of a source you can borrow or quote from. According to Section 107 of the Copyright Act of 1976—the *fair use provision*—available on the Library of Congress Web site at **http://lcweb.loc.gov/copyright/title17**, writers can use copyrighted materials for purposes of "criticism, comment, news reporting, teaching (including multiple copies for classroom use), scholarship, or research." You can usually use up to 10 percent of a source, although this amount can be substantially less for songs or poetry and substantially more for images.

If you're not sure whether a source can be used under the fair use provision of the copyright law, ask its author or publisher for permission to use it. Remember that in all cases you must cite the source of the material you use under the fair use provision.

■ Working in Groups: Plagiarism, Peer Review, and Collaboration

Peer review and other collaborative activities raise important questions about plagiarism:

- If another writer suggests changes to your document and you subsequently incorporate them into your document, are you plagiarizing?
- What if those suggestions significantly change your document?
- If you work with a group of writers on a project, do you need to individually identify the parts that each of you wrote?
- Is it ethical to list yourself as a coauthor if another writer does most of the work on a collaborative writing project?

The answers to these questions will vary from situation to situation. In general, however, it's appropriate to use comments from reviewers in your document without citing them. If a reviewer's comments are particularly helpful, acknowledge their contributions in your document—writers often thank reviewers in a footnote or endnote or in an acknowledgments section. It is also appropriate to list coauthors on a collaboratively written document without individually identifying the text that was written by each coauthor.

■ Some Final Thoughts on Plagiarism

In addition to the ethical, legal, and technical aspects of plagiarism, you should also remember the potential impact of plagiarism on the effectiveness of your document. Because plagiarized material will often differ in style, tone, and word choice from the rest of your document, your readers are likely to notice these differences and wonder whether you've plagiarized the material or, if not, why you've written a document that's so difficult to read. If your readers react negatively, it's unlikely that your document will be successful.

 ON THE WEB SITE

You can complete this checklist online in the **Research Log** on the *Bedford Researcher* Web site at **http://www.bedfordresearcher.com**. It can also be printed or downloaded.

Checklist for Avoiding Plagiarism

- When taking notes, place quotation marks around any direct quotations, use ellipses and brackets appropriately, and identify the source and the page number (if any) of the quotation.
- When taking notes, make sure paraphrases differ significantly in word choice and sentence structure from the passage being paraphrased and identify the source and page number from which you took the paraphrase.
- When taking notes, make sure summaries are not just series of passages copied from the source.
- In your document, use signal phrases to distinguish between your ideas and those from your sources.
- In your document, make sure you've acknowledged your sources and correctly attributed your quotations.
- In your document, make sure you've used a bibliography or references list and clearly identified all sources in some way (using footnotes, endnotes, or in-text citations).
- Make sure that you haven't quoted so much of a source that it exceeds the fair use provision guidelines.

Your Research Project

UPDATE YOUR PROJECT TIMELINE

As you move into the next stage of your research writing project—writing your document—review your project timeline. At this point, you've completed eight project milestones.

PROJECT TIMELINE		
ACTIVITY	START DATE	COMPLETION DATE
Select your topic		
Explore your topic		
Narrow your topic to a single conversation		

Develop your research question
Develop your plan to collect and manage information
Collect information
Read and evaluate information
Take notes
Organize your information
Create your document outline
Develop your thesis statement
Write the first draft of your project document
Review and revise your first draft
Review and revise additional drafts
Edit your draft
Finalize in-text and end-of-text citations
Design your document
Publish and submit your project document

If you'd like to complete this activity online, use the **Research Log** activity "Create a Project Timeline" at **http://www .bedfordresearcher.com**. If you have created a research log using a notebook or a word processor, you can print or download this activity.

With the difficult work of locating, critically reading, evaluating, and taking notes on your sources completed, you're ready to move on to the most challenging—and rewarding—part of your research writing project: writing your project document. The next part of this book discusses the major research writing processes you'll use as you move from notes to a final project document. You'll find discussions of organizing your ideas and information, planning and drafting, revising and editing, and designing your project document. When you've completed work on these processes, you'll have a polished, well-supported project document that represents your contribution to the conversation you've decided to join.

Part Four

Writing Your Document

11. **Organizing and Outlining**
12. **Drafting Your Document**
13. **Integrating Source Information into Your Document**
14. **Revising and Editing**
15. **Designing Your Document**

After you read critically, evaluate, and take notes on your sources, you'll have a better understanding of the conversation you've decided to join. Your working thesis statement will become less preliminary and will begin to resemble the final thesis statement you will use to shape your contribution to the conversation. In the chapters that follow, you'll learn how to use your notes and outline to create a well-written, well-designed document.

CHAPTER 11

Organizing and Outlining

As a research writer, you're ready to shift your attention away from collecting and working with sources and toward crafting your own contribution to the conversation—your project document. Writing your document begins with organizing and outlining, two processes that build on the note-taking strategies you learned in the previous chapter.

Organizing involves reviewing your notes, revising your working thesis statement, and choosing an organizing strategy. It also involves selecting an organizing principle that is appropriate for your purposes and your readers' needs and interests. Organizing your ideas and information allows you to create an outline, which serves as a blueprint for your project document. In this chapter, you'll learn about these processes by answering the following questions.

Key Questions

11a

How should I organize my information and ideas?

To begin organizing your information and ideas, review your notes, review and revise your working thesis statement, and choose an organizing strategy.

■ Step 1: Review Your Notes

Up to this point in your research process, you've been focusing on the voices of individual sources and might not have taken much time to

ORGANIZING YOUR INFORMATION AND IDEAS	
Step 1	Review your notes
Step 2	Review and revise your working thesis statement
Step 3	Select an organizing strategy

analyze what your sources are saying, as a group, about the conversation you've decided to join. The first step toward organizing your information and ideas should be to read quickly through your notes to gain an overall sense of your sources.

■ Step 2: Review and Revise Your Working Thesis Statement

IN THIS BOOK

Read more about your working thesis statement on p. 200.

As you've collected, read, and evaluated information about your project, you've gained a more complete understanding of your conversation. Working with this information may have changed your working thesis statement. Use the following questions to determine whether you should revise your working thesis statement:

- After collecting and working with your sources, have you found it necessary to alter your argument or approach?
- Have your purposes—the reasons you are working on this project—changed since you started your project?
- Has the role you are adopting changed? Are you informing your readers? Reporting the results of an investigation? Entertaining them? Arguing with them? Will you adopt multiple roles?

■ Step 3: Select an Organizing Strategy

IN THIS BOOK

Read about creating an outline on p. 190.

An *organizing strategy* is a process you can use to organize your information and ideas. The organizing strategies discussed in this chapter include labeling your notes and sources, grouping your notes and sources, and clustering or mapping ideas. Each of these strategies will help you explore the relationships among your ideas and information and will help you later as you develop your outline.

Your selection of an organizing strategy will depend on the kind of information you've collected and how you've taken notes. If you've collected all of your information in electronic form (as Web pages, downloaded files, email messages, and so on), you'll probably make different decisions about how to organize your ideas than you will if you've saved your sources and notes in paper form (books, articles, printouts, and so on). Similarly, if you've written all of your notes on note cards or in a notebook, you might choose a different organizing strategy than if you've taken all of your notes in a word processor.

Labeling Your Notes and Sources. One of the simplest organizational strategies is to label your notes and sources. The label should help you understand at a glance how you will use each note or where in your project you plan to position it. For example, you might label all of the notes that support your argument as "Support for my argument." Or you might label the notes that you want to use in your introduction as "Introduction," and so on. If you are using note cards as featured writer Jenna Alberter did, you might want to label each card with a Post-it Note. If you have taken electronic notes, as featured writer Aaron Batty did, you have a number of options, depending on how you have saved your notes (see Figure 11.1).

Occasionally, you might find that a note or source contains information you want to use for multiple purposes. For instance, a note might include a quotation that you want to use in your introduction and a paraphrase that you want to support your argument. Labels don't take up a lot of room on a note or source, so you can apply more than one label. Once you've labeled your notes and sources, you can organize them into groups or put them in order according to the outline you will create.

Grouping Your Notes and Sources. Grouping — putting your notes and sources into categories — is perhaps the most frequently used organizational strategy. To group your *printed* notes and sources, you can put paper materials into related piles, folders, or envelopes or attach related notes and sources to one another with paper clips, binder clips, or rubber bands. To group your *electronic* notes and sources, you can create word processing files into which you insert related material, folders on your computer into which you move notes or sources, or folders in your Bookmarks or Favorites list into which you move related items.

As with labeling, you might run into problems if you want to place notes or sources in two or more groups. If you're working with a paper note or source, you can put it in both groups by making a photocopy or printing out another copy. Or you can create a cross-reference note, such as "See note on Jackson's article in the opposing viewpoints group." If you're working with an electronic source or note, simply copy the material into the relevant folder or file.

Clustering and Mapping Information and Ideas. Clustering and mapping are organizing strategies that provide a graphical overview of the ideas and information you've collected and plan to use in your document. An important advantage of clustering and mapping is that they allow you to see at a glance which ideas and information are related (clustering) and how they are related (mapping).

Clustering is similar to grouping: It shows related ideas and information as clusters, or networks, of related material. Clustering,

ON THE WEB SITE
Read more about Jenna Alberter, Aaron Batty, and the other student writers discussed in this chapter in Featured Writers on the *Bedford Researcher* Web site at **http://www .bedfordresearcher .com.**

IN THIS BOOK
Read about organizing electronic information and notes on p. 235.

RESEARCH ASSISTANT
Use the worksheet Grouping Your Sources to place your sources into categories.

> **A** ***Reactions to White Paper***
>
> On February 21, 2000, China shocked the world with its release of the white paper "The
> One-China Principle and the Taiwan Issue." In this 18-page document, the Beijing government
> outlined its case for Taiwan being the rightful property of the People's Republic of China (PRC),
> and, most surprisingly, its intent to use force if Taiwan did not move to "reunite" with the mainland.

Figure 11.1 Labeling Electronic Notes and Sources

A Aaron typed a label at the top of a note he took in a word processing file.

B In Microsoft Internet Explorer, Aaron renamed the titles of his Favorites items to be recognizable labels, such as "China's Position on Taiwan, June 1988."

C In Netscape Navigator, Aaron could have added a label to the DESCRIPTION field in the PROPERTIES dialog box for Bookmark items. (On the Mac, he would have used the DESCRIPTION field in the GET INFO dialog box.)

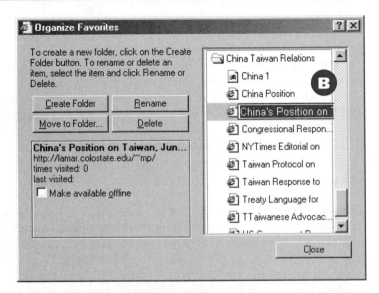

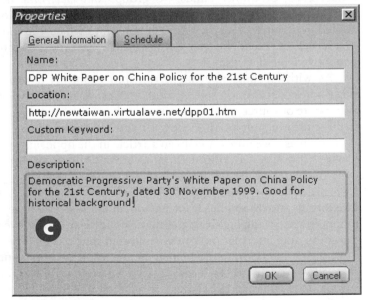

however, allows you to visualize the relationships of information and ideas more easily than grouping. Clustering is useful at many points during your research writing process. As you began to explore your topic, you might have used clustering as a type of brainstorming to come up with ideas. Now, after you've taken notes on your sources, you can use clustering to help explore relationships among the ideas and information you've collected.

Clusters can show how key ideas or supporting points might relate to a main idea. The most important ideas are closest to the center of the cluster, while less important points are farther out (see Figure 11.2). Clusters can be drawn on a piece of paper or with graphics tools in a word processing program or image editor.

IN THIS BOOK
Read about using clustering to generate ideas about a topic on p. 14.

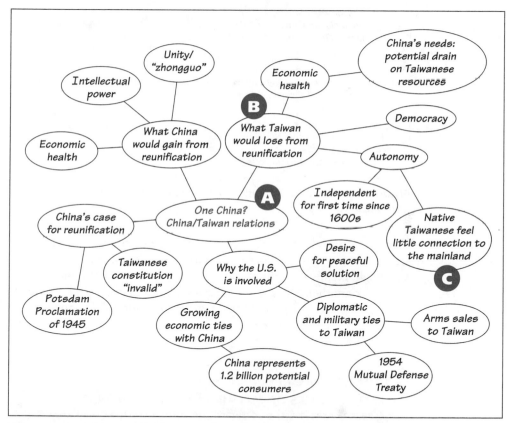

Figure 11.2   Clustering Ideas

A Clusters typically build around a central idea. In featured writer Aaron Batty's cluster, the central idea is "One China? China/Taiwan Relations" at the center of his cluster.

B Clusters are sets of related information and ideas. This cluster includes ideas about what reunification with China would mean for Taiwan. Other clusters include Chinese and U.S. perspectives.

C The least important information is farthest from the center and connected to a related cluster.

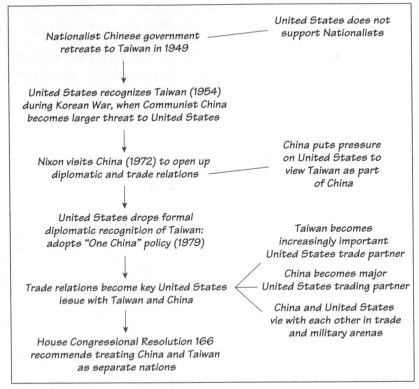

Figure 11.3 A Map Showing a Timeline of Key Events in Taiwanese History

While clustering is based on a grouping principle, *mapping* might show how you can sequence information in a document. For instance, you might create a map that shows how your argument builds on one idea after another. Or you might create a map that lays out a timeline of events related to your topic. Figure 11.3 shows a map featured writer Aaron Batty created to organize his thoughts about key events in Taiwanese history.

Your Research Project

CREATE CLUSTERS OR MAPS IN *RESEARCH ASSISTANT*

Research Assistant, the software program included on a CD-ROM at the back of this book, will help you organize your information and ideas. To create clusters or maps in *Research Assistant,* do the following:

- Open the Clustering worksheet and follow the directions for creating a cluster.
- Open the Timeline worksheet to map your ideas and information chronologically.

- Open one of the Causes and Effects worksheets to create a cause/effect map of ideas and information.
- Open a blank worksheet and create a map or cluster by dragging sources from your collection bin onto the new worksheet and using *Research Assistant*'s graphics and text tools. You can draw lines, circles, and boxes, use colors, and make notes on your worksheet.

  To learn more about *Research Assistant,* see p. 403 or visit the Research Assistant section of the *Bedford Researcher* Web site at **http://www.bedfordresearcher.com.**

11b

What organizing principle should I use?

Before you create an outline, think about how you might organize the information in your project document. No matter what your research writing situation, most project documents, whether print or online, contain some sort of introduction, body, and conclusion. Almost all research essays written for college courses follow this general organization. You can read more about drafting these sections of your document in the next chapter, but for now it's important that you decide on an *organizing principle,* or pattern, to organize your information and ideas.

 ON THE WEB SITE
Read about the typical sections of print and electronic research project documents in the research writing manual Sections Typically Found in Research Project Documents.

Your selection of an organizing principle will affect both the structure of your project document and the way you think about the information and ideas you will ultimately use in your document. You can choose from a number of organizing principles:

- **Chronological.** Paragraphs in a print document or pages in a Web document track the sequence in which events occur over time.
- **Cause/Effect.** Paragraphs or pages identify the factors that lead to (cause) an outcome (effect).
- **Pro/Con.** Paragraphs or pages identify each side of an argument. In many cases, these are followed by an argument in favor of one side or the other or by an alternative resolution to the issue.
- **Multiple Perspectives.** Paragraphs or pages identify a range of perspectives about an issue. These are frequently followed by an analysis supporting one perspective.
- **Comparison/Contrast.** Paragraphs or pages identify similarities and differences among the information and ideas in your sources.
- **Strengths/Weaknesses.** Paragraphs or pages contrast the strengths and weaknesses of one or more arguments about an issue. These

are typically followed by an argument about the superiority of one argument over the others.

- **Problem/Solution.** Paragraphs or pages define a problem and discuss the appropriateness of one or more solutions to the problem. If multiple solutions are proposed, an argument is usually made for the appropriateness of one solution.

📖 **IN THIS BOOK**

Read more about defining your role as a writer on p. 202.

Your choice of organizing principle will largely depend on the role or roles you adopt as a writer:

- If you're investigating an issue as an *inquirer,* you might choose an organizing principle that lends itself to a document reflecting the kind of investigation you're conducting, such as cause/effect. You might be asking, as featured writer Gaele Lopez asked about the causes of low turnout among younger voters, "What causes something to happen?"

- If you're adopting the role of *informant* or *interpreter,* you might select an organizing principle that allows you to clearly and easily convey information, such as chronology, cause/effect, or comparison/contrast. You might be suggesting, as featured writer Aaron Batty did in his analysis of the effects of the "one China" policy on the United States, a likely outcome (or effect) of a particular set of events (or causes).

- If you're adopting the role of *advocate,* you might opt for an organizing principle that is well suited to argumentation, such as pro/con or strengths/weaknesses. Featured writer Rianne Uilk, for example, used the pro/con organizing principle in her research paper about the effects of education reform legislation on Colorado public schools.

- If you're attempting to amuse or intrigue your readers as an *entertainer,* you'll probably be combining your goal of entertaining your audience with a goal of informing or persuading them. As a result, you should use one of the organizing principles associated with informing or persuading, such as pro/con, cause/effect, or comparison/contrast.

11c

What kind of outline should I create?

An *outline* represents the sequence in which your ideas and information will appear in your project document. Outlines range from informal lists of ideas to detailed instructions. Outlines are most effective when they build on organizational strategies such as labeling, grouping, clustering, or mapping and when they reflect your thoughtful decisions about the most appropriate organizing principle for your document. It's best, then, to create your outline *after* you've spent time organizing your notes and selecting an organizing principle.

■ Using Informal Outlines

Informal outlines can take many forms: a brief list of words, a series of short phrases, or even a series of sentences. You can use informal outlines to remind yourself of key points to address in your document or of notes you should refer to when you begin drafting. Featured writer Jenna Alberter, who wrote a research essay about images of women in seventeenth-century Dutch art, created the following informal outline. In her outline, each item represents a section she planned to include in her paper.

ON THE WEB SITE
Read more about Janna Alberter and the other student writers discussed in this chapter in Featured Writers on the *Bedford Researcher* Web site at **http://www .bedfordresearcher .com**.

Jenna Alberter's Informal Outline

1. Introduction
2. Role of women in Dutch society
3. Jacob Cats's important book *Houwelick* (or *Marriage*)
4. Overview of women's stages of life (with examples from seventeenth-century literature and art)
5. Young women and courtship
6. Women as wives and mothers
7. Elderly women and widows
8. Conclusion

Since the purpose of an informal outline is to serve largely as a reminder, rather than as a detailed blueprint for a document, many informal outlines are incomplete. They typically consist of brief labels or phrases rather than complete sentences and seldom have subpoints as formal outlines do (see the next section).

Not all informal outlines, however, are incomplete. Featured writer Patrick Crossland wrote the following detailed "thumbnail outline," a type of informal outline, as he worked on his research essay about college admissions standards. Patrick's teacher assigned the outline to help students in Patrick's class organize ideas and information before writing rough drafts of their essays. Patrick identified the major sections he would include in his research essay and noted which sources he would use to provide background information and to support his argument.

Patrick Crossland's Thumbnail Outline

Intro

Present problem; offer an introductory look at the question of who's getting into college and what the factors are that affect this. Introduce the various admittance issues to be examined.

Section 1

Examine the notion of competition through the "Caleb" analogy. Look at the college application process through the perspective of a game (therefore beating the competitors). Present the tier system and analogy by Miller.

Section 2

Look at the issue of race, the history of the problem, and the introduction of equal opportunity policies. Present the Krauthammer view of who it hurts or helps (is it fair in that sense?).

Section 3

Discuss family situations and their relation to the ability to succeed in higher education. Use Lillard and Gerner source covering the issues of family makeup.

Section 4

Examine the role that gender plays in getting accepted and succeeding in college. Look at issues of equality of the sexes.

Section 5

Look at mental/physical capabilities and their relation to college success. Discuss a change in curricula to suit people of all different mental capabilities.

Conclusion

■ Using Formal Outlines

A *formal outline* provides a complete and accurate list of the points you want to address in your research document. Writers who use formal outlines depend on a system of numbers and letters and varying amounts of indentation to identify the hierarchy of ideas and information. You can use formal outlines to identify

- your working thesis statement
- the key points you want to make in your document
- the sequence in which those points should be presented
- support for your points
- the notes and sources you should refer to as you work on your document

The most common types of formal outlines are topical outlines and sentence outlines.

Topical Outlines. Topical outlines present the topics and subtopics you plan to include in your research document as a series of words and phrases. Items at the same level of importance should be phrased in parallel grammatical form.

Featured writer Gaele Lopez prepared the following topical outline for his research essay on low voter turnout among 18-to-24-year-olds. Notice that he includes his working thesis statement, suggests the key points he wants to make in his document, maps out the support for his points, and uses a conventional system of numbers and letters to convey the organization of the information.

Gaele Lopez's Topical Outline

Working thesis statement: Turnout among voters under age 25 is low because they do not understand why it is important to vote.

I. Lack of trustworthy political information
   A. Internet: primary source of information
      1. Difference between Internet and other media
      2. Difficulty sustaining attention to issues
   B. General distrust of traditional news media
      1. Issue of "reportability"
      2. Withholding of information
II. A generation of nonvoters
   A. Lack of motivation to register
      1. Thriving economy
      2. Benefit of participation questionable
   B. Lack of motivation to vote if registered
      1. Unaffected by leadership
      2. Little concern for civic affairs
III. Distrust of government institutions
   A. Youth's refusal to let others make decisions for them
      1. No identification with candidates
      2. Belief that officials are in politics for the wrong reasons
   B. Party platform disconnect
      1. Youths interested in jobs, wages
      2. Candidates talking eldercare, social security
IV. Decrease in political knowledge/awareness/action
   A. Erosion of knowledge base
      1. Unaware of decrease in national debt
      2. Misinformed on important current political issues
   B. Consequences of underrepresentation
      1. Underevaluation of needs of 18-to-24-year-olds
      2. Possible loss of voting rights

Not all topical outlines use arabic numerals, letters, and roman numerals to indicate the hierarchy of information. An alternative approach, commonly used in business and the sciences, uses numbering with decimal points:

1.
   1.1
      1.1.1
      1.1.2

RESEARCH ASSISTANT
Use the worksheet Outline & Bibliography Builder to create your outline.

ON THE WEB SITE
Use the research writing manual Using Your Word Processor at **http://www .bedfordresearcher .com** to learn how to use bullets, numbering, and indentation to create outlines.

    1.2
        1.2.1
        1.2.2
  2.

Sentence Outlines. Sentence outlines use complete sentences to identify the points you want to cover. Sentence outlines typically serve two purposes:

1. They begin the process of converting an outline into a draft of your document.
2. They help you assess the structure of a document that you have already written.

Section of Gaele Lopez's Topical Outline Turned into a Sentence Outline

Thesis statement: Turnout among voters under age 25 is low because they do not understand why it is important to vote.

  I. Young voters have not found a trustworthy source of political information.
    A. Under-25-year-olds actively use the Internet as their primary source of information.
      1. While it is easy for newspaper readers or TV viewers to be drawn into a political issue while reading or viewing, most users of the Internet—largely a "search-specific" information source—miss finding something they weren't looking for.
      2. The difficulty young voters have sustaining attention to political issues may result from reading Web pages for information, which often means reading snippets, headlines, sensational quotes, and brief commentary rather than substantive discussion.
    B. Younger voters in general tend to distrust news media.
      1. Along with many of his peers, one 18-year-old college student asks, "What makes some [stories] reportable and others not?"
      2. Young adults begrudge the media for what they perceive as withholding information: "I know they won't lie to me, but I'm concerned about what they don't want me to know," one 19-year-old said.

You can also create a sentence outline *after* you've written a document. In that case your outline consists of the topic sentence of each paragraph. Using this approach, you can determine the effectiveness of the document's organization and content.

■ **Reviewing Your Outline**

Whether you created an informal or a formal outline, ask yourself whether it is adequate:

- Does your outline provide an effective organization for your document?
- Have you covered all of your key points?
- Does the outline suggest sufficient detail in your coverage of key points?
- Do any sections seem out of order?

Creating an outline helps clarify your ideas about the organization of your project document. As you review your outline, ask whether it can serve as a blueprint for the first draft of your project document. If you don't feel confident about your outline, spend more time on it. Taking the time to create an effective outline will reduce the time needed to write your first draft.

■ **Understanding the Relationship between Notes and Outlines**

Outlines are not intended to replace your notes. Instead, an outline refers you to the more detailed information contained in your notes and sources. Your outline acts as a guide to the structure of your project document, while your notes help you to develop the sections within the document. It is important, as a result, to create links between your outline and your notes. The following techniques can help you link your outline to your notes.

- *Create direct references within your outline to a particular note or group of notes.* Some writers find it helpful to make direct references to the sources they intend to use by placing the name of the source in parentheses next to each item in their outline.
- *Create a parallel arrangement between your notes and your outline.* Organize your notes so that they correspond to the order in which they appear in your outline.
- *If your notes and outline are on paper, create a physical link between them.* Attach notes to your outline using paper clips or staples.
- *If your notes and outline are on paper, create groups of notes that correspond to major headings in your outline.*
- *If your notes and outline are saved as word processing documents, create electronic links between them.* Copy the text of a note and insert it into the outline as a comment (annotation) or as a footnote or endnote. Or create a hypertext link to the file containing your note. If you are using the OUTLINE VIEW in your

ON THE WEB SITE

Use the research writing manual Using Your Word Processor to learn how to use comments, endnotes, footnotes, hypertext links, and the OUTLINE VIEW to create links between your outline and your notes.

word processor, you can also insert the note as a lower-level heading.

- If you've saved your notes in the Research Log on the *Bedford Researcher* Web site, use the ORDER field to place your notes in a sequence that corresponds to the key points in your outline.

- If you've saved your notes in *Research Assistant,* use the Outline template to create your outline and drag the icons representing your notes next to the points in your outline.

Your Research Project

CREATE YOUR OUTLINE IN RESEARCH ASSISTANT
To create an outline and organize your notes in *Research Assistant:*

- Open the Outline worksheet and follow the directions for creating an outline.

- Drag icons representing your sources onto the outline worksheet. Each icon has a related note card that allows you to save your notes about the source. You can also use the note card to evaluate and rank your sources.

To learn more about *Research Assistant,* see p. 403 or visit the Research Assistant section of the *Bedford Researcher* Web site.

Organizing your ideas and information, selecting an organizing principle for your project document, and creating an outline prepares you to plan and draft your project document. In the next chapter, you will read about strategies you can use to create your document.

CHAPTER 12

Drafting Your Document

If you're new to research writing, you might be surprised at how long it's taken to get to the chapter about "writing." If you are not new to research writing, you know that you've been writing all along. Research writing isn't so much the act of putting words to paper or screen as it is the process of identifying and learning about a conversation, reflecting on what you've learned, and making your contribution to that conversation. This chapter focuses on how to draft your contribution—your project document. The key questions addressed in this chapter include:

Key Questions

12a

What are my readers' expectations about my project document?

As you've worked on your research writing project so far, you've thought about how to achieve your purposes as a writer and address your readers' needs and interests. When you begin to draft your project document, ask yourself an additional question: What will my readers expect from this document?

ON THE
WEB SITE
View the research
writing manual
Sections Typically
Found in Research
Project Documents
on the *Bedford Re-
searcher* Web site,
at **http://www
.bedfordresearcher
.com**, to learn
about sections
typically found in
print and electronic
research project
documents.

Some readers will have expectations about the structure and style of your document. If you are writing a research essay for a class, for instance, your readers will expect it to be similar to other research essays. At a minimum, the essay will have an introduction, a thesis statement, a body, a conclusion, and a list of works cited. Your readers will also expect a serious tone. You will inform them or argue with them about an aspect of the conversation you've decided to join, and you'll cite your sources. If you're creating an informative Web site, your readers will have a different set of expectations: an opening page, a detailed contribution to the conversation, a list of works cited or direct links to those sources, a system for navigating among the pages on your site, and effective use of images and other media elements. Your readers will have yet another set of expectations about a feature article, a marketing plan, or a scientific report, all of which have characteristic sections and styles.

Even in a writing class in which your instructor has left the topic for a research project open, he or she will nonetheless have expectations about what you'll be writing about and what sections you should include in your document. If your readers have no knowledge of your document until they read it, they'll look for clues to learn what it's about. They'll scan the title and introduction, for instance, to find out what the document addresses. If they're interested, they'll start to read. If your document coincides with their needs and interests, they'll probably keep reading.

IN THIS
BOOK
Read more about
common knowl-
edge on p. 176.

If your readers are involved in the conversation, they'll expect you to avoid unnecessary references to commonly accepted information and to show an awareness of the issues other writers have raised. If your readers have not been involved in the conversation—or are unfamiliar with the topic—think carefully about what you can treat as common knowledge and what information you'll have to provide to help your readers understand the conversation.

When deciding what to include in your research writing document, imagine your readers' expectations about the structure of your document; the clarity and effectiveness of your introduction, thesis statement, and conclusion; the support you offer for your points; the organization of your document; the quality of your writing; and the accuracy and completeness of your documentation.

12b

How can I create my thesis statement?

Your research question guided you through the process of searching for, locating, and collecting information. After you collected that information, your working thesis statement provided a basis for reading critically, evaluating, taking notes on and organizing your sources, and creating your outline. Your research question and your working thesis statement helped *you* focus your efforts to learn about and decide how best to contribute to the conversation.

Your thesis statement, in contrast, is designed to help *your readers* understand how you view the conversation and how they should view it as well. Your thesis statement presents your main point. It answers your research question and is less tentative than your working thesis statement. If you've asked, for example, about the causes of a problem, then your thesis statement should identify those causes. If you've asked what the best solution to a problem might be, your thesis statement should identify that solution.

Sample Research Question:

What is the cause of the decline in the population of brown trout in the state's rivers?

Sample Thesis Statement:

The decline in the population of brown trout in the state's rivers is a result of disease introduced by rainbow trout grown in the state's fish hatcheries.

In addition to answering your research question, your thesis statement might invite your readers to learn something new, suggest that they change their attitudes or beliefs, or argue that they should take action of some kind.

Sample Research Question:

How can we eliminate disease in brown trout in the state's rivers?

Sample Thesis Statement:

State fish hatcheries must take steps to eliminate disease in the rainbow trout they release into state streams.

This thesis statement urges the state agency that controls fish hatcheries to take action. It also encourages readers to accept that argument and, possibly, to change their attitudes and beliefs about state-supported fish hatcheries.

 ON THE WEB SITE

To learn more about drafting your thesis statement, view the tutorial How to - Develop a Thesis Statement on the *Bedford Researcher* Web site at **http://www .bedfordresearcher .com**.

IN THIS BOOK

Read more about research questions on p. 47 and about working thesis statements on p. 184.

DEVELOPING AN EFFECTIVE THESIS STATEMENT	
Step 1	Build on your research question and your working thesis statement
Step 2	Consider your purpose and roles
Step 3	Adapt your thesis statement to the needs and interests of your readers
Step 4	Determine the scope of your thesis statement

A variation of this thesis statement could urge readers to take action:

> Citizens should contact their state legislators and ask them to direct state fish hatcheries to eliminate disease in the rainbow trout released into state streams.

 ON THE WEB SITE
Read more about the student writers discussed in this chapter in Featured Writers on the *Bedford Researcher* Web site at **http://www .bedfordresearcher .com**.

Table 12.1 presents the eight featured writers' movements from research question to working thesis statement to thesis statement. Note how each thesis statement answers its research question as well as directs readers' attention to one aspect of the conversation, encourages them to change their attitudes or beliefs, or urges them to take action of some kind.

Developing an effective thesis statement involves four steps.

◼ Step 1: Build on Your Research Question and Your Working Thesis Statement

As you learned, your thesis statement is an answer to your research question. You can begin to develop that answer by identifying key words and phrases in your research question and working thesis statement. For example,

Research Question:
What is the **cause of recent declines** in the **state's brown trout population**?

Working Thesis Statement:
Disease linked to **hatchery-raised rainbow trout** seems to be **causing the** decline.

Thesis Statement:
The Department of Natural Resources should determine whether the **recent decline** of **brown trout populations** in **state** streams is **caused by disease** spread by **rainbow trout released from state fish hatcheries**.

Identifying key words and phrases provides you with a set of terms that focus on the specific aspect of the conversation. Use these words and phrases to craft your thesis statement.

TABLE 12.1 THE FEATURED WRITERS' MOVEMENTS FROM RESEARCH QUESTION TO THESIS STATEMENT

FEATURED WRITER	RESEARCH QUESTION	WORKING THESIS STATEMENT	THESIS STATEMENT
Jenna Alberter	What was the relationship between seventeenth-century Dutch paintings of women and the culture in which they were created?	Seventeenth-century Dutch paintings reflected society's expectations of women and helped women understand their roles in society.	Dutch Baroque genre paintings did not simply reflect the reality surrounding them; they also helped shape that reality.
Aaron Batty	What are the implications for the United States of differences in China's and Taiwan's interpretations of the "one China" policy?	The United States might be drawn into a war over the "one China" policy.	As we venture into the twenty-first century, with its quickly developing world economy and global culture, the final definition of "one China" will shape the course of not only the Asia-Pacific region but the whole world.
Patrick Crossland	What cultural, academic, and regional factors affect college admissions decisions?	Factors affecting college admissions decisions include race, gender, and intellectual ability.	What many college applicants like Caleb don't realize is that getting into college is much like entering a contest in which each applicant is pitted against thousands of others.
Kevin Fahey	How is Nick Adams characterized by Ernest Hemingway?	Nick Adams is a flawed character with whom readers can identify.	By portraying Nick Adams as befuddled, intimidated, and even self-serving, Hemingway gives us a hero with whom most readers can identify.
Gaele Lopez	Why is turnout low among 18-to-24-year-old voters?	Turnout among voters under age 25 is low because they don't understand why it's important to vote.	Turnout among voters under age 25 is low because they do not understand why it is important to vote.
Holly Richmond	Who are my ancestors and what did they do during their lifetimes?	My parents, grandparents, and great-grandparents lived rich and varied lives.	The Richmond family has a rich and varied history.
Maria Sanchez-Traynor	How is English taught to foreign-language speakers at the Intensive English Program?	Teachers use immersion techniques and explain the theory of the English language to help students at the IEP learn to speak and write English.	Moffie and her colleagues at the Intensive English Program (IEP) at Colorado State University use a variety of motivational strategies to teach English to non-native speakers.
Rianne Uilk	What are the likely effects of Colorado Senate Bill 186 on education reform in Colorado public schools?	Schools, teachers, and students will be negatively affected by Colorado Senate Bill 186.	Despite its few merits, Senate Bill 186, which became Colorado state law on April 10, 2000, will actually hurt the educational welfare of the very students it is intended to help.

■ Step 2: Consider Your Purpose and Role

Make sure your thesis statement is consistent with the purpose for your research writing project. Your thesis statement should also be consistent with the role (or roles) you've adopted as a research writer. Featured writer Gaele Lopez, for example, wanted to explain the causes of low turnout among younger voters. His thesis statement, "Turnout among voters under age 25 is low because they do not understand why it is important to vote," answered the research question "Why is turnout low among 18-to-24-year-old voters?" His thesis statement was consistent with his purpose (to explain low voter turnout) and his roles (informant and interpreter).

■ Step 3: Adapt Your Thesis Statement to the Needs and Interests of Your Readers

A thesis statement should invite your readers to learn something new, change their attitudes or beliefs about a topic, or take action of some kind. It should do so, however, in a way that respects their concerns and their ability to do what you suggest.

Featured writer Aaron Batty wanted his readers to understand the potential global impact of the "one China" policy. Because his research project was published as a Web site, he expected that his readers would visit the site only if they were interested in relations between China and Taiwan. He did not assume, however, that his readers would know about the "one China" policy or its implications. His thesis statement calls attention both to the existence of the policy and to the global implications of that policy.

> As we venture into the twenty-first century, with its quickly developing world economy and global culture, the final definition of "one China" will shape the course of not only the Asia-Pacific region but the whole world.

In contrast, featured writer Patrick Crossland could assume that his readers—classmates in his composition class—had experienced the college admissions process. He knew, however, that they might not understand fully the factors that affect admissions decisions. Most important, if any of his classmates were thinking of transferring to another school, they might need to be aware of those factors. Patrick wrote a thesis statement that addressed the nature of the admissions process—a process he characterized as a contest.

> What many college applicants like Caleb don't realize is that getting into college is much like entering a contest in which each applicant is pitted against thousands of others.

■ Step 4: Determine the Scope of Your Thesis Statement

A thesis statement should call your readers' attention to a *specific* aspect of the conversation you've joined. A broad thesis statement does not encourage your readers to learn anything new, change their attitudes or beliefs, or take action. The following thesis statement is too broad:

Broad Thesis Statement:

We should protect the health of state wildlife.

There's no conversation to be had about this topic because few people would argue with such a thesis. A more focused thesis statement would define what should be done and who should do it.

Focused Thesis Statement:

The state's Department of Natural Resources should place a moratorium on the release of rainbow trout from state fish hatcheries until they are no longer a danger to the wild brown trout population.

This thesis statement focuses more narrowly on a problem: diseases spread by hatchery-raised rainbow trout that threaten the survival of brown trout.

Your Research Project

DRAFT YOUR THESIS STATEMENT
In your research log, complete the following activity to draft your thesis statement.

1. My research question:
2. My working thesis statement:
3. My purpose for writing:
4. I want my thesis statement to reflect the following needs and interests of my readers:
5. I want my readers to do one or more of the following:
   - learn about . . .
   - change their attitudes or beliefs about . . .
   - take the following action:
6. I want my thesis statement to be consistent with one or more of the following role(s):
   - Informant
   - Interpreter

(continued)

- Advocate
- Inquirer
- Entertainer

7. The most important words and phrases in my research question:

8. The most important words and phrases in my working thesis statement:

9. Building on my research question and working thesis statement, my thesis statement:

10. I can narrow the scope of my thesis statement by rephrasing it:

If you'd like to complete this activity online, use the **Research Log** activity "Draft Your Thesis Statement" at **http://www .bedfordresearcher.com**. If you have created a research log using a notebook or a word processor, you can print or download this activity.

12c

How can I use my outline to draft my project document?

IN THIS BOOK
Read more about creating an outline on p. 190.

Your outline—whether formal or informal—provides a framework you can use to begin drafting your project document. If you created an informal outline, it can be the skeleton of your document, and you can now begin fleshing out sections. Translate a bulleted list of items, for instance, into a series of brief sentences or write paragraphs based on the key points in the outline.

If you created a formal outline, such as a topical outline or a sentence outline, you can use it as the basis for the first draft of your document. As you write, use each main point in the outline as a topic sentence for a paragraph. Use subpoints under each main point to form supporting sentences. Featured writer Gaele Lopez used his topical outline as a guide while he drafted each paragraph.

Partial Topical Outline:

Thesis statement: Turnout among voters under age 25 is low because they do not understand why it is important to vote.

I. Lack of trustworthy political information
   A. Internet: primary source of information
      1. Difference between Internet and other media
      2. Difficulty sustaining attention to issues

Paragraph Based on Shaded Portion of the Outline:

One reason explaining the lackluster voting tendencies of America's youth is that they have not found a trustworthy source of information about the political process. Without such a trustworthy information channel, many find it impossible to build the sense of civic pride and sense of community it takes to be motivated to vote. This is in large part due to the Internet. Whereas baby-boomers over the years have been drawn to television, print, and radio as sources for reliable political information, youths aged 18 to 25 use the Internet as their primary source of information, and are thus subject to its shortcomings. While newspaper and television viewers are exposed regularly to political candidates and issues, Net surfers can easily avoid political issues entirely. Because the Internet is predominantly a "search-specific" device—giving users the ability to control what they view and read—users are less apt to be exposed to news they don't specifically search for.

If your outline contains references to specific notes or sources, make sure that you use those notes in your draft. Take advantage of the time you spent thinking about which sources are most appropriate for a particular section of your document.

As you work on your document, you might find it necessary to reorganize your ideas. Think of your outline as a flexible guide rather than a rigid blueprint.

12d

How can I introduce my project document?

Without exception, readers expect documents to include some sort of introduction. Whether they are reading a home page on a Web site or an opening paragraph in a research report, readers want to learn quickly what a document is about. As you begin to draft, think about how you can help your readers to understand swiftly and easily what your document is about. In addition, ask how your readers might react to different types of introductions.

■ Strategies for Introducing Your Document

You can introduce your document using one of several strategies:

State the Topic.   Tell your readers what your topic is, what conversation you are focusing on, and what your document will tell them about it. Featured writer Jenna Alberter began her introduction with the following direct statement:

IN THIS BOOK

Read featured writer Jenna Alberter's research paper in Appendix A on p. 362.

Artists and their artwork do not exist in a vacuum. The images artists create help shape and in turn are shaped by the society and culture in which they are created. The artists and artworks in the Dutch Baroque period are no exception.

Define Your Argument.   If your research document presents an argument, use your introduction to get right to your main point—the point you are trying to persuade your readers to accept. In other words, you can introduce your project document by leading with a thesis statement, as in the following introduction:

> While the private tragedies of its central characters have public implications, William Shakespeare's *Julius Caesar* is more about personal struggles than political ambition. It is easy to see the play as one whose focus is the political action of public events. The title character, after all, is at the height of political power. However, the interior lives of Julius Caesar, Marcus Brutus, and their wives offer a more engaging storyline. Shakespeare alternates between public and private scenes throughout the play to emphasize the conflict between duties of the Roman citizenry and the feelings and needs of the individual, but it is the "private mind and heart of the individual" (Edwards 105) that the reader is compelled to examine.

 ON THE WEB SITE

Read Gaele Lopez's research paper in Featured Writers on the *Bedford Researcher* Web site at http://www .bedfordresearcher .com.

Define a Problem.   If your research has led you to propose a solution to a problem, you might begin your document by defining the problem. Featured writer Gaele Lopez used this strategy to introduce his research paper:

> Ever since 1972, when 18-year-olds gained the right to vote, voter turnout among America's youth has been on the decline. Only 32 percent of the nation's registered voters under age 24 voted in the 1996 presidential election (Capuano), and among this same age group, who make up some 22 percent of the total voting population, only 38 percent voted in the incredibly tight 2000 elections (Berman). Labeled lazy and apathetic by the popular press, America's youngest voters have refused their right to vote out of political ignorance. Turnout among voters under age 25 is low because they do not understand why it is important to vote.

ON THE WEB SITE

Use the **Research Log** activity Define and Respond to a Problem at http://www .bedfordresearcher .com to define and respond to a problem.

Ask a Question.   Asking a question invites your readers to become participants in the conversation. Featured writer Rianne Uilk encouraged her readers to take an interest in education reform legislation by asking key questions in the first paragraph of her research paper:

> But what if teachers were forced to grade every student based on a set of strict guidelines, making no exceptions at all for special student situa-

tions? What if all schools were themselves graded on student academic performance, regardless of whether they were impoverished inner-city schools or wealthy suburban schools? How would this affect the students and the way in which they are taught? What would it do to student self-esteem and teacher motivation? These are the questions facing Colorado teachers as their districts move to implement the new Senate Bill 186. Despite its few merits, this bill, which became Colorado State law on April 10, 2000, will actually hurt the educational welfare of the very students it is intended to help.

IN THIS BOOK
Read Rianne Uilk's research paper in Appendix A on p. 373.

Tell a Story.   Everyone loves a story, assuming it's told well and has a point. Featured writer Patrick Crossland began his research project with a story about his brother Caleb, a high school student and a star athlete who was applying to colleges and universities:

> Caleb is a junior in high school. Last night his mom attended his varsity wrestling match, cheering him on as he once again defeated his competitors. On the way home, they discussed his busy schedule, in which he balances both schoolwork and a job at his father's company. Caleb manages to get good grades in his classes while at the same time he learns a trade in the woodworking industry. . . .

ON THE WEB SITE
Read featured writer Patrick Crossland's research paper in Featured Writers on the *Bedford Researcher* Web site at **http://www.bedfordresearcher.com**.

Provide a Historical Account.   Historical accounts can help your readers understand the origins of a situation and how the situation has changed over time. Featured writer Aaron Batty introduced his research project with a historical account:

> On February 21, 2000, the People's Republic of China (PRC) shocked the world with its release of the white paper "The One-China Principle and the Taiwan Issue." In this 18-page document, the Chinese government outlined its case that, in keeping with the "One China" principle to which the United States and Taiwan had allegedly agreed, Taiwan is the rightful property of the People's Republic of China, and revealed that it intended to use force if Taiwan did not move to reunite with the mainland.

IN THIS BOOK
See excerpts from featured writer Aaron Batty's informative Web site in Appendix A on p. 370. Read the complete document in Featured Writers on the *Bedford Researcher* Web site.

Lead with a Quotation.   A quotation allows your readers to learn about the issue from someone who knows it well or has been affected by it. Featured writer Maria Sanchez-Traynor used the following quotation to introduce her feature article about the Intensive English Program at Colorado State University:

> Attached to Heather Moffie's copy of the syllabus for her intermediate grammar class is a note reading, "Emphasize that you're here to help them — benefit comes from participation."

ON THE WEB SITE
Read featured writer Maria Sanchez-Traynor's feature article in Featured Writers on the *Bedford Researcher* Web site.

Review the Situation.   A brief review of the situation can draw on other sources or on your own synthesis of information about the issue. A brief review can be combined with other strategies, such as asking a question, defining a problem, or defining your argument.

12e

How can I support my points?

Using sources to support your points is the essence of research writing. Whether you are making your main point or a minor one, readers will expect evidence to back it up. In print documents and in linear electronic documents (such as email messages and word processing files), support is usually provided in the body of the document—the text between the introduction and the conclusion. On a Web site, support can be provided in a variety of locations. Fortunately, readers will not bring hard and fast expectations about *where* support should be located on a Web site. Remember, however, that they *will* expect you to support your points.

Depending on the point you want to make, some types of support might be more effective than others. The key is how your readers will react to the support you provide. In some cases, for example, statistical evidence might lend better support for a point than a quotation. The following are some of the most effective ways to support your points.

IN THIS BOOK

Read more about using quotations on p. 218.

Direct Quotation.   Quotations from experts or authorities can lend weight to your argument. Quotations from people who have been affected by an issue can provide concrete evidence of the impact of the issue. Featured writer Patrick Crossland used a quotation from an admissions expert to support his point about the competitiveness of the college admissions process:

> Duke University Director of Undergraduate Admissions Christoph Guttentag uses a baseball analogy in describing how students advance in the admission process. "Think of it as a baseball game. Everybody gets [his] time at bat. The quality of [students'] academic work that we can measure through test scores and analysis of high school courses gets about 10 percent of the applicants to third base, 50 percent to second base, and about 30 percent to first base. And 10 percent strike out" (qtd. in "College Admissions").

Statistical and Other Numerical Evidence.   Much of the support you'll use in your project document is textual, typically presented in the form of quotations, paraphrases, and summaries. But your topic may lend itself to numerical evidence. Featured writer Gaele Lopez used statistical evidence throughout his research paper:

> Meanwhile, many young Americans don't even register to vote, let alone make it to voting booths. In fact, only 65 percent of voters age 18 to 25 were registered for the 2000 presidential election, according to a Project Vote Smart survey, compared to the 80 percent or so of older citizen voters who are registered, according to the United States Census Bureau.

Example.   It's often better to show with an apt example than to tell with a general description. Examples provide concrete evidence in your document. Featured writer Aaron Batty used an example to illustrate a point in his document:

> This sense of cohesiveness is ancient. To find evidence of that, one need look no further than the name of the country. The two characters that spell the name of the nation we call "China" mean "central kingdom."

Definition.   Definitions explain what something is, how a defined process works, or what you mean by a statement. Featured writer Maria Sanchez-Traynor used a definition to explain a teaching strategy:

> Instead, they use a strategy called "immersion" to teach their classes. The goal is to *immerse,* or surround, the participants with the English language. Immersion means that all classes, no matter their level, are taught solely in English.

Qualification.   You can use qualifications to make your meaning more precise and reduce the possibility that your readers might misunderstand your point. Qualifications allow you to narrow the scope of a statement. In the conclusion of her research paper, featured writer Jenna Alberter used a qualification to clarify the relationship between painting and culture in seventeenth-century Dutch society:

> Because of their faithful depiction of the world and their painstaking attention to detail, seventeenth-century Dutch paintings of domestic scenes can be called realistic. However, it is important to remember that these images do not always simply depict the people and their world exactly as they were. Instead, these works served multiple purposes—to spread and promote ideas about domestic virtue, to instruct viewers about women's roles, and, finally, to entertain viewers (Franits, *Paragons* 9).

Amplification.   Amplification expands the scope of your point. Featured writer Gaele Lopez used amplification to broaden his discussion of the consequences of low turnout among younger voters:

> The consequences of youth not voting are dire. Not only are they left underrepresented, but they may eventually lose their right to vote, as some critics have questioned whether, by not showing up to polls, young Americans are telling the nation the right is not important to them.

Analogy.   One of the most common ways to support a point is to describe similarities between one thing and another. You've encountered analogies throughout this book. Here's another: "Drafting a research document is similar to cooking. Without the proper tools, ingredients, and knowledge, it won't turn out as well as you'd like."

Association.   If you remember the advertising slogan "I want to be like Mike," you're already familiar with association. Through association you can support a point by associating it—connecting it—with something or someone else. When you support your argument using a quotation from an expert, you're using a form of association. It's as if you're saying, "Look, this intelligent person agrees with me."

Contrast.   Contrasts are similar to association, but in reverse. You can use contrasts to show that something is *not* like something else.

📖 **IN THIS BOOK**
Read more about using images and other illustrations on p. 229.

Illustration.   Visual elements can help your readers understand your points more clearly. In print documents, illustrations are usually photos, drawings, or charts. Electronic documents can also include video, audio, and animations. Featured writer Maria Sanchez-Traynor used photographs in her article about the Intensive English Program.

12f

How can I ensure my project document is well organized?

📖 **IN THIS BOOK**
Read more about clustering and mapping on p. 185. Read more about outlining on p. 190.

In addition to supporting your points, readers expect you to organize your document in a sensible way that allows them to read and understand it easily. Fortunately, you've already spent time organizing your ideas. Perhaps you've clustered or mapped them and created an outline. In addition, it's likely that you've continued to refine your organization as you've planned your document.

A well-organized document allows a reader to anticipate — to predict — what will come next, which helps readers understand your goals more easily. The test of good organization is whether your readers can move smoothly through your document without saying, "Where did that come from?" As you draft, check whether your document is organized consistently and predictably. You might find the following techniques useful.

Provide a Map.   The most direct way of signaling the organization of your document is to provide a map in your introduction. You might write something like "This report will cover three approaches to treating cancer of the bladder: chemotherapy, a combination of chemotherapy and radiation, and surgical removal of the organ."

Use a Table of Contents, a Home Page, or a Menu.   Tables of contents, home pages, and menus are similar to maps. If you are writing a print document, ask yourself whether your document is long enough to justify using a table of contents. If you are writing an electronic document such as a Web site, you can lay out the key elements of your document on a home page. Similarly, you can provide a menu on the side, top, or bottom of your pages that readers can see as they work through your site. Featured writer Aaron Batty provided a menu to help readers understand the organization of his Web site and to move to particular pages within it. He placed the menu on every page of his site except his works cited page (see Figure 12.1).

Use Headings and Subheadings. As your readers read through your document, you can help them keep their place by using headings and subheadings. Your formatting should distinguish between headings (major sections) and subheadings (subsections).

Provide Forecasts and Cross-References. Forecasts prepare your readers for a shift in your document, such as the boundary between one section and the next. Forecasts that appear at the end of a major section might take the form of a sentence beginning with "In the next section, you can read about . . ." Cross-references tell your readers that they can find related information in another section of the document or let them know that a particular issue will be addressed in greater detail elsewhere. On a Web site, forecasts and cross-references might take the form of small images, flags or statements such as "Continue to next section" or "Follow this link for more information."

IN THIS BOOK

You can read more about formatting your document in Chapter 15 on p. 246.

IN THIS BOOK

See p. 268 for a discussion of informational flags.

A The navigation menu, similar to a table of contents, on each page of Aaron Batty's Web site helps readers understand the organization of the site.

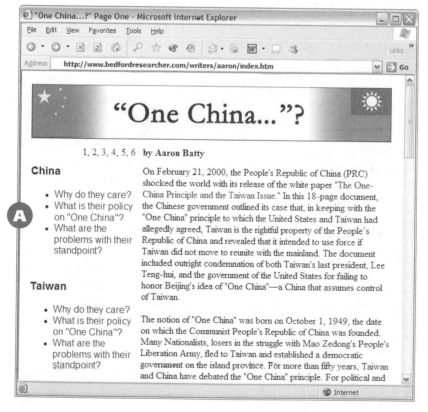

**Figure 12.1
A Navigation Menu on Aaron Batty's Web Site**

12g

How can I make my project document more readable?

IN THIS BOOK
See pp. 238–39 for discussions of editing for accuracy, consistency, and economy.

Even a thoughtful, well-researched project document will be ineffective if it's difficult to read. As you draft your project document, give attention to paragraphing and paragraph structure, transitions between sentences and paragraphs, tone and style, and economy. These issues are discussed briefly in this section and then more fully in Chapter 14, Revising and Editing.

■ Use Effective Paragraphing and Paragraph Structure

Your readers will expect you to break your document into paragraphs, each of which should focus on a single idea. Paragraphs often have a topic sentence in which a writer makes an assertion or observation or asks a question. The rest of the sentences in the paragraph develop—or flesh out—the topic identified in the topic sentence. Your readers will also expect you to present your paragraphs in a coherent and sensible order. As you draft, keep in mind the logic of your argument or discussion.

■ Create Effective Transitions

Good writers provide clear directions to their readers. These directions often take the form of a transition, the point at which one section or paragraph ends and another begins. Effective transitions smooth readers' movement from one idea to another. Some transitions might be sentences, such as "A sudden job loss creates not only a financial burden but a psychological one as well." Others come in the form of headings and subheadings, which explicitly signal a change in topic. Still others are signal words or phrases, such as *however, on the other hand, in addition,* and *first.*

■ Use Appropriate and Consistent Tone and Style

In many cases, readers and writers never meet and have little or no personal knowledge of each other. Your document might be the only point of contact between you and your readers. Your readers, as a result, will judge you and what you have to say not only on *what* you say but *how* you say it. Ensure that your readers will judge you positively by paying attention to the following:

- **Word Choice.** Make sure that your readers understand your words, and use technical language appropriate for your readers.

How will your readers react to slang? Ask yourself whether they will find your words too stiff and formal.

- **Sentence Length and Complexity.** A sentence can be grammatically correct yet incomprehensible. A sentence that is too complex will make your readers work overtime to figure out what it means. Can a complex concept be more simply stated?
- **Variety.** A steady stream of sentences written in exactly the same way will have the same effect as a lecture delivered in a monotone. Best bet: Vary your sentence length and structure.

■ Strive for Economy

An effective document says enough to meet the writer's goals, and no more. As you draft your document, ask yourself whether you've written enough to make your point. Then ask whether you could make your point more economically without compromising your ability to meet your goals.

12h

How should I cite my sources?

Your readers will expect you to cite, or give credit to, your sources. They will also expect you to use a consistent style to do so, such as the Modern Language Association (MLA) documentation system, the American Psychological Association (APA) documentation system, or the documentation system described in the *Chicago Manual of Style* or by the Council of Science Editors (formerly the Council of Biology Editors, from which the style, CBE, derives its name). Documentation systems define everything from whether to use footnotes, endnotes, or parenthetical citations to the format of the entries in your works cited list. You can learn more about the reasons for documenting your sources in Chapter 16. The MLA, APA, *Chicago,* CBE, and Columbia Online Style documentation systems are illustrated in Chapters 17–21.

IN THIS BOOK
Read more about documentation systems on p. 283.

12i

How can I conclude my project document?

Your conclusion provides an opportunity to reinforce your message. It offers one last chance to achieve your purposes as a writer and to share your final thoughts about the issue with your readers.

You've probably read conclusions that simply summarize the document. These summaries can be effective, especially when the document has presented complex ideas and information. A conclusion can do more, however, than simply summarize your points. It can also give your readers an incentive to continue thinking about what they've read, to take action about the issue, or to read more about it.

As you draft, think about what you want to accomplish with your conclusion. You can choose from a range of strategies to draft an effective conclusion.

Sum Up Your Argument.   Summarize the argument you've made in your document. Featured writer Jenna Alberter concluded her analysis of the relationship between society and painting in seventeenth-century Holland by using this technique.

> Because of their faithful depiction of the world and their painstaking attention to detail, seventeenth-century Dutch paintings of domestic scenes can be called realistic. However, it is important to remember that these images do not always simply depict the people and their world exactly as they were. Instead, these works served multiple purposes— to spread and promote ideas about domestic virtue, to instruct viewers about women's roles, and, finally, to entertain viewers (Franits, *Paragons* 9). Just as in the art of every culture in history, the art of the Dutch Baroque period was both a mirror of the world in which it was created and a shaper of that world.

Offer Additional Analysis.   Extend your analysis of the issue by supplying additional insights. Featured writer Aaron Batty's conclusion addressed two key issues he had raised in his Web site about the "one China" policy.

> China's economy does need a boost, but gobbling up a rich neighboring country is not the solution. With luck, we may see China realizing that the only way to really strengthen its economy is to enter the world market and adhere to its guidelines. As far as China's cultural idealism is concerned, it really is time to abandon the age-old philosophy of *zhongguo,* or "central kingdom." This way of thinking is anachronistic, and will only continue to hurt China, a land of rich culture and history that deserves a much more important role in world affairs. But this can never happen until its government takes a more open, pragmatic approach to foreign policy. The PRC is right about one thing, though. There *is* only "one China." Taiwan, however, is not a part of it.

Speculate about the Future.   Reflect on what might happen next. Featured writer Gaele Lopez presented his thoughts on whether turnout would remain low among younger voters and what will be required to increase it.

While a repeal of voting rights for 18- to 21-year-olds may be unlikely, other effects will certainly be felt: younger people's interests will not be properly evaluated, and the "cycle of mutual neglect" will continue. Clearly, the demographic group of 18- to 24-year olds in America has shown less of an interest in participating in the political process than everyone else. This will remain true until younger voters feel they have trustworthy sources of information as well as candidates to choose from whom they feel listen to them. Finally, they must understand the importance of their vote, and why it is not just a right, but a civic duty.

Close with a Quotation.   Select a quotation that does one of the following:

- sums up the points you've made in your document
- points to the future of the issue
- suggests a solution to a problem
- illustrates what you would like to see happen
- makes a further observation about the issue

Featured writer Maria Sanchez-Traynor used a quotation from a former student to underscore her main point about the dedicated teaching available from the Intensive English Program at Colorado State University.

> Former student Munehito Endo says he is still benefiting from the IEP: "Whenever I have a problem they still help me out, even though I'm not in the program anymore." Students enrolled in the Intensive English Program benefit from the energy and methodology of the program's teachers—teachers who are truly "here to help."

Close with a Story.   Tell a story about the issue you've discussed in your document. The story might suggest a potential solution to the problem, offer hope about a desired outcome, or illustrate what might happen if a desired outcome isn't realized. Featured writer Patrick Crossland continued the story he used to introduce his research paper.

> Thus, in the midst of Caleb Crossland's busy schedule, he applies to various colleges he wants to attend. He continues to get good grades, studies for the SAT, and stays involved in extracurricular activities. He researches schools and plans to apply early. And with the support of his family, Caleb should have an edge over the many other students competing against him for a spot at the nation's top colleges.

Link to Your Introduction.   This technique is sometimes called a "bookends" approach since it positions your introduction and conclusion as related ends of your document. The basic idea is to turn your conclusion into an extension of your introduction.

- If your introduction used a quotation, end with a related quotation or respond to the quotation.
- If your introduction used a story, extend that story or retell it with a different ending.
- If your introduction asked a question, answer the question, restate the question, or ask a new question.
- If your introduction defined a problem, provide a solution to the problem, restate the problem, or suggest that readers need to move on to a new problem.

 ON THE WEB SITE

This checklist can be completed online in the **Research Log** on the *Bedford Researcher* Web site at **http://www .bedfordresearcher .com**. It can also be printed or downloaded.

Drafting Checklist

- Include sections that your readers will expect or that your assignment requires.
- Write an effective introduction. Ask yourself:
  - Have I introduced the conversation clearly?
  - Is the strategy I've used (leading with a quotation, defining the problem, and so on) appropriate for my purpose, my role, and my readers?
  - Have I included a clear, strong thesis statement?
- Provide adequate support for your points. Ask yourself:
  - Do my evidence and analysis back up my points sufficiently?
- Make sure your document is well organized. Ask yourself:
  - Is my project document organized clearly?
  - Have I made it possible for my readers to anticipate the organization of my document?
- Use effective paragraphing and paragraph structure. Ask yourself:
  - Have I broken up the document into clear paragraphs?
  - Does each paragraph have a topic sentence?
  - Have I presented my paragraphs in a coherent order?
- Create effective transitions. Ask yourself:
  - Have I provided smooth and effective transitions in my paragraphs?
  - Have I made use of headings and subheadings to signal a change in topic?
- Use an appropriate and consistent tone and style. Ask yourself:
  - Will my readers understand my words?
  - Will they question whether my words are technical enough?
  - Will they react poorly to slang?

- Will they find my words too stiff or formal?
- Are my sentences grammatically correct and comprehensible?
- Have I varied my sentence length and structure?
- Strive for economy. Ask yourself:
  - Have I written enough to make my point?
  - Can I make my point more economically without reducing my ability to meet my goals?
- Document your sources correctly.
- Write an effective conclusion. Ask yourself:
  - Does my conclusion reinforce my message?
  - Does it do more than simply restate my argument?

Drafting your project document is the beginning of the final phase of your work on your research project. The next chapter discusses strategies for integrating information and ideas from your sources into your project document.

CHAPTER 13

Integrating Source Information into Your Document

As you draft your project document, remember the range of strategies you can use to support your points, convey your ideas, and illustrate positions taken by other authors. This chapter discusses the primary techniques research writers use to integrate source information into their documents: quotation, paraphrase, and summary. It also looks at techniques for working with numerical information and information conveyed through images, audio, and video. Keep the following questions in mind as you begin to think about how best to use information from your sources in your project document.

Key Questions

13a

How can I integrate quotations into my project document?

Using quotations, or exact words found in a source, is among the most common techniques used by research writers to integrate information into their own writing. Quotations can serve a variety of purposes and range in form from brief, partial quotations to extended, block quotations. As you integrate quotations into your document, remember to

- blend quotations smoothly
- acknowledge the source of the quotation in a way that clearly differentiates the quotation from your own ideas
- provide a context that shows the relevance of the quotation
- punctuate each quotation properly

■ Understanding the Purposes of Quotations

Quotations can be used to introduce an idea, to support or clarify a point, or to illustrate positions on an issue. A well-chosen quotation can have a powerful impact on your readers' perception of your argument and on the overall quality of your document. Quotations can also provide a sense of immediacy by bringing in the voice of someone who has been affected by an issue or lend a sense of authority to your argument by conveying the words of an expert.

ON THE WEB SITE
View the tutorial How to Integrate Quotations into a Draft at **http://www .bedfordresearcher .com** to learn more about using quotations in your project document.

Using Quotations to Introduce an Idea.   Quotations are frequently used to introduce an idea. In the following example, featured writer Aaron Batty quotes a professor from whom he'd taken a political science course. Aaron uses the quotation to indicate that he has reservations about the point he is about to make. The professor's observation is striking and thought-provoking and, as such, is likely to pique the interest of Aaron's readers in his project document.

> Some Americans feel strongly that the United States does not belong in discussions of Asian politics, for, as one of my political science professors in Japan said, "Most Americans put the center of Asia somewhere between New York and Los Angeles" (Scott, 1999).

Aaron has attributed the source of the quotation using APA style.

Using Quotations to Support a Point.   Writers often use quotations to support the points they make in their project documents. After making a point about themes in the works of two Dutch artists, featured writer Jenna Alberter quotes art scholar Mariët Westermann:

> Westermann describes the work of Vermeer and de Hooch in this way: "Their paintings invite contemplation of domestic virtue, of the quiet and harmonious household prescribed by Cats and others" (124).

Since Jenna names the source of the quotation in a signal phrase, she includes only the page number in the citation, following MLA guidelines (see p. 288).

Using Quotations to Illustrate a Position.   Research writers can use direct quotations to present someone else's position on an issue, as featured writer Rianne Uilk does in her essay on education legislation in Colorado:

A raised number following the quote refers readers to the source information in the writer's Chicago-style endnotes.

Another state legislator, Paul Zimmerman, D-Thornton, condemns the bill, saying, "It digs a hole, it kicks these kids in, and then it allows no escape."[8]

■ Understanding Partial, Complete, and Block Quotations

Quotations can be parts of sentences (partial), whole sentences (complete), or long passages (block). Reasons for choosing one type of quotation over another include

- the length of the passage
- the complexity of the ideas and information in the passage
- the obligation to convey ideas and information fairly

Partial Quotations. *Partial quotations* can be a single word, phrase, or most of a sentence. These types of quotations are often used to convey a well-turned phrase or to complete a sentence using important words from a source, as in the following example.

> However, there are those who, according to William H. Gray III, "contend that preferences based upon race are illegal and unfair" (2).

Complete Quotations. *Complete quotations* are typically one or more complete sentences that are integrated into a paragraph of your project document. Research writers most often use complete quotations when the meaning of the passage cannot be conveyed adequately by a few well-chosen words. The following quotation was drawn from a personal interview.

> "Many students who come in at the intermediate level often have studied English for ten years," Gough says. "However, their grammar is textbook-based and oftentimes leaves few options to speak or hear the language."

IN THIS BOOK

Read more about documentation systems in Chapters 17 (MLA), 18 (APA), 19 (*Chicago*), 20 (CBE), and 21 (Columbia Online Style).

Block Quotations. *Block quotations* are extended quotations, often several sentences, that are set off in a block from the rest of the text. In general, use a block quotation if the quotation runs more than four typed lines. Format the blocked quotation by indenting the entire quotation one inch, or ten spaces, from the left margin. Do not place quotation marks around the quotation. Typically, a colon is used to introduce the quotation. You should include source information following the documentation system you are using in your project document, such as MLA, APA, *Chicago*, CBE, or Columbia Online Style. Featured writer Patrick Crossland used the following block quotation in his MLA-style research essay:

In the article "In the Best Interest of America, Affirmative Action in Higher Education Is a Must," William H. Gray III states:

> At many colleges it is acceptable to use preferences in admissions based on student characteristics such as special talents, geographic origin, and alumni legacy. The most publicized and debated preference, however, is race.

Quotation marks are not necessary for block quotations.

No page numbers provided for an online source.

■ Identifying the Sources of Your Quotations

You should identify the source of a quotation for three reasons. First, it fulfills your obligation to document your sources. Second, it helps you (and your readers) distinguish between your ideas and those of your sources. Third, it can help you strengthen your overall argument by calling attention to the qualifications or experiences of the person you are quoting. Featured writer Jenna Alberter introduced a quotation in her MLA-style essay in a way that clearly indicated who had made the statement and what his qualifications were:

> In *Paragons of Virtue*, art historian Wayne Franits calls attention to this distinction between the ideal and the real, noting "[Both] art and literature present an exemplary image, a topos that does not necessarily reflect the actual situation of young women in seventeenth-century Dutch culture" (25).

Source of the quotation is identified as an authority.

Square brackets indicate an altered quotation.

IN THIS BOOK

Read more about documentation systems in Chapters 17 (MLA), 18 (APA), 19 (*Chicago*), 20 (CBE), and 21 (Columbia Online Style).

Research writers who use MLA or APA documentation format include citations, or acknowledgments of source information, within the text of their document. These citations, in turn, refer readers to a list of works cited or a list of references at the end of the document. Both systems use a combination of signal phrases and parenthetical information to refer to sources. Note the following examples:

MLA Style:

Ann Gill argues, "Education reform is the best solution for fixing our public schools" (22).

"Education reform is the best solution for fixing our public schools" (Gill 22).

MLA-style in-text citations include the author's name and exact page reference.

APA Style:

Ann Gill (2001) has argued, "Education reform is the best solution for fixing our public schools" (p. 22).

"Education reform is the best solution for fixing our public schools" (Gill, 2001, p. 22).

APA-style in-text citations include the author's name, publication date, and exact page reference.

If you are using MLA format, be sure to cite page numbers for paraphrased and summarized information as well as for direct quotations. The following paraphrase of Ann Gill's comments about education reform includes the page number of the original passage in parentheses.

> Ann Gill argues that public schools would benefit significantly from education reform (22).

Providing a Context for Your Quotations.   Skilled research writers know the importance of providing a context for the quotations they include in their documents. It's not enough to simply put text within two quotation marks and move on to the next phase of drafting. Readers can be confused by "orphan quotations"—quotations that are inserted into a paragraph without introduction.

To introduce a quotation effectively, provide sufficient background information about the source of your quotation and use signal phrases or colons to integrate the quotation into your document. Doing so gives your reader a frame for understanding how you are using the source information.

The writer describes the subject of debate.

A signal phrase identifies the speaker as an expert.

Following MLA style, the writer cites the source in parentheses. The writer includes the abbreviation "qtd. in" to indicate that the expert's words are quoted in the source, an article by Kathleen Reid.

> Many refute the idea that computer use is as damaging to children as television viewing. According to child development expert Jennifer Doyon, "Even a preschooler can benefit from simple computer activities, which by their very nature promote interactivity in a way that television shows cannot" (qtd. in Reid 89).

Your decision about how to introduce your quotations will depend in large part on the type of document you are writing and the expectations of your readers. In writing classes, ask your instructor for guidance on how to introduce quotations and whether you will be expected to conform to a specific style, such as MLA or APA.

Varying Your Attributions.   Research writing involves attribution—the act of crediting the source of information or ideas. Become familiar with both the following common forms of attribution and a number of potentially more precise alternatives.

Common Attributions:	Alternative Attributions:	
asked	according to . . .	confirmed
said	affirmed	inquired
stated	alleged	mused
wrote	assumed	observed
	believed	reported
	commented	wondered

Your attributions can convey important shadings of meaning—for example, the difference between saying that someone "alleged" something and someone "confirmed" something.

■ Modifying Quotations

Research writers have an obligation to quote their sources accurately and fairly. You should avoid quoting sources in ways that distort the original meaning of the quotation. The most common sources of problems with modified quotations are failing to indicate that you have deleted words and deleting words in a way that significantly alters the meaning of the original passage.

IN THIS BOOK

For an extended discussion about avoiding plagiarism, see p. 173.

An obligation to quote accurately and fairly, however, does not mean that you can't modify your quotations to fit your draft. Some of the most useful strategies writers can use to modify quotations include

IN THIS BOOK

Read more about modifying quotations on p. 168.

- using ellipses (. . .) to indicate deleted words
- using brackets [ ] to clarify meaning
- adding *emphasis*

Using Ellipses. Ellipses are frequently used to shorten a quotation. A lengthy quotation, for instance, might be shortened using an ellipsis without significantly changing its meaning.

IN THIS BOOK

Read more about using ellipses on pp. 169–70.

Original Text:

Ask Americans how things are *really* going and you'll hear stories of burnout and quiet desperation, of fifty- and sixty-hour weeks with no letup in sight.

Modified Quotation Using Ellipses:

According to critic Joe Robinson, Americans are overworked: "Ask Americans how things are *really* going and you'll hear stories of [. . .] fifty- and sixty-hour weeks with no letup in sight" (467).

The writer shortened the original, taking only as much information as she needed to make her point but without misrepresenting her source.

Note that the Modern Language Association (MLA) recommends placing brackets around an ellipsis [. . .] when you shorten a quotation to indicate that the ellipsis did not appear in the original text. Brackets are not required of writers using other documentation styles, such as APA, *Chicago*, and CBE.

Using Brackets. Brackets can be used to clarify meaning when part of a quotation refers to information not contained in the quotation itself and which would not be available to readers who saw only the quotation. In the following example, featured writer Aaron Batty modified a quotation with brackets so that his readers would know what the "it" of the original passage refers to.

IN THIS BOOK

Read more about using brackets on p. 169.

Original Text:

It meets all prerequisites for statehood.

Brackets Used to Add Information:

"[Taiwan] meets all prerequisites for statehood."

Research writers can also use brackets to change the capitalization or the tense of a word or to blend a quotation more smoothly into their own sentence. In the following examples, the original quotation is changed slightly for a better grammatical fit.

Brackets Used to Change Capitalization:

It is clear that "[it] meets all prerequisites for statehood."

Brackets Used to Change Tense:

"It [has met] all prerequisites for statehood."

■ Punctuating Quotations

The rules for punctuating quotations are as follows:

- Use double quotation marks (" ") around partial or complete quotations. Do not use quotation marks for block quotations.
- Use single quotation marks (' ') to indicate quoted material within a quotation that is punctuated using double quotation marks:

    "We pragmatically identify the current cross-Strait relations as a 'special state-to-state relationship.'"

- In most cases, place punctuation marks such as commas, periods, question marks, and exclamation points *inside* quotation marks:

    Dawn Smith asked an important question: "Do college students understand the importance of voting?"

    "Although I'm nineteen, I don't think I'll vote in the next election," said one college sophomore. "I don't like either candidate."

- Colons and semicolons are placed *outside* quotation marks:

    Many young voters consider themselves "too busy to vote"; they say that voting takes too much time and effort.

- Do not put a sentence-ending punctuation mark inside quotation marks if doing so will alter the meaning of the quotation:

    But what can be gained from following the committee's recommendation that the state should "avoid, without exceptions, any proposed tax hike"?

- When citation information is provided in parentheses following a quotation, place the punctuation mark (comma, period, semicolon, colon, or question mark) after the parentheses.

- Use a four-point ellipsis with no space before the ellipsis and a space following it to indicate an omission at the end of a sentence.

- Use a three-point ellipsis, with a space before and after, to indicate an omission within a sentence.

13b

How can I integrate paraphrases into my project document?

A paraphrase is a restatement, in your own words, of a passage from a source. Unlike summaries, which are shorter than the text being summarized, paraphrases are about as long as the text on which they are based. Like quotations, paraphrases can be used to illustrate or support a point you make in your document. You can also use them to illustrate another author's argument about an issue. Like quotations and summaries, you need to identify the sources of your paraphrases. (Consult the documentation system you are using in your project document for specific requirements.)

Since a paraphrase is a restatement of the information, ideas, or argument in a source, make sure your paraphrase is an accurate and fair representation of the source. Most paraphrasing errors occur when writers misread a source. If you're uncertain about the accuracy and fairness of your paraphrase, reread the source.

Your notes are likely to include a number of paraphrases of information and arguments from your sources. Since you've already taken the time to transform the information into a paraphrase, you may be able to insert the paraphrase directly into your project document. Or you may need to revise the paraphrase so that it fits the context and tone of your document. Also, for a smoother transition from your ideas to the ideas found within your sources, use signal phrases. In the following example, note how featured writer Jenna Alberter lets her reader know where her statement ends and the support for her statement begins:

ON THE WEB SITE

View the tutorial How to Integrate Paraphrases into a Draft at **http://www .bedfordresearcher .com** to learn more about using paraphrases in your project document.

IN THIS BOOK

Read about documentation systems in Chapters 17 (MLA), 18 (APA), 19 (*Chicago*), 20 (CBE), and 21 (Columbia Online Style).

IN THIS BOOK

Read more about and see examples of paraphrasing sources on pp. 168–72.

> During the seventeenth century, the concept of domesticity appears to have been very important in all levels of Dutch society; literally hundreds of surviving paintings reflect this theme. Such paintings depict members of every class and occupation, and according to Wayne Franits, a specialist in seventeenth-century Dutch art, they served the dual purpose of both entertaining and instructing the viewer. They invite the viewer to inspect

The writer's idea.

A signal phrase provides a transition from the writer's idea to ideas gained from source information.

A paraphrase of source material, with a citation in parentheses. MLA requires the page number for paraphrased material, and because Jenna cited two sources by Franits in her paper, she included in her citation a brief version of the source title.

and enjoy their vivid details, but also to contemplate the values and ideals they represented ("Domesticity" 13).

The biggest danger in paraphrasing from notes comes not during drafting but when you create the original note. If you neglect to include quotation marks around a direct quotation, you might assume it is a paraphrase and insert it directly into your project document with no quotation marks. Or, if you misread a passage during note taking and create an inaccurate paraphrase, you run the risk of using that inaccurate paraphrase when you draft your document.

The best approach, of course, is to take careful notes. Clearly indicate in your notes whether you are quoting or paraphrasing and carefully assess the accuracy of your paraphrases. Since even the most conscientious writer can make a mistake, it's wise to review the original source whenever possible as you draft.

IN THIS BOOK

Read about avoiding plagiarism as you take notes on p. 173.

13c

How can I integrate summaries into my project document?

IN THIS BOOK

Read more about summaries on p. 172.

ON THE WEB SITE

View the demonstration How to Integrate Summaries into a Draft at **http://www .bedfordresearcher .com** to learn more about using summaries in your project document.

A summary is a concise statement, written in your own words, of information found in a source. In combination with quotation and paraphrase, summaries allow you to work economically with even the most comprehensive sources.

As you condense the ideas found in source material, check whether the summary you've created is written in an appropriate style and tone or whether it should be revised to better fit your project document. You should also take care to identify properly the source of your summary. Finally, make sure that your summary is an accurate and fair representation of the ideas in the original source.

You can summarize an entire source, ideas and information within a particular source, or a group of sources.

■ Summarizing an Entire Source

Research writers frequently summarize an entire work. In some cases, the summary might be as brief as a single sentence. In other cases, the summary might occupy one or more paragraphs or be integrated into a discussion contained in one or more paragraphs.

Featured writer Aaron Batty's Web site includes a brief summary (highlighted) of the key points found in the white paper "The One-China Principle and the Taiwan Issue":

On February 21, 2000, the People's Republic of China (PRC) shocked the world with its release of the white paper "The One-China Principle and the Taiwan Issue." In this 18-page document, the Chinese government outlined its case that, in keeping with the "One China" principle to which the United States and Taiwan had allegedly agreed, Taiwan is the rightful property of the PRC and revealed that it intended to use force if Taiwan did not move to reunite with the mainland.

Rather than using a "nutshell" approach, featured writer Rianne Uilk spread her summary of Colorado Senate Bill 186 across three paragraphs, interrupting her summary with interpretive comments. The focus of these three paragraphs, as a result, is not simply a summary of the bill, but also Rianne's reflections on its meaning and implications. This extended summary serves as the basis for discussion in a significant portion of her research essay:

Colorado Senate Bill 186 mandates that every public school be assessed, or tested, and given two grades: one based on test scores in reading, writing, and arithmetic, and one based on safety.[1] Schools that receive an academic performance grade of "A" will be awarded more grant money for their schools. They will also be required to vote on whether to become "charter schools" — semi-autonomous schools operated by a group of people (including parents, teachers, and community members) that make their own decisions about what, how, and whom to teach. Meanwhile, schools that receive an academic performance grade of "F" will be without needed funding and will be forced to become charter schools if their grades do not improve within three years, and schools that receive a "D" will be subject to intervention by the state. As many as 30 percent of Colorado public schools will be forced to change in some way after the first year of the bill's implementation.

Senate Bill 186 was the brainchild of Colorado Governor Bill Owens as part of his "Putting Children First" agenda, which includes expanding standardized testing, grading schools based on performance, and initiating a "Read to Achieve" program to improve elementary school literacy.[2] With Senate Bill 186, Owens, who has made education his number one priority, claims he hopes to wake up the state — in particular, school administrators and parents — and call attention to the problems within Colorado's education system. Owens and other supporters of the bill argue that students' grades have shown little improvement, and in fact they have slid in recent years, and that school administrators are to blame. Owens asserts: "I'm not willing to let the present system continue on its inexorable road to mediocrity."[3]

In essence, the bill claims that the many different teaching practices and alternative curriculum initiatives among school districts throughout the state make it increasingly difficult to measure whether there is a "thorough and uniform system of schools" in the state. It also claims that most parents find it difficult to determine whether public schools are providing "quality academic instruction in an environment that is conducive to learning." Thus, the bill requires that the department of education compile "objective indicators" of public schools' academic

Source cited in a Chicago-style note.

The main point of the bill.

Identification of additional key points from the source.

Shift from summary to interpretation in the second paragraph.

Illustrative quotation cited in a note.

Additional information about the bill, interspersed with interpretation throughout the third paragraph of the extended summary.

performance and make these compilations readily available. Such report cards, the bill's drafters claim, will assist parents and taxpayers in making choices that will enable all children to have an opportunity for a quality education. These report cards will also help parents and taxpayers monitor the progress schools are making toward providing students with an opportunity for a quality education in "a safe learning environment."4

■ Summarizing Specific Ideas and Information from a Source

You can also use summaries to convey key information or ideas from a source without summarizing the entire source. In his research essay, featured writer Patrick Crossland summarized a brief section of a book about college admissions. His summary is highlighted in the following passage:

To introduce his summary, Patrick identified the author of the book and its title, as well as the source of the specific ideas he is summarizing.

Bill Paul, author of *Getting In: Inside the College Admissions Process*, a book that tells the stories of several students applying to an elite Ivy League institution, shares three suggestions for students who want to get into a college. Paul bases these suggestions on his discussions with Fred Hargadon, who in 1995 was dean of admissions at Princeton. Hargadon suggested that the best way students can enhance their chances for acceptance into the college of their choice is to read widely, learn to speak a second language, and engage in activities that interest and excite them and that also help them develop their confidence and creativity (238–49).

Following MLA style, Patrick cited exact page numbers.

■ Summarizing a Group of Sources

In addition to summarizing a single source, research writers often summarize groups of sources. It's not unusual, for instance, to encounter phrases such as "Numerous authors have argued . . ." or "The research in this area seems to indicate that . . ." within research documents. Such collective summaries allow you to establish a point briefly and with authority. They are effective particularly at the beginning of a research project document, when you are establishing a foundation for your argument, and can serve as a transitional device when you move from one major section of the document to another.

When you are summarizing a group of sources, separate the citations with a semicolon. MLA guidelines require including author and page information, as in the following example:

Several critics have argued that the Hemingway code hero is not always male (Graulich 217; Sherman 78; Watters 33).

APA guidelines require including author and date information, as in the following example:

The benefits of early detection of breast cancer have been well documented (Page, 1999; Richards, 2000; Vincent, 2002).

13d

How can I integrate numerical information into my project document?

Depending on the issue you are addressing, you might use numerical information, such as statistics, in your document. Sometimes you might present this information within sentences. At other times, you might use tables, charts, or graphs. Although numerical information differs from the textual information found in quotations, paraphrases, and summaries, you still need to ensure that you've accurately and fairly presented the information in your document and that you've clearly identified the source of the information.

> **IN THIS BOOK**
> Read about formatting illustrations, including tables, charts, and graphs, on p. 259.

Featured writer Aaron Batty used numerical information—in the form of dollars and cents—to support his argument about why Mainland China would prefer to incorporate Taiwan:

> China stands to make three primary gains if Taiwan is incorporated into the PRC. The first of these is money. When the Nationalists fled to Taiwan, they took much of the country's wealth with them, and that has affected China's economy ever since. Despite early Sovet backing—which they lost due to ideological differences—and recent capitalistic reforms, China's per capita gross domestic product still hovers around a meager $770, while that of Taiwan is $12,009 (U.S. Department of State [USDOS], 1999a, 1999b). In addition, Taiwan's foreign reserves are ranked at number three in the world (United Nations [UN], 1999). China, of course, would benefit significantly from Taiwan's economic standing.

13e

How can I integrate images, audio, and video information into my project document?

Images, audio, and video can add significantly to the effectiveness of your project document. If you are distributing your research project document in printed form, you can include images. If you are distributing your project document electronically—for instance, as a Web site or a word processing document—you can include an image, audio, or video file in your document. You can also create links between your Web page and another Web page that contains a media element.

Use caution, however, when taking images and audio or video from other sources. Since a photograph is a complete source in and of itself, simply copying the image into your document might be a form of plagiarism. The same is true of audio and video files. Jenna Alberter, for example, used images she found in books and on the Web in her

ON THE WEB SITE

This checklist can be completed online in the **Research Log** on the *Bedford Researcher* Web site at **http://www .bedfordresearcher .com**. It can also be printed or downloaded.

Integrating Source Information Checklist

- Integrate quotations appropriately. Ask yourself:
  - Have I modified quotations correctly?
  - Have I identified the sources of all quotations?
  - Have I punctuated quotations properly?
- Integrate paraphrases appropriately. Ask yourself:
  - Have I accurately paraphrased my sources?
  - Have I identified the source of my paraphrases?
- Integrate summaries appropriately. Ask yourself:
  - Have I accurately summarized my sources?
  - Have I identified the sources I summarize?
- Use numerical information appropriately. Ask yourself:
  - Have I used charts, graphs, and figures when appropriate?
  - Have I identified the sources of numerical information?
- Use images, audio, and video appropriately. Ask yourself:
  - Have I identified the authors of these materials?
  - Have I respected the fair use guidelines for reproducing copyrighted materials? (See p. 177.)

IN THIS BOOK

To see how featured writer Jenna Alberter used images in her research essay, turn to p. 362.

research essay. She carefully documented the sources of those images, and since she was writing an academic paper—rather than a document intended for publication and wide distribution—she did not seek permission to use them. (In contrast, the publisher of this book sought and received permission to publish those images.)

If you are creating an electronic document, it is usually best to make a link between your document and a document that contains an image, sound clip, or video clip—rather than simply copying the image and placing it in your document. If it isn't possible or appropriate to create a link to another document, you should contact the owner of the image, sound clip, or video clip. If you cannot contact the owner, review the fair use guidelines discussed on page 000 for guidance about using the material. Like the other sources you cite in your document, make sure you fairly present the information and identify its author or creator.

Making sure that you have effectively integrated ideas and information from your sources is an essential part of drafting your project document. As you move on to the next phase of your research writing process—revising and editing—continue to think about how you can refine and improve your use of sources in your document.

Organizing and
Outlining

Drafting Your
Document

Integrating
Source
Information into
Your Document

► Revising and
Editing

Designing Your
Document

CHAPTER 14

Revising and Editing

Revising and editing are shorthand terms for processes writers use to evaluate the effectiveness of their drafts and, if necessary, to change them. *Revising* allows you to rethink and re-envision your project document. It provides you with an opportunity to look at such big-picture issues as whether the document you've drafted is appropriate for your research writing situation, whether your argument is sound and well supported, and whether you've organized and presented ideas and information clearly.

Editing, in contrast, focuses on the effectiveness and accuracy of your words and sentences. When you edit, you address issues such as the clear and concise expression of ideas and information, the balance between consistency and variety, and the proper use of punctuation, spelling, and grammar.

This chapter examines revising and editing—as well as how these processes can be supported by your word processor—by asking the following questions:

Key Questions

14a

How should I revise my project document?

Ideally, revision is an orderly process in which you assess your writing situation and how effectively your document responds to it. Experienced writers will tell you that using a systematic approach is the best way to revise. Systematic revision involves following a number of steps

REVISING YOUR PROJECT DOCUMENT	
Step 1	Consider your research writing situation
Step 2	Consider your use of information
Step 3	Consider the structure and organization of your document
Step 4	Consider your integration and documentation of sources
Step 5	Ask for feedback
Step 6	Create a to-do list

to examine your writing situation, your use of information, your organization and structure, and your integration and documentation of sources. By following these steps, you'll ensure that you haven't overlooked something in the revision process.

■ Step 1: Consider Your Research Writing Situation

IN THIS BOOK
Read about elements of your research writing situation on p. 5.

Begin revising by asking yourself whether your document helps you achieve your purposes. If your assignment directed you to inform readers about a particular subject, see whether you've presented appropriate information, whether you've presented enough information, and whether that information is presented clearly. If your purpose is to convince readers in some way, ask whether you have presented your argument clearly and effectively.

Second, think about your readers' needs and interests. It's useful during revision to imagine how your readers will react to your document by asking these questions:

• Will my readers trust what I have to say? How can I establish my credibility?

• Will my readers have other ideas about how to address this issue? How can I convince them that they should believe what I say?

• Will my readers think that my proposed solution to the problem is too expensive? How can I convince them that it's cost-effective?

Finally, identify your requirements, limitations, and opportunities. Ask yourself whether you've met the specific requirements of the assignment, such as length and number of sources. Evaluate how well you've worked around any limitations, such as lack of access to information. Ask whether you've fully taken advantage of your opportunities and whether any new opportunities have come your way. Reflecting on these issues can help you identify useful directions for revision.

Step 2: Consider Your Use of Information

Whether you are making an argument, posing questions about an issue, informing your readers, or entertaining them, think about how you've used source information in your document. First, check the clarity of your thesis statement. Next, review the amount of support you've provided for your points and the appropriateness of that support for your purpose and readers. Finally, if you are arguing about an issue, determine whether you've identified and addressed reasonable opposing viewpoints.

IN THIS BOOK

Read about supporting your argument as you draft your project document on p. 208. Read about integrating information and ideas from your sources into your project document on p. 218.

Step 3: Consider the Structure and Organization of Your Document

Ideally, your readers should be able to locate information and ideas easily. As you read your introduction, ask whether it clearly and concisely conveys your main point and whether it helps your readers anticipate the structure and organization of your document. Consider the appropriateness of your organizing principle for your purpose and readers? If you've used headings and subheadings, evaluate their effectiveness.

Make sure your document is easy to read. Check for effective paragraphing and paragraph structure. If you have a number of small paragraphs, you might think about combining them. If you have a number of long paragraphs, you might need to break them up using transitions. Finally, ask whether your conclusion leaves your readers with something to think about. The most effective conclusions typically provide more than a document summary.

IN THIS BOOK

Read about organizing your project document on p. 184.

IN THIS BOOK

Read about improving the readability of your project document on p. 212.

Step 4: Consider Your Integration and Documentation of Sources

It's important that you integrate your sources effectively into your project document and acknowledge them according to the style guidelines you are following. Ensure that you have documented all of your sources and that you've clearly distinguished between your ideas and those of other writers. Review your works cited or reference list for completeness and accuracy. Remember that improper documentation can reduce your document's effectiveness and your credibility.

IN THIS BOOK

Read about distinguishing between your ideas and those drawn from your sources on p. 221. Read about documentation systems in Chapters 17 (MLA), 18 (APA), 19 (*Chicago*), 20 (CBE), and 21 (Columbia Online Style).

Step 5: Ask for Feedback

After spending long hours on a project, you may find it difficult to identify problems your readers might have with your draft. You might read the same paragraph eight times, failing to notice that *pargraph* is misspelled. Or you might not notice that a document is organized in a way that could confuse your readers. You can ask for feedback on your draft from a friend, relative, colleague, or writing center tutor. It's generally a good idea to ask for help from someone who will be frank as well as supportive. Hearing "it's just fine" from a reviewer will not help you to revise.

When you ask for feedback, be specific about the kinds of comments you're looking for. There's little point getting detailed editing comments when you're still wrestling with the overall organization of your document. Similarly, if you're on deadline and no longer have time for a major revision, let your reviewer know that you're looking primarily for editing comments.

 ON THE WEB SITE

This checklist can be completed online in the **Research Log** on the *Bedford Researcher* Web site at **http://www .bedfordresearcher .com**. It can also be printed or downloaded.

Revision Checklist

- Review your research writing situation. Ask yourself:
  - Does my document help me achieve my purposes?
  - Does my document address my readers' needs and interests?
  - Does my document meet any requirements and effectively work around my limitations?
  - Does my document take advantage of my opportunities?
- Consider your use of information. Ask yourself:
  - Have I provided a clear and appropriate thesis statement?
  - Have I offered adequate support for my points?
  - Have I considered reasonable opposing viewpoints, if appropriate?
- Consider the structure and organization of your document. Ask yourself:
  - Is my introduction clear and concise?
  - Is my document well organized? Can I map or outline it?
  - Can readers follow my organization?
  - Have I made use of an organizing principle?
  - Is my text easy to read?
  - Do I use effective paragraphing and paragraph structure?
  - Are my transitions smooth?
  - Does my conclusion provide more than a summary of my document?
- Consider your use of sources. Ask yourself:
  - Are my sources integrated and acknowledged in my text and in a works cited or reference list?
  - Have I distinguished between my work and that of other writers?

Step 6: Create a To-Do List

Each time you review your document, you're likely to think of ways to improve it. Some of these ideas might have to do with revision, while some might affect other aspects of the document, such as formatting. Because you won't necessarily want to make these changes right away, create a to-do list in your research log. Each time you have an idea, write it on your list.

ON THE WEB SITE

Use the To-Do List tool in the **Research Log** to keep track of your work outline. You can find the Research Log on the *Bedford Researcher* web site at **http://www.bedfordresearcher.com**.

14b

How can I use my word processor when I revise?

By working with your word processor as you revise, you can easily move text within a document or from one document to another using the drag and drop or copy/cut/paste functions. You can view your document in alternative ways—using draft (normal), print, and outline views—and you can split your document using the Split Window tool. In addition, you can

ON THE WEB SITE

You can learn more about using your word processor in the research writing manual Using Your Word Processor on the *Bedford Researcher* Web site at **http://www.bedfordresearcher.com**.

- use the Highlighting tool to keep track of and compare information
- use the Comments tool to note ideas for revision
- save multiple versions of your drafts

Using the Highlighting Tool to Keep Track of and Compare Information

Most word processors provide a Highlighting tool that allows you to color passages of text, as you might do with a highlighting marker on paper (see Figure 14.1). You can use the Highlighting tool to identify

- points made in your document
- support for each point
- different types of support in your document, such as quotations, paraphrases, and summaries
- support drawn from specific sources

Using the Comment Tool to Note Ideas for Revision

Microsoft Word's Comment tool allows you to insert comments in your document and easily keep track of ideas for revision, as featured writer Maria Sanchez-Traynor did (see Figures 14.2 and 14.3).

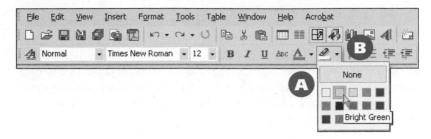

Figure 14.1 The HIGHLIGHT Button on the Microsoft Word Formatting Toolbar

A Click on the HIGHLIGHT button to activate the Highlighting tool and select a color. You can then drag your cursor across the text to highlight it in the color you chose. To deactivate the Highlighting tool, click on the HIGHLIGHT button again.

B To select a different color, click on the arrow next to the HIGHLIGHT button and a color palette will appear. Select a color, the palette automatically closes, and you can drag your cursor across some text to highlight it.

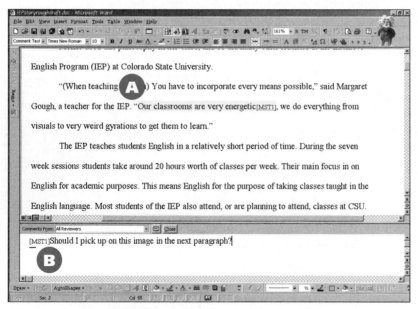

Figure 14.2 Inserting a Comment in Your Document

A In your Word document, select text or place your cursor where you want your comment to appear. From the INSERT menu, select COMMENT.

B A COMMENT box will open. (If you are using Word XP, the box will open in the margin. If you are using an older version of Word, the box will open at the bottom of the page.) Type your comment in this space. If you are using your own copy of Word, the comment will show your name or initials. You can control this setting in the USER INFORMATION tab in the TOOLS→OPTIONS menu (in Windows) or the OPTIONS→PREFERENCES menu (on the Mac).

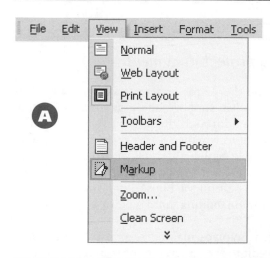

Figure 14.3 Viewing Comments in a Word Document

A If you are using Word XP, you can view comments using the VIEW→ MARKUP command. If you are using an older version of Word, you can view comments using the VIEW→ COMMENTS command. You can also double-click on a comment to open the Comment box.

B You can also float your cursor over a comment to view it.

English Program (IEP) at Colorado State University.

"(When teaching Engli
> **Maria Sanchez-Traynor:**
> Should I pick up on this image in the next paragraph?

ate every means p

Gough, a teacher for the IEP. "Our classrooms are very energetic[MST1], w

visuals to very weird gyrations to get them to learn."

The IEP teaches students English in a relatively short period of ti

---

■ Saving Multiple Versions of Your Drafts

It's possible that you will not be happy with every revision you make. To avoid wishing that you hadn't made extensive revisions to a draft of your document, save a new copy of your draft before every major revising session. You can name your drafts by number, as in Draft1.doc, Draft2.doc, and so on. You can also name drafts by date, as in Draft-April6.doc and Draft-April10.doc. Or come up with a naming system that works for you. What's important is that you save multiple versions of your drafts in case you don't like the changes you've made.

14c

How should I edit my project document?

When you edit, you focus on the words and sentences in your document rather than on its main idea, support, and organization. Editing is best conducted after you've addressed the larger issues involved in revising. If you're uncertain about whether you've organized your document as effectively as possible or whether you've provided enough support for your argument, deal with those issues first. In the same way that you wouldn't start painting a house until you've finished building the walls, hold off on editing until you're confident that you're finished revising.

Thorough editing often involves making several passes through your document. Be sure to edit for accuracy, economy, and consistency; edit to avoid sexist language; edit for tone and style; edit spelling, grammar, and punctuation; and obtain feedback from a reader.

■ Editing for Accuracy

You'll risk damaging your credibility if you provide inaccurate information in your document. To reduce this risk, do the following:

- **Check Your Facts and Figures.** Your readers might think you're deliberately misleading them if you fail to provide accurate information. As you edit, return to your original sources or your notes to check any facts and figures.

- **Check Every Quotation.** Return to your original sources or consult your notes to ensure that you have quoted each source exactly. Make sure that you have noted any changes to a quotation with an ellipsis or brackets, and make sure that those changes haven't altered the original meaning of the passage.

- **Check the Spelling of Every Name.** Don't rely on electronic spelling checkers, which provide the correct spelling for only the most common or prominent names.

■ Editing for Economy

Editing for economy involves reducing the number of words needed to express an idea or convey information to your readers. The following strategies are often helpful:

- **Remove Unnecessary Modifiers.** Unnecessary modifiers are words that provide little or no additional information to a reader, such as *fine, many, somewhat, great, quite, sort of, lots, really,* and *very*.

- **Remove Unnecessary Introductory Phrases such as *there are* and *it is*.** Sentences beginning with *there are* and similar phrases allow you to emphasize a point, as in "There are a number of reasons to use *there are* at the beginning of a sentence." However, you can often recast such sentences more concisely by simply stating the point, as in "You can use *there are* at the beginning of a sentence for several reasons." Keep your eye out for phrases such as *there are, there is, these have, these are, here are, here is, it has been reported that, it has been said that*, and so on.

- **Eliminate Stock Phrases.** Search your document for phrases that you can replace with single words, such as the following:

Stock Phrase	Alternative
at that point in time	then
at the present time	now
at this point in time	now
by means of	by
in order to	to
in the event that	if

Editing for economy generally reduces the effort your readers expend to understand your meaning. However, you should use care when you edit for economy. Reducing the length of a sentence won't necessarily make it easier to understand, and it can reduce the amount of information you provide your readers.

■ Editing for Consistency

Editing your project document for consistency helps you present information in a uniform way. Use the following strategies to edit for consistency:

- **Treat Concepts Consistently.** Check your document for consistent treatment of concepts, information, ideas, definitions, and anecdotes.

- **Use Numbers Consistently.** Check the documentation system you are using for guidelines concerning treatment of numbers. Typically, you'll find that you should spell out the numbers zero through ten and use arabic numerals for numbers larger than ten.

- **Treat Your Sources Consistently.** Avoid referring to some sources using first names and to others using honorifics, such as Dr., Mr., or Ms. Also check that you have cited your sources appropriately for the documentation style you are using, such as MLA or APA. Check each reference for consistent presentation of names, page numbers, and publication dates.

IN THIS BOOK
For information on using documentation systems, see Chapters 17 (MLA), 18 (APA), 19 (*Chicago*), and 20 (CBE).

IN THIS BOOK

Read about designing your document in Chapter 15.

- **Format Your Document Consistently.** Avoid any inconsistencies in your use of fonts, headings and subheadings, and tables and figures.

Editing to Avoid Sexist Language

As you draft your document, avoid using sexist language, language that stereotypes men or women. For instance, although it is technically correct to use male pronouns, such as *he, him,* and *his* when the gender of a noun is unspecified, many readers find the usage unacceptable. The simplest way to avoid using sexist language is to revise your sentences so that generic references, such as *the writer,* are plural: *the writers,* as in the following example:

Sexist Language:

Today's research writer finds at least half of his source information on the Internet.

Nonsexist Language:

Today's research writers find at least half of their source information on the Internet.

Editing for Tone and Style

Your readers will judge you—and what you have to say—not only on *what* you say but on *how* you say it. Apply the following strategies regarding tone and style as you edit your document:

- **Use Appropriate Words.** As you edit, make sure that your language is appropriate for your audience. If you are writing a technical report, your language will be much different than if you are writing a feature article for a magazine.
- **Rewrite Complex Sentences.** A sentence can be grammatically correct yet incomprehensible. A sentence that is too complex will make your readers work overtime to figure out what it means.
- **Vary Your Sentence Length and Structure.** A steady stream of sentences written in exactly the same way will have the same effect as a lecture delivered in a monotone. Best bet: Vary your sentence length and structure.

Editing for Spelling, Grammar, and Punctuation

Editing your spelling is right up there with dressing appropriately for weddings and funerals. It doesn't necessarily affect your ability to get your point across—in most cases your readers will understand even the most atrociously spelled document—but it does affect what your readers think of you. Ignore enough spelling errors in your document and you'll erode their confidence in your ability to present information or make an argument. The same goes for grammar and punctuation. If you haven't made sure your subjects and verbs agree and that sentences all end with the appropriate punctuation, a reader might not trust that you have presented your facts correctly.

Find Someone Else to Read Your Project Document

One of the biggest challenges writers face is reading a draft of their own work as a reader rather than as the writer. Because you know

---

Editing Checklist

- Ensure that your document is accurate. Ask yourself:
  - Are the facts and figures in my document accurate?
  - Are my quotations accurate?
  - Are names spelled correctly?
- Strive for economy. Ask yourself:
  - Have I removed unnecessary modifiers (*very, really, somewhat*)?
  - Have I removed unnecessary introductory phrases (*there are, it is*)?
  - Have I removed or reduced my use of stock phrases (*at the present time, in order to*)?
- Ensure that your document is consistent. Ask yourself:
  - Have I treated concepts consistently?
  - Have I used numbers consistently?
  - Have I treated my sources consistently?
  - Have I formatted my document consistently?
- Remove sexist language from your document.
- Use appropriate tone and style. Ask yourself:
  - Have I used appropriate words?
  - Have I rewritten overly complex sentences?
  - Have I varied my sentence length and structure?
- Check for correct spelling, grammar, style, and punctuation. Ask yourself:
  - Have I used my word processor's built-in spelling, grammar, and style tools?
  - Have I asked a friend, relative, or colleague to proofread my draft?
  - Have I consulted a handbook and a dictionary?

ON THE WEB SITE

This checklist can be completed online in the **Research Log** on the *Bedford Researcher* Web site at **http://www .bedfordresearcher .com**. It can also be printed or downloaded for use in your word processor.

what you're trying to say, you'll find it easy to understand your draft. And because you've read and reread your document so many times, you're likely to overlook errors in spelling, punctuation, and grammar. After you've edited your project document, ask a friend, relative, or classmate to proofread it and to make note of any problems.

14d

How can I use my word processor when I edit?

By working with your word processor as you edit, you can

- check for consistency with the Split Window and Find tools
- find misspellings with the spelling checker tool
- edit for grammar, punctuation, and style using the grammar and style tools

■ Checking for Consistency with the Split Window and Find Tools

ON THE WEB SITE

You can learn more about using your word processor in the research writing manual Using Your Word Processor on the *Bedford Researcher* Web site at **http://www .bedfordresearcher .com.**

Some word processors allow you to split your window so that you can view different parts of your document at the same time (see Figure 14.4). This can be useful when you want to ensure that you are referring to a concept in the same way throughout your document or when you want to check for inconsistent uses of fonts, headings, subheadings, illustrations, and tables.

To use the Split Window view in Word, select SPLIT from the WINDOW menu. Featured writer Jenna Alberter's final draft appears in Figure 14.4, with page 2 in the top window and page 8 in the bottom window.

You can also use the Find tool to locate concepts, names, numbers, and titles in your document and check them for consistency. Once you've identified a word or phrase that you'd like to check or change, you can search for it throughout your document. If you are referring to sources using a parenthetical style, such as MLA or APA, you can also use the Find tool to search for an opening parenthesis. Most word processors use the EDIT→FIND or EDIT→SEARCH menu commands to start the Find tool.

■ Find Misspellings with the Spelling Checker Tool

The spelling checker in most word processors allows you to check your spelling anytime. In addition, these spelling checkers can operate as you type, indicating potential spelling errors by inserting a colored line underneath suspect words.

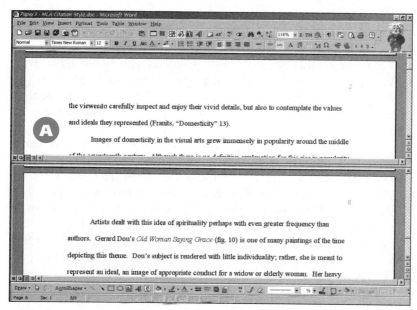

Figure 14.4   Viewing Two Parts of a Document Using the Split Window Tool

A The SPLIT command (in the WINDOW menu) allows you to view two parts of the same document simultaneously. Identify a word or phrase that you want to check for consistency in one part of your document and then locate other occurrences of that word or phrase in other parts of your document. Compare the two windows to ensure consistency.

Although spelling checkers work well to help you locate spelling errors, they have two primary limitations. First, they can't identify words that are spelled correctly but misused—such as *to/two/too, their/they're/there,* and *advice/advise.* Second, spelling checkers are ineffective when they run into a word they don't recognize. If a word isn't in their dictionary, they mark the word as misspelled. This can happen with proper names, technical and scientific terms, and unusual words. To compound this problem, spelling checkers often suggest replacement words. If you take the advice, you'll end up with a paper full of incorrect words.

If you have any doubts about advice from your spelling checker, consult a dictionary.

■ Editing for Grammar, Punctuation, and Style with Grammar and Style Tools

As word processors have grown more complex, they've also become more effective at checking grammar, punctuation, and style. If you are confident about your knowledge of grammar, punctuation, and style, you can use the grammar and style-checking tools in your word processor to identify potential problem areas in your document. You'll find that these tools can point out problems you might have overlooked, such as a subject-verb disagreement that occurred when you revised a sentence. However, if you don't have a strong knowledge of grammar, punctuation, and style, you can easily be misled by inaccurate advice.

Most word processors, such as Microsoft Word and Corel WordPerfect, provide built-in grammar and style checkers. To use these tools, select GRAMMAR from the TOOLS menu. The default setting for Word and WordPerfect is to check grammar and style as you type. When the word processing program detects a potential problem, it places a colored line underneath it. If you find this distracting, you can change the rules that the grammar and style checker uses. If you find that your grammar and style tools are giving you bad advice in a particular area, you can turn that rule off (see Figure 14.5).

Figure 14.5 Fine-Tuning Your Grammar and Style Checker

A In the TOOLS menu in Microsoft Word, select OPTIONS (if you are using a Mac, select PREFERENCES . . . from the TOOLS menu). The OPTIONS or PREFERENCES dialog box will open. Click on the SPELLING & GRAMMAR tab. To change settings, add or clear the check marks to indicate which rules you want to include or ignore.

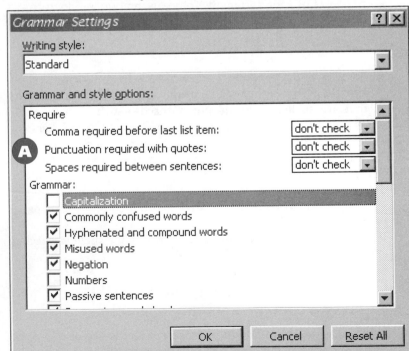

The spelling, grammar, and style checking tools in your word processor are convenient and easy to use. Unfortunately, they're not always as accurate as they could be. You can overcome their limitations, however, by carefully proofreading your document or by asking a friend or colleague to proofread it and by regularly consulting a good handbook and an up-to-date dictionary.

When you've completed the work of planning, drafting, revising, and editing, you are ready to turn to the tasks of designing and publishing your document. Although what you say is the most important factor in the overall success of your document, you shouldn't overlook the importance of its appearance. In Chapter 15, you'll find a discussion of how design and formatting can enhance the effectiveness of your project document and how you can distribute your document once you've completed it.

CHAPTER 15

Designing Your Document

Some writers view document design—the format and layout of a document—as little more than icing on the cake. However, design contributes in important ways to the readability and effectiveness of a document. Writers who ignore document design are missing out on a powerful tool for sharing information and ideas with readers.

This chapter discusses strategies you can use to design your project document. By answering the following questions, you'll learn how these strategies can help you enhance the readability and effectiveness of your document.

Key Questions

15a

How does my research writing situation affect the design of my document?

Regardless of its content, a well-designed document

- is easy to read. Readers do not have to strain to read the text or decode illustrations. The text, images, and other features

work together to make it easy for readers to move through the
document.

- helps readers locate information. In a well-designed document,
  readers can find what they need or what interests them quickly.
- adapts to the limitations of and takes advantages of the opportunities associated with the medium (paper, Web site, word processing document) in which it is published.

Designing a document with these qualities begins with understanding your research writing situation—your purposes, your readers' needs and interests, the context in which your document will be
read, and your requirements, limitations, and opportunities.

Your Purposes.   Like providing adequate support for your points
or using a particular organization for your document, your design
decisions will affect the overall effectiveness of your document. Ask
yourself what primary message you want to get across to your readers
and how you might reinforce that message through document design.
Think about how design elements such as illustrations (tables, charts,
and images) can help you highlight key ideas or more easily convey
complex information.

Your Readers' Needs and Interests.   Thoughtful document design
involves much more than adding visual flash to your document. Ask
how your readers will react to specific design decisions, such as type
size, colors, and the format of tables and charts. Also consider how the
inclusion of images or audio or video materials might affect your readers' understanding of and attitude toward your main idea.

The Context in Which Your Document Will Be Read.   If you are
printing your document, focus your attention on design choices that
are best suited to print. If you are designing a Web site or a document
that will be read on an electronic mailing list or a newsgroup, focus on
the impact of screen size and resolution on readability or consider the
speed of downloading an image.

Your Requirements, Limitations, and Opportunities.   If you are
writing for a class, your instructor might ask you to format your project document in a specific way, prescribing type size, margins, line
spacing, and so on. Even if you are working within a strict set of formatting guidelines, however, remember your limitations and opportunities. If you have access to a high-quality color printer, you'll have
greater flexibility in designing a print document than if you have
access only to a black-and-white printer. If you have expertise in coding Web pages or know someone who does, you might be able to take
on greater challenges as you design your site. Also keep in mind the

software tools you have available—your word processing program, desktop publishing software, and HTML editing software. Your word processing program might be ideal for working with fonts, alignment, and spacing but might offer a weak set of tools for creating and formatting tables or charts. Understanding the opportunities and limitations of your software can help you save time, avoid wasted effort, and reduce frustration. Most important, it can help channel your energies into activities for which your programs are well suited.

Your readers will inevitably compare your document with others. Increase the chance that it will compete well by noting how other documents are designed. Glance through magazines, newspapers, books, and Web sites to get an idea of your formatting and design options. Collect examples of good designs by photocopying or obtaining print sources, by saving online documents, and by adding interesting Web sites to a design folder in your Bookmarks or Favorites list. When you see a well-designed document, note which particular design elements are most effective.

ON THE WEB SITE

For alternative designs, check out the Research Projects Gallery on the *Bedford Researcher* Web site at **http://www.bedfordresearcher.com**.

15b

How can I design my document to improve its readability?

You can make your project document more readable by choosing appropriate fonts and laying out your document effectively.

■ Choose Appropriate Fonts

A font is type of a specific size and face, such as 12-point Times New Roman or 10-point Helvetica. To learn how to choose appropriate fonts, you must understand some font basics.

Typeface. Typeface refers to the name and design of a font, such as Arial, Garamond, or Times New Roman.

Style. Font style refers to regular body text, *italic text*, **bold text**, and ***bold italic text***.

Family. A font family is a set of fonts in different styles. The Arial family, for example, includes *Arial Italic*, **Arial Bold**, ***Arial Bold Italic***, Arial Narrow, **Arial Rounded Bold**, and **Arial Black**.

Effects.   Font effects refer to deviations from standard type, such as underlining or superscripting. Common effects include

Underline	ALL CAPS	Superscript[12]
~~Strike Through~~	SMALL CAPS	Subscript$_{12}$

ON THE WEB SITE
Use the research writing manual *Using Your Word Processor* at **http://www.bedford researcher.com** to learn about formatting fonts in your word processor.

Size.   Font size is measured in *points,* with 72 points to an inch. Typically, body text is 10 or 12 points, while heading type is 14 points or larger.

Fixed-Width and Variable-Width Fonts.   In a fixed-width font, the space given to each letter, number, and symbol has the same width: The letter *l* and the letter *w* take up the same width. Fixed-width fonts are useful when you need to align text in columns, such as in a table of descriptive statistics (populations, percentages). Most fonts, however, are variable-width fonts in which letters, numbers, and symbols take up different amounts of space based on their natural width. Notice the difference between the following fixed-width and variable-width fonts.

Fixed-Width Fonts:

Courier

Letter Gothic

Variable-Width Fonts:

Times New Roman

Arial

Leading.   Leading is the space between lines of text. Historically, the term refers to thin bars of lead that typesetters used to create space between lines of handset type. The following two sentences have different leading:

These are lines of text in 10-point Garamond separated by 12-point leading.

These are lines of text in

10-point Garamond separated

by 18-point leading.

In word processing, you can set leading in the FORMAT → PARAGRAPH dialogue box or by selecting single-, one-and-a-half, or double-line spacing.

Categories of Fonts.   The two main categories of fonts are serif and sans-serif. *Serif fonts,* such as Times New Roman, have small strokes or lines (serifs) at the end of each stroke. Serif fonts are more readable for longer passages of text and thus are often used for body text. *Sans-serif* fonts, such as Arial and Helvetica, have straight ends. Many writers use sans-serif fonts for headings and subheadings. Other font categories are *decorative fonts* and *symbol fonts.* The following are examples of all four categories.

ABCDEF serifs — **Serif fonts:** Times, Times New Roman, Garamond, Century Schoolbook, Bookman Old Style, Goudy Old Style

ABCDEF — **Sans-serif fonts:** Helvetica, Arial, Univers, Verdana, Gill Sans, Tahoma, Zurich Light

ABCDEF — **Decorative fonts:** Algerian, Bernhard Fashion, Brush Script, Monotype Corsiva, Isadora

✡✣•✥✦✥✦ — **Symbol fonts:** Wingdings, Common Bullets, Zapf Dingbats

To increase the readability of your document, keep the following guidelines in mind.

Select Fonts That Are Easy to Read. Word processors default to certain fonts because they are easy to read. Times New Roman, for instance, is much easier to read than Arcadia.

The medium in which your readers will read your document also should play a part in your design decisions. On paper, serif fonts are generally easier to read. Some research suggests, however, that sans-serif fonts may be easier to read on the screen. Verdana, for instance, is a sans-serif font that was developed specifically for reading on a computer monitor.

Finally, remember that variable-width fonts make it easier to read body text while fixed-width fonts make it easier to read columns of numbers.

Select Fonts That Complement Each Other. If you prefer to use a sans-serif font for body text, consider using a serif font for headings. A serif body font may work well with a sans-serif heading font.

ON THE WEB SITE

Read more about Aaron Batty and the other student writers whose work is discussed in this chapter in Featured Writers on the *Bedford Researcher* Web site at **http://www .bedfordresearcher .com.**

Avoid Using Too Many Fonts, Styles, and Effects. Don't go overboard with fonts. As a rule of thumb, use no more than three different fonts in a document. You can use one for your body, another for your headings, and another for figure or table headings. Choosing fonts at random or because they are "interesting" can make your document look chaotic. Similarly, extensive use of *italics*, **bold**, underline, SMALL CAPS, or any of the other styles and effects makes it harder to read a document. Use styles and effects for their intended purpose: to emphasize your points and to signal the function of particular parts of your text, and remember to think about which typographical elements

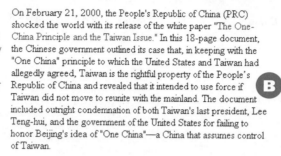

1, 2, 3, 4, 5, 6 **by Aaron Batty**

China

- Why do they care?
- What is their policy on "One China"?
- What are the problems with their standpoint?

A

On February 21, 2000, the People's Republic of China (PRC) shocked the world with its release of the white paper "The One-China Principle and the Taiwan Issue." In this 18-page document, the Chinese government outlined its case that, in keeping with the "One China" principle to which the United States and Taiwan had allegedly agreed, Taiwan is the rightful property of the People's Republic of China and revealed that it intended to use force if Taiwan did not move to reunite with the mainland. The document included outright condemnation of both Taiwan's last president, Lee Teng-hui, and the government of the United States for failing to honor Beijing's idea of "One China"—a China that assumes control of Taiwan.

Figure 15.1 Content from Aaron Batty's Web Site, Showing Appropriate Use of Fonts

A Aaron used a sans-serif font for links in his menu. All are the same size and face.

B Aaron used a serif font for body text.

are most appropriate for both your purpose and audience. Figures 15.1 and 15.2 show featured writer Aaron Batty's font choices for his Web site.

Note. Word processing and desktop publishing programs provide a great deal of control over fonts. If you are planning to distribute your document in electronic format, however, be aware that the fonts you use may not travel with your document. Web pages suffer from the same limitation. If the readers of your Web site do not have the same fonts on their computer as you used in your site, their Web browsers will use substitute fonts. The resulting page, as it appears on their browsers, could have a markedly different appearance than you intended.

ON THE WEB SITE
Use the research writing manual Writing the Web: HTML Coding and Web Design to learn about using fonts effectively on Web pages at http://www .bedfordresearcher .com.

■ Lay Out Your Document Effectively

Spacing, alignment, margins, and columns are important elements of both print and online documents. These elements allow you to control the layout of your document or the display of text and graphics on the page or screen.

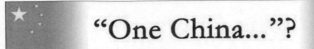

1, 2, 3, 4, 5, 6   **by Aaron Batty**

China

- **Why do they care?**
- *What is their policy on "One China"?*
- What are the problems with their standpoint?

On February 21, 2000, the **People's Republic of China (PRC)** shocked the world with its release of the white paper "The One-China Principle and the Taiwan Issue." In this 18-page document, the Chinese government outlined its case that, in keeping with the *"One China"* principle to which the **United States** and **Taiwan** had allegedly agreed, **Taiwan** is the *rightful property* of the **People's Republic of China** and revealed that it intended to use force if Taiwan did not move to reunite with the mainland. The document included *outright condemnation* of both **Taiwan's** last president, Lee Teng-hui, and the government of the **United States** for failing to honor Beijing's idea of *"One China"*—a China that assumes control of Taiwan.

Figure 15.2   Content from Aaron's Batty's Web Site, Showing Too Many Fonts

A Multiple fonts, styles, and effects create a confused look.

B A combination of serif and sans-serif fonts and italic and bold text creates a distracting passage of text.

Spacing.   In addition to setting the leading, or space between lines of text (p. 249), you can specify the space before and after paragraphs. In most word processors spacing can be set precisely, using points (there are 72 points per vertical inch of text), or relatively, using lines (single spacing, double spacing, triple spacing, and so on). In Web pages, spacing can be controlled using cascading style sheets (p. 259).

Alignment.   Alignment refers to the placement of text and illustrations (such as photos and drawings) on the page. Figure 15.3 shows the four types of alignment: left justified, right justified, centered, and justified.

Margins.   Margins are the space between the edge of the page or screen (top, bottom, right, and left) and the beginning of the text or graphics in your document. In most word processors and desktop publishing programs, you can set the margins using a menu command such as FILE → PAGE SETUP. You can also set margins using the ruler.

You can format parts of your document so that they have larger or smaller right or left margins than the rest of your text. This is useful for setting off long quotations, for calling attention to specific passages of text, and for setting text outside the standard margins (as is often

ON THE WEB SITE
Use the research writing manual *Using Your Word Processor* at **http://www .bedfordresearcher .com** to learn how to control spacing, alignment, and margins.

One of the greatest monsters to slay before an applicant can enter through college doors is that of the standardized testing used by colleges to assess capability. Many colleges use the traditional forms of testing such as the SAT's, ACT's, and other college entrance exams as a standard procedure in evaluating academic capability. In the book *Getting In,* Levine and May state that "a college entrance examination is one of the two most significant factors in getting into college, the other being high school grades" (116).

One of the greatest monsters to slay before an applicant can enter through college doors is that of the standardized testing used by colleges to assess capability. Many colleges use the traditional forms of testing such as the SAT's, ACT's, and other college entrance exams as a standard procedure in evaluating academic capability. In the book *Getting In,* Levine and May state that "a college entrance examination is one of the two most significant factors in getting into college, the other being high school grades" (116).

Figure 15.3
Text
Alignments

One of the greatest monsters to slay before an applicant can enter through college doors is that of the standardized testing used by colleges to assess capability. Many colleges use the traditional forms of testing such as the SAT's, ACT's, and other college entrance exams as a standard procedure in evaluating academic capability. In the book *Getting In,* Levine and May state that "a college entrance examination is one of the two most significant factors in getting into college, the other being high school grades" (116).

One of the greatest monsters to slay before an applicant can enter through college doors is that of the standardized testing used by colleges to assess capability. Many colleges use the traditional forms of testing such as the SAT's, ACT's, and other college entrance exams as a standard procedure in evaluating academic capability. In the book *Getting In,* Levine and May state that "a college entrance examination is one of the two most significant factors in getting into college, the other being high school grades" (116).

A *Left-justified* text is the most appropriate option for most college research documents. When alignment is *left justified,* the lines of text and illustrations are aligned flush to the left margin and ragged, or unaligned, at the right margin.

B Alignment is *right justified* when lines of text and illustrations are aligned flush to the right margin and ragged at the left margin.

C *Centered* alignment has lines of text and illustrations centered on the page.

D When alignment is *justified,* lines of text and illustrations are aligned at both the right and left margins, usually by inserting extra spacing between words.

done for pull quotes—quotations that are pulled out from the text and placed elsewhere on the page—in magazine and newspaper articles).

Columns.   Columns provide additional design opportunities, allowing you greater freedom over where to place illustrations and other elements on a page. You can use columns in most word processors (typically the FORMAT → COLUMNS menu command) and desktop publishing programs to create two or more columns of text on a single page. You can also achieve this effect on a Web page by using a table.

Figures 15.4 and 15.5, which depict the opening page of featured writer Maria Sanchez-Traynor's article about the Intensive English Program at Colorado State University, illustrate decisions about spacing, alignment, margins, and columns.

This document is designed to maximize the amount of text on a page. The page appears crowded, uses very little white space, and is hard to read.

The margins are very small (only .2 inch on each side).

The line spacing is 11 points and the font size is 11 points. The small amount of leading between the lines makes the text difficult to read. There is no extra space before paragraphs.

The alignment of the text is justified. This makes the text difficult to read. In addition, the lines of text are extremely long and therefore hard for the eye to follow.

Figure 15.4
A Crowded Page Design

This document is designed to make it easier for the reader to locate information. It uses a two-column layout to increase the amount of white space on the page. Columns reduce the amount of distance the reader's eye must travel across the page, thus increasing reading speed and efficiency. Note that the photograph is reduced to fit the column width.

The margins of the page are .8 inch on all sides.

The alignment of the columns is left justified, making the text more evenly spaced and easier to read.

The line spacing is a reader-friendly 15 points, and there are 6 points of extra space before paragraphs.

Figure 15.5   An Open, Readable Page Design Using Columns

Typically, writers have greater control over spacing, alignment, margins, and columns in print documents. However, the growing sophistication of Web design tools offers increasing control for Web site writers.

15c

How can I design my document to help readers locate information easily?

You can help your readers locate information in your document by adopting a consistent design, calling attention to information through headings and subheadings, using color, using borders and shading, inserting illustrations, and providing navigation aids, such as tables of contents and indexes.

Adopt a Consistent Design

Adopting a consistent design means treating text and illustrations uniformly throughout your document. For instance, left-justifying body text throughout the document rather than left-justifying some passages of body text and right-justifying other passages helps create a consistent design. Similarly, formatting headings using a sans-serif font and body text using a serif font helps maintain a consistent design.

Use a consistent design to help your readers recognize differences in the function of text, such as headings, body text, block quotations, captions for illustrations, and notes. When readers understand the function of text that is formatted in a particular way, they'll find it easier to locate the information they seek.

Use Headings and Subheadings

Headings and subheadings signal sections and subsections to your readers. By scanning headings and subheadings, readers can easily locate information in your document. Headings and subheadings also serve as transitional devices, signaling a shift from one subject to another. Generally, bigger, bolder fonts are assigned to headings, while smaller fonts are assigned to subheadings. To use headings effectively, follow these guidelines.

Clearly Distinguish Headings from Subheadings. To help your readers follow your document's organization, format headings and subheadings clearly and consistently. The following example shows the difference between effective and ineffective formatting:

Effective Formatting	Ineffective Formatting
The Problem	The Problem
Causes of the Problem	Causes of the Problem
Lack of Funding	*Lack of Funding*
Lack of Trained Staff	*Lack of Trained Staff*
Effects of the Problem	Effects of the Problem
On Staff	*On Staff*
On Students	**On Students**

Phrase Your Headings Consistently.   Headings and subheadings work together best when they use similar grammatical constructions. The following example shows the difference between effective and ineffective phrasing.

Effective Phrasing	Ineffective Phrasing
The Problem	The Problem
Causes of the Problem	Causes of the Problem
Lack of Funding	Lack of Funding
Lack of Trained Staff	Trained Staff Have Not Been Available
Effects of the Problem	The Problem Has Had Two Effects
On Staff	Effects on Staff
On Students	Students Have Also Been Affected

ON THE WEB SITE
Use the research writing manual *Using Your Word Processor* at **http://www.bedford researcher.com** to learn about defining and using styles.

Use Styles.   One of the best ways to ensure consistent formatting of headings and subheadings is to use the Style tool in your word processor or desktop publishing program. The Style tool (available through the FORMAT → STYLE menu command in Microsoft Word) allows you to assign specific formatting commands to a style, such as Heading 1, Heading 2, Heading 3. You can define a style using font size, typeface, style, and effect as well as spacing, indentation, and color. In Web documents, you can define styles by using cascading style sheets (p. 259).

■ Use Color

Using color in your document has several advantages over using only black, white, and shades of gray.

- Color can call attention to specific parts of your document, such as headings and subheadings, charts, tables, and pull quotes.
- Color can signal your overall organizational scheme if you color-code headings, subheadings, borders, and backgrounds.

- Color can signal the function of particular types of text in your document, such as long quotations, examples, and captions.
- Color can increase the overall attractiveness of your document.

Figure 15.6 shows how color increases the attractiveness of and calls attention to specific parts of the first page of Maria Sanchez-Traynor's feature article.

Some Cautions about Using Color. As you work with color, use the following guidelines.

- Avoid using more than four colors on a page, unless you are using a color photo.
- Use color consistently. Use the same color for top-level headings throughout your document, another color for lower-level headings, and so on.
- Make sure you have sufficient contrast between your colors. For instance, avoid using light colors on white or light-colored

Figure 15.6 Using Color to Call Attention to Important Information on a Page

A The color headline and byline stand out in the example on the right, while they fade into the background in the example on the left.

B The effect of the "drop cap"—the large capitalized first letter in the first paragraph—is enhanced with color.

C Although the photo is black and white, the color caption stands out from the black body text.

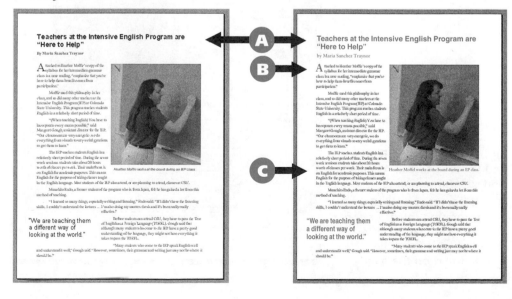

backgrounds and avoid using red or blue on dark-colored backgrounds.

- Restrain yourself. Use your colors for effect, not just because you know color-formatting commands.
- Seek advice from your instructor when designing a document for an academic assignment.

■ Use Borders and Shading

ON THE WEB SITE

Use the research writing manual Using Your Word Processor at **http:// www.bedford researcher.com** to learn how to create tables and to format borders and shading.

Borders and shading can help readers locate key information and identify the functions of different kinds of text. You can use borders and shading, for instance, to set off sidebars—brief discussions of information related to but not a central part of your document (see Figure 15.7).

Borders and shading function like color in a document, and the cautions about using them are the same: Avoid overusing borders and shading and make sure that you've provided sufficient contrast between your text and background shading.

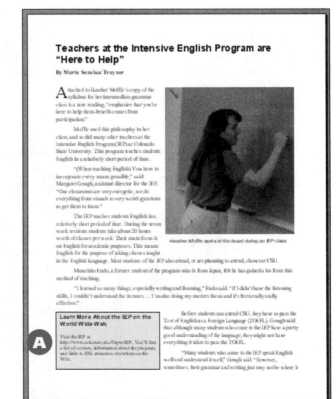

Figure 15.7 Using Borders and Shading to Call Attention to Information

A A border and a shaded background call attention to this sidebar by differentiating it from the other text on the page.

Using Borders and Shading on the Web.   Most word processing and desktop publishing programs provide abundant tools for formatting borders and shading. Web development tools lag behind in this area, largely because of the limitations of the HTML coding language. However, you can achieve effects similar to those provided by word processors and desktop publishing programs by using tables or cascading style sheets (CSS).

**ON THE
WEB SITE**
Use the research
writing manual
*Writing the Web:
HTML Coding and
Web Design* at
**http://www
.bedfordresearcher
.com** to learn
about formatting
Web pages.

■ Use Illustrations

Illustrations—photos, drawings, charts, graphs, tables, animations, audio clips, and video clips—can expand on or demonstrate points made in the text of your document. Illustrations are often further categorized as figures (which include photos, drawings, charts, and graphs) or tables. You can use illustrations for the following purposes.

Demonstrate or Emphasize Points Made in Your Document.   Illustrations allow you to explain your points more fully than you can do with text alone. Although readers seldom appreciate the repetition of key points in the text of your document, they welcome well-designed and helpful illustrations that complement your text. For example, if you were writing about different kinds of wildflowers, the illustration shown in Figure 15.8 would complement a description of the flower.

Reduce the Amount of Text Needed to Make Your Point.   Illustrations help you make your point succinctly. In many cases, a well-designed chart can take the place of several paragraphs of explanatory text. A pie chart, for instance, might illustrate the results of a survey, as is shown in Figure 15.9.

Help Your Readers Better Understand Your Points.   Showing something is usually more effective than describing it. You can enhance your readers' understanding by using illustrations. Featured writer

Figure 15.8   A Hand-Painted Illustration of the Wildflower Bitterroot to Complement Text Describing the Flower

Figure 15.9 A Pie Chart That Makes a Point More Succinctly than Words

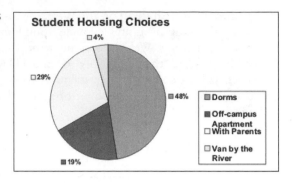

Jenna Alberter used photographs of the paintings she discussed in her research paper to illustrate her points (see p. 362).

Increase the Appeal of Your Document. Page after page of unbroken text is far less appealing than pages containing a mix of text and illustrations. In addition to attracting your reader's eye to key information, well-placed and well-designed illustrations can break up the monotony of a text document.

ON THE WEB SITE

Use the research writing manuals Writing the Web: HTML Coding and Web Design and Using Your Word Processor at **http://www .bedfordresearcher .com** to learn how to work with illustrations in your print and electronic documents.

Formatting Illustrations According to Style Guides. The major style guides discussed in this book—MLA, APA, *Chicago*, and CBE—provide formatting guidelines for illustrations. These style guides agree on several key points.

- Place an illustration as close as possible to the part of the text to which it relates.
- Distinguish between tables and figures.
- Number tables and figures in the order in which they appear in the document.
- Use compound numbering of figures and tables in longer documents. For example, the second table in Chapter 5 would be labeled Table 5.2.

The style guides differ on the placement of labels, captions, notes, and source material in tables and figures (see Table 15.1). Remember that although these guidelines vary, they share the goal of using illustrations consistently and presenting them effectively.

As word processing, desktop publishing, and Web editing software grows more sophisticated, it continues to be easier to insert and work with illustrations in print and electronic documents. Remember, however, that illustrations are best used when they serve a clear function in your document. Avoid including illustrations simply because you think it might make your document look better.

TABLE 15.1	SELECTED MLA, APA, *CHICAGO*, AND CBE INSTRUCTIONS FOR ILLUSTRATIONS			
ELEMENT	MLA	APA	*CHICAGO*	CBE
Table Labels	Type label flush left above the table. Capitalize the first word, all important words, and proper nouns.	Type label flush left above the table. Format the label as you would a title. Capitalize the first word and proper nouns.	Type label flush left above the table. Capitalize the first word and all important words *or* use a sentence.	Type label flush left above the table. Format the label as you would a title. Capitalize the first word and proper nouns.
Table Notes and Source Information	Place source information and notes below the table, in that order.	Place notes and source information below the table, in that order.	Place source information and notes below the table, in that order.	Place source information and notes below the table, in that order.
Figure Labels	Type figure number and caption below the figure. Capitalize the first word and all proper nouns.	Type figure number and caption below the figure. Capitalize the first word and all proper nouns.	*Caption* refers to titles and *legend* refers to explanatory text. Place both below the figure. Capitalize the first word and all proper nouns.	Type figure number and caption below the figure. Capitalize the first word and all proper nouns.
Figure Notes and Source Information	Place notes and source information in the caption.	Place notes and source information in the caption.	Source information follows the caption and, if present, the legend.	Place source information in parentheses at the end of the caption.

■ Provide Navigation Support

If your document is long and complex, your readers may find it difficult to locate information. In longer print documents and linear documents distributed online (such as word processing files and files saved in Portable Document Format), use navigation devices such as tables of contents and indexes to help your readers locate information. On Web sites, provide pulldown menus, navigation menus (such as button bars), navigation headers and footers, and site maps (see Figure 15.10). Depending on the complexity of your Web site, you can also provide tables of contents, indexes, and search tools to help your readers.

A Navigation header
B Site map
C Navigation menu (table of contents)
D Site search
E Navigation footer

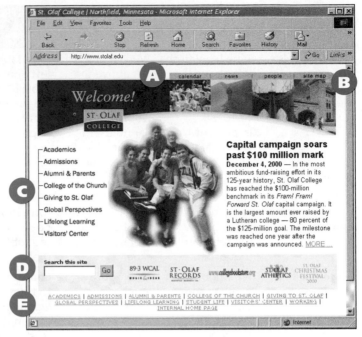

Figure 15.10 A Web Site with Multiple Navigation Tools

15d

How should I design a research essay?

When designing a research essay, consider the needs of your readers. Most often, you'll think of your instructor as your reader. Occasionally, you'll also address your project document to your classmates or to the other writers and readers involved in the conversation you've decided to join. As featured writer Patrick Crossland designed his research essay, he noted the expectations of his instructor and the four classmates who worked with him in a collaborative group. He followed his instructor's directions about line spacing, margins, documentation system (MLA), page numbers, and title page. He also recognized his readers' needs by using headings to help them locate information. Figures 5.11 through 5.14 show sample pages of Patrick's essay.

Who's Getting into College?

A

Patrick Crossland

B

COCC192: College Writing
Professor Doerr
5 December 2000

C

IN THIS BOOK

For another sample essay formatted in MLA style, turn to p. 362.

ON THE WEB SITE

To read Patrick Crossland's complete essay, visit the Featured Writers area of the *Bedford Researcher* Web site at **http://www .bedfordresearcher .com**.

Figure 15.11   Title Page of Patrick Crossland's Research Essay
A Title of document in large type and boldface font
B Author's name
C Course, instructor, and date

Crossland 2

Who's Getting Into College?

 Caleb is a junior in high school. Last night his mom attended his varsity wrestling match, cheering him on as he once again defeated his competitors. On the way home, they discussed his busy schedule, in which he balances both schoolwork and a job at his father's company. Caleb manages to get good grades in his classes while at the same time he learns a trade in the woodworking industry. Both of his parents are proud of him and support him as he accomplishes the various feats of yet another busy day.

As his senior year of high school approaches, Caleb is bombarded with information and applications from various colleges he is interested in attending. However, the more he studies the applications and their requirements, the more he is confused. He knows he wants to go to college, he's just not sure how to best position himself to get into his top choices. As he stares at the many essay questions, he wonders what exactly the colleges are looking for and who is getting in.

What many college applicants like Caleb don't realize is that getting into college is much like entering a contest in which each applicant is pitted against thousands of others. The objective of the college contest is to beat out the other competitors by getting good grades and scoring high on standardized tests, participating in academic or extracurricular activities, and having a particular economic background and race.

Grades and Standardized Test Scores

If you ask high-school students what they worry most about in terms of getting into the college of their choice, most will answer their grades and standardized test scores. Indeed, experts agree that a student's intellect is an important admissions decision factor, as colleges

Figure 15.12 First Page of Patrick Crossland's Research Essay

A The writer's last name and the page number appear in the upper right-hand corner of every page.

B The title is repeated on the first page of the text. Patrick used a larger sans-serif font for his title and a serif font for the body text.

C One-inch left and right margins and double-spaced lines provide space for the teacher to write comments on the paper.

D Patrick used a sans-serif font larger than the body text to distinguish section headings from the body text.

Crossland 3

tend to admit the students they feel have the greatest potential for academic success. Mary Lee Hoganson, College Consultant for Homewood-Flossmoor High School in Flossmoor, Illinois, says that many colleges won't make a decision about a student's admittance until they have received their first semester senior grades, and many schools' offers of admission are contingent upon a student's continued high performance over the course of their senior year. According to Hoganson:

> [Colleges] expect to see a performance that indicates you
> are ready for college-level work. [. . .] Admissions letters
> often contain [contingency clauses requiring] continued
> successful performance. It is not at all rare for a college
> to withdraw an offer of admission when grades drop sig-
> nificantly over the course of the senior year. (qtd. in
> "Experts")

And it's not just grades that matter—admissions staff also look at the kind of courses students are taking. Nadine K. Maxwell, Coordinator of Guidance Services for Fairfax County Public Schools in Fairfax, Virginia, says that college admissions staff are looking to see whether a student's high school academic profile "indicates that [he or she has] the potential for academic success on their campus" ("Experts"). Maxwell says admission staff take into consideration whether the student has taken rigorous courses such as AP or honors courses. In addition, some admissions offices will consider the student's class rank and the quality of their high school as they decide whether to admit someone or not.

Of course, one of the greatest monsters applicants must slay before they can enter college is to take an entrance exam or standardized test, such as the SAT and ACT. These tests are used by many colleges to assess student aptitude and academic capability. According

Figure 15.13   The Second Page of Patrick Crossland's Research Essay
A Patrick set off block quotations by indenting one inch from the left margin. Quotation marks are not used for long quotations.

Crossland 7

Ⓐ Works Cited

Ⓑ "Experts Answer Your Application Questions: Get the Inside Scoop on Applying to College." Collegeboard.com. 2000. 10 Nov. 2000 <http://www.collegeboard.com/article/0,1120,5-26-0-8487,00.html?orig=sec>.

Gray, William III. "In the Best Interest of America, Affirmative Action in Higher Education Is a Must." The Black Collegian (1 Feb. 1999): 144–146. The Electric Library, Morgan Library, Colorado State University, Fort Collins, CO. 24 Oct. 2000. <http://www .elibrary.com/education>.

"How College Admission Works: SAT Scores." 2000. 14 Nov. 2000. <http://www.howstuffworks.com/college-admission4.htm>.

"Interview with Derek Bok." Secrets of the SAT. 1999. PBS Online. 12 Nov. 2000. <www.pbs.org/wgbh/pages/frontline/shows/sats/ interviews/bok.html>.

Krauthammer, Charles. "Lies, Damn Lies, and Racial Statistics: Figures from all the University of California Campuses Paint Another Picture." Time 151.15 (April 20, 1998). October 20, 2000: 86–88.

Levine, Joel, and Lawrence May. Getting In. New York: Random, 1972.

Lillard, Dean, and Jennifer Gerner. "Getting into the Ivy League: How Family Composition Affects College Choice." Journal of Higher Education (November/December 1999): 709–710.

Paul, Bill. Getting In: Inside the College Admissions Process. Reading, MA: Addison-Wesley, 1995.

Figure 15.14 Works Cited Page of Patrick Crossland's Research Essay

A "Works Cited" heading is centered and appears in a boldface sans-serif font larger than the body text.

B Double spacing is used throughout. The first line of each entry is at the left margin, and additional lines are indented one-half inch.

15e

How should I design a Web site?

Designing an effective Web site involves six steps: considering available design options, planning your site, coding your pages, putting your site online, testing your site, and announcing your site.

■ Step 1: Consider Design Elements Unique to Web Sites and Other Electronic Documents

Most of the design features discussed so far in this chapter—fonts, line spacing, text alignment, margins, columns, color, borders, shading, and illustrations—apply to print and electronic documents. Web sites and some types of electronic documents, however, can take advantage of additional design features, including frames, pop-up windows, informational flags, links, and audio, video, and animations.

Frames.   *Frames* divide the document into independent parts on-screen (see Figure 15.15). A table of contents might be displayed in one frame, a page containing text in another, and a navigation menu in yet another.

Most Web site designers who use frames use two frames: one for a menu or a set of navigation tools and a second for displaying pages that contain content. Research suggests that a two-frame design that keeps a navigation menu in front of readers is more effective than a design with no frames.

Although frames can aid your readers' ability to navigate your Web site, they also pose problems for users. It can be difficult to add a framed Web page to a Bookmarks or Favorites list. It can also be difficult to search sites that use frames. In addition, printing pages displayed in frames can be difficult.

ON THE WEB SITE

For a more detailed discussion of designing and coding a Web site, view the research writing manual *Writing the Web: HTML Coding and Web Design* on the *Bedford Researcher* Web site at **http://www .bedfordresearcher .com**.

IN THIS BOOK

Read more about Bookmarks and Favorites lists on p. 70.

DESIGNING A WEB SITE	
Step 1	Consider design elements unique to Web sites and other electronic documents
Step 2	Plan your site
Step 3	Code your pages
Step 4	Put your site online
Step 5	Test your site
Step 6	Announce your site

**Figure 15.15
A Web Page
Using a Four-
Frame Design
to Separate
Content from
Navigation
Aids**

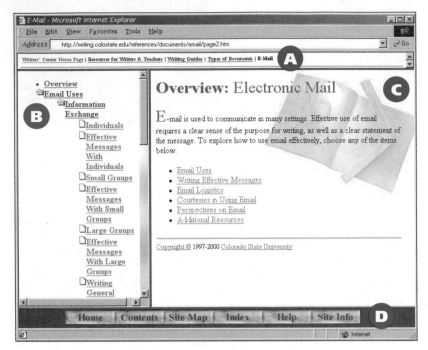

A Navigation header frame
B Navigation menu (table of contents) frame
C Main frame
D Navigation footer frame

Pop-Up Windows.   Sometimes called floating windows, pop-up windows appear on top of the current page you are viewing when you click on a link (see Figure 15.16). Pop-up windows often function in the same way that endnotes do in a print document. Instead of having to turn pages to view a note, however, you simply click on a link to open the window. Pop-up windows offer an important advantage over links that replace the current page with a new page: The page you are reading doesn't go away. This increases the likelihood that readers will return to the current page after opening the pop-up window.

Informational Flags.   In many cases, you don't need to click on a link to learn something. Simply moving your mouse over some links and images can cause an informational flag to pop up (see Figure 15.17). This gives readers a preview of what they might find if they clicked on the link.

Links.   The ability to link documents is the defining feature of the Web. Links allow readers to move directly from one document to another with the click of a mouse. The ability to create links means

Figure 15.16
A Pop-Up
Window

Interaction Among Classmates and Between Students and Teachers

One of the biggest differences between the two classroom settings was interaction during class. Our observations of the classrooms, along with student and teacher reports of their interactions, indicate that students in the [...]
classmates and [...]
Our observati[...]
the interaction [...]
on writing, rat[...]
interactions an[...]

Teacher Comment - Microsoft Internet Ex... _ □ ✕

"I think it's different just because you get to walk around while they're drafting, and you can interact with them very much during the drafting phase. . . I try to do that in the traditional classroom when they're in workshop, but I think it's harder because they do less up-front drafting and revising in the classroom." - Jen

Close This Comment

In comparing t[...]
classroom sett[...]

In-Class Contact with Teachers

A Button clicked to open pop-up window.
B Pop-up window.

that you are not limited to a sequential ordering of text. You can create complex documents in which the "next page" differs according to a reader's needs and interests. As you design a document that uses links, keep in mind the need to anticipate the options your readers are

A An informational flag (white text box) appears when the cursor is moved over "Resources for Writers & Teachers."

Figure 15.17
An Informa-
tional Flag
That Appears
When the
Cursor Moves
over an
Image

The Writers' Center
at Colorado State University

◊ Resources for Writers & Teachers
◊ Cou[...]
◊ Questions[...]
◊ Send Your Draft to a Consultant
◊ Campus Location, Hours & Services

View Online Resources for Writers and Teachers, including Interactive Tutorials, Demonstrations, Reference Guides, and Links to Other Web Resources

Member, Online Writing Center Consortium

Site Information. Copyright © 1997, 1998, 1999 Colorado State University. Last modified 9-99. Note: This site uses frames and scripts and is best viewed at 800x600 resolution in 256 colors using Netscape Navigator 3.x or MS Internet Explorer 3.x or higher. / Text Only.

most likely to choose. If you want them to follow a particular path through your document—a specific sequence of pages—consider how you can use links to define that path.

Audio Files, Video Files, and Animations.   In an online publication you can include a wider range of illustrations than in a print document, including audio files, video files, and animations. Your use of these illustrations, however, can be complicated by factors such as the speed with which your readers will access your document, the capabilities of your readers' computers, and the possibility that these elements might distract your readers from the information you want them to view.

■ Step 2: Plan Your Site

The major steps in planning your Web site include creating content, selecting an organizational structure for your site, assigning content to your pages, and selecting navigational tools to help your readers locate information on your site.

Create Content.   Every chapter preceding this one has focused on how you can develop and refine content for your project document. It is worth repeating that even the most attractive Web site will fail without good content—content that has a clear purpose and addresses readers' needs and interests.

Select an Organizational Structure for Your Web Site.   Web sites typically use one or a combination of three organizational structures: linear, hierarchical, and interlinked. Each organizational pattern offers advantages for writers depending on their specific purposes and their readers' needs and interests.

Linear Organization.   A linear, or sequential, organizational pattern is similar to that found in a book or a long essay. Readers' choices are limited: they can go either forward or backward (see Figure 15.18). A scientific report presented on the Web, for instance, might use a linear organization in which the title page is linked to the abstract, the abstract is linked to the introduction, the introduction is linked to the methods section, and so on. Linear Web sites are also well suited to step-by-step instructions, in which each page builds on the one before it.

**Figure 15.18
A Web Site
Using a
Linear Orga-
nization**

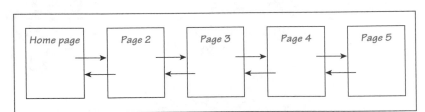

Hierarchical Organization. In a hierarchical structure, pages are linked to each other according to their level in a hierarchy. This organizational pattern is frequently used for sites that provide information, such as instructional sites, government sites, and commercial sites. Like a linear structure, however, a strict hierarchy offers limited navigational choices to readers: They can move up to a higher level or down to pages lower in the hierarchy (see Figure 15.19). They cannot, however, move across the site to other pages at the same level in the hierarchy. Few sites follow a strict hierarchical structure. Instead, they modify it through navigation tools such as menus, tables of contents, and *cross links*—links that move across levels or to other parts of the hierarchy.

IN THIS BOOK

Read more about selecting navigational tools for your Web site on pp. 272–73.

Interlinked Organizations. In an interlinked site, it is possible to reach every other page in the Web site from a given page (see Figure 15.20). This organizational structure is sometimes used in smaller sites or in sites that provide a navigational menu on each page. This organizational structure becomes difficult to support when the site grows to more than a handful of pages. In a site composed of nine pages, for instance, each page would have eight links on it. In a site composed of one hundred pages, each page would need ninety-nine links. Sites that use a predominantly interlinked organizational structure often modify it by reducing the number of links.

Combined Organizational Structure. Larger sites frequently use a mix of the three organizational structures. A site that is organized in a more or less hierarchical structure, for instance, might incorporate linear and interlinked structures in some parts of the site.

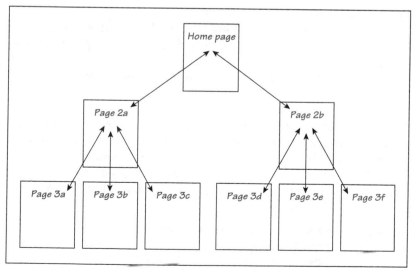

Figure 15.19 A Web Site Organized in a Hierarchical Structure

**Figure 15.20
A Web Site
Organized in
an Interlinked
Structure**

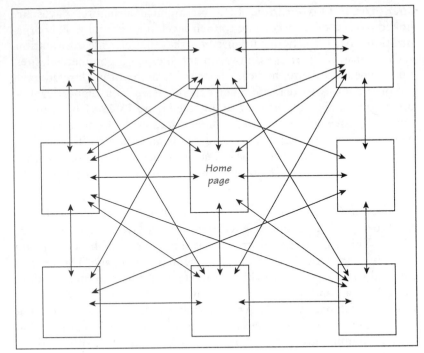

Assign Content to the Pages on Your Site. Once you've chosen an organizational structure, decide what you'll put on each page. Most Web sites have a home page, which serves as the main entrance to the site. Depending on the size and complexity of your site, you might also create main pages for categories of information on your site. Once you've selected these pages, you can determine where the remaining information on your site should be placed.

Experienced Web site designers debate whether it is best to select an organizational pattern before deciding where to place content. Most likely, you will move back and forth between these steps until you've arrived at an appropriate organization and division of content on your site.

Select Your Navigation Tools. Your choice of navigational tools will depend on the size and complexity of your site, your organizational structure, and your knowledge of your readers' familiarity with the Web. At a minimum, you should provide links to and from related pages. However, there are advantages to providing additional support, such as the following.

Persistent Menus. These are buttons or links that appear in the same place on all pages. Thus readers will know where to find them no matter what part of your site they visit (see Figure 15.21).

Figure 15.21
Examples of a
Navigation
Header and a
Persistent
Menu

A This navigation header allows readers to return to a previous page and to see the path they've taken to arrive at a page.

B This persistent navigation menu appears on every page in the Web site.

Navigation Headers. A navigation header is a line of links running along the top of a page that mirrors the path the reader took to reach the page (see Figure 15.21).

Navigation Footers. A navigation footer is a set of links running along the bottom of the page.

Tables of Contents. Similar to those found in print documents, online tables of contents can help even readers who are relatively unfamiliar with the Web.

Site Maps. These graphical representations are familiar to most people because they are like road maps.

Drop-Down Menus. Drop-down menus, which can be created using HTML forms and scripting languages, such as javascript, have the dual advantage of functioning much like the menus on word processing and other software programs and of taking up relatively little space on your page (see Figure 15.22).

Follow Proven Principles of Web Site Design. Designing your site involves focusing on the overall look and feel of the site, which builds on the decisions you've made in Step 1 regarding content, organiza-

Figure 15.22
Drop-Down Navigation Menu

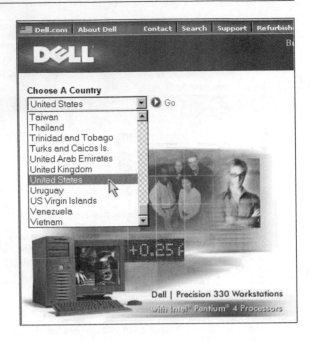

tion, and navigation tools. It also involves focusing on the function and appearance of individual pages in your site. The following principles underlie the design of an effective Web site.

Strive for a consistent design across your pages. Since one Web page is usually as easy to visit as another, avoid different designs on your pages. Different page designs can lead readers to think they've left your site and jumped to another. If you need to differentiate among your pages, use subtle variations in an overall design, such as differences in color, navigation aids, or placement of text on a page. Differences in your page designs should reflect differences in the functions of the pages.

Simple is better. Don't try to cram too much on a single page.

Keep important information on the screen. Readers often jump to another Web page if they don't find what they're looking for on the screen quickly. Although it's relatively easy to scroll down a page, few readers are willing to scroll down more than one screen to find the information they're seeking.

Avoid overuse of graphics. Graphics increase the time it takes for a browser to open a Web page. A well-designed home page usually contains less than 40K of text and images. (To test the size of your home page, view the details of the HTML and image files used for the page. In Windows, use My Computer or Windows Explorer to view file sizes. On a Macintosh, view files in a folder.) In addition, research suggests that readers of Web pages are drawn to textual information as opposed to graphical information—a behavior that is strikingly different from readers' typical behaviors with print documents.

As you begin to design your Web site, browse the Web for sites that attempt to accomplish a purpose similar to your own. Evaluate their site and page designs, noting features and layouts that you might want to incorporate into your own site. Then begin sketching designs on paper or in a graphics program. When you're satisfied with your design, get ready to code your pages.

■ Step 3: Code Your Pages

Web browsers, such as Netscape Navigator and Microsoft Internet Explorer, read files that are formatted using hypertext markup language (HTML). HTML sounds more complicated than it is. In essence, it consists of tags inserted into your text. These tags tell the browser how to interpret a particular section of text—as a heading or a paragraph, as a bold or italic font, as a link to another Web document, and so on. The tags are easy to learn: Each starting tag turns a particular effect on, and a corresponding ending tag turns that effect off. Tags that turn on an effect are placed within angle brackets < > and those that turn off an effect are preceded by a forward slash and placed within angle brackets: </ >. Table 15.2 lists a number of frequently used HTML tags.

ON THE WEB SITE

Read about 12 issues to consider as you design your Web site in the research writing manual Writing for the Web: HTML Coding and Web Design on the *Bedford Researcher* Web site at **http://www .bedfordresearcher .com**.

TABLE 15.2 FREQUENTLY USED HTML TAGS		
TAG	**WHAT THE TAG DOES**	**HOW THE TAGGED TEXT APPEARS ON THE WEB PAGE**
<html> </html>	Tells the browser that an HTML document is starting and ending.	
<head> </head>	Tells the browser that code between the tags is part of the document's header—which can contain identifying information, links to style sheets, and scripts—and should not be displayed in the body of the document. (See *body*.)	
<title>My Home Page</title>	Displays the title of the document in the browser title bar.	
<body> </body>	Tells the browser that the text of an HTML document is starting and ending.	

TABLE 15.2   FREQUENTLY USED HTML TAGS

TAG	WHAT THE TAG DOES	HOW THE TAGGED TEXT APPEARS ON THE WEB PAGE
<p>This is what a paragraph tag looks like. It starts and ends with the "p" tag.</p>	Tells the browser to start and end a paragraph.	This is what a paragraph tag looks like. It starts and ends with the "p" tag.
<h1>Heading 1</h1>	Tells the browser that the text between the tags is a first-level (largest) heading.	**Heading 1**
<h2>Heading 2</h2>	Tells the browser that the text between the tags is a second-level heading.	**Heading 2**
<h3>Heading 3</h3>	Tells the browser that the text between the tags is a third-level heading.	**Heading 3**
Hello	Bold text.	**Hello**
<i>Goodbye</i>	Italic text.	*Goodbye*
<u>See You Soon</u>	Underlined text.	See You Soon
<a href="URL">Link</a>	Tells the browser that the text between the tags is a link (or an "anchor," thus the "a"). When the mouse clicks on the link, a new Web page is opened in the browser. The URL should be a Web address, such as **http://writing.colostate.edu**.	Link
A line break. A new line.	A line break. (One of the few tags that has no ending tag.)	A line break. A new line.

Typically, it takes an afternoon to gain a basic understanding of how to code an HTML document. You can create HTML documents using a variety of software programs. You can use a plain-text editor, such as Notepad, to code your documents by hand. You can use an HTML editor, such as Macromedia's HomeSite, to create documents using built-in HTML coding tools, and you can use WYSIWIG Web editors, such as Macromedia's Dreamweaver and Microsoft's Front-Page, to create Web pages in much the same manner that you can create word processing documents. You can also use the built-in HTML conversion tools in your word processor. The latter option is the easiest for most writers. The only drawback to relying on built-in HTML conversion tools is that it can be difficult to revise the code in your files if anything goes wrong. To avoid this problem, it's usually best to preserve your original word processing files. If you need to change the page on your Web site, make changes to the word processing file, convert the revised file to HTML, and then replace the old HTML file with the revised one.

Naming Files for the Web.   Some Web browsers have a difficult time reading files that have names containing spaces. Before sending a file to a Web site, make sure that you've renamed it so that it no longer contains spaces. You might replace spaces with underscores _ or dashes -. *my research project.html* might be renamed as *my_research_project* *.html* or *my-research-project.html*.

Similarly, some Web servers—the computer where the HTML files for a Web site are stored—are case sensitive. If you've named your file *File2.html* but link to *file2.html,* the Web server will send an error message to your browser that the file cannot be found. To avoid unnecessary headaches caused by trying to figure out why your links aren't working, always use lowercase file names.

ON THE WEB SITE

For a detailed discussion of HTML coding, see the research writing manual Writing for the Web: HTML Coding and Web Design on the *Bedford Researcher* Web site at **http://www .bedfordresearcher .com**.

■ Step 4: Put Your Site Online

Putting your site online involves obtaining a Web account, transferring your files to that account, and in some cases, setting permissions on your files so that they are available on the Web.

Obtain an Account.   A Web site account provides you with a URL (Web address) for your site, a folder on a server in which to place your files, and a user name and password so that you can access that folder. Many colleges and universities provide Web accounts to students at no cost. You can usually learn whether your college or university provides free or low-cost Web accounts by visiting your institution's main Web site.

Transfer Your Files to Your Web Server.   Most Web site designers code their documents on their computers and then send the files to a Web server. This process is called *transferring files* and is carried out using a program, such as Ipswitch's WS_FTP (**http://www.ipswitch .com**) or CuteFTP (**http://www.cuteftp.com**), that uses the File Transfer Protocol (FTP). These programs create a connection between your computer and your Web server, allowing you to copy files in a manner similar to copying them from your hard drive to a floppy disk or a Zip disk.

Your Web account provider will tell you how to transfer files to and from your Web server.

If Necessary, Set Permissions.   Some Web accounts are set up so that you must specify the files you want the public to view. All other files are hidden—that is, they can't be viewed using a Web browser. If your Web account uses this approach, you will need to give Web browsers "permission" to view your files. Your Web account provider will tell you how to do this.

■ Step 5: Test Your Site

Once you've set up your site so that Web browsers can view your documents, test it by viewing it in your browser, making sure that

- each page can be opened by your browser
- your text displays properly (in particular, headings, paragraphs, formatting, line breaks, and tables)
- each link works
- each image is placed appropriately and appears in the browser
- any audio or video files work
- any animations work

You should also pay attention to how quickly your pages appear in the browser. Your readers will understand that the Web is a fairly slow medium. However, don't strain their patience. On a computer that uses a 56K modem, your pages should load within ten to twenty seconds. If they take longer, reduce the size of images. If necessary, eliminate some images.

If you've included audio and video files on your Web page, test the speed at which these files open in your browser. If you can, test your files on a computer that connects to the Web at the same speed as that used by your readers. If you are connecting to the Web with a high-speed connection, you might not notice that a page takes a long time to load or that audio and video files don't run well on computers that connect using phone modems.

■ Step 6: Announce Your Site

ON THE WEB SITE

View Research Links on the *Bedford Researcher* Web site at **http://www .bedfordresearcher .com** to locate specialized search sites and directories.

Once you've created your site, let your readers know that it's online. You can inform your readers by sending an email message containing the URL or posting a message on a newsgroup. You can list your site on popular search engines, such as *Lycos* (**http://www.lycos.com**), *AltaVista* (**http://www.altavista.com**), and *Google* (**http://www.google .com**); on directories, such as *Open Directory* (**http://dmoz.org**) and *Yahoo!* (**http://www.yahoo.com**); and on specialized search sites and directories that are related to your topic.

15f

How can I publish my document?

Your options for publishing your project document include

- printing your document
- distributing it as a computer file
- publishing it on the Web

Your choice of publication medium will be based on your purposes as a writer, your knowledge of your readers' preferences, and your access to publication resources, such as printers, software programs, and Web server accounts.

■ Printing Your Document

Printing options include sending your document to a printer attached to your computer, creating copies of your document on a copy machine, and bringing your document to a professional printer. For most writers, printing means sending their documents to a laser or inkjet printer attached to their computer.

Printing to a computer printer allows you to maintain a great deal of control over the appearance of your document. If you don't like the way your document looks, you can reformat your document and print another copy. Better yet, you can test the appearance of your document before you print using the PRINT PREVIEW command (usually found in the PRINT dialog box and also available in many word processing and desktop publishing programs through the FILE → PRINT PREVIEW menu command).

■ Distributing Your Document as a Computer File

Rather than printing your document and sending it to your readers on paper, you can send them the file and ask them to open it on their own computers. This saves paper. It can also save time and money.

Prepare Your File. Before you send your document as a file, ask whether your readers are likely to have the software needed to open it. If they have the same program you use (your word processor or desktop publishing program, for example) or if they have another program that can read your file, you can send them the file as is. If you suspect they might not have software that can open your file, save your file in a format they can read, such as rich text format (RTF), a format supported by most word processing programs. If you own Adobe Acrobat, you can publish your document as a PDF (portable document format) file. Most Web browsers can open documents saved as PDF files.

IN THIS BOOK

Read more about adding files to a Web site on p. 277. Read about URLs on p. 38.

Send Your File.   You can send a file in three ways:

- On a diskette or other removable storage medium, such as a Zip disk, SuperDisk, or writable CD.

- As an attachment to an email message. Recipients save the attached file on their computer and then open it for viewing.

- As a file on a Web site. If your file is too large to send as an attachment, place it on your Web site (assuming, of course, that you have one and that you have enough room on the site to store a large file). Link the file to a page on your site and send your readers the URL for the file.

Helping Your Readers Get in Touch with You

Whether you print your document, distribute it electronically, or publish it on the Web, provide contact information so that your readers can get in touch with you. For print documents, provide your mailing address and, if you like, your email address and Web URL. For electronic documents, provide an email address or Web URL.

Designing and publishing your project marks the end of your research writing process. The remaining sections of this book provide reference materials you can consult throughout that process. In the next section, you'll find detailed descriptions of the MLA, APA, Chicago, CBE, and Columbia Online Style documentation systems. Appendix A presents project documents created by three of the featured writers. Appendix B provides a list of resources you can use to collect information for topics in specific disciplines, such as biology, history, and film studies.

Joining the Conversation

Collecting Information

Working with Sources

Writing Your Document

▶ Documenting Sources

Part Five

Documenting Sources

As you complete your work on your project document, you can turn your attention fully to the task of citing and documenting your sources. This section of *The Bedford Researcher* discusses reasons to document your sources and describes five major documentation systems: MLA, APA, *Chicago,* CBE, and COS.

CHAPTER 16

Understanding Why You Should Document Your Sources

Research writers document their sources to avoid plagiarism, demonstrate accountability to others who have written about a topic, and create a record of their work that others can follow and build upon. These reasons illustrate the concept of writing as participation in a community of writers and readers. By documenting your sources, you show that you are aware that other writers have contributed to the conversation you've joined and that you respect them enough to acknowledge their contributions. In turn, you expect that writers who read your document will cite your work.

Documenting your sources can also help you achieve your purposes as a writer. If your readers find that you haven't documented your sources, they'll suspect that you're careless, or they'll decide that you're dishonest. In either case, they won't trust what you have to say. In this chapter, you'll find answers to the following questions.

Key Questions

16a

How should I document my sources?

How you document sources will depend on the discipline in which you are writing (such as anthropology or chemical engineering), your audience, and the type of document you are writing. Most often, you will

1. provide a reference to your source within the text
2. provide a complete set of citations, or formal acknowledgments, for your sources in a works cited or reference list

The specific format of your in-text citations will depend on the documentation system you use. You might use a parenthetical style, such as the American Psychological Association (APA) or the Modern Language Association (MLA) styles. Or you may choose the footnote/endnote citation style described in *The Chicago Manual of Style* (*Chicago*) or the citation-sequence style recommended in *Scientific Style and Format* (known as CBE style).

If you are writing an electronic document that cites other online sources, you might simply link to your sources. Table 16.1 presents examples of in-text citations and works cited or reference list entries for each of these major documentation styles.

As Table 16.1 shows, although each style differs from the others, particularly in the handling of in-text citation, they share a number of

TABLE 16.1   EXAMPLES OF IN-TEXT CITATIONS AND BIBLIOGRAPHIC ENTRIES FOR MAJOR DOCUMENTATION STYLES

STYLE	IN-TEXT CITATION	WORKS CITED OR REFERENCE LIST ENTRY
MLA Style	China has had a strong sense of nationalism (Borthwick 13).	Borthwick, Mark. *Pacific Century: The Emergence of Modern Pacific Asia.* 2nd ed. Boulder: Westview, 1998.
APA Style	China has had a strong sense of nationalism (Borthwick, 1998).	Borthwick, M. (1998). *Pacific century: The emergence of modern Pacific Asia* (2nd ed.). Boulder, CO: Westview Press.
***Chicago* Style: Footnote System**	China has had a strong sense of nationalism.[3]	Note: The citation is placed in a footnote. 3. Mark Borthwick, *Pacific Century: The Emergence of Modern Pacific Asia,* 2nd ed. (Boulder, Co.: Westview Press, 1998), 13.
CBE Style: Citation-Sequence System	China has had a strong sense of nationalism.[3]	Note: Numbered citations are placed in the reference list in the order they appear in the text. 3. Borthwick M. *Pacific century: the emergence of modern Pacific Asia.* 2nd ed. Boulder (CO): Westview Press; 1998. 582 p.
Web Style	<u>Borthwick</u> observes that China has had a strong sense of nationalism.	Many Web documents will link directly to a cited work, as shown here. Or they may use a style such as MLA, APA, *Chicago*, CBE, or COS.

similarities. With the exception of Web style, key publication information is usually provided in a works cited or reference list, which includes the following information about each source:

- author(s) and/or editor(s)
- title
- publication date
- publisher and city of publication (for books)
- periodical name, volume, issue, and page numbers (for articles)
- URL and access date (for online publications)

These documentation systems create an association between citations in the text of a document and the works cited page. In the case of Web publications, the link is often made directly to the source itself.

16b

Which documentation system should I use?

Your choice of documentation system will be guided by the discipline or field within which you are writing and any requirements associated with your research writing project.

If your research writing project has been assigned to you, ask the person who assigned the project or someone who has written a similar document what documentation system you should use. If you are writing a research project for a writing class, your instructor will most likely tell you which documentation system to follow.

If you don't have access to advice about which documentation system is best for your project, consider the discipline in which you are writing. In humanities courses such as composition, literature, art, and philosophy, the MLA or *Chicago* system is often used. In social science courses, such as psychology and sociology, APA style is typically used. The sciences often follow CBE style. In engineering and business, a wide range of documentation styles are used, many of which are specific to scholarly journals or specializations within the discipline.

16c

What are the benefits of using a documentation system?

Documentation systems benefit readers and writers alike. Readers benefit because documents that adhere to a documentation system provide information that allows readers to locate the sources referred to in the document. Writers benefit in two ways. First, if you follow a documentation system when you create your working bibliography, you'll find it easier to locate your sources later in your research project. Second, documentation systems call attention to differences among types of sources, focusing your attention as a writer on the fact that your sources may have widely varying characteristics.

Your Research Project

USE THE RESEARCH LOG TO ENTER PUBLICATION INFORMATION FOR YOUR SOURCES

The Working Bibliography tool in the **Research Log** at **http://www.bedfordresearcher.com** allows you to enter information about print, online, and field sources. You can

- add, update, or delete entries in your working bibliography
- display your working bibliography in MLA, APA, *Chicago,* or CBE style
- print your working bibliography, save it as a downloadable file, or send it via email

To use the Working Bibliography tool, follow these steps:

1. Log in to your **Research Log** account and click on the Update Your Working Bibliography link.
2. Click on the Add New Sources to Your Working Bibliography link.
3. Select the type of source you want to add, such as a book, a Web site, or an article.
4. Enter the publication information for your source, such as the author, publication date, and title, into the publication information form. Examples of complete citations are provided at the top of the form in MLA, APA, *Chicago,* and CBE styles.
5. Add notes about the source. If you prefer, you can leave this field blank or update it later.
6. Click on the ADD CITATION button. You will be returned to the main page of the Working Bibliography.

You can also create a bibliography in *Research Assistant* (included on a CD-ROM at the back of this text), although you will find it most useful for electronic sources. *Research Assistant* automatically saves source information, such as the source URL and the date you visited the source on the Web, when you drag a source into its collection bin. Consult the online help in *Research Assistant* for information about using its bibliography tool.

The following chapters provide detailed descriptions of five documentation systems: the MLA citation system, the APA citation system, the footnote system recommended by The Chicago Manual of Style, *the citation-sequence style recommended in* Scientific Style and Format, *and the Columbia Online Style documentation system.*

CHAPTER 17

Using MLA Style

Modern Language Association (MLA) style, used primarily in the humanities, emphasizes the authors of a source and the pages on which information is located in the source. Writers who use the MLA documentation system cite, or formally acknowledge, source information within their text using parentheses, and they provide a list of sources in a works cited list at the end of their document. For more information about MLA style, consult the *MLA Handbook for Writers of Research Papers*. Information about the *MLA Handbook* can also be found at **http://www.mla.org/**.

To see featured writer Jenna Alberter's research essay, formatted in MLA style, turn to page 362.

17a

How do I cite sources within the text of my document?

MLA uses a parenthetical approach to in-text citation to acknowledge the use of another author's words, facts, and ideas. When you refer to a source within your text, place the author's last name and specific page number(s), if the source is paginated, within parentheses. Your reader then can go to the works cited list at the end of the document and find a full citation there. The example on page 291 shows sample pages from a student essay and illustrates the connection between the in-text citation and the entry in the list of works cited.

1. Basic Format for Direct Quotation. It is often desirable to name the author of a source within your sentence rather than in a parenthetical citation. By doing so, you create a context for the material (words, facts, ideas) you are including and indicate where the information from the author begins. When you are using a direct quotation from a source and have named the author in your sentence, place only the page number in parentheses after the quotation. Punctuation marks follow the parentheses.

Lai   6

notes that the benefits of a well-designed work space cannot be over-rated. William Collier, work space designer and inventor, says, "Cubicles aren't the answer" (qtd. in Anderson). His most notable invention to date, the Aura Workstation, which sells for over $7,000.00, is "a free-standing environment engineered to give the user control over airflow, lighting, temperature, seating and even orientation on the compass" (Anderson). Though many American workers haven't felt the need for global positioning, the interest with which Collier's inventions are met reflects the American worker's desire to inhabit a work space that is flexible and, to some degree, customizable.

Lai   12

Works Cited

Anderson, Porter. "William Collier: Aura Workstation." *CNN.com* 11 Dec. 2001. Cable News Network. 17 Dec. 2001 <http://www.cnn.com/ 2000/CAREER/jobenvy/12/08/aura/index.html#chart>.

Kapai points out that "more than half of all Americans now carry at least one personal wireless communication device" (46), a fact that illustrates our growing dependence on technology.

When you have not mentioned the author in your sentence, you must place the author's name and the page number in parentheses after the quotation.

It is important to note that "more than half of all Americans now carry at least one personal wireless communication device" (Kapai 46).

When you are using a block (or extended) quotation, the parenthetical citation comes after the final punctuation and a single space.

If you continue to refer to a single source for several sentences in a row within one paragraph—and without intervening references to another source—you may reserve your reference to the end of the paragraph. However, be sure to include all of the relevant page numbers.

2. Basic Format for a Summary or Paraphrase. When you are summarizing or paraphrasing information gained from a source, you are still required to cite the source. If you name the author in your sentence, place only the page number in parentheses after the quotation. Punctuation marks follow the parentheses. When you have not mentioned the author in your sentence, you must place the author's name and the page number in parentheses after the quotation.

> Kapai reminds us that ownership of electronic items such as cell phones and pagers is now over fifty percent (46).

> Ownership of electronic items such as cell phones and pagers is now over fifty percent (Kapai 46).

3. Entire Source. If you are referring to an entire source rather than to a specific page number, you will not need a parenthetical citation.

> The articles that Fields and Fricker edited for Medical Problems in Athletes extend far beyond the predictable torn ACL or bruised Achilles tendon.

4. Corporate or Group Author. Cite the corporation or group as you would an individual author. You may use abbreviations for the source in subsequent references if you add the abbreviation in parentheses at the first mention of the name.

> The Modern Language Association (MLA) has taken a strong stance on the issue of plagiarism and academic dishonesty (27). The MLA statement on academic dishonesty calls our attention to the need to better address the problem in our teaching (29).

5. Unknown Author. If you are citing a source that has no known author, such as the article "Censorship in the United States: 1620–2000," use a brief version of the title in the parenthetical citation.

> Despite First Amendment freedoms, even in the United States, censorship has a long history ("Censorship" 22).

6. Two or More Works by the Same Author. For references to authors with more than one work in your works cited list, insert a short title between author and page number, separating the author and the title with a comma.

> (Morrison, Paradise 147)

> (Morrison, Song 320)

7. Two or Three Authors. Include the last name of each author in your citation.

Casting physically attractive actors wins points with film audi-ences: "Primitive as the association between outward strength and moral force may be, it has its undeniable appeal" (Clarke, Johnson, and Evans 228).

8. Four or More Authors. Use only the last name of the first author and the abbreviation "et al." (Latin for "and others"). Note that there is no comma between the author's name and "et al."

(Hafen et al. 62)

9. Two or More Works. Use a semicolon to separate entries.

Films with biblical subject matter have been simultaneously praised by conservative religious viewers and criticized by the-ologians (Black 163; Clarke, Johnson, and Evans 46-57).

10. Source Quoted in Another Source. Ideally, you will be able to find the primary, or original, source for material used in your research project document. If you quote or paraphrase a secondary source—a source that contains information about a primary source—use the abbreviation "qtd. in" (for "quoted in") when you cite the source.

By laying out the roles and duties of the woman, Jacob Cats's book "encompasses also the masculine counter-duties" (qtd. in Westermann 119).

11. Source with No Page Numbers. Many Web sources lack stable page numbers. In such cases, treat the source as unpaginated and list only the author's name in parentheses.

Especially for teenagers and young adults, eating disorders are desperate attempts to control a world that feels uncontrollable (Harrison).

17b

How do I prepare the list of works cited?

MLA-style research documents include a reference list titled "Works Cited," which is placed at the end of the document. If you wish to acknowledge sources that you read but did not cite in your text, you may title the list "Works Consulted" and include them.

 ON THE WEB SITE

Use the working bibliography tool in the **Research Log** (at **http://www .bedfordresearcher .com**) to record bibliographic infor-mation for your sources. When you select the docu-mentation style in which you are writ-ing—MLA, APA, *Chicago,* or CBE— your bibliography will be automati-cally formatted.

12. Placement, Formatting, and Arrangement of Works Cited Entries. In print documents and linear documents that are distributed electronically (such as a word processing file or a newsgroup post), the list of works cited usually appears at the end of the document. In the case of longer documents, the list of works cited might appear at the end of chapters or sections. In electronic documents that use links, such as a Web site, the list of works cited often appears as a separate page to which other pages are linked. Figure 17.1 shows a works cited list in MLA style.

Figure 17.1 A Works Cited List in MLA Style

A The works cited list begins on a new page. The title "Works Cited" is centered.

B The list of works cited is alphabetized by author. If the author's name is unknown, alphabetize using the title of the source.

C All entries in the list are double-spaced, with no extra space between entries. Entries are formatted with a hanging indent: The first line of an entry is flush with the left margin and subsequent lines are indented one-half inch or five spaces.

D To cite more than one work by the same author, use the author's name in the first entry. Thereafter, use three hyphens followed by a period in place of the author's name. List the entries alphabetically by title.

Alberter 15

 Works Cited

Alpers, Svetlana. "De Hooch: A View with a Room." Art in America 86.6
(1999): 92-99.

Franits, Wayne E. "Domesticity, Privacy, Civility, and the Transformation
of Adriaen van Ostade's Art." Images of Women in Seventeenth-
Century Dutch Art: Domesticity and the Representation of the
Peasant. Ed. Patricia Phagan. Athens: U of Georgia P, 1996. 3-25.

---. Paragons of Virtue: Women and Domesticity in Seventeenth-Century
Dutch Art. Cambridge: Cambridge UP, 1993.

Kleiner, Fred S., and Richard G. Tansey. Gardner's Art through the Ages.
10th ed. New York: Harcourt, 1996.

Westermann, Mariët. A Worldly Art: The Dutch Republic 1585-1718.
London: Calmann, 1996.

Books, Conference Proceedings, and Dissertations

Provide three main pieces of information, each piece followed by a period and one space:

- author (last name first)
- title and subtitle (underlined)
- publication data (place, publisher, and year)

For major cities such as Boston, Chicago, Los Angeles, New York, and London, you need not identify the state or country. If more than one city is listed in the source, give only the first. Shorten publishers' names to the first main word (Wiley, Harcourt), and omit "Press," "Inc.," "Co.," and the like. For university presses, use the abbreviation UP. You will find basic publication information for books on the title and copyright pages.

13. One Author.

> Black, Gregory. The Catholic Crusade against the Movies,
> 1940–1975. Cambridge: Cambridge UP, 1998.

> Morrison, Toni. Jazz. New York: Knopf, 1992.

14. Two or Three Authors. List all the authors in the same order as on the title page, last name first for only the first author listed. Use commas to separate authors' names.

> Zimmerman, Donald E., and Michel Lynn Muraski. The Elements of
> Information Gathering: A Guide for Technical Communicators,
> Scientists, and Engineers. Phoenix: Oryx, 1995.

> Jowett, Garth S., Ian C. Jarvie, and Kathryn H. Fuller. Children
> and the Movies: Media Influence and the Payne Fund Contro-
> versy. Cambridge: Cambridge UP, 1996.

15. Four or More Authors. Provide the first author's name (last name first) followed by a comma, and then the abbreviation "et al." (Latin for "and others").

> Hafen, Brent Q., et al. Mind/Body Health: The Effects of Atti-
> tudes, Emotions, and Relationships. Boston: Allyn, 1996.

16. Corporate or Group Author. Write out the full name of the corporation or group, and cite the name as you would an author. This name is often also the name of the publisher.

> Joint Association of Classical Teachers. <u>The World of Athens: An Introduction to Classical Athenian Culture</u>. Cambridge: Cambridge UP, 1984.

> Reference Press. <u>Hoover's Guide to Computer Companies</u>. Austin: Reference, 1995.

17. Unknown Author. When no author is listed on the title or copyright page, begin the entry with the title of the work. Alphabetize the entry by the first word of the title other than *A*, *An*, or *The*.

> <u>The International Who's Who 2000</u>. 63rd ed. London: Europa, 1999.

18. Translated Book. List the author first and then the title, followed by the name of the translator and publication information.

> Aeschylus. <u>Oresteia</u>. Trans. Peter Meineck. Indianapolis: Hackett, 1998.

19. Edition Other Than the First. Include the number of the edition and the abbreviation "ed." after the title.

> Freitag, Wolfgang M. <u>Art Books: A Basic Bibliography of Monographs on Artists</u>. 2nd ed. New York: Garland, 1997.

20. Multivolume Work. Include the total number of volumes and the abbreviation "vols." after the title.

> Gaze, Delia, ed. <u>Dictionary of Women Artists</u>. 2 vols. London: Fitzroy, 1997.

If you have used only one of the volumes in your document, include the volume number after the title. List the total number of volumes after the publication information.

> Wright, Christopher, comp. <u>The World's Master Paintings: From the Early Renaissance to the Present Day</u>. Vol. 1. London: Routledge, 1997. 2 vols.

21. Book in a Series. If a series is named on the title page, include that name just before the publication information. Include the series number after a period. If the word "Series" is part of the series name, abbreviate it "Ser."

> Segal, Charles. <u>Oedipus Tyrannus: Tragic Heroism and the Limits of Knowledge</u>. Twayne's Masterwork Studies. Ser. 108. New York: Twayne, 1993.

22. Republished Book. Indicate the original date of publication after the title.

> Bradley, Andrew Cecil. Shakespearean Tragedy: Hamlet, Othello,
>   King Lear, Macbeth. 1905. New York: Meridian, 1955.

If anything has been added (a foreword, introduction, or afterword, for example), note that information after the date of original publication. If the republished work has a new title, include all basic bibliographic information for the new title. Then include the abbreviation "Rpt. of" (for "reprint of") followed by the original title and year of publication.

23. Author with an Editor. Include the name of the editor (first name first) after the title.

> Faulkner, William. New Orleans Sketches. Ed. Carvel Collins. New
>   York: Random, 1958.

24. Anthology. To cite an anthology of essays, stories, or poems or a collection of articles, list the editor or editors first (as on the title page), followed by the abbreviation "ed." or "eds."

> Fields, Karl B., and Peter A. Fricker, eds. Medical Problems in
>   Athletes. Malden, MA: Blackwell, 1997.

25. Foreword, Introduction, Preface, or Afterword. Begin with the author and the name of the part you are citing. Continue with the title of the work and the author (first name first), following "By." At the end of the entry, list the inclusive page numbers on which the part of the book appears.

> Jones, Peter V. Preface. The World of Athens: An Introduction to
>   Classical Athenian Culture. By Joint Association of Classical
>   Teachers. Cambridge: Cambridge UP, 1984. vii-viii.

If the author of the foreword or other part is also the author of the work, use only the last name after "By."

> Morrison, Toni. Afterword. The Bluest Eye. By Morrison. New York:
>   Plume-Penguin, 1994. 209-16.

If the foreword or other part has a title, include the title in quotation marks between the author and the name of the part.

> Gates, Henry Louis, Jr. "Toni Morrison (1931–)." Preface. Toni
>   Morrison: Critical Perspectives Past and Present. Ed. Gates
>   and K. A. Appiah. New York: Amistad, 1993. ix-xiii.

26. Chapter in an Edited Book or Selection in an Anthology. Begin your citation with the author and the title of the chapter or selection. Follow this with the title of the anthology or collection, the abbreviation "Ed." or "Eds.," and names of the editors (first name first) as well as publication information. At the end of your entry, list the inclusive page numbers for the selection or chapter.

> Anderson, Arnold E. "Eating Disorders in Males: Critical Ques-
> tions." Eating Disorders: A Reference Sourcebook. Ed. Ray-
> mond Lemberg. Phoenix: Oryx, 1999. 73-79.

27. Two or More Works from One Anthology. To avoid repeating the same information about the anthology several times, include the anthology itself in your list of works cited.

> Lemberg, Raymond, ed. Eating Disorders: A Reference Sourcebook.
> Phoenix: Oryx, 1999.

In the entries for individual selections or chapters, cross-reference the anthology by giving the editor's name and the page numbers on which the selection appears.

> Pelch, Bonnie L. "Eating Disordered Families: Issues between the
> Generations." Lemberg 121-23.

28. Published Proceedings of a Conference. Provide information as you would for a book, adding information about the conference sponsors, place, and dates before the publication data.

> Brack, Duncan, ed. Trade and Environment: Conflict or Compati-
> bility? Proc. of the Royal Inst. of Intl. Affairs, Apr. 1997,
> Chatham House, London. London: Earthscan, 1998.

29. Paper Published in Proceedings of a Conference. Treat a selection from conference proceedings as you would a selection in an edited collection.

> Lee, James. "Trade-Related Environmental Measures: How Much Is
> a Dolphin Worth?" Trade and Environment: Conflict or Com-
> patibility? Proc. of the Royal Inst. of Intl. Affairs, April
> 1997, Chatham House, London. Ed. Duncan Brack. London:
> Earthscan, 1998.

30. Sacred Text. Include the title of the version as it appears on the title page. If the title does not identify the version, place that information directly after the title:

The Jerusalem Bible. Garden City, NY: Doubleday, 1966.

The Holy Bible: New Revised Standard Version. New York: Amer.
Bible Soc., 1989.

31. Published Dissertation or Thesis. Cite as you would a book, but include information specific to the dissertation, such as the school and, if relevant, the University Microfilms International (UMI) order number.

Higgins, John W. Tracing the Vision: A Study of Community
Volunteer Producers, Public Access Cable Television, and
Empowerment. Diss. Ohio State U, 1994. Ann Arbor: UMI,
1995. 9517017.

32. Unpublished Dissertation or Thesis. Place the title of the thesis or dissertation in quotation marks and add information about the type of dissertation, the school, and the date.

Corney, Jeffrey R. "Writing Science for Audience: A Comparison of
Professional Reports and Popular Essays." Thesis. Colorado
State U, 1995.

33. Abstract of a Dissertation or Thesis. Treat an abstract as you would an article in a journal. First give the information for unpublished dissertations. Then add the source, abbreviated either *DA* or *DAI* (for *Dissertation Abstracts* or *Dissertation Abstracts International*), volume number, year (in parentheses), and page number.

Hurley, Michael Edgar. "The Role Conflict and Academic Performance of College Student-Athletes." Diss. U of Miami, 1993.
DAI 54 (1993): 2067.

■ Sources in Journals, Magazines, and Newspapers

The basic information you will provide for articles in magazines, scholarly journals, and newspapers includes

- author (last name first)
- title of article (enclosed in quotation marks)
- journal, magazine, or newspaper title (underlined)
- date of publication
- inclusive page numbers for the article

If the journal, magazine, or newspaper title begins with *The,* omit that in your entry. Publication dates for journals include the volume number and, sometimes, the issue number. Do not include volume and issue information for magazines or newspapers.

34. Article in a Journal Paginated by Volume. Most journals continue pagination for an entire year, beginning again at page 1 only in the first volume of the next year. After the journal title, list the volume number, year of publication in parentheses, a colon, and inclusive page numbers.

> Boag, Peter. "Thomas Moran and Western Landscapes: An Inquiry into an Artist's Environmental Values." Pacific Historical Review 67 (1998): 41-66.

35. Article in a Journal Paginated by Issue. Some journals begin at page 1 for every issue. After the volume number, add a period and the issue number, with no space.

> Plantinga, Carl. "Spectacles of Death: Clint Eastwood and Violence in Unforgiven." Cinema Journal 37.2 (1998): 65-83.

36. Article in a Monthly or Bimonthly Magazine. After the author's name and title of the article, list the title of the magazine, the date (use abbreviations for all months except May, June, and July), and the inclusive pages.

> Swerdlow, Joel L. "The Power of Writing." National Geographic Aug. 1999: 110-32.

If the article does not appear on consecutive pages, write only the first page number and a plus sign (+), with no space between.

> Vollers, Maryanne. "Razing Appalachia." Mother Jones July-Aug. 1999: 36+.

37. Article in a Weekly or Biweekly Magazine. Give the exact date of publication, inverted.

> Levy, Steven, and Brad Stone. "Hunting the Hackers." Newsweek 21 Feb. 2000: 38-44.

38. Article in a Daily Newspaper. If the title of the newspaper begins with *The*, omit the word. If the newspaper is not a national newspaper (such as the *Wall Street Journal, Christian Science Monitor,* or *Chronicle of Higher Education*) or the city of publication is not part of its title, give the name of the city in square brackets [Salem, OR] after the title. List the date in inverted order and, if the masthead indicates that the paper has more than one edition, give this information after the date ("natl. ed.," "final ed."). Follow with a colon and a space, and end with the page numbers (use the section letter before the page number if the newspaper uses numbered sections). If the article does not appear on consecutive pages, write only the first page number and a plus sign (+), with no space between.

> Gosselin, Peter J. "Federal Investigators Focus on Hard Drives, Workers with Access." <u>Seattle Times</u> 18 June 2000: A2.

39. Unsigned Article in a Newspaper or Magazine. Begin with the title of the article. Alphabetize by the first word other than *A*, *An*, or *The*.

> "Energy Secretary Faces Tough Questions on Los Alamos." <u>New York Times</u> 22 June 2000, natl. ed.: A22.

40. Editorial in a Newspaper. Include the word "Editorial" after the title.

> "Rethinking Welfare Reform." Editorial. <u>Washington Post</u> 18 June 2000: B6.

41. Letter to the Editor. Include the word "Letter" after the author.

> Hamilton, Kendra. Letter. <u>Washington Post</u> 18 June 2000: B6.

42. Review. After the author and title of the review, include the words "Rev. of," followed by the title of the work under review; a comma; the word "by" (for a book) or "dir." (for a play or film); and the name(s) of the author or director. Continue with publication information for the review.

> Laird, Pamela Walker. "Consuming Smoke: Cigarettes in American Culture." Rev. of <u>Cigarette Wars: The Triumph of "The Little White Slaver,"</u> by Cassandra Tate. <u>Reviews in American History</u> 28 (2000): 96-104.

> Welsh, Jim. "'Ill Met by Moonlight': Michael Hoffman's <u>Dream</u>." Rev. of <u>A Midsummer Night's Dream</u>, dir. Michael Hoffman. <u>Literature/Film Quarterly</u> 27 (1999): 159-61.

43. Published Interview. Begin with the person interviewed. If the published interview has a title, give it in quotation marks. If not, write the word "Interview" (no quotation marks or underline). If an interviewer is identified and relevant to your project, give that name next. Then supply the publication data.

> Stafford, Kim. "Listening to the Future: A Conversation with Kim
> Stafford." Interview with Eric Todd Smith. Northwest Review
> 37.1 (1999): 102-14.

■ Print Reference Works

44. Encyclopedia, Dictionary, or Thesaurus. Cite as you would a book (see p. 295).

45. Handbook or Almanac. Cite as you would a book (see p. 295).

46. Entry in an Encyclopedia, Dictionary, Thesaurus, Handbook, or Almanac. In many cases, the entries and articles in reference works are unsigned. Therefore, begin your citation with the title of the entry in quotation marks, followed by a period. Give the title of the reference work, underlined, and the edition and year of publication. If the work is arranged alphabetically, you may omit the volume and page numbers.

> "Censorship." The New Encyclopaedia Britannica: Macropaedia.
> 15th ed. 1993.

> Suber, Howard. "Hitchcock, Alfred." The Encyclopedia Americana.
> Intl. ed. 1998.

If you cite a specific definition, include that information after the title of the entry, adding the abbreviation "Def." and the number of the definition.

> "Nunnery." Def. 1b. The Oxford English Dictionary. 2nd ed. 1989.

If a reference work is not well known (perhaps because it includes highly specialized information), provide all of the bibliographic information.

> Porter, Roy. "Great Chain of Being." The Harper Dictionary of
> Modern Thought. Ed. Alan Bullock and Stephen Trombley. Rev.
> ed. New York: Harper, 1988.

47. Map or Chart. Generally, treat a map or chart as you would a book without authors. Give its title (underlined), the word "Chart" or "Map," and publication data. For a map in an atlas, give the map title followed by publication information for the atlas and page numbers for the map. If the creator of the map or chart is listed, use his or her name as you would an author's name.

> The Middle East and North Africa. Map. Washington: AMIDEAST,
> 1991.

"Greece and the Aegean." Map. National Geographic Atlas of the World. 6th ed. Washington: Natl. Geographic Soc., 1992. 65-66.

48. Government Publication. In most cases, cite the government agency as the author. If there is a named author, editor, or compiler, provide that name after the title. Use the abbreviations "Dept." for department, "Cong." for Congress, "S" for Senate, "H" or "HR" for House of Representatives, "Res." for resolution, "Rept." for report, "Doc." for document, and "GPO" for Government Printing Office.

United States Dept. of Education. Office of Educ. Research and Improvement. Natl. Center for Educ. Statistics. Literacy behind Prison Walls: Profiles of the Prison Population from the National Adult Literacy Survey. By Karl O. Haigler et al. Washington: GPO, 1994.

If you are citing from the *Congressional Record,* the entry is simply Cong. Rec. followed by the date, a colon, and the page numbers.

49. Pamphlet. Format the entry as you would for a book (see p. 295).

■ Electronic Sources

The publication information you provide for electronic sources should allow your readers to retrace your steps electronically to locate the source. In general, entries for electronic sources include

IN THIS BOOK
Read more about URLs on p. 38.

- author
- title of work (underlined) or description of site (for example, Home page)
- publication date or date on which the site was last updated
- name of institution or organization associated with the site, if any
- date on which you accessed the site (read the source)
- URL (in angle brackets < >)

50. World Wide Web Site. Provide publication information followed by the access date and the URL in angle brackets. Place a period after the final angle bracket.

Partenheimer, David. Exercise Helps Keep Your Psyche Fit. 13 June 1999. Amer. Psychological Assn. 21 Nov. 2000 <http://www .apa.org/releases/exercise.html>.

Darling, Jill. Alchemy. 11 May 2001. 8 Nov. 2001 <http://writing .colostate.edu/gallery/darling/alchemyhome.htm>.

51. Article in an Online Periodical. Provide information as you would for a print periodical, adding the date of access and the URL. Since the article was published online, it is unlikely to have page numbers.

> Slatin, John. "La Zambinella Meets the Cyborg: Barthes, S/Z, and Print-Based Literary Studies." CWRL: The Electronic Journal for Computers, Writing, Rhetoric, and Literature 3 (1997). 12 Nov. 1999 <http://www.cwrl.utexas.edu/~cwrl/v3n1/ zambinella/index.html>.

52. Email message. Cite the sender of the message; the title (from the subject line, in quotation marks); a phrase indicating the recipient of the message; and the date of the message.

> Holm, Janine. "Last-minute Revisions." E-mail to the author. 17 July 1999.

> Richards, Jessica. "Ideas for Revisions." E-mail to Alice Walters. 5 Nov. 2001.

53. Message Posted to a Newsgroup, Electronic Mailing List, or Online Discussion Forum. Cite the name of the person who posted the message; the title (from the subject line, in quotation marks); the phrase "Online posting"; the date of the message; the name of the newsgroup, list, or forum; the access date; and the URL.

> Carbone, Nick. "Re: E Text Readers." Online posting. 30 Oct. 2001. TechRhet list. 8 Nov. 2001 <http://groups.yahoo.com/ group/TechRhet/message/5122>.

54. Source Obtained through Telnet, FTP, or Gopher. Cite as you would a Web page.

> Marks, Karen T. "More Oedipal Theory." 13 Jan. 2000. 14 Jan 2000. <telnet://hamlet.psu.edu/oed.txt>.

55. CD-ROM Issued in a Single Edition. Treat a CD-ROM as you would a book, noting "CD-ROM" after the title.

> Crane, Gregory, ed. Perseus. CD-ROM. 2.0. New Haven: Yale UP, 1996.

56. CD-ROM Issued Periodically. Treat a CD-ROM that is issued periodically as you would a print periodical, noting its electronic publication date at the end of the citation. In the following note, the CD-ROM is a database, *MLA International Bibliography,* distributed by SilverPlatter.

Singer, Armand, and Michael Lastinger. "Themes and Sources of
Star Wars: John Carter and Flash Gordon Enlist in the First
Crusade." Popular Culture Review 9.2 (1998): 65-77.
MLA International Bibliography, 1991-2000/06. CD-ROM.
SilverPlatter. May 2000.

57. Online Scholarly Project. Provide as much of the following information as possible:

- author and title of the work (and original publication date, if any)
- name of the project or database
- editor or producer
- publication date
- project sponsor
- date of access
- URL (in angle brackets)

Schreiner, Olive. "Dreams." 1898. The Victorian Women Writers
Project. Ed. Perry Willett. 2001. Indiana University. 27 Mar.
2002 <http://www.indiana.edu/~letrs/vwwp/schreiner/
dreams.html>.

58. Work from a Subscription Service. Libraries subscribe to reference databases such as Lexis-Nexis and InfoTrac. If you access a work from a subscription service, list in your citation as much of the following information as possible:

- author, title, and other publication information for the source
- name of the database
- name of the service, if any
- name of the library where you accessed the article
- date of access

Rosenberg, Norman J., and Roberto C. Izaurralde. "Storing Carbon
in Agricultural Soils to Help Head-off a Global Warming."
Climatic Change 51.1 (2001): 1-10. Article First. OCLC
FirstSearch. Morgan Library, Colorado State University,
Fort Collins, CO. 9 Feb. 2002.

59. Abstract in an Online Database. Provide the publication information for the source, followed by the word "Abstract," information about the database, the library from which you accessed it, and the date you accessed it.

> Olsen, Francis. "The Promise and Problems of a New Way of Teach-
> ing Math." <u>Chronicle of Higher Education</u> 8 Oct. 1999: A31+.
> Abstract. <u>Educational Research Information Clearinghouse</u>.
> FirstSearch. Colorado State U Lib., Fort Collins. 18 July 2000
> <http://firstsearch.oclc.org/>.

60. Computer Software. Cite computer software as you would a book. Provide additional information about the medium on which it is distributed and the version.

> <u>Microsoft Office XP Professional</u>. CD-ROM. Redmond: Microsoft,
> 2001.

■ Field Sources

61. Personal Interview. Place the name of the person interviewed first, words to indicate how the interview was conducted, and the date.

> Davies, Eleanor. Telephone interview. 14 Feb. 2000.

62. Letter. Give the writer's name, the words "Letter to the author" (no quotation marks or underline), and the date the letter was written.

> Hammersmith, Sharon. Letter to the author. 14 Nov. 1999.

If the letter was written to someone else, give that name rather than "the author" and provide information about where you read the letter.

63. Lecture or Public Address. Give the speaker's name and the title of the lecture (if there is one) or the form ("Lecture," "Panel discussion," "Reading"). If the lecture was part of a meeting or convention, identify that. Conclude with the event data, including venue, city, and date.

> Wills, Garry. "Government and the Arts: Athens to Washington."
> Willamette U, Salem, OR. 30 Sept. 1999.

■ Media Sources

64. Film or Video Recording. You will generally begin with the title of the film or recording (underlined). Always supply the name of the director (following the abbreviation "Dir."), the distributor, and the year of original release. You may also insert other relevant information, such as the names of performers or screenplay writers, before the distributor.

> <u>Hamlet</u>. Dir. Franco Zeffirelli. Perf. Mel Gibson. Warner, 1990.

If you wish to emphasize an individual's role in the film or movie, such as the director or screenplay writer, you may list that name first.

> Olivier, Laurence, dir. and perf. <u>Hamlet</u>. Paramount, 1948.

For media other than film (such as videotape and DVD), identify the media before the distributor.

> Branagh, Kenneth, dir. and perf. <u>Hamlet</u>. Videotape. Columbia, 1996.

65. Television Program. Include the title of the program (underlined), the network, the station's call letters and city (if any), and the date on which you watched the program. If there are relevant persons to name (such as an author, director, conductor, narrator, or actor), include that information after the title. If the program has named episodes or segments, list those in quotation marks. If the program is part of a series, include that information before the network.

> "An Unsuitable Job for a Woman." <u>Mystery!</u> PBS. KETC, Minneapolis. 30 June 2000.

66. Radio Program. Cite as you would cite a television program.

> <u>Fresh Air</u>. Host Terry Gross. Natl. Public Radio. KOAC, Corvallis. 17 May 1999.

67. Radio or Television Interview. Provide the name of the person interviewed and the title of the interview. If there is no title, write "Interview" and, if relevant, the name of the interviewer. Then provide the name of the program, the network, the call letters of the station, the city, and the date.

> Fox, Vicente. Interview with Ted Koppel. <u>Nightline</u>. ABC. KATU, Portland, OR. 3 July 2000.

68. Sound Recording. Begin with the name of the person whose work you want to highlight: the composer, the conductor, or the performer. Next list the title followed by names of other artists (composer, conductor, performers), with abbreviations indicating their roles, after the title. The recording information includes the manufacturer and the date. If the recording is not a compact disc, identify its form (such as Audiocassette, Audiotape, LP, or MP3) before the recording data.

> Mozart, Wolfgang Amadeus. <u>The Symphonies: Salzburg</u> 1772-1773. Acad. of Ancient Music. Dir. Jaap Schroeder and Christopher Hogwood. LP. Decca, 1979.

If you wish to cite a particular track on the recording, give its performer and title (in quotation marks) and then proceed with the information about the recording. For recordings that contain rerecorded material, include the date of the performance between the title and the recording data.

> Rattle, Simon, Cond. <u>Gustav Mahler Symphony No. 10 in F Sharp</u>.
> Bournemouth Symphony Orch. 1980. EMI Classics, 1992.

69. Musical Composition. Give the composer and title. Underline the title unless it identifies the composition by form ("symphony," "suite"), number ("Opus 39," "K.231"), or key ("E flat").

> Gilbert, W. S., and Arthur Sullivan. <u>H.M.S. Pinafore, or The Lass
> That Loved a Sailor</u>.

If you are referring to a published score, provide publication data as you would for a book. Insert the date of composition between the title and the publication data.

> Brahms, Johannes. <u>Walzer für Klavier zu Vier Händen</u>. Opus 39.
> 1865. Munich: Henle, 1955.

70. Live Performance. Generally, begin with the title of the performance (underlined). Then give the author and director; the major performers; and theater, city, and date.

> <u>Henry V</u>. By William Shakespeare. Dir. Libby Appel. Oregon Shake-
> speare Festival, Ashland. 30 Apr. 2000.

71. Work of Art. Give the name of the artist, the title of the work (underlined), the date of completion, and the name of the collection, museum, or owner, and the city.

> Rodin, Auguste. <u>The Thinker</u>. 1880. Musée Rodin, Paris.

72. Advertisement. Provide the name of the product, service, or organization being advertised, followed by the word "Advertisement." Then provide the usual publication information.

> FTD. Advertisement. <u>Time</u> 19 Apr. 1999: 33.

73. Cartoon. Treat a cartoon like an article in a newspaper or magazine. Give the cartoonist's name, the title of the cartoon if there is one (in quotation marks), the word "Cartoon," and the publication data for the source.

> Browne, Mark. "The Back Page." Cartoon. <u>New Yorker</u> 15 May
> 2000: 108.

CHAPTER 18

Using APA Style

American Psychological Association (APA) style, used primarily in the social sciences and in some of the natural sciences, emphasizes the author(s) and publication date of a source. Writers who use the APA documentation system cite, or formally acknowledge, information within their text using parentheses and provide a list of sources, called a reference list, at the end of their document. For more information about APA style, consult the *Publication Manual of the American Psychological Association* and *Mastering APA Style: Student's Workbook and Training Guide*. Information about these publications can also be found on the APA Web site at **http://www.apa.org**.

To see pages from featured writer Aaron Batty's APA-style research document, an informative Web site about Taiwan-China relations, turn to page 370.

18a

How do I cite sources within the text of my document?

APA uses an author-date form of in-text citation to acknowledge the use of another author's words, facts, or ideas. When you refer to a source, insert a parenthetical note that gives the author's last name and the date of the publication, separated by a comma. Even when your reference list includes the day or month of publication, the in-text citation should include only the year. For a quotation, the parenthetical citation also includes the page(s) on which the quotation can be found, if the source has page numbers. Note that APA style requires using the past tense or present perfect tense to introduce the material you are citing: *Renfrew argued* or *Renfrew has argued*.

You should provide the minimum amount of information necessary to allow your reader to find the source in your reference list. The following sample pages from a student essay illustrate the connection between the in-text citation and the entry in the list of references.

American Welfare   4

recipients are unhappy given the current economic downturn. Workfare, designed to be an improvement over traditional hand-out welfare by granting temporary work situations that lead to long-term employment, does not work when a community is suffering from increasing unemployment. Critics of such programs have argued that they are nothing but "a dead end for many poor people in need of education and training, a way to cut and divert people from public benefits and create a tide of cheap labor that has swept thousands of paying jobs from city payrolls" (Bernstein, 2001, p. A20). Changing economic times require changing the models.

American Welfare   11

References

Bernstein, N. (2001, December 17). As welfare comes to an end, so do the jobs. *The New York Times*, pp. A1, A20.

1. Basic Format for Direct Quotation. When you are using a direct quotation from a source and have named the author in your sentence, place the publication date in parentheses directly after the author's last name. Include the page number (with "p." for page) in parentheses after the quotation.

> Oakley (1992) put the question succinctly: "When women have children, what is the role of professionalized health care on the one hand, and of the social environment on the other, in helping them to do so?" (p. viii).

If you are using a direct quotation from a source and have not mentioned the author's name in your sentence, place the author's name, the publication date, and the page number in parentheses: (Oakley, 1992, p. viii).

2. Basic Format for Summary or Paraphrase. When you are summarizing or paraphrasing, place the author's name and date either in the sentence or in parentheses at the end of the sentence. Include a page or chapter reference if it would help readers find the original material in a longer work.

> Oakley (1992) has suggested that research has not yet satisfactorily shown *how* social support actually works (chap. 2).

> But research has not yet satisfactorily shown *how* social support actually works (Oakley, 1992, chap. 2).

3. Two Authors. List the names of both authors in every mention in the text. If you mention the authors' names in a sentence, use the word "and" to separate the last names, as shown in the first example. If you place the authors' names in the parenthetical citation, use an ampersand (&) to separate the last names, as shown in the second example.

> Vest and Long (1995) have found that graduates of electrical engineering programs placed a high value on communication skills.

> The survey found that interpersonal communication skills were ranked more highly than written communication skills (Vest & Long, 1995).

4. Three, Four, or Five Authors. In parentheses, name all the authors the first time you cite the source, using an ampersand (&) before the last author's name. On subsequent references to the source, use the last name of the first author followed by the abbreviation "et al." (Latin for "and others").

Farming families have not usually been correctly represented in popular television series (Garkovich, Bokemeier, & Foote, 1995). The problem of misrepresentation has drawn a great deal of fire from researchers (Garkovich et al., 1995).

5. More Than Five Authors. In all references to the source, give the first author's last name followed by "et al."

Zimmerman et al. (1995) reported the results of an extensive study of communication practices by faculty and students in an engineering program.

6. Corporate or Group Author. In general, cite the full name of the corporation or group the first time it is mentioned in your text. If you put an abbreviation for the group in square brackets the first time you cite the source, you can use the abbreviation in subsequent citations.

The number of graduate programs a prospective student in psychology may consider could be quite overwhelming (American Psychological Association [APA], 1998). A student might narrow the search to programs that offer the PhD (APA, 1998).

7. Unknown Author. Sources with unknown authors are listed by title in the list of references. In your in-text citation, shorten the title as much as possible without introducing confusion. Add quotation marks to article titles and italicize book titles.

Recent scientific discoveries continue to inflame the evolution-creationism debate ("Fossil," 2000).

If the author of the source is identified as "Anonymous," cite the author of the source as Anonymous.

The rise in water levels along the Missouri River has been referred to as a national crisis (Anonymous, 2001).

8. Two or More Works. List the sources in alphabetical order and separate them with semicolons. If you are referring to two or more sources by the same author, order those sources chronologically.

The studies of social and cultural factors in shaping how men respond to a variety of stressors have not ignored biology (Mackey, 1996; Renfrew, 1997, 2001).

9. Source Quoted in Another Source. Ideally, you will be able to find the primary, or original, source for material used in your research project document. If you quote or paraphrase a secondary source—a source that contains information about a primary source—mention the primary source and indicate that it was cited in the secondary source.

> According to Cats (1625), by laying out the roles and duties of the woman, his book "encompasses also the masculine counter-duties" (as cited in Westermann, 1996, p. 119).

10. Source with No Page Numbers. Many Web sources lack stable page numbers. In such cases, indicate the paragraph number or section heading in which the cited passage exists.

> Garcia (2000) estimates that from 30 to 50 percent of anorexia nervosa patients also have the symptoms of bulimia nervosa (para. 4).

18b

How do I prepare the reference list?

 ON THE WEB SITE
Use the working bibliography tool in the **Research Log** (at **http://www .bedfordresearcher .com**) to record bibliographic information for your sources. When you select the documentation style in which you are writing—MLA, APA, *Chicago,* or CBE—your bibliography will be automatically formatted.

The reference list contains publication information for all sources that you have cited within your document, with one exception. Personal communication, such as correspondence, email messages, and interviews, is cited only in the text of the document.

11. Placement, Formatting, and Arrangement of Reference List Entries. In print documents and linear documents that are distributed electronically (such as a word processing file or a newsgroup post), the reference list usually appears at the end of the document. In the case of longer documents, the reference list might appear at the end of chapters or sections. In electronic documents that use links, such as Web sites, the reference list often appears as a separate page to which other pages are linked. Figure 18.1 shows an example of a reference list in APA style.

■ Books, Conference Proceedings, and Dissertations

Provide four main pieces of information, each piece followed by a period and a single space:

- author or editor (last name first, initials for first and middle name)
- date of publication (in parentheses)

Batty 15

References

(A) Anonymous. (2000, March 18). China: No independence for Taiwan. *BBC News Online.* Retrieved March 20, 2000, from http://news.bbc.co .uk/hi/english/in_depth/asia_pacific/2000/taiwan_election/ newsid_682000/682190.stm

(B) Borthwick, M. (1998). *Pacific century* (2nd ed.). Boulder, CO: Westview Press.

(C) Eckholm, E. (2000, March 11). China, citing tensions, asks U.S. to end Taiwan arms sales. *The New York Times,* p. B1.

(D) Eckholm, E., & Myers, S. L. (2000, March 1). Taiwan asks U.S. to let it obtain top-flight arms. *The New York Times,* p. A6.

Fang, L. (1990). The Chinese amnesia. P. Link (Trans.), M. Borthwick (Ed.), *Pacific Century,* (2nd ed.) (pp. 415-416). Boulder, CO: Westview Press.

Joint communiqué on arms sales to Taiwan. (1982). *Taiwan documents project.* Retrieved March 13, 2000, from http://newtaiwan .virtualave.net/communique03.htm

Olivier, B. V. (1996, September 29). *Ancient Asian History.* Lecture presented at Colorado State University. Fort Colins, CO.

Figure 18.1 A Reference List in APA Style

A The reference list begins on a new page. The title "References" is centered at the top of the page.

B The reference list is ordered alphabetically by author. If a source's author is an organization, alphabetize the source by the name of the organization.

C All entries are double-spaced, with no extra space between entries. Entries are formatted with a hanging indent: The first line of an entry is flush with the left margin and subsequent lines are indented one-half inch or five spaces.

D All major words in the titles of periodicals are capitalized. Only initial words of the main title and subtitle and proper nouns and proper adjectives are capitalized in book and article titles. Book titles are italicized; article titles are not italicized and do not have quotation marks.

- title of the book (italicized, capitalizing only the first word of the title, first word of the subtitle, and any proper nouns or proper adjectives)
- place and publisher (separated by a colon)

APA style does not abbreviate or omit such terms as "University" or "Press" in publishers' names; however, it does omit words such as "Inc." or "Co." You will find basic publication information for books on the title and copyright pages.

12. One Author.

> Mackey, W. C. (1996). *The American father: Biocultural and developmental aspects.* New York: Plenum Press.

13. Two or More Authors. List the authors in the same order as the title page does, both with last name first. Use commas to separate authors and use an ampersand before the final author's name. List every author up to six; for a work with more than six authors, give the first six names followed by "et al." (Latin for "and others").

> Garkovich, L., Bokemeier, J. L., & Foote, B. (1995). *Harvest of hope: Family farming/farming families.* Lexington: University Press of Kentucky.

14. Corporate or Group Author. Write out the full name of a corporate or group author. Cite the name of the corporation or group as you would an author. If the corporation is also the publisher, use "Author" for the publisher's name.

> American Psychological Association. (1998). *Graduate study in psychology 1998–1999.* Washington, DC: Author.

15. Unknown Author. When there is no author listed on the title or copyright page, begin the entry with the title of the work. Alphabetize the entry by the first significant word of the title (not including *A*, *An*, or *The*).

> *The new international atlas.* (1994). Chicago: Rand McNally.

16. Translated Book. List the author first followed by the year of publication, the title, and the translator (in parentheses, identified by the word "Trans."). Place the original date of the work's publication at the end of the entry.

> Freud, S. (1957). *Civilization and its discontents* (J. Riviere, Trans.). London: Hogarth Press. (Original work published 1930)

17. Book in an Edition Other Than the First. Note the edition ("2nd ed.," "Rev. ed.") after the title.

> Grimes, R. (1995). *Beginnings in ritual studies* (Rev. ed.). Columbia: University of South Carolina Press.

18. Multivolume Work. Include the number of volumes in parentheses after the title.

> Massarik, F. (Ed.). (1990). *Advances in organization development* (Vols. 1–3). Norwood, NJ: Ablex.

If you have used only one volume in a multivolume work, identify that volume, by number and by title.

> Hickman, L. A., & Alexander, T. M. (Eds.). (1998). *The essential John Dewey: Vol. 2. Ethics, logic, psychology*. Bloomington: Indiana University Press.

19. Author with an Editor. Include the editor's name and the word "Ed." in parentheses after the title.

> James, W. (1980). *The selected letters of William James* (E. Hardwick, Ed.). Boston: NonPareil.

20. Anthology. To cite an anthology of essays or a collection of articles, list the editor or editors first, followed by the abbreviation "Ed." or "Eds." in parentheses.

> Kaya, Y., & Yokobori, K. (Eds.). (1997). *Environment, energy, and economy: Strategies for sustainability*. Tokyo: United Nations University Press.

21. Chapter in an Edited Book or Selection in an Anthology. Begin the entry with the author, the publication date, and the title of the chapter or selection (not italicized). Follow this with the names of the editors (initials first) and the abbreviation "Ed." or "Eds." in parentheses, the title of the anthology or collection (italicized), inclusive page numbers for the chapter or selection (in parentheses, with abbreviation "pp."), and place and publisher.

> Johansson, T. B. (1997). Global warming and renewable energy. In Y. Kaya & K. Yokobori (Eds.), *Environment, energy, and economy: Strategies for sustainability* (pp. 232–247). Tokyo: United Nations University Press.

22. Foreword, Introduction, Preface, or Afterword. Treat as you would a chapter in a book (see p. 317).

23. Published Proceedings of a Conference. Cite information as you would for a book, capitalizing the name of the conference, meeting, or symposium (if there is one).

> *Schools and religion: Proceedings before the United States Commission on Civil Rights.* (2000). Executive summary and transcripts of proceedings held in Washington, DC, New York City, and Seattle, WA, Spring/Summer 1998. Washington, DC: United States Commission on Civil Rights.

24. Paper Published in the Proceedings of a Conference. Treat a conference paper as you would a selection from an edited collection.

> Zimmerman, D. E., Palmquist, M., & Muraski, M. (1998). Students as WWW surfers: A brief look at students and the WWW. In *IPCC 1998: A contemporary renaissance: Changing the way we communicate: Vol. 2. Technical papers: Proceedings of the IEEE International Professional Communication Conference.* Quebec City, Canada, September 23–25, 1998. Piscataway, NJ: IEEE.

25. Sacred Text. Treat as you would a book (see p. 316).

26. Published Dissertation or Thesis. Cite as you would a book, but include information about the college or university that granted the degree. Follow with the *Dissertation Abstracts International* information obtained from University Microfilms International (UMI).

> Higgins, J. W. (1994). *Tracing the vision: A study of community volunteer producers, public access cable television, and empowerment* (Doctoral dissertation, Ohio State University, 1994). *Dissertation Abstracts International, 56-01A,* 9517017.

27. Unpublished Dissertation or Thesis. Format as you would a book, replacing the publisher information with the phrase "Unpublished doctoral dissertation" or "Unpublished master's thesis," followed by information about the college or university.

> Corney, Jeffrey R. (1995). *Writing science for audience: A comparison of professional reports and popular essays.* Unpublished master's thesis, Colorado State University, Fort Collins.

28. Abstract of a Dissertation or Thesis. Treat an abstract as you would an article in a journal. Follow with the *Dissertation Abstracts International* information obtained from UMI.

Hurley, M. E. (1993). The role conflict and academic performance of college student-athletes. *Dissertation Abstracts International, 54*(06A), 2067.

■ Sources in Journals, Magazines, and Newspapers

The basic information for articles in journals, magazines, and newspapers includes the following:

- author (last name first)
- publication date (in parentheses)
- title of article (no quotation marks)
- for journals, title of journal (italicized), followed by volume number (italicized) and inclusive page numbers
- for magazines or newspapers, title of publication (italicized), followed by page numbers

Note that you should capitalize all significant words in journal titles.

29. Article in a Journal Paginated by Volume. Most journals continue page numbers throughout an entire annual volume, beginning again at page 1 only in the first volume of the next year. After the author and publication year, provide the article title, the journal title, the volume number (italicized), and the inclusive page numbers.

Smith, K. H., & Stutts, M. A. (1999). Factors that influence adolescents to smoke. *Journal of Consumer Affairs, 33,* 321–357.

30. Article in a Journal Paginated by Issue. Some journals begin at page 1 for every issue. Include the issue number (in parentheses, not italicized) after the volume number.

Wilcox, R. V. (1999). There will never be a "very special" *Buffy: Buffy* and the monsters of teen life. *Journal of Popular Film and Television, 27*(2), 16–23.

31. Article in a Magazine. The author's name and the publication date are followed by the title of the article, the magazine title (italicized), and the volume number, if any (also italicized). Include all page numbers.

Critser, G. (2000, March). Let them eat fat: The heavy truths about American obesity. *Harper's, 298,* 41–47.

32. Article in a Newspaper. List the author's name and the complete date (year first). Next give the article title followed by the name of the newspaper (italicized). Include all page numbers, preceded by "p." or "pp."

> Colvin, R. L. (2000, June 18). Marion Joseph: The force behind phonics predicts a reading renaissance. *Los Angeles Times,* p. M3.

33. Unsigned Article in a Newspaper. Begin with the article title, and alphabetize in the reference list by the first significant word in the title. Precede page numbers with "p." or "pp."

> Recession shouldn't mean the end of research. (2002, Feb. 10). *The Boston Globe,* p. D12.

34. Letter to the Editor. Include the words "Letter to the editor" in square brackets after the title of the letter, if any. Note that the page numbers in the example indicate that the letter was printed on non-consecutive pages.

> Raine, E. S. (2000, Jan./Feb.). Not so sweet charity [Letter to the editor]. *Public Health Reports, 115,* pp. 6, 77.

35. Review. After the title of the review, include the words "Review of the book . . ." or "Review of the film . . ." and so on in brackets, followed by the title of the work reviewed.

> Yagoda, B. (2000, May/June). Coloring public opinion [Review of the book *The black image in the white mind: Media and race in America*]. *The New Leader, 78*(2), 27–28.

When the review is untitled, follow the date with the bracketed information.

> Eisenman, R. (2000). [Review of the book *Brushing back Jim Crow: The integration of minor league baseball in the American south*]. *Multicultural Review, 9*(2), 74.

36. Published Interview. Cite a published interview like a journal article (see p. 319).

■ Print Reference Works

37. Encyclopedia, Dictionary, Thesaurus, Handbook, or Almanac. Cite a reference work, such as an encyclopedia or a dictionary, as you would a book.

> Lindberg, C. A. (Ed.). (1998). *The Oxford American desk thesaurus.* New York: Oxford University Press.

38. Entry in an Encyclopedia, Dictionary, Thesaurus, Handbook, or Almanac. Begin your citation with the name of the author or, if the entry is unsigned, the title of the entry. Proceed with the date, the title of the reference work, and the edition number. If the contents of the reference work are arranged alphabetically, omit the volume and page numbers.

> Hitchcock, Alfred. (1998). In *The encyclopedia Americana* (pp. 508–510). Danbury, CT: Grolier.

39. Government Publication. Give the name of the department (or office, agency, or committee) that issued the report as the author. If the document has a report or special file number, place that in parentheses after the title.

> U.S. Senate Committee on Commerce, Science, and Transportation. (1998). *Children's Protection from Violent Programming Act: Report of the Committee on Commerce, Science, and Transportation on S. 363*. Washington, DC: U.S. Government Printing Office.

40. Pamphlet. Format the entry as you would a book (see p. 316).

■ Electronic Sources

In general, entries for electronic sources include

IN THIS BOOK
Read more about URLs on p. 38.

- author, if known
- date of publication or latest update (if there is no date listed, use "n.d.")
- title
- publication information
- retrieval date
- online location: the URL, database, or information service where you located the document (The URL is not followed by a period.)

This information should allow your readers to retrace your steps electronically to locate the source. Page numbers cannot be provided for most electronic sources. When there is no author listed for an electronic source, begin your entry with the title.

41. Nonperiodical Web Document. For a stand-alone Web source, such as a report or an online brochure, cite as much of the following information as possible: author, publication date, document title, retrieval data (date you read the source), and the URL.

> Partenheimer, D. (1999, June 13). *Exercise helps keep your psyche fit*. American Psychological Association. Retrieved Nov. 21, 2000, from http://www.apa.org/releases/exercise.html

For a chapter or section within a Web document, identify the section as well as the main document.

> Calambokidis, J., Evenson, J., Steiger, G., & Jeffries, S. (1994). Watching gray whales. In *Gray whales of Washington state* (chap. 4). Retrieved December 19, 2001, from http://www.cascadiaresearch.org/gray/whale7.pdf

For a document within a government agency Web site or other complex site, include the name of the agency or organization before the URL.

> National Institutes of Health. (2001, December). *NIH human embryonic stem cell registry*. Retrieved December 19, 2001, from the National Institutes of Health Web site: http://escr.nih.gov/

42. Article in an Online Periodical. Publication information follows the retrieval date and the URL. Since the article was published online, it is unlikely to have page numbers. Note that the journal in the first example provides volume and issue numbers while the second does not.

> Brent, D. (1997). Rhetorics of the Web: Implications for teachers of literacy. *Kairos: A Journal for Teachers of Writing in Webbed Environments, 2*(1). Retrieved July 18, 2000, from http://english.ttu.edu/kairos/2.1/features/brent/bridge.html

> Barber, J. F. (2000). All watched over by machines of loving grace: Promoting cybernetic ecology in writing classrooms. *Academic.Writing*. Retrieved July 18, 2000, from http://aw.colostate.edu/articles/barber2000/bridge.html

43. Online Article Originally Published in a Print Periodical. Publication information is followed by the retrieval date and the URL. Include [Electronic version] after the title.

> Amato, J. (1992). Science-literature inquiry as pedagogical practice: Technical writing, hypertext, and a few theories, part I [Electronic version]. *Computers and Composition 9*(2), 41–54. Retrieved July 18, 2000, from http://www.cwrl.utexas.edu/~ccjrnl/Archives/v9/9_2_html/9_2_3_Amato.html

44. Email Message. Because email messages are difficult or impossible for your readers to retrieve, APA does not recommend including them in your reference list. You should treat them as personal communications and cite them parenthetically in your text (see p. 314).

45. Message Posted to a Newsgroup, Electronic Mailing List, or Online Discussion Forum. List the author, posting date, message title, name of the list or forum, and URL, as well as any additional identifying information such as message number.

> Carbone, N. (2001, October 30). Re: E text readers. Message
>   posted to TechRhet electronic mailing list, archived at
>   http://groups.yahoo.com/group/TechRhet/message/5122

46. Source Obtained through Telnet, FTP, or Gopher. Cite as you would a Web page.

> White, E. G. (2000, April 14). Molds. Retrieved July 18, 2000,
>   from gopher://hamlet.psu.edu/somethings/rotten/oed.txt

47. Article or Abstract Obtained through a Database. Provide publication information about the source obtained through a database, the date the source was retrieved, and the database in which the information was found. It is not necessary to indicate the format of the database (CD-ROM, network, and so on). If you are referring to an abstract in a database, include the word "Abstract" in square brackets (no quotation marks or italics) following the title of the source.

> Grower, T. (2000, July 10). Healthy man: Chemicals good for your
>   lawn could be bad for you. *Los Angeles Times,* S1. Retrieved
>   July 18, 2000, from Academic Universe database.

> Olsen, F. (1999, October 8). The promise and problems of a new
>   way of teaching math [Abstract]. *Chronicle of Higher Educa-*
>   *tion, 46*(7), A31-A32, A34. Retrieved July 18, 2000, from
>   ERIC database.

48. Computer Software. If an individual has rights to the program, software, or language, name him or her as the author; otherwise, begin the entry with the name of the program. In square brackets after the name, identify the source as "Computer software." Treat the organization that produces the software as the publisher. If you're referring to a specific version that isn't included in the name, put this information last.

> Reference Manager Professional Edition [Computer software].
>   (2000). Berkeley, CA: ISI ResearchSoft. Version 9.5.

■ Field Sources

49. Personal Interview. Treat unpublished interviews as personal communications and include them in your text only (see p. 311). Do not cite personal communications in your reference list.

50. Letter. Cite a personal letter as a personal communication in the text only (see p. 314), not in the reference list.

51. Lecture or Public Address. Cite a lecture or public address the same way you would cite an unpublished paper presented at a conference.

> Wills, G. (1999, September 30). *Government and the arts: Athens to Washington*. Lecture presented at Willamette University, Salem, OR.

■ Media Sources

52. Film or Video Recording. List the director and producer (if available), the date of release, the title followed by "Motion picture" in square brackets, and the studio or distributor.

> Zeffirelli, F. (Director). (1990). *Hamlet* [Motion picture]. Burbank, CA: Warner Brothers.

53. Television Program. List the director (if available), the broadcast date, the title followed by "Television broadcast" or "Television series episode," in square brackets, and the producer.

> Innes, L. (Director). (2000, November 22). *Shibboleth* [Television series episode]. In A. Sorkin (Producer), *The West Wing*. Burbank, CA: Warner Brothers Television.

54. Radio Program. List the host, the broadcast date, the title followed by "Radio broadcast," or "Radio series episode," in square brackets, and the producer.

> Gross, T. [Host]. (1999, May 17). *Fresh Air* [Radio series episode]. Washington, DC: National Public Radio.

55. Sound Recording. Name the artist as author; the date; the title (italicized), the medium (in square brackets); and the production data.

> Gray, M. (1999). I Try. On *On How Life Is* [CD]. New York: Sony/ Epic.

■ Other Sources

56. General Advice about Other Sources. APA provides general guidance for citing additional sources, suggesting that you use as a guide a source type listed in their manual that most closely resembles the type of source you want to cite.

CHAPTER 19

Using Chicago Style

The documentation style described in *The Chicago Manual of Style: The Essential Guide for Writers, Editors, and Publishers* (14th ed.) is used in the humanities and in some of the social sciences. Its primary system for documenting sources is a note system in which researchers acknowledge their sources in footnotes or endnotes. Footnotes appear at the bottom of a printed page, whereas endnotes appear at the end of the document. Although it is permissible to omit a bibliography when using the note system (since all relevant publication information is provided in the notes), the manual encourages authors to provide a bibliography or list of works cited in documents where more than a few sources are cited. For more information about this system, consult *The Chicago Manual of Style*. Information about the manual can also be found at **http://www.press.uchicago.edu**.

To see featured writer Rianne Uilk's research essay, formatted in *Chicago* style, turn to page 373.

The Chicago Manual of Style provides limited instructions for citing electronic sources. The suggestions presented in this chapter for formatting online documents are based on models from the *Columbia Guide to Online Style* (see Chapter 21).

CITATIONS WITHIN YOUR TEXT	
1. Numbering	328
2. Placement of note numbers in the text	328
3. Placement of notes	329
4. Including page numbers in a note	329
5. Cross-referencing notes	329
6. Citing the same source in multiple notes	330

NOTES AND ENTRIES IN YOUR BIBLIOGRAPHY OR LIST OF WORKS CITED

19a

How do I cite sources within the text of my document?

The Chicago Manual of Style's system for citing sources within the text of your document uses footnotes or endnotes. Notes can also be used to expand on points made in the text—that is, notes can contain both citation information and commentary on the text. For electronic documents such as Web sites that consist of multiple "pages" of text, footnotes can take the form of links to notes at the end of a "page" or to pop-up windows that display the notes. Endnotes in multipage electronic documents can be linked to a separate notes page.

The first time you refer to a source in a note, provide complete publication information for the source. In subsequent references, you may shorten the note to the author's last name and the page numbers (if the source has page numbers) to which you refer. Separate the elements with commas and end with a period. *Chicago* style italicizes titles of books and periodicals.

The following examples illustrate the most common ways of citing sources within the text of your document using *Chicago*'s note system.

1. Numbering. Notes should be numbered consecutively throughout your work, beginning with 1.

2. Placement of the Note Numbers in the Text. Place the number for a note at the end of the sentence containing the reference after punctuation and outside any parentheses. If you are using an em-dash (or two hyphens) to separate parts of a sentence, the note number should precede the dash. Note numbers are set as superscripts.

Liang calls attention to the significance of "the unprecedented presence of Europeans in Southeast Asia in the early decades of the twentieth century."[1]

This point is central to Kellerman's[2] argument—and should not be overlooked by critics.

3. Placement of Notes. You may choose between footnotes, which appear at the foot of the page containing corresponding note numbers (as shown in Figure 19.1), and endnotes, which appear at the end of the document in a section titled "Notes." Longer works, such as books, typically use endnotes. The choice, however, depends on the expectations of your readers and your preferences. Regardless of placement, notes are numbered consecutively throughout the document (if you use a bibliography, it follows the last page of text or the last page of endnotes).

Model notes for various types of sources appear in section 19b, which begins on p. 330.

4. Including Page Numbers in a Note. Use page numbers whenever you refer to a specific page of a source rather than to the source as a whole. The use of page numbers is required for quotations.

> 3. Mariët Westermann, *A Worldly Art: The Dutch Republic 1585–1718* (London: Calmann and King, 1996), 119.

5. Cross-Referencing Notes. If you are referring to a source identified in a previous note, you can refer to that note instead of repeating the information.

> 16. See note 5 above.

Figure 19.1 **Example of a Numbered Note and Its Corresponding Footnote**

Senate Bill 186 is also discriminatory to students in low-income communities. Representative Gloria Leyba, D-Denver, comments that the report cards mandated by the bill punish low-income and inner-city school districts for circumstances they cannot control.[6] Because the residents of low-income communities do not make as much money as do residents in high-income communities, the taxes collected for the school districts in these low-income communities are not as high.

----

6. Fred Brown, "Retooled School Bill Goes Back to Senate: Grading System Concerns House Democrats," *Denver Post,* 22 March 2000, A14.

6. Citing the Same Source in Multiple Notes. If you refer to the same source in several notes, provide a full citation in the first note.

> 1. Lucille Granger, *A History of Magic* (New York: Pantheon Books, 2000), 146.

Then provide simply the author's last name and the page number in subsequent notes.

> 4. Granger, 162.

Chicago style no longer recommends the use of Latin abbreviations ("ibid." and "op. cit.") to refer to works cited in previous notes.

19b

How do I format notes and prepare the bibliography?

ON THE WEB SITE
Use the working bibliography tool in the **Research Log** (at **http://www .bedfordresearcher .com**) to record bibliographic information for your sources. When you select the documentation style in which you are writing—MLA, APA, *Chicago*, or CBE—your bibliography will be automatically formatted.

The Chicago Manual of Style provides guidelines for formatting notes and entries in a bibliography of works that are relevant to but not necessarily cited within your document.

7. Placement, Formatting, and Arrangement of Bibliography and Works Cited Entries. In print documents and linear documents that are distributed electronically (such as a word processing file or a newsgroup post), the bibliography appears at the end of the document. In the case of longer documents, a bibliography might appear at the end of each chapter or section. In electronic documents that use links, such as a Web site, the bibliography often appears as a separate page to which other pages are linked. Figure 19.2 shows an example of a *Chicago*-style bibliography.

8. Basic Format for *Chicago*-style Notes and Bibliography Entries. For notes, include the number of the note, indented and not superscript, followed by these elements:

- author's name (first name first)
- title (followed by the title of the complete work if the source is an article, chapter, or other short work contained in a larger work)
- publisher (for a book) or publication title (for a journal, magazine, or newspaper)
- date
- page(s)

For entries in the bibliography, include these elements:

- author's name (last name first)
- title (followed by the title of the complete work if the source is an article, chapter, or other short work contained in a larger work)

Uilk 10

A Bibliography

Bartels, Lynn. "Owens Likes Furor over Education Reform Plan." *Rocky Mountain News* 18 March 2000, A7.

B

Brown, Fred. "Retooled School Bill Goes Back to Senate: Grading System Concerns House Democrats." *Denver Post* 22 March 2000, A14.

Gutierrez, Hector. "Teachers Protest Grading Proposal." *Rocky Mountain News* 26 March 2000, A20.

C Newcomb, JoElyn, and Linda Shoemaker. "Owens' Risky Experiment for Children." *Denver Post* 17 February 2000, B11.

Owens, Bill. "Announcement of 'Putting Children First: A Plan for Safe and Excellent Public Schools.'" *State of Colorado Home Page.* 8 December 1999. http://www.state.co.us/childrenfirst/ChildrenFirstRemarks.htm (16 April 2000).

D ———. "Open Letter to Colorado's Teachers from Governor Owens." *State of Colorado Home Page.* 15 December 1999. http://www.state.co.us/childrenfirst/teacher_letter_amd_23.pdf (15 April 2000).

Pascoe, Pat. "School Reform Will Do Little to Help Children Learn." *The Pascoe Express,* 15 March 2001. http://home.earthlink.net/~dambois/latest.html (16 April 2000).

"Putting Children First: A Plan For Safe and Excellent Public Schools." *State of Colorado Home Page.* 19 November 1999. http://www.state.co.us/childrenfirst (15 April 2000).

E

Figure 19.2   A *Chicago*-Style Bibliography

A Center the title Bibliography.

B Entries should be double-spaced, with no extra space between entries. Use a hanging indent: Type the first line of a citation flush with the left margin and indent subsequent lines one-half inch or five spaces.

C Titles of books and periodicals are italicized. All major words in titles are capitalized.

D Alphabetize the list by authors' last names. Successive sources by the same author or editor should be listed using 3 em-dashes (or 6 hyphens) in place of the name of the author or editor. Place the earliest entry first. In cases where the author's name is unknown, alphabetize using the title (ignoring the words *A, An,* and *The*).

E A source with an unknown author should be listed by title. Alphabetize the entry by the first significant word (ignoring the words *A, An,* and *The*).

- publisher (for a book) or publication title (for a journal, magazine, or newspaper)
- date
- page(s) (if the source is a shorter work included in a complete work)

Note: For each type of source, a pair of models is presented in this section: a model note followed by a model bibliographic entry.

9. Source Quoted in Another Source.

> 1. Edmund Hillary, *High Adventure* (London: Hodder & Stoughton, 1955), 175, quoted in Jon E. Lewis, *The Permanent Book of the 20th Century* (New York: Carroll & Graf, 1994), 507.

> Hillary, Edmund. *High Adventure*. London: Hodder & Stoughton, 1955. Quoted in Jon E. Lewis, *The Permanent Book of the 20th Century* (New York: Carroll & Graf, 1994), 507.

■ Books, Conference Proceedings, and Dissertations

10. One Author. Use the basic format described on page 330.

> 2. Barbara Evans Clements, *Bolshevik Women* (Cambridge: Cambridge University Press, 1997), 85.

> Clements, Barbara Evans. *Bolshevik Women*. Cambridge: Cambridge University Press, 1997.

11. Two or Three Authors. List the authors in the order on the title page. In a note, list all authors' first names first. In the bibliography, list the first author's last name first and list the other author's first name first:

> 2. W. Barnett Pearce and Stephen W. Littlejohn, *Moral Conflict: When Social Worlds Collide* (Thousand Oaks, Calif.: Sage, 1997), 144.

> Pearce, W. Barnett, and Stephen W. Littlejohn. *Moral Conflict: When Social Worlds Collide*. Thousand Oaks, Calif.: Sage, 1997.

12. Four or More Authors. In a note, give only the first author's name followed by "et al." (Latin for "and others"). In the bibliography, list the authors as they appear on the title page, although it is permissible to shorten the list to the first author and "et al."

3. Milton M. R. Freeman et al., *Inuit, Whaling, and Sustainability* (Walnut Creek, Calif.: Sage-Altamira, 1998), 71.

Freeman, Milton M. R., Lyudmila Bogoslovskaya, Richard A. Caulfield, Ingmar Egede, Igor I. Krupnik, and Marc G. Stevenson. *Inuit, Whaling, and Sustainability*. Walnut Creek, Calif.: Sage-Altamira, 1998.

13. Corporate or Group Author. Use the corporation or group as the author; it may also be the publisher.

7. American Psychological Association, *Graduate Study in Psychology 1998–1999* (Washington, D.C.: American Psychological Association, 1998), 4.

American Psychological Association. *Graduate Study in Psychology 1998–1999*. Washington, D.C.: American Psychological Association, 1998.

14. Unknown Author. When no author is listed on the title or copyright page, begin the entry with the title of the work. In the bibliography, alphabetize the entry by the first word other than *A*, *An*, or *The*.

4. *National Geographic Atlas of the World,* Rev. 7th ed. (Washington, D.C.: National Geographic Society, 1999), 16.

National Geographic Atlas of the World. Rev. 7th ed. Washington, D.C.: National Geographic Society, 1999.

15. Translated Book. List the author first and the translator after the title. Use the abbreviation "trans." in a note, spell the abbreviation in the bibliography.

7. Franz Kafka, *The Castle,* trans. Mark Harman (New York: Schocken Books, 1998), 26.

Kafka, Franz. *The Castle*. Translated by Mark Harman. New York: Schocken Books, 1998.

16. Edition Other Than the First. Give edition information after the title.

8. W. Lance Bennett, *News: The Politics of Illusion,* 3rd ed. (White Plains, N.Y.: Longman, 1996), 188.

Bennett, W. Lance. *News: The Politics of Illusion*. 3rd ed. White Plains, N.Y.: Longman, 1996.

17. Untitled Volume in a Multivolume Work. In the bibliography, if you have used all the volumes, give the total number of volumes after the title, using the abbreviation "vols." ("2 vols." or "4 vols."). If you have used one volume, give the abbreviation "Vol." and the volume number after the title. In the notes, give the volume number and page number, separated by a colon, for the specific location of the information referred to in your text.

9. Roscoe R. Hill, ed., *Journals of the Continental Congress, 1774–1789* (New York: Johnson Reprint, 1968), 1:39–62.

Hill, Roscoe R., ed. *Journals of the Continental Congress, 1774–1789.* Vol. 1. New York: Johnson Reprint, 1968.

18. Titled Volume in a Multivolume Work. Give the title of the volume to which you refer, followed by the volume number and the general title for the entire work.

10. Henrik Ibsen, *Pillars of Society, A Doll's House, Ghosts,* vol. 5 of *The Oxford Ibsen,* ed. and trans. James Walter McFarlane (Oxford: Oxford University Press, 1961), 273.

Ibsen, Henrik. *Pillars of Society, A Doll's House, Ghosts.* Vol. 5 of *The Oxford Ibsen.* Edited and translated by James Walter McFarlane. Oxford: Oxford University Press, 1961.

19. Book in a Series. The series name follows the title and is capitalized as a title but is not italicized. If the series numbers its volumes, include that information as well.

11. Andrea Minoretti, *A Walker's Guide to Mt. Chocorua,* Appalachian Mountain Club's Pocket Guides (Concord, N.H.: Appalachian Mountain Club, 1998), 46–49.

Minoretti, Andrea. *A Walker's Guide to Mt. Chocorua.* Appalachian Mountain Club's Pocket Guides. Concord, N.H.: Appalachian Mountain Club, 1998.

20. Republished Book. Place the original publication date before the publication information for the reprint.

12. Andrew Cecil Bradley, *Shakespearean Tragedy: Hamlet, Othello, King Lear, Macbeth* (1905; reprint, New York: Meridian Books, 1955), 156.

Bradley, Andrew Cecil. *Shakespearean Tragedy: Hamlet, Othello, King Lear, Macbeth.* 1905. Reprint, New York: Meridian Books, 1955.

21. Author with an Editor. List the author at the beginning of the citation and add the editor's name after the title. In notes, use the abbreviation "ed." before the editor's name. In the bibliography, include the phrase "Edited by" before the editor's name.

> 13. Richard Irving Dodge, *The Powder River Expedition Journals of Colonel Richard Irving Dodge,* ed. Wayne R. Kime (Norman: University of Oklahoma Press, 1997), 91–92.

> Dodge, Richard Irving. *The Powder River Expedition Journals of Colonel Richard Irving Dodge.* Edited by Wayne R. Kime. Norman: University of Oklahoma Press, 1997.

22. Anthology or Collection with an Editor. To cite an anthology or a collection of articles, give the editor(s) before the title of the collection, adding a comma and the abbreviation "ed." or "eds."

> 14. Donna Reiss, Dickie Selfe, and Art Young, eds., *Electronic Communication across the Curriculum* (Urbana, Ill.: National Council of Teachers of English, 1998), 39.

> Reiss, Donna, Dickie Selfe, and Art Young, eds. *Electronic Communication across the Curriculum.* Urbana, Ill.: National Council of Teachers of English, 1998.

23. Foreword, Introduction, Preface, or Afterword. Give the name of the writer of the foreword, introduction, preface, or afterword followed by the phrase "introduction to," "preface to," and so on before the title of the book. After the title insert the word "by" and the author's name.

> 15. Daniel J. Boorstin, introduction to *A Lady's Life in the Rocky Mountains,* by Isabella L. Bird. (Norman: University of Oklahoma Press, 1960), vii.

> Boorstin, Daniel J. Introduction to *A Lady's Life in the Rocky Mountains,* by Isabella L. Bird. Norman: University of Oklahoma Press, 1960.

24. Chapter in a Book or Selection in an Anthology. Give the author and title (in quotation marks) for the chapter or selection. Then give the title, editor, and publication data for the book or anthology. Give the inclusive page numbers before the publication data in the bibliography.

> 16. Arnold E. Anderson. "Eating Disorders in Males: Critical Questions," in *Eating Disorders: A Reference Sourcebook,* ed. Raymond Lemberg (Phoenix: Oryx Press, 1999), 76.

> Anderson, Arnold E. "Eating Disorders in Males: Critical Questions." In *Eating Disorders: A Reference Sourcebook,* edited by Raymond Lemberg, 73–79. Phoenix: Oryx Press, 1999.

25. Published Proceedings of a Conference. Provide information as for an anthology or collection with an editor (see p. 335).

26. Paper Published in the Proceedings of a Conference. Cite as a chapter in an edited book (see p. 335).

27. Sacred Text. Cite sacred texts within the text of your document. A note should include the book, chapter, and verse, but not a page number.

28. Published Dissertation or Thesis. Give the author and title, the phrase "Ph.D. diss." or "master's thesis," followed by information about the institution that granted the degree and the year. Include information from *Dissertation Abstracts International* if appropriate.

> 17. John W. Higgins, *Tracing the Vision: A Study of Community Volunteer Producers, Public Access Cable Television, and Empowerment* (Ph.D. diss., Ohio State University, 1994), Ann Arbor: UMI, 1995, 9517017, 49.

> Higgins, John W. *Tracing the Vision: A Study of Community Volunteer Producers, Public Access Cable Television, and Empowerment.* Ph.D. diss., Ohio State University, 1994. Ann Arbor: UMI, 1995. 9517017.

29. Unpublished Dissertation or Thesis. Give the author and title, in quotation marks. Then include the phrase "Ph.D. diss." or "master's thesis," information about the institution that granted the degree, and the date.

> 18. Jeffrey R. Corney, "Writing Science for Audience: A Comparison of Professional Reports and Popular Essays" (master's thesis, Colorado State University, 1995), 26.

> Corney, Jeffrey R. "Writing Science for Audience: A Comparison of Professional Reports and Popular Essays." Master's thesis, Colorado State University, 1995.

30. Abstract of a Dissertation or Thesis. Treat the abstract of a dissertation or thesis as you would an article in a journal (see p. 337). Add information about *Dissertation Abstracts International*.

19. Michael E. Hurley, "The Role Conflict and Academic Performance of College Student-athletes" (Ph.D. diss., University of Miami, 1993), abstract in *Dissertation Abstracts International* 54 (1993): 2067.

Hurley, Michael E. "The Role Conflict and Academic Performance of College Student-athletes." Ph.D. diss., University of Miami, 1993. Abstract in *Dissertation Abstracts International* 54 (1993): 2067.

■ Sources in Journals, Magazines, and Newspapers

Provide the following information for articles in journals, magazines, and newspapers:

- author
- title of article (in quotation marks)
- title of periodical (italicized)
- date
- pages

In notes, give the author's first name first, separate the elements by commas, and refer to a specific page or pages. In the bibliography, give the author's last name first, separate the elements by periods, and give inclusive pages.

31. Article in a Journal Paginated by Volume. Most journals number pages throughout an entire annual volume, beginning at page 1 only in the next year. Include the volume number before the year.

20. James Magee, "Crusading at the Court of Charles VI, 1388–1396," *French History* 12 (1998): 372.

Magee, James. "Crusading at the Court of Charles VI, 1388–1396." *French History* 12 (1998): 367–83.

32. Article in a Journal Paginated by Issue. If numbering begins at page 1 for each issue in a volume, indicate the issue number with the abbreviation "no." after the volume.

21. Janice Brown, "Oba Minako—Telling the Untellable," *Japan Quarterly* 45, no. 3 (1998): 53.

Brown, Janice. "Oba Minako—Telling the Untellable." *Japan Quarterly* 45, no. 3 (1998): 50–59.

33. Article in a Monthly Magazine. Magazines are cited by their dates rather than by volume and issue.

> 22. Christina Hoff Sommers, "The War against Boys," *Atlantic Monthly*, May 2000, 62.

> Sommers, Christina Hoff. "The War against Boys." *Atlantic Monthly*, May 2000, 59–74.

34. Article in a Weekly Magazine. Cite like a monthly magazine, but provide the day of publication.

> 23. Brian Thomas Gallagher, "Teaching (Native) America," *The Nation*, 5 June 2000, 37.

> Gallagher, Brian Thomas. "Teaching (Native) America." *The Nation*, 5 June 2000, 37.

35. Article in a Newspaper. If the name of the newspaper does not include the city, insert the city before the name (and italicize it). If an American city is not well known, give the state (in parentheses, abbreviated). Identify newspapers from other countries with the city in parentheses (not italicized) after the name of the newspaper.

> *Eugene (Ore.) Register-Guard*

> *Sunday Times* (London)

If a paper comes out in more than one edition, identify the edition after the date.

> 24. Francis X. Clines, "Call to Arms to Save Lincoln's Camp David," *New York Times*, 26 June 2000, National edition, A1.

> Clines, Francis X. "Call to Arms to Save Lincoln's Camp David." *New York Times*, 26 June 2000, National edition, A1, A13.

36. Unsigned Article in a Newspaper or Magazine. If no author is given, begin with the title of the article.

> 25. "Agency Issues New Rules to Protect West Coast Salmon," *Los Angeles Times*, 21 June 2000, A22.

> "Agency Issues New Rules to Protect West Coast Salmon." *Los Angeles Times*, 21 June 2000, A22.

37. Letter to the Editor. Treat as a newspaper article. If no title is provided, place "Letter to the Editor" in the title position.

26. Kevin Foskin, "Slow This Fast Track," *Fort Collins Coloradoan,* 10 November 2001, A8.

Foskin, Kevin. "Slow This Fast Track." *Fort Collins Coloradoan,* 10 November 2001, A8.

38. Review. Give the author of the review, the review title, if any, and then the words "review of" followed by the title and author of the work reviewed.

27. Roseanne Castellino, review of *Boston Confronts Jim Crow, 1890–1920,* by Mark Schneider, *Library Journal* 122 (1997): 147.

Castellino, Roseanne. Review of *Boston Confronts Jim Crow, 1890–1920,* by Mark Schneider. *Library Journal* 122 (1997): 147.

Print Reference Works

39. Entry in an Encyclopedia, Dictionary, Thesaurus, Handbook, or Almanac. In notes, provide the title of the work (italicized), the edition, the abbreviation "s.v." for (*sub verbo,* or "under the word"), and the title of the entry.

28. *Encyclopedia Americana,* international ed., s.v. "Lomond, Loch."

Chicago does not recommend including reference works such as encyclopedias or dictionaries in the bibliography.

40. Government Publication. In general, give the issuing body, then the title and any other information (such as report numbers) that would help your readers locate the source. Follow with the publication data and the page numbers if relevant. You may abbreviate "Government Printing Office" to GPO.

29. U.S. Congress, Congressional Budget Office, *Water Use Conflicts in the West: Implications of Reforming the Bureau of Reclamations' Water Supply Policies* (Washington, D.C.: GPO, 1997), 7.

U.S. Congress. Congressional Budget Office. *Water Use Conflicts in the West: Implications of Reforming the Bureau of Reclamations' Water Supply Policies.* Washington, D.C.: GPO, 1997.

■ Electronic Sources

📖 **IN THIS BOOK**
Read more about URLs on p. 38.

The *Chicago Manual of Style* provides limited instruction for citing electronic sources. The basic format presented here is adapted from the *Columbia Guide to Online Style* (see Chapter 21).

To cite online sources in notes, arrange entries as you would printed sources: note number, author, date, title, and publication data. Then add the document's online location (the URL, database, or information service where you located the document) and the date you accessed the source. Publication information should allow your readers to retrace your steps electronically to locate the source. Note that page numbers cannot be provided for most electronic sources. To list online sources in your bibliography, see the humanities-style models on pp. 353–60 in Chapter 21.

41. Basic Format for Citing an Electronic Source.

> 30. Mark Harden, "Rembrandt: Abraham and Isaac," *One Man Show: Rembrandt,* 16 Mar. 2000. http://www.artchive .com/rembrandt/abraham.html (22 Oct. 2000).

> 31. Doug Brent, "Rhetorics of the Web: Implications for Teachers of Literacy," *Kairos: A Journal for Teachers of Writing in Webbed Environments* 2.1 (1997), http://english.ttu.edu/kairos/ 2.1/features/brent/bridge.html (18 July 2000).

42. Email Message. *Chicago* recommends that personal communication not be included in the bibliography, although it can be cited in your text. Email should be treated in the same manner.

> 32. Brad B. Donahue, "Research on Cell Phone Use," personal email (6 December 1998).

■ Field Sources

43. Personal Interview. Give the location and date in a note. Do not include unpublished interviews in the bibliography.

> 33. Philip S. Bryant, interview by author, St. Peter, Minn., 29 March 1998.

44. Letter or Other Personal Communication. Do not include personal communications such as letters or phone calls in the bibliography. In a note, give the name of the person with whom you communicated, the form of communication, and the date.

> 34. Johann Floria, conversation with the author, 5 September 1999.

> 35. Marilyn Smith, letter to the author, 17 April 1997.

45. Survey. *Chicago* does not specify how to cite survey results. Cite them in your text as you would personal communication. (See p. 340.)

46. Observation Note. *Chicago* does not specify how to cite observation notes. Cite them in your text as you would personal communication. (See p. 340.)

47. Lecture or Public Address. *Chicago* does not specify how to cite lectures or public addresses. Cite them in your text as you would personal communication. (See p. 340.)

■ Media Sources

48. Film or Video Recording. Provide the title first, the names of either the director or the starring performers (with abbreviations), the length of the film, the company, the year it was filmed, and the medium (film, videocassette, DVD).

> 36. *Casablanca,* dir. Michael Curtiz, perf. Humphrey Bogart and Ingrid Bergman, 1 hr. 44 min., MGM/UA, 1942, videocassette.

> *Casablanca.* Directed by Michael Curtiz. Performed by Humphrey Bogart and Ingrid Bergman. 1 hr. 44 min. MGM/UA. Video-cassette.

49. Television Program. *Chicago* does not specify how to cite a television program. Cite as you would a video recording, identifying the medium as "television program" or "television broadcast."

50. Radio Program. *Chicago* does not specify how to cite a radio program. Cite as you would a video recording, identifying the medium as "radio program" or "radio broadcast."

51. Sound Recording. Give the composer and title of the recording, the performers and conductor, the label, and identifying number.

> 37. Gustav Mahler, *Symphony No. 10 in F sharp,* Bournemouth Symphony Orchestra, Simon Rattle, EMI Classics compact disc 7544062, 1997.

> Mahler, Gustav. *Symphony No. 10 in F sharp.* Bournemouth Symphony Orchestra, Simon Rattle. EMI Classics compact disc 7544062, 1997.

CHAPTER 20

Using CBE Style

Scientific Style and Format: The CBE Manual for Authors, Editors, and Publishers provides guidelines for citing sources in the sciences. The *CBE Manual* recommends two systems:

- a citation-sequence system, which lists sources in the reference list according to the order in which they appear in the document
- a name-year system, which is similar to the author-date system used by the APA (see Ch. 18).

This chapter describes and provides models for the citation-sequence system. For more information on CBE style, visit the Council of Science Editors Web site at **http://www.councilscienceeditors.org**. (The Council of Biology Editors changed its name to the Council of Science editors in 2000 to more accurately reflect its expanding membership.)

Note that the *Manual*, last published in 1994, provides little guidance on citing online sources. However, you can obtain information about citing sources in the sciences in Chapter 21, which presents the Columbia Online Style.

20a

How do I cite sources within the text of my document?

The CBE citation-sequence system uses sequential numbers to refer to sources within a document. These numbers, in turn, correspond to numbered entries in the reference list. This approach to citing sources reduces distraction to the reader and saves space within a document.

1. Format and Placement of the Note. Sources are cited in the citation-sequence system using superscript numbers or numbers placed in parentheses. Superscript numbers should be formatted in a font one or two points smaller than the body text:

> These results[4] suggest a need to reconfigure the device.

> These results (4) suggest a need to reconfigure the device.

2. Citing a Previously Mentioned Source. Use the first number assigned to a source when citing the source for the second time. In the following examples, the author is referring to sources earlier numbered 4, 12, and 17:

> These results[4,12,17] suggest the need for additional analysis.

> These results (4,12,17) suggest the need for additional analysis.

3. Citing a Source within a Source. When referring to a source cited in another source, use the phrase "cited in":

> The data that were originally collected[17(cited in 6)] indicate . . .

> The data that were originally collected (17 cited in 6) indicate . . .

20b

How do I prepare the references list?

ON THE WEB SITE

Use the working bibliography tool in the **Research Log** (at **http://www.bedfordresearcher.com**) to record bibliographic information for your sources. When you select the documentation style in which you are writing—MLA, APA, *Chicago*, or CBE— your bibliography will be automatically formatted.

CBE style specifies that you should create a list of works that are cited in your document or that contributed to your thinking about the document. Sources cited in your document should be identified in a section titled References. Sources that contributed to your thinking about your document should be presented in a section titled Additional References.

With two exceptions, sources cited within your document must be listed in the reference list and sources in the reference list must be referred to in your document. Personal communication, such as correspondence and interviews, is cited only in the text of your document, using the term *unreferenced* to indicate that it is not found in the reference list, as shown in the following example:

> . . . this disease has proven to be resistant to antibiotics under specific conditions (a 2000 letter from Asterson to me; unreferenced, see "Notes").

Typically, information about personal communication is placed in a Notes or Acknowledgments section. Similarly, oral presentations at conferences that are not available in any form (such as microform, reference database, conference proceedings, or online) should be cited in the text of your document but not included in your reference list.

4. Placement and Formatting. The *CBE Manual* does not specify the location of the reference list, deferring instead to the formatting guidelines of individual journals in the sciences. In general, however, the reference list usually appears at the end of print documents and linear documents that are distributed electronically (such as word processing files or newsgroup posts). In the case of longer documents or documents in which sections of a book (such as chapters) are intended to stand on their own, the reference list might appear at the end of sections or chapters. In electronic documents that use links, such as Web sites, the reference list often appears as a separate page to which other pages are linked. Figure 20.1 shows an example of a CBE-style reference list.

Figure 20.1   A Reference List in CBE Citation-Sequence Style

A The reference list is titled References.

B The reference list is double-spaced and formatted using smaller type than that used in the rest of the document. Individual references are formatted flush left.

C Note that the reference list is not alphabetical. The sources are numbered and listed in the order in which they appear in the document.

D Titles of books and periodicals are neither underlined nor italicized. All major words in the titles of periodicals are capitalized. For all other sources, only initial words of the main title and proper nouns and adjectives are capitalized.

A **REFERENCES**

B 1. Kinzey WG, editor. New world primates: ecology, evolution and behavior. New York: Aldine de Gruyter; 1997. 436 p.

2. Krashen S. Effects of phonemic awareness training on delayed tests of reading. Perceptual and Motor Skills 1999;89:79-82.

C 3. Burros F, Chen RY. Training in phonemic awareness: three case studies. Perceptual and Motor Skills 1999;89:186-202.

D 4. Snowdon CT. Is speech special? lessons from new world primates. In: Kinzey WG, editor. New world primates: ecology, evolution and behavior. New York: Aldine de Gruyter; 1997. p 75-93.

5. Tomasello M, Call J. Primate cognition. New York: Oxford Univ Pr; 1997. 517 p.

■ Books, Conference Proceedings, and Dissertations

Using the information from the title and copyright pages, provide the following four elements (the order may change depending on the source type):

- the author (last name followed by first initial(s) with no intervening punctuation)
- the title (capitalize first word only; no underline, italics, or quotation marks)
- the publication information (place, publisher, date)
- the number of pages in the book (abbreviated only as *p*)

5. One Author. Use the standard style just described.

> 1. Garrett L. The coming plague: newly emerging disease in a world out of balance. New York: Farrar, Straus, Giroux; 1994. 750 p.

6. Two or More Authors. List the authors in the order in which they appear on the title page, each of them last name first. Separate authors by commas.

> 2. Tomasello M, Call J. Primate cognition. New York: Oxford Univ Pr; 1997. 517 p.

7. Corporate or Group Author. Identify the organization as the author.

> 3. Flora of North America Editorial Committee. Flora of North America. New York: Oxford Univ Pr; 1993. 371 p.

8. Unknown Author. Identify the author as [Anonymous].

> 4. [Anonymous]. The new international atlas. Chicago: Rand McNally; 1994. 560 p.

9. Translated Book. Identify the translator after the title.

> 5. Freud S. Civilization and its discontents. Riviere J, translator. London: Hogarth; 1957. 221 p.

10. Book in an Edition Other than the First. Note the edition (for instance, "2nd ed" or "New rev ed") after the title and with a separating period.

6. Grimes R. Beginnings in ritual studies. Rev ed. Columbia (SC): Univ of South Carolina Pr; 1995. 299 p.

11. Multivolume Work. Include the total number of volumes if you are making a reference to all volumes in the work, or "volume" followed by the specific volume number followed by the title of that volume (if that volume is separately titled).

7. Massarik F, editor. Advances in organization development. Volume 1. Norwood (NJ): Ablex; 1990. 238 p.

12. Authored Book with an Editor. Identify the editor before the publication information.

8. James W. The selected letters of William James. Hardwick E, editor. Boston: NonPareil; 1980. 271 p.

13. Anthology or Collection with an Editor. To cite an anthology of essays or a collection of articles, treat the editor's name as you would an author's name. Identify with the word "editor."

9. Kinzey WG, editor. New world primates: ecology, evolution and behavior. New York: Aldine de Gruyter; 1997. 436 p.

14. Chapter in an Edited Book or a Work in an Anthology. List the author and title of the section; then include the word "In" followed by a colon, the editor's name (last name first followed by initials) and the word "editor." Include the book title, place, and publisher, and note the inclusive pages of the section rather than the number of pages in the book.

10. Snowdon CT. Is speech special? lessons from new world primates. In: Kinzey WG, editor. New world primates: ecology, evolution and behavior. New York: Aldine de Gruyter; 1997. p 75-93.

15. Foreword, Introduction, Preface, or Afterword of a Book. If the part is written by someone other than the author of the book, treat it as you would a chapter in an edited book (see above), but do not identify the author of the book as an "editor."

16. Chapter of a Book. If you wish to refer to a chapter of a book, identify the chapter of the book following the publication information. Identify the inclusive pages of the chapter.

11. Tomasello M, Call J. Primate cognition. New York: Oxford Univ Pr; 1997. Chapter 8, Social strategies and communication; p 231-72.

17. Published Proceedings of a Conference. List the editors of the proceedings as authors. Give the title of the publication and, if different, the name of the conference that produced it; date and place of the conference; publication data; and number of pages.

> 12. Wang Y, Neuendorf KKE, editors. Earthquakes: converging at Cascadia. Association of Engineering Geologists, 40th Annual Meeting; 1997 Sep 30-Oct 4; Portland, OR. Portland (OR): Department of Geology and Mineral Industries; 1997. 90 p.

18. Paper Published in the Proceedings of a Conference. Format the citation as you would a chapter in an edited book.

> 13. Zimmerman DE, Palmquist M, Muraski M. Students as WWW surfers: a brief look at students and the WWW. In: Smith J, editor. IPCC 1998, a contemporary renaissance: changing the way we communicate. Volume 2, Technical papers. Proceedings of the IEEE International Professional Communication Conference; 1998 Sep 23-25; Quebec City. Piscataway (NJ): IEEE; 1998. p 102-11.

19. Published Dissertation or Thesis. Use the general format for a book, adding the word "dissertation" or "thesis" in square brackets after the title. Treat the institution granting the degree as the publisher. Follow with the phrase "Available from" followed by a colon, followed by the *Dissertation Abstracts International* information.

> 14. Higgins JW. Tracing the vision: a study of community volunteer producers, public access cable television, and empowerment [dissertation]. Columbus (OH): Ohio State University; 1994. 212 p. Available from: University Microfilms, Ann Arbor, MI: 9517017.

20. Unpublished Dissertation or Thesis. Use the general format for a book, adding the word "dissertation" or "thesis" in square brackets as a final element of the title. Treat the institution granting the degree as the publisher.

> 15. Corney JR. Writing science for audience: a comparison of professional reports and popular essays [thesis]. Fort Collins (CO): Colorado State University; 1995. 123 p.

■ Sources in Journals, Magazines, and Newspapers

The basic information you provide for articles in journals, magazines, and newspapers includes:

- author
- title of article (not underlined, italicized, or placed in quotation marks)
- title of periodical (conventionally abbreviated)
- date
- inclusive page numbers

21. Article in a Journal Paginated by Volume. If a journal is paginated continuously through a volume, cite only the volume number and then the page numbers. A semicolon separates the year and volume number. There are no spaces between the year, volume number, and page numbers.

> 16. Phillips RL, Cummings JL, Notah G, Mullis C. Golden eagle predation on domestic calves. Wildlife Society Bull 1996;24:468-70.

22. Article in a Journal Paginated by Issue. If a journal begins each issue at page 1, include the issue number (in parentheses) directly following the volume number. As with an article in a journal paginated by volume, there are no spaces between the year, issue number, and page numbers.

> 17. Forsyth T. Technology transfer and the climate change debate. Environment 1998;40(9):16-20,39-43.

23. Article in a Weekly Journal. Provide the date (year, month, day) as well as the issue number (in parentheses after the volume number). As with an article in a journal paginated by volume, there are no spaces between the year, issue number, and page numbers.

> 18. Monastersky R. Fossil jaw tells tale of whale evolution. Science News 1998 Oct 10;154(15):229.

24. Article in a Magazine. Magazines are not identified by volume; give only the date (year, month, day).

> 19. Cohen P. No more kicks. New Scientist 2000 June 10:2-26.

25. Article in a Newspaper. Treat newspaper articles as you would magazine articles, identifying their pages by section, page, and column on which they begin.

> 20. Pollack A. New ventures aim to put farms in vanguard of drug production. New York Times, early ed. 2000 May 14;Sect 1:26(col 1).

26. Unsigned Article in a Newspaper. Format as you would an article that lists an author, using "[Anonymous]" in place of the author's name.

> 21. [Anonymous]. Energy secretary faces tough questions on Los Alamos. New York Times, natl ed. 2000 June 22;Sect A:22.

■ Print Reference Works

27. Encyclopedia, Dictionary, Thesaurus, Handbook, or Almanac. Begin with the title of the reference work and information about the edition. Identify the editor, if listed. Provide publisher and publication date.

> 22. CRC handbook of chemistry and physics. 74th ed. Boca Raton (FL): CRC Pr; 1993.

> 23. The Oxford companion to the English language. McArthur T, editor. New York: Oxford Univ Pr; 1992.

28. Map or Chart. Use area information in place of an author. Follow with the title, place of publication and publisher, and a physical description. If the map is part of a larger document, such as an atlas, provide publication information for the document.

> 24. Middle East, North Africa. The Middle East and North Africa. Washington (DC): AMIDEAST; 1991. 1 sheet.

> 25. Greece. Greece and the Aegean. In: National Geographic atlas of the world. Rev 6th ed. Washington (DC): National Geographic Soc; 1992. p 65-66.

29. Pamphlet. Format entries as you would for a book (see p. 346).

■ Electronic Sources

CBE style does not provide guidelines for many electronic sources. The following entries are all the guidelines cover. For additional information, consult the guidelines for APA style (Chapter 18) or Columbia Online Style (Chapter 21).

30. Electronic Book. Cite an electronic book as you would a print book, adding the following information.

- medium, in square brackets following the title
- name of organization that has posted the book

- notification that the electronic version has been revised or updated, if appropriate, in square brackets just before the access information
- access date

> 26. McLeod SH, Soven M, editors. Writing across the curriculum: a guide to developing programs [World Wide Web]. Fort Collins (CO): The WAC Clearinghouse; 2000. Available from: http://wac .colostate.edu/books/mcleod_soven/. Accessed 2002 July 20.

31. Electronic Journal Article. Cite electronic journals as you do print journals, giving the medium and adding the URL and access date to the end.

IN THIS BOOK Read more about URLs on p. 38.

> 27. Barber JF. All watched over by machines of loving grace: promoting cybernetic ecology in writing classrooms [World Wide Web]. The WAC Clearinghouse, 2000. Available from: http://wac.colostate.edu/articles/barber2000/bridge.html. Accessed 2002 July 18.

32. Computer Software. If no author is identified, place the title in the first position in the reference.

> 28. Reference Manager Professional Edition [computer program]. Version 9.5. Berkeley (CA): ISI ResearchSoft; 2000.

■ Media Sources

33. Film or Video Recording. Place the title in the first field with the type of medium identified in brackets, followed by individuals listed as authors, editors, performers, conductors, and so on. Identify the producer if different from the publisher. Provide publication information.

> 29. Hamlet [videotape]. Zeffirelli F, director. Burbank (CA): Warner Bros; 1990.

34. Television Program. CBE style does not provide guidance on citing television programs. Cite as you would cite a film or video recording.

35. Radio Program. CBE style does not provide guidance on citing radio programs. Cite as you would cite a film or video recording.

36. Sound Recording. Cite as you would a film or video recording.

■ Field Sources

37. Personal Interview. Treat unpublished interviews as personal communication (p. 344). Cite them in the text only; do not cite them in the reference list.

38. Personal Letter. Cite personal letters as personal communication (p. 344). Cite them in the text only; do not cite them in the reference list.

39. Lecture or Public Address. Like an unpublished paper presented at a meeting, lectures or public addresses are treated as personal communication (p. 344).

CHAPTER 21

Using Columbia Online Style

The guidelines presented in this chapter are taken from *The Columbia Guide to Online Style* by Janice R. Walker and Todd Taylor. Columbia Online Style (COS) was designed specifically for researchers faced with the challenge of citing electronic sources. COS is not a substitute for other major documentation systems (MLA and *Chicago* style in the humanities; APA style in the social sciences; and CBE style in the sciences); instead, it complements each of these styles by being adaptable. This chapter presents two models for each source type: an author-page style that you can use in humanities documents and an author-date style that you can use in scientific documents. To see COS adapted to the *Chicago*-style footnote/endnote system, see Chapter 19. Information about Columbia Online Style is available on the Web at **http://www.columbia.edu/cu/cup/cgos/idx_basic.html**.

Like all of the major documentation styles, COS requires writers to include in-text citations as well as a list of works cited or references at the end of the document.

21a

How do I cite sources within the text of my document?

Humanities guidelines require research writers to acknowledge within their text the author of source material and the page on which the information was found. Scientific guidelines require that in-text references include an author's name and date of publication. The following examples—both for humanities and for scientific documents—illustrate the most common ways of citing electronic sources within the text of your document in COS style. (The humanities examples that follow are adapted from the MLA-style author-page in-text citation system. See Chapter 19 if you are using the *Chicago Manual of Style* footnote/endnote system.)

1. Basic Format for an In-text Citation. For a humanities document (**Hum**), include the author's name in parentheses following the source. Since most electronic documents have no page numbers, you will not include one in the citation. For scientific documents (**Sci**), include the name and date.

> **Hum**
>
> According to consumer trend analysts, "robust e-commerce activity has proven no replacement for the idle foot traffic at America's shopping malls" (Rigazio).

> **Sci**
>
> According to consumer trend analysts, "robust e-commerce activity has proven no replacement for the idle foot traffic at America's shopping malls" (Rigazio, 2001).

2. Author Named in the Sentence. If you name the author within your sentence, include the date of publication in parentheses following the name for scientific documents. For humanities documents, give no additional parenthetical information.

Hum

Williamson notes that the benefits of yoga are psychological as well as physical.

Sci

Williamson (2000) notes that the benefits of yoga are psychological as well as physical.

3. Unknown Author. If you cannot identify the author or creator of an electronic document, include a brief version of the title in parentheses. Use italics for book titles and quotation marks for journal titles.

Hum

A recent study revealed that "nearly 8 out of 10 American children have had a violent encounter at school by the time they reach seventh grade" ("Bullies").

Sci

A recent study revealed that "nearly 8 out of 10 American children have had a violent encounter at school by the time they reach seventh grade" ("Bullies," 1999).

4. Unknown Publication Date. If you are writing a scientific document and cannot identify the date of publication or latest update for an electronic source, use the date you accessed the source.

Griffin and Reid (9 July 2000) have argued for increased federal funding for stem cell research.

5. Section, Chapter, or Paragraph within a Document. If an electronic document contains numbered subsections, list the numbers at the end of the citation.

Hum

Because Columbia Online Style was compiled by two experts, it's more detailed than the mainstream systems and the advice is better for citing Internet sources (Carbone, sec. 4).

Sci

Because Columbia Online Style was compiled by two experts, it's more detailed than the mainstream systems and the advice is better for citing Internet sources (Carbone, 2001, sec. 4).

21b

How do I prepare the list of works cited or references?

If you are writing a print document, begin the list of works cited (humanities style) or list of references (scientific style) on a new page. If you are creating a Web site or other electronic document, your list of works cited or references may be a separate file to which readers may link directly from the in-text citations. Publication information should allow your readers to retrace your steps electronically to locate the source. Note that page numbers cannot be provided for most electronic sources.

6. Basic Format for an Entry in the List of Works Cited or References. To cite online sources in a humanities style document (**Hum**), include as much of the following information as available.

- Author's last name and first name
- Title of document (followed by title of complete work, in italics, if any)
- Version or file number, if any
- Date (if different from date accessed)
- URL or online location
- Date accessed

> Gandi, Sunil. "Benefits of Yoga for Hypertension." 14 May 2001. http://tn.essortment.com/hypertensionyo_rmlz.htm (21 Dec. 2001).

To cite online sources in a scientific style document (**Sci**), include as much of the following information as available.

- Author's last name and initials
- Date (if different from date accessed)
- Title of document (followed by title of complete work, in italics, if any)
- Version or file number, if any
- URL or online location
- Date accessed

> Gandi, S. (2001, May 14). Benefits of yoga for hypertension. http://tn.essortment.com/hypertensionyo_rmlz.htm (21 Dec. 2001).

7. World Wide Web Site. Provide publication information followed by the URL and the access date. Do not place a period after the URL.

Hum

Harden, Mark. "Rembrandt: Abraham and Isaac." *One Man Show: Rembrandt.* 16 Mar. 2000. http://www.artchive.com/ rembrandt/abraham.html (22 Oct. 2000).

Sci

Harden, M. (2000, March 16) Rembrandt: Abraham and Isaac. *One man show: Rembrandt.* http://www.artchive.com/rembrandt/ abraham.html (22 Oct. 2000).

8. Article in an Online Periodical. Provide publication information followed by the URL and the access date. Do not place a period after the URL. Since the article was first published online, it is unlikely to have page numbers.

Hum

Brent, Doug. "Rhetorics of the Web: Implications for Teachers of Literacy." *Kairos: A Journal for Teachers of Writing in Webbed Environments* 2:1(1997). http://english.ttu.edu/kairos/ 2.1/features/brent/bridge.html (18 July 2000).

Sci

Brent, D. (1997). Rhetorics of the Web: Implications for teachers of literacy. *Kairos: A Journal for Teachers of Writing in Webbed Environments, 2*(1). http://english.ttu.edu/kairos/2.1/ features/brent/bridge.html (18 July 2000).

9. Article Originally Published in Print and Obtained Online. Provide publication information followed by the URL and the access date. Do not place a period after the URL.

Hum

Amato, Joe. "Science-Literature Inquiry as Pedagogical Practice: Technical Writing, Hypertext, and a Few Theories, Part I." *Computers and Composition* 9:2(1992): 41-54. http:// www.cwrl.utexas.edu/~ccjrnl/Archives/v9/9_2_html/ 9_2_3_Amato.html (18 July 2000).

Sci

> Amato, J. (1992). Science-literature inquiry as pedagogical prac-
> tice: Technical writing, hypertext, and a few theories, part I.
> *Computers and Composition, 9*(2), 41-54. http://www.cwrl
> .utexas.edu/~ccjrnl/Archives/v9/9_2_html/9_2_3_Amato
> .html (18 July 2000).

10. Email Message. For humanities papers, include the words "personal email" and the date after the author and subject line.

> Donahue, Brad. "Writing Center Upgrades." Personal email (6 Dec.
> 2001).

Personal communication, such as email, is not included in the list of
references in scientific style documents.

11. Message Posted to a Newsgroup or Online Discussion List. List
the author's name or electronic alias followed by either the subject line
of the post and then the date (humanities) or the date on which the
message was posted and then the subject (scientific). Then list the
name of the forum (if any), the online address, and the date of access.

Hum

> Lorhan, Rachel. "Re: darkness." 16 June 2000.
> news://news.colostate.edu/alt.angst (8 Oct. 2001).

Sci

> Lorhan, R. (2000, June 16). Re: darkness.
> news://news.colostate.edu/alt.angst (8 Oct. 2001).

12. Source Obtained through Telnet, FTP, or Gopher. Cite these
sources as you would a Web site (see p. 357).

Hum

> Marks, Kyle T. "More Oedipal Theory." 13 Jan. 2000.
> telnet://hamlet.psu.edu/oed.txt (18 July 2000).

Sci

> Marks, K. T. (2000, January 13). More oedipal theory.
> telnet://hamlet.psu.edu/oed.txt (18 July 2000).

13. Source from an Information Service or Database. Provide the
standard publication information for a publication found in a data-

base or online service, followed by the specific database in which the information was found, the name of the information service or company, and the URL at which the service or database can be found. Follow this with the access date.

Hum

Grower, Thomas. "Healthy Man: Chemicals Good for Your Lawn
Could Be Bad for You." *Los Angeles Times* 10 July 2000: S1.
Academic Universe. Lexis-Nexis. http://web.lexis-nexis
.com/universe (18 July 2000).

Sci

Grower, T. (2000). Healthy man: Chemicals good for your lawn
could be bad for you (*Los Angeles Times,* 10 July 2000,
p. S1). *Academic Universe. Lexis-Nexis.* http://web.lexis-
nexis.com/universe (18 July 2000).

Note: If you are referring to an abstract in a database, indicate that it is an abstract by including the word "Abstract" in square brackets following the title of the source.

14. Information from a Database Accessed through CD-ROM. Use the same structure for a source obtained through a database or online information service.

Hum

DuVerlie, Claud A. "Satellite-Assisted Instruction for Foreign Languages: An Emerging Model in French." *ADFL-Bulletin:* 19:3
(1988): 28-31. *MLA International Bibliography.* SilverPlatter.
(16 Feb. 2002)

Sci

DuVerlie, C. A. (1988). Satellite-assisted instruction for foreign
languages: An emerging model in French. *ADFL-Bulletin,*
19(3), 28-31. *MLA International Bibliography.* SilverPlatter.
(16 Feb. 2002)

15. Computer Software. If an individual has rights to the program, software, or language, name him or her as the author; otherwise, begin the entry with the name of the program. The organization that produces the software is treated as the publisher. If you're referring to a specific version that isn't included in the name, put this information last.

Hum

Microsoft Office XP Professional. Redmond, WA: Microsoft Corporation, 2001.

Reference Manager Professional Edition. Vers. 9.5. Berkeley, CA: ISI ResearchSoft, 2000.

Sci

Microsoft office XP professional. (2001). Redmond, WA: Microsoft Corporation.

Reference manager professional edition. (Version 9.5). (2000). Berkeley, CA: ISI ResearchSoft.

APPENDIX A

Three Sample Research Projects

This appendix presents three student research projects. To read interviews with the writers about their research and writing processes and to see early versions of these project documents, visit the Featured Writers area of the *Bedford Researcher* Web site at **http://www.bedfordresearcher.com,** where you can also read five additional student research project documents.

MLA-style Research Essay

Alberter   1

Heading includes writer's name, instructor's name, course, and date.

Jenna Alberter
Professor Coronel
AR414
27 April 2000

Images of Women in Seventeenth-Century
Dutch Art and Literature

Title is centered, and essay is double-spaced with one-inch margins.

Artists and their artwork do not exist in a vacuum. The images artists create help shape and in turn are shaped by the society and culture in which they are created. The artists and artworks in the Dutch Baroque period are no exception. In this seventeenth-century society of merchants and workers, people of all classes purchased art to display in their homes. As a result, artists in the period catered to the wishes of the people, producing art that depicted the everyday world (Kleiner and Tansey 864). It is too simplistic, however, to assume that this relationship was unidirectional. Dutch Baroque genre paintings did not simply reflect the reality surrounding them; they also helped to shape that reality. For instance, members of seventeenth-century Dutch society had very specific ideas regarding the roles of women. These ideas, which permeated every level of society, are represented in the literature and visual art of the period (Franits, Paragons 17).

MLA style in-text citations include author(s) of source and page number.

Thesis states Jenna Alberter's main point.

During the seventeenth century, the concept of domesticity appears to have been very important in all levels of Dutch society; literally hundreds of surviving paintings reflect this theme. Such paintings depict members of every class and occupation, and according to Wayne Franits, a specialist in seventeenth-century Dutch art, they served the dual purpose of both entertaining and instructing the viewer. They invite the viewer to inspect and enjoy their vivid details, but also to contemplate the values and ideals they represent (Franits, "Domesticity" 13).

Jenna includes a brief title to distinguish two sources by the same author.

Images of domesticity in the visual arts grew immensely in popularity around the middle of the seventeenth century. Although there is no definitive explanation for this rise in popularity, there is a long history in Dutch art and literature of focusing on domestic themes. In the early sixteenth century, Protestant reformers and humanists wrote books and treatises on domestic issues. Their main focus was the roles and responsibilities of members of the family, especially the women. This type of literature continued to be produced, and flourished, in the first half of the seventeenth century (Franits, "Domesticity" 13).

Perhaps the most well-known and influential work of literature of this type is Jacob Cats's book Houwelyck, or Marriage. Published in

Summary of Jacob Cats's book Houwelyck. Because she learned about Houwelyck in Wayne Franits's book Paragons of Virtue, Jenna cites Franits as the source. Houwelyck is also discussed in Mariët Westermann's book A Worldly Art.

Alberter   2

1625, this was a comprehensive reference book for women of all ages, but especially young women, regarding matters of marriage and family. Although many other similar books were being published in the Nether-lands and England during this period, Cats's work was perhaps the most extensive; it even contained an alphabetical index for quick reference (Franits, Paragons 5).

Houwelyck, which by mid-century had sold over 50,000 copies, making it a best-seller for its time, contained instruction for women on the proper behavior for the six stages of life: Maiden, Sweetheart, Bride, Housewife, Mother, and Widow. It is particularly telling that these stages of life were defined in reference to the roles of men. Although Cats's book specifically addressed women, it had implications for men as well (Westermann 119). According to Cats, by laying out the roles and duties of the woman, his book "encompasses also the mascu-line counter-duties" (qtd. in Westermann 119).

Cats's six stages of life are used as the organizing principle for the research essay.

Jenna cites an indirect source: words quoted in another source.

The illustration on the title page of the first edition of Cats's work shows what was considered the ideal role for a woman at this time. Created by Adriaen van de Venne, Stages of Life (Fig. 1) depicts several figural groups arranged on a hill. It shows life as a large hill, with marriage as its pinnacle, and then heading down toward widow-hood and death (Westermann 120). This depiction seems to reflect the expectations society held for its women--that a woman's goal in life should be to provide a man with a good, proper wife and, once that duty has been fulfilled, to wait dutifully for death.

Reference to an illustration found later in the text.

Images of young women are numerous in the visual art of this period. Gerard Dou's Portrait of a Young Woman (Fig. 2) exemplifies this

Fig. 1 **Pieter de Jode after Adriaen van de Venne, *Stages of Life*, engraved frontispiece to Jacob Cats's Hou-welyck (Marriage), 1625, private collection (Westermann 120).**

Illustration cap-tion includes fig-ure number and source informa-tion.

type of work. This painting demonstrates that portraiture was highly influenced by contemporary ideals of feminine virtue. The young woman's pose is passive, self-contained, and somewhat rigid, communicating her dignity, humility, and modesty, which were all considered very important in a young girl. She holds a songbook in her lap, which not only indicated her skill in the arts but was also considered a symbol of docility. Near her rest two additional books, one of which is a Bible. Besides the obvious reference to the importance of piety, these items also were indicative of the practical value of literacy. Young women were brought up with the sole purpose of becoming wives and mothers, and the ability to read was crucial for the management of an efficient household (Franits, Paragons 19).

Effective transition between paragraphs creates coherence.

Another common element in images of young women is needlework, such as in Nicolaes Maes' Young Girl Sewing. This theme was meant to represent ideals of docility, domesticity, and diligence, all highly prized virtues in future wives. In addition, proper training of young women was considered very important, and activities such as sewing and lace making were thought to prevent laziness and prepare young women for their future as wives and mothers (Franits, Paragons 21). According to scholar Mariët Westermann, women would also sometimes sell their cloth, yarn, and lace to bring extra income into the households. Occasionally, women who sold their goods would form guilds of workers, although this was rare in the male-dominated guild system of the time (125).

Jenna names the author of the source in her text sentence. She cites her source even when paraphrasing the author's words.

The young women in such pieces are beautifully rendered. Elegant and refined, they are obviously of the middle or upper classes; their clothes are made of expensive, luxurious cloth and their beautiful,

Fig. 2   Gerard Dou, Portrait of a Young Woman, oil on panel, date unknown, private collection (Franits 20).

Alberter   4

braided hair is laced with shiny, smooth ribbon. Their skin looks like porcelain, smooth and clear. While these images were designed and painted to look very realistic, it is important to remember that, like the literature of the time, they represented an ideal, not necessarily the reality. In Paragons of Virtue, art historian Wayne Franits calls attention to this distinction between the ideal and the real, noting, "[Both] art and literature present an exemplary image, a topos that does not necessarily reflect the actual situation of young women in seventeenth-century Dutch culture" (25).

Brackets indicate a modified quotation.

   In the large number of paintings depicting young women, probably commissioned by their parents, another popular theme is that of courtship. These works, such as Jacob van Loo's Wooing, are often an appreciation or celebration of love and romance but also serve to instruct about expected and appropriate behavior of young women in such situations.

   Contemporary literature of this period also concerns courtship. In Houwelyck, for example, Cats discusses the "rules" and etiquette of courtship as well as the virtues a young woman should possess in order to acquire a good husband (Franits, Paragons 18). Cats argues that women should show only limited initiative in the relationship; for the most part, they should follow the lead of the suitor. Women should meet with suitors only in the safe confines of their own homes, under the watchful eye of their parents. They should avoid the use of very showy clothing or jewelry to attract men; instead, they should utilize the "jewels" of humility, modesty, piety, and so forth. And of course, the decision regarding the choice of spouse is ultimately left to the parents (Franits, Paragons 34).

   Jan Soet's work Maagden-Baak, or Maiden's Beacon, published in 1642, deals with the courtship theme in even greater detail than Cats's book. The frontispiece to Soet's book depicts several young women standing on the shore, where they have been watching a ship coming into harbor. They have turned to look at a veiled figure, thought to be an allegory for Chastity. The metaphor is that women, like the ship in the drawing, must endure the storms and dangers of courtship before they can enter the secure harbor of marriage. To accomplish this, women must have the guidance of a beacon, in this case Soet's book (Franits, Paragons 33).

Transitional sentence carries readers from one idea to the next.

   Once the maiden navigated the perilous seas of courtship, she could enter into the safety and security of marriage and motherhood, where she found for herself a very rigid, prescribed role. The marriage portraiture of Johannes Verspronck illuminates the status of men and women in their roles in marriage. In Portrait of a Man and Portrait of a Woman (Figs. 3 and 4), Verspronck provides visual cues to the

Alberter   5

Fig. 3   Johannes Verspronck,
Portrait of a Man, oil on canvas,
1641, Rijksmuseum Twenthe,
Enschede (Westermann 132).

Fig. 4   Johannes Verspronck,
Portrait of a Woman, oil on
canvas, 1640, Rijksmuseum
Twenthe, Enschede (Westermann 132).

differences between the roles of husband and wife. The separate portraits are meant to hang side by side, the partners turned toward each
other. Though nearly identical composition may suggest equality, the
woman's pose is conservative and self-contained, while the man's is
bold and engaging. He has pulled off his glove, as if preparing to greet
the viewer; in contrast, the woman waits, quietly and expectantly, to
be approached. In the same way, shadows play on the man's face, creating depth, while the woman's face is smoothed by soft, direct light.
Such visual cues reinforce the social and cultural norms and expectations of husbands and wives (Westermann 133).

　　Both men and women had prescribed roles and responsibilities in
the home and community. The workplace, usually separate from the
home, was generally the domain of the husband, especially in upper-
and middle-class families. Women, in contrast, spent most of their time
in the private, domestic space of the home. A wife's main duties were
to help her husband, care for the children, run the household, and
supervise the servants (Franits, Paragons 64).

Two well-known Dutch Baroque painters, Johannes Vermeer and Pieter de Hooch, specialized in painting scenes from everyday life (Russell). Much of their work depicts the interiors of typical middle- and upper-class Dutch homes as quiet, serene, orderly domestic spaces. De Hooch's Woman and Child in an Interior reflects such a space, where the woman is adept at her role as wife and mother and runs the household efficiently. In these works, the man is often absent, as the home is not considered his domain (Alpers 95). Westermann describes the work of Vermeer and de Hooch in this way: "Their paintings invite contemplation of domestic virtue, of the quiet and harmonious household prescribed by Cats and others" (124).

These pervasive ideas about gender status and roles were reinforced by theological views of the time. Protestant and humanist philosophers wrote extensively about domestic life, outlining specific roles and duties for each member of the family, focusing much of their attention on the wife and mother. Marriage was considered to be a natural and honorable state instituted by God; the primary goal was companionship, not procreation. (Indeed, children were often viewed as the inevitable danger of married life, rather than its purpose.) Wives, like Eve, were meant to act as helpmates for their husbands. In short, marriage was "viewed as a covenantal alliance between spouses who agreed to fulfill particular obligations appropriate to their sex" (Franits, Paragons 66-67).

A surprisingly large number of Dutch Baroque paintings depict images of the elderly, especially as compared with work in other European countries at the time. Dutch authors of the Baroque period also often explored themes of aging and widowhood. The final chapter in Cats's Houwelyck discusses these topics at length and in a very sensitive and moving manner. The chapter is divided into two sections. The first focuses on issues of the fleeting nature of human existence and the need for the elderly to turn away from worldly matters and toward the spiritual realm; the second section provides practical advice and instruction for widows regarding their roles and behavior (Franits, Paragons 161). Many authors, including Cats, argued that growing older and deteriorating physically could have positive consequences as well. They believed that aging forced elderly people to turn their minds to death and the afterlife. Older people were thought to possess prized virtues such as moderation and simplicity and therefore would be favored by God and looked upon with compassion. Because of this spiritual wisdom, it was thought that aging allowed a person to contemplate death without fear (Franits, Paragons 163-64).

Artists dealt with this idea of spirituality perhaps with even greater frequency than authors. Gerard Dou's Old Woman Saying Grace

Alberter   7

(Fig. 5) is one of many paintings of the time depicting this theme. Dou's subject is rendered with little individuality; rather, she is meant to represent an ideal, an image of appropriate conduct for a widow or elderly woman. Her heavy garments and pious disposition are typical of this type of painting. Dou also included several symbolic elements that seventeenth-century viewers would have immediately understood: the spinning wheel and sewing basket representing domestic virtue and the burned-out candle signifying the transitory nature of life (Franits, Paragons 171).

Widows of this time were expected to do more than live simple, pious lives. Authors, philosophers, and artists of the time also encouraged elderly women to be virtuous role models for young women and girls. Artists such as Gerard ter Borch were known to place young and elderly women side by side. Such works probably served to instruct older women to act as guides and teachers to their younger family members.

Because of their faithful depiction of the world and their painstaking attention to detail, seventeenth-century Dutch paintings of domestic scenes can be called realistic. However, it is important to remember that these images do not always simply depict the people and their world exactly as they were. Instead, these works served multiple purposes—to spread and promote ideas about domestic virtue, to instruct viewers about women's roles, and, finally, to entertain viewers (Franits, Paragons 9). Just as in the art of every culture in history, the art of the Dutch Baroque period was both a mirror of the world in which it was created and a shaper of that world.

Conclusion reinforces Jenna's thesis statement.

Fig. 5   Gerard Dou, Old Woman Saying Grace, oil on panel, date unknown, Alta Pinakothek, Munich (Franits, Paragons 171).

Alberter 8

WORKS CITED

Alpers, Svetlana. "De Hooch: A View with a Room." Art in America 86.6 (1999): 92-99.

Franits, Wayne E. "Domesticity, Privacy, Civility, and the Transformation of Adriaen van Ostade's Art." Images of Women in Seventeenth-Century Dutch Art: Domesticity and the Representation of the Peasant. Ed. Patricia Phagan. Athens: U of Georgia P, 1996. 3-25.

---. Paragons of Virtue: Women and Domesticity in Seventeenth-Century Dutch Art. Cambridge: Cambridge UP, 1993.

Kleiner, Fred S., and Richard G. Tansey. Gardner's Art through the Ages. 10th ed. New York: Harcourt, 1996.

Russell, Lynn P. "Johannes Vermeer: Legacy of Light." Natl. Gallery of Art. 18 Apr. 2000 <http://www.nga.gov/education/schoolarts/vermeer.htm>.

Westermann, Mariët. A Worldly Art: The Dutch Republic 1585-1718. London: Calmann, 1996.

Heading, "Works Cited," is centered.

Three hyphens indicate that a source was written by the author of the previously cited source.

First line of each entry is flush with left margin; additional lines are indented one-half inch, or five spaces.

List is double-spaced and alphabetized by authors' last names.

Titles of publications are underlined.

Since there was no indication of when the Web site was created, Jenna provides only the date of access.

APA-style Research Web Site

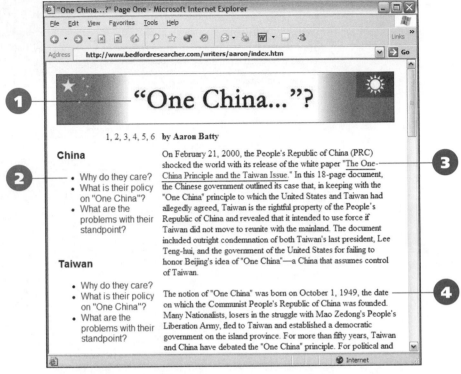

1 Title is centered.

2 Aaron provides a navigation menu that functions as a guide to the organization of his Web site. He placed this menu on every page except the References page.

3 Aaron built links into his Web site to make it easier for readers to visit source documents on the Web.

4 Presentation of historical background provides a context for Aaron's discussion.

5 Because the author (Borthwick) is not named in a signal phrase, his name and the date appear in parentheses, along with the page number.

6 Name and date are given for a lecture or other public discussion.

7 Aaron provides a navigation footer, corresponding to each of the six main pages on the site, and a "Next" link to carry readers to subsequent pages.

8 List of references is a separate page on the site. Heading is centered.

9 List is alphabetized by author's name, or by title in the case of Web sources that list no author.

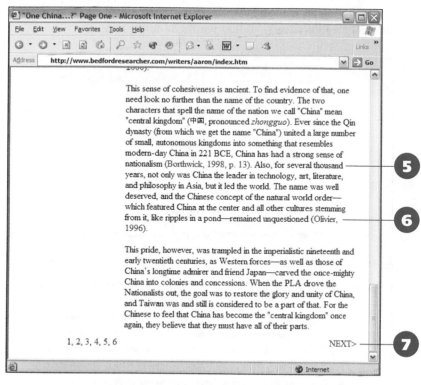

"One China...?" Page One - Microsoft Internet Explorer

File Edit View Favorites Tools Help

Address http://www.bedfordresearcher.com/writers/aaron/index.htm Go

This sense of cohesiveness is ancient. To find evidence of that, one need look no further than the name of the country. The two characters that spell the name of the nation we call "China" mean "central kingdom" (中国, pronounced *zhongguo*). Ever since the Qin dynasty (from which we get the name "China") united a large number of small, autonomous kingdoms into something that resembles modern-day China in 221 BCE, China has had a strong sense of nationalism (Borthwick, 1998, p. 13). Also, for several thousand years, not only was China the leader in technology, art, literature, and philosophy in Asia, but it led the world. The name was well deserved, and the Chinese concept of the natural world order— which featured China at the center and all other cultures stemming from it, like ripples in a pond—remained unquestioned (Olivier, 1996).

This pride, however, was trampled in the imperialistic nineteenth and early twentieth centuries, as Western forces—as well as those of China's longtime admirer and friend Japan—carved the once-mighty China into colonies and concessions. When the PLA drove the Nationalists out, the goal was to restore the glory and unity of China, and Taiwan was and still is considered to be a part of that. For the Chinese to feel that China has become the "central kingdom" once again, they believe that they must have all of their parts.

1, 2, 3, 4, 5, 6   NEXT>

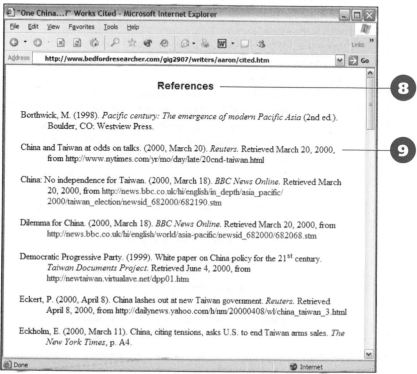

"One China...?" Works Cited - Microsoft Internet Explorer

File Edit View Favorites Tools Help

Address http://www.bedfordresearcher.com/gig2907/writers/aaron/cited.htm Go

References

Borthwick, M. (1998). *Pacific century: The emergence of modern Pacific Asia* (2nd ed.). Boulder, CO: Westview Press.

China and Taiwan at odds on talks. (2000, March 20). *Reuters*. Retrieved March 20, 2000, from http://www.nytimes.com/yr/mo/day/late/20cnd-taiwan.html

China: No independence for Taiwan. (2000, March 18). *BBC News Online*. Retrieved March 20, 2000, from http://news.bbc.co.uk/hi/english/in_depth/asia_pacific/2000/taiwan_election/newsid_682000/682190.stm

Dilemma for China. (2000, March 18). *BBC News Online*. Retrieved March 20, 2000, from http://news.bbc.co.uk/hi/english/world/asia-pacific/newsid_682000/682068.stm

Democratic Progressive Party. (1999). White paper on China policy for the 21st century. *Taiwan Documents Project*. Retrieved June 4, 2000, from http://newtaiwan.virtualave.net/dpp01.htm

Eckert, P. (2000, April 8). China lashes out at new Taiwan government. *Reuters*. Retrieved April 8, 2000, from http://dailynews.yahoo.com/h/nm/20000408/wl/china_taiwan_3.html

Eckholm, E. (2000, March 11). China, citing tensions, asks U.S. to end Taiwan arms sales. *The New York Times*, p. A4.

Done   Internet

If Aaron Batty were submitting a traditional research essay, his title page and first page of text would look like this:

Title and page number appear at the top of each page.

One China...?   1

One China...?

Aaron Batty

C0200

Professor Palmquist

April 28, 2000

Title page includes full title, writer's name, course, instructor's name, and date.

One China...?   2

One China...?

On February 21, 2000, the People's Republic of China (PRC) shocked the world with its release of the white paper "The One-China Principle and the Taiwan Issue." In this 18-page document, the Chinese government outlined its case that, in keeping with the "One China" principle to which the United States and Taiwan had allegedly agreed, Taiwan is the rightful property of the People's Republic of China and revealed that it intended to use force if Taiwan did not move to reunite with the mainland. The document included outright condemnation of both Taiwan's last president, Lee Teng-hui, and the government of the United States for failing to honor Beijing's idea of "One China"--a China that assumes control of Taiwan.

The notion of "One China" was born on October 1, 1949, the date on which the Communist People's Republic of China was founded. Many Nationalists, losers in the struggle with Mao Zedong's People's Liberation Army, fled to Taiwan and established a democratic government on the island province. For more than fifty years, Taiwan and China have debated the "One China" principle. For political and economic reasons, the United States has been involved in the debate as well. All three want to find a common answer to the question, Is there really only "one China," and is Taiwan a part of it? As we venture into the 21st century, with its quickly developing world economy and global culture, the final definition of "One China" will shape the course of not only the Asia-Pacific region but the whole world.

Aaron's thesis statement identifies the main point of his discussion.

What China Gains from Reunification

The Chinese, with the most to gain from reunification, are driving the debate. China stands to make three primary gains if Taiwan is incorporated into the PRC. The first of these is money. When the Nationalists fled to Taiwan, they

Headings throughout, centered, help readers follow the document's organization.

Chicago-style Research Essay

Title of essay. ──────────────────── The Impact of Senate Bill 186

Writer's name. ──────────────────── Rianne Uilk

Title of course,
instructor's name, ──────────────────── C0150 Sec130
and date.   Professor Barribeau
                                         28 April 2000

Uilk   1

For as long as the United States has had an organized public school system, students have been assessed and given grades based on the skills and knowledge they demonstrate to their teachers. When assigning grades to students, American teachers have always acknowledged that each student is unique. They therefore take into consideration any special circumstances related to the student's educational experience--such as a nonnative English background, a particular learning disability, or a special artistic talent--that cannot always be measured in terms of grades and test scores. But what if teachers were forced to grade every student based on a set of strict guide-lines, making no exceptions at all for special student situations? What if all schools were themselves graded on student academic performance, regardless of whether they were impoverished inner-city schools or wealthy suburban schools? How would this affect the students and the way in which they were taught? What would it do to student self-esteem and teacher motivation? These are the questions facing Colorado teachers as their districts move to implement the new Senate Bill 186. Despite its few merits, this bill, which became Colorado state law on April 10, 2000, will actually hurt the educa-tional welfare of the very students it is intended to help.

Thesis states Rianne Uilk's main point.

Colorado Senate Bill 186 mandates that every public school be assessed, or tested, and given two grades: one based on test scores in read-ing, writing, and arithmetic, and one based on safety.[1] Schools that receive an academic performance grade of A will be awarded more grant money for their schools. They will also be required to vote on whether to become "charter schools"--semiautonomous schools operated by a group of people (including parents, teachers, and community members) that make their own decisions about what, how, and whom to teach. Meanwhile, schools that receive an academic performance grade of F will be without needed funding and will be forced to become charter schools if their grades do not improve within three years, and schools that receive a D will be subject to inter-vention by the state. As many as 30 percent of Colorado public schools will be forced to change in some way after the first year of the bill's implemen-tation.

Summary of a source is cited with an endnote.

Senate Bill 186 was the brainchild of Colorado Governor Bill Owens as part of his "Putting Children First" agenda, which includes expanding stan-dardized testing, grading schools based on performance, and initiating a "Read to Achieve" program to improve elementary school literacy.[2] With Sen-ate Bill 186, Owens, who has made education his number one priority, claims he hopes to wake up the state--in particular, school administrators and par-ents--and call attention to the problems within Colorado's education system. Owens and other supporters of the bill argue that students' grades have shown little improvement, and in fact have slid in recent years, and that school administrators are to blame. Owens asserts: "I'm not willing to let the present system continue on its inexorable road to mediocrity."[3]

Direct quotation is cited with an endnote.

Uilk   2

In essence, the bill claims that the many different teaching practices and alternative curriculum initiatives among school districts throughout the state make it increasingly difficult to measure whether there is a "thorough and uniform system of schools" in the state. It also claims that most parents find it difficult to determine whether public schools are providing "quality academic instruction in an environment that is conducive to learning." Thus, the bill requires that the department of education compile "objective indicators" of public schools' academic performance and make these compilations readily available. Such report cards, the bill's drafters claim, will assist parents and taxpayers in making choices that will enable all children to have an opportunity for a quality education. These report cards will also help parents and taxpayers monitor the progress schools are making toward providing students with an opportunity for a quality education in "a safe learning environment."[4]

All of the partial quotations in the paragraph come from a single source, which is cited at the end of the paragraph.

While Governor Owens may have awakened parents and administrators with his bill, critics--myself included--argue that the bill is prejudiced and discriminatory and will only segregate schools, subjecting some schools and their students to ridicule. Ultimately, the bill will reward schools in affluent areas and punish those in poorer parts of the state--those schools that need resources the most. Indeed, the bill does not seek to change the circumstances that produced the problem of students who are poor learners; instead, it merely assesses the schools' academic performance and then punishes or rewards the schools based on these grades. How exactly this is supposed to help such already challenged students as second-language learners and students in low-income schools is unclear.

First, Senate Bill 186 is prejudiced toward children who are not native English speakers. As many teachers will attest, children who do not speak English as their first language generally do not perform as well on standardized tests as do native English speakers. The standardized tests are given in English, and translated versions are not available to students whose native language is not English. If children can't understand the test they are taking, they cannot reasonably be expected to perform at their best. And when those students do poorly on these tests, their scores affect the entire school's average. According to Patty Smith, a Colorado public school teacher,

The phrase "according to" helps to integrate a direct quotation with the writer's ideas.

"Bill 186 does not consider that many students who have just entered the school system and who do not yet speak English are very bright kids--their English is just not at the level it needs to be. Given time, their test scores will improve. But it's not fair to discriminate against these kids."[5] Obviously, these are matters that the students cannot control, and it is certainly not the fault of the teachers or the schools, who are in all likelihood doing their utmost to help the students assimilate and learn English. To penalize schools for including children who do not yet have a full grasp of the English language, as Senate Bill 186 does, is unfair and does little to promote improved teaching.

Uilk   3

Transition sentence carries readers from one main point to the next.

Senate Bill 186 is also discriminatory to students in low-income communities. Representative Gloria Leyba, D-Denver, comments that the report cards mandated by the bill punish low-income and inner-city school districts for circumstances they cannot control.[6] Because the residents of low-income communities do not make as much money as do residents of high-income communities, the taxes collected for the school districts in low-income communities are not as high. Thus, low-income schools often lack appropriate books, supplies, and technology--as well as adequately prepared and compensated teachers. While some students are capable of doing well in such low-resource schools, socioeconomic factors strongly contribute to their ability or inability to excel. State Senator Pat Pascoe goes so far as to say that if he ranked the state's schools from the lowest socioeconomic level to the highest, they would match almost exactly the schools' test scores from lowest to highest. According to Pascoe, "giving schools a letter grade without considering the socioeconomic background of the children merely measures the knowledge the children bring to school with them. I believe schools should be measured on what they add to a child's knowledge."[7] The amount of funding a school district receives directly affects the level of education that children within it will receive. However, Senate Bill 186 does nothing to address this discrepancy in resources--it provides little if any financial aid to help failing schools improve themselves. Instead it contributes to the disparity between low-income and high-income schools--and the stigmatization of the children who attend poorer schools. Another state legislator, Paul Zimmerman, D-Thornton, condemns the bill, saying, "It digs a hole, it kicks these kids in, and then it allows no escape."[8] Children who have no control over where they were born and what economic level they were born into are being penalized for these very factors.[9]

Senate Bill 186's grading system will also encourage the segregation and stigmatization of poorer schools. Because most schools will strive to receive an academic performance grade of A, they are not going to want students who will bring their average down. And if the school is a charter school, it can determine who gets in and who doesn't. Colorado public school teacher Andrew Mays asks, "Are these schools going to want students who are not proficient in English, who have mental or physical handicaps, or who come from families with limited economic means? Probably not, so they will begin discriminating against children who might bring test averages down."[10] Soon children will be fighting to get into schools in which they were earlier guaranteed a place. Meanwhile, parents trying to decide which school would be best for their children will avoid "problem" schools, preferring to send their children to an A-graded school, if they are allowed, rather than a school that, perhaps unfairly, has received a grade of D or F. This only furthers the cycle of discrimination, segregation, and stigmatization. How will this improve schools?

Uilk   4

Meanwhile, the bill's use of charter schools as a solution to the problems found in many public-run schools is weak at best. Senator Pascoe asserts, "There is no reason to believe a charter school takeover would improve educational achievement. State studies have not shown that charter schools are any more effective than other schools, if one compares schools with children at the same socioeconomic level."[11] Public school teacher Patty Smith furthers the argument: "Although charter schools have shown to be effective in some areas, many have failed to improve student learning, and many once-successful charter schools have now closed. It's not the solution to this complex problem. It's only a Band-Aid."[12]

Governor Owens argues that his bill addresses the lack of parental involvement in many schools. Owens wants parents to become more involved with their children's education and, therefore, take more steps to improve their children's schools on their own.[13] However, Owens does not understand the challenges some parents face in certain communities. Many lower-income parents are not as aware of educational issues as more affluent parents are, and some do not have the same educational expectations for their children. Meanwhile, parents of bilingual students may not even speak English themselves. It's not that they don't *want* to understand, but rather that they *can't*. Other parents simply must work longer hours to support their families and are therefore not home to supervise their children. These parents have been forced to decide that it's more important to feed their children than to focus on their schooling. To penalize those children whose parents, for whatever reason, are unable to be more involved in their education is doubling the disadvantage.

Damon Smith, a teacher at Kepner Middle School in Denver, which probably would get a D or F under the bill's plan, agrees with Governor Owens that there needs to be some kind of educational reform. However, he believes that Bill 186 unfairly targets certain schools, while praising others.[14] Smith says that soon there will be no reward for teaching at-risk youth. Teachers will be punished because their class averages aren't high enough, although those teachers may have a large number of bilingual students or students with disabilities. Take, for example, a teacher who loves helping hard-to-teach children get excited about school. She likes working with students from challenging backgrounds because she wants to help at-risk students succeed. The students don't fare well on tests--at least not yet--but they are learning more than they ever have before, and they are enjoying the process. When the test results come in and the averages are low, what actions might be taken against that teacher? The administration may start considering whether to even keep her on staff. Will removing such a teacher improve student test scores? More important, will removing such a teacher help these children learn any better?

I agree there needs to be something done about Colorado's education

Uilk   5

system, but Senate Bill 186 is not the way to do it. As a community, we can come up with a better plan. Test scores do not always show progress in the classroom. If we choose not to step back and look at the bigger picture, children might become numbers and not individuals. Legislators should take the money they are holding over school administrators' heads--as well as the money it will take to set up the bill's program--and instead provide programs, resources, and teachers in needy school districts. Instead of closing down schools or turning them into charter schools, legislators should provide teachers with training on how to teach the disadvantaged. Instead of taking away valuable resources from low-income schools, legislators should provide students with equal resources in all classrooms. Research also indicates that successful reform requires a major investment in our very young children with quality child care and preschool.[15] These efforts would help improve schools more than any report card or label will.

As a society, our main concern should be that *all* students are well educated, regardless of their class or background. Senate Bill 186 is an effective way to wake people up, but that's all it's good for. It is prejudiced, discriminatory, and it will hurt the children who need the most help. American public schools have produced over two centuries' worth of productive and intelligent citizens, and we need to concentrate today on the schools that are not living up to this proud history--not by grading them, however, but by imagining and implementing better ways to educate our children.

Conclusion reinforces the writer's thesis.

Uilk   6

Notes

First line of each note is indented one-half inch, or five spaces.

1. State of Colorado General Assembly, *Senate Bill 00-186*, 31 January 2000, http://www.leg.state.co.us/inetcbill.nsf/fsbillcont/ 222894FAE70D5C6E872568460071E6D3?Open&file=186_enr.pdf (15 April 2000).

Note numbers are not raised.

2. Bill Owens, "Open Letter to Colorado's Teachers from Governor Owens," *State of Colorado Home Page*, 15 December 2000, http://www.state .co.us/childrenfirst/teacher_letter_amd_23.pdf (15 April 2000).

Authors' names are listed first name first.

3. Lynn Bartels, "Owens Likes Furor over Education Reform Plan," *Rocky Mountain News*, 18 March 2000, A7.

4. State of Colorado.

5. Patty Smith, interview by author, 25 March 2000.

6. Fred Brown, "Retooled School Bill Goes Back to Senate: Grading System Concerns House Democrats," *Denver Post*, 22 March 2000, A14.

7. Pat Pascoe, "School Reform Will Do Little to Help Children Learn," *The Pascoe Express*, 15 March 2000, http://home.earthlink.net/~dambois/ latest.html (16 April 2000).

Last name and page number refer to an earlier source by the same author.

8. Brown, A14.

9. Hector Gutierrez, "Teachers Protest Grading Proposal," *Rocky Mountain News*, 26 March 2000, A20.

10. Andrew Mays, interview by author, 25 March 2000.

Last names without page numbers refer to a source with no page numbers.

11. Pascoe.

12. Smith.

13. Owens.

14. Bartels, A7.

15. Pascoe.

Entries are double-spaced and follow the same numerical order as in the text.

Uilk   7

Bibliography

First line of each entry is flush with left margin. Additional lines are indented one-half inch, or five spaces.

Bartels, Lynn. "Owens Likes Furor over Education Reform Plan." *Rocky Mountain News* 18 March 2000, A7.

Brown, Fred. "Retooled School Bill Goes Back to Senate: Grading System Concerns House Democrats." *Denver Post* 22 March 2000, A14.

Gutierrez, Hector. "Teachers Protest Grading Proposal." *Rocky Mountain News* 26 March 2000, A20.

Newcomb, JoElyn, and Linda Shoemaker. "Owens' Risky Experiment for Children." *Denver Post* 17 February 2000, B11.

Owens, Bill. "Announcement of 'Putting Children First: A Plan for Safe and Excellent Public Schools.'" *State of Colorado Home Page*. 8 December 1999. http://www.state.co.us/childrenfirst/ChildrenFirstRemarks.htm (16 April 2000).

---. "Open Letter to Colorado's Teachers from Governor Owens." *State of Colorado Home Page*. 15 December 1999. http://www.state.co.us/childrenfirst/teacher_letter_amd_23.pdf (15 April 2000).

Pascoe, Pat. "School Reform Will Do Little to Help Children Learn." *The Pascoe Express,* 15 March 2001. http://home.earthlink.net/~dambois/latest.html (16 April 2000).

"Putting Children First: A Plan For Safe and Excellent Public Schools." *State of Colorado Home Page*. 19 November 1999. http://www.state.co.us/childrenfirst (15 April 2000).

State of Colorado General Assembly. *Senate Bill 00-186*. 31 January 2000. http://www.leg.state.co.us/inetcbill.nsf/fsbillcont/222894FAE70D5C6E872568460071E6D3?Open&file=186_enr.pdf (15 April 2000).

Entries are double-spaced and alphabetized by authors' last names.

Government body listed as the source author.

APPENDIX B

Guide to Resources in the Disciplines

Use this guide as a starting point for finding resources in specific disciplines. A more comprehensive guide containing over 1,000 hyperlinked entries can be found on the *Bedford Researcher* Web site (**http://www.bedfordresearcher.com**). Each category that follows is organized into three subcategories: print resources, databases, and Web sites.

CONTENTS

GENERAL

Print Resources

Book Review Index. Detroit: Gale, 1965–.
Over 100,000 reviews of books, periodicals, and journals.

New York Times Index. New York: New York Times, 1948–.
Easy access to all material from the *New York Times.* Abstracts provided of significant news events.

Readers' Guide to Periodical Literature. New York: Wilson, 1900–.
Index to English-language periodicals.

Databases

ArticleFirst (OCLC, available through OCLC FirstSearch)
Over 12,000 articles from 1990 to the present.

Biography Index (Wilson, available through OCLC FirstSearch)
Covers biographical information for books and periodicals for a wide range of subject areas.

Dissertation Abstracts Online (Bell & Howell, available through OCLC FirstSearch)
Includes dissertations and theses on a wide range of academic subjects.

Electric Library (Infonautics)
Articles on a wide range of subjects. Sources include books, newspapers, magazines, TV/radio transcripts, and pictures.

FactSearch (Pierian, available through OCLC FirstSearch)
Emphasis on sources with date-linked and statistical evidence. Includes over 99,000 records on subjects such as economics, the environment, health, political issues, and social issues. Some full-text sources.

Lexis-Nexis Academic Universe
Provides sources on legal, medical, news, business, and reference issues. Many entries full-text sources.

Newspaper Abstracts (Bell & Howell, available through OCLC FirstSearch)
Includes all types of newspaper articles, editorials, commentaries, and reviews from over 50 newspapers. Most entries include abstracts.

Periodical Abstracts (Bell & Howell, available through OCLC FirstSearch)
Contains abstracts from general and academic publications.

Readers' Guide Abstracts (Wilson, available through OCLC FirstSearch)
Bibliographic citations of articles from popular magazines from 1983 to the present. Many include abstracts, and listings cover a wide range of topics.

Readers' Guide to Periodical Literature (Wilson, available through SilverPlatter)
Electronic equivalent of the print version of the *Readers' Guide to Periodical Literature.*

Web Sites

About.com: http://www.about.com/
Boasts depth and breadth, with 700 guide sites organized into 36 channels—ultimately covers over 50,000 subjects.

Academic Info: http://www.academicinfo.net/
No-nonsense, information-only site provides online college-level research material via its subject directory.

Open Directory: http://dmoz.org/
Subject directory managed by volunteer editors provides organization missing in automated search engines.

Yahoo!: http://www.yahoo.com/
Popular directory directs you to categorized and reviewed indexes to sites. Provides daily updated links to news and topics of interest.

ARTS AND HUMANITIES

General

Print Resources

The American Humanities Index. Albany: Whitston, 1974–.
Indexes English-language humanities journals and periodicals. Limits entries to articles from American publications.

Humanities Index. New York: Wilson, 1974–.
Indexes English-language periodicals for all areas of the humanities.

Databases

Arts and Humanities Citation Index (Web of Science—Institute for Scientific Information)
A multidisciplinary database that contains sources from 1975 to the present.

Humanities Abstracts (Wilson, available through OCLC FirstSearch)
This database includes abstracts of book reviews, original fiction, articles, and play reviews.

Web Sites

Academic Info's Humanities Directory: http://www.academicinfo.net/subhum.html
Humanities section of collegiate-level research searchable by keyword or subject index.

Links2Go Arts and Humanities Directory: http://www.links2go.com/search?search=Art+and+Humanities
Uses automated technology that compiles and prioritizes links to relevant Internet content.

Open Directory's Arts Directory:
http://dmoz.org/Arts/
Contains a varied subject index, including individual links to topics such as body art, animation, and native and tribal arts, in addition to typical categories such as dance and literature.

Search Engine Guide's Arts Links: http://www
.searchengineguide.com/pages/Arts/
Subcategorized by architecture, artists, crafts, humanities, performing arts, and photography.

Art

Print Resources

Art Index. New York: Wilson, 1929–.
Covers both foreign and domestic art publications. Entries are listed by author and subject, and cover a wide range of art topics.

Concise Oxford Dictionary of Art and Artists.
Ed. Ian Chilvers. 2nd ed. Oxford: Oxford UP, 1996.
Covers art from the fifth century b.c. to the present. Includes biographies of notable artists as well as information on topics such as techniques, styles, museums, galleries, and more.

Contemporary Artists. Ed. Joann Cerrito.
4th ed. New York: St. James, 1996.
Biographical profiles of over 800 contemporary artists. Covers painting, sculpture, performance art, graphic arts, and more.

Dictionary of Art. Ed. Jane Turner. 34 vols.
New York: Grove's Dictionaries, 1996.
Thirty-four volumes of information on general art topics and artists. Entries appear alphabetically. The final volume is a cumulative index.

Databases

Art Abstracts (Wilson, available through OCLC FirstSearch)
Covers a range of art subjects including painting, sculpture, photography, film, and folk arts.

Art Index (SilverPlatter)
Index includes entries from over 350 journals.

Bibliography of the History of Art (J. Paul Getty Trust and the Centre National de la Recherche Scientifique, available through Research Libraries Group)
Covers European and American art. Entries include a citation and an abstract.

Web Sites

Internet Resources for Art Historians: http://
www.wisc.edu/arth/otherresources.html
Specifically geared to aid students and scholars in locating art history resources.

Open Directory's Arts Directory:
http://dmoz.org/Arts/
Contains a varied subject index, including links to topics such as body art, animation, and native and tribal arts in addition to typical categories such as dance and literature.

World Wide Art Resources: http://wwar.com/
Access to arts services, artist portfolios, and global arts resources.

Architecture

Print Resources

Dictionary of Architecture and Construction.
Ed. Cyril M. Harris. 3rd ed. New York: McGraw, 2000.
An alphabetical list of short definitions of architecture terms, people, and events. Includes many illustrations.

Kidder Smith, G.E. *Source Book of American Architecture.* New York: Princeton Architectural, 1996.
Includes information and descriptions of over 500 buildings. Also provides historical surveys of the development of American architecture.

Packard, Robert T., and Balthazar Korab. *Encyclopedia of American Architecture.* 2nd ed.
New York: McGraw, 1995.
Alphabetical list of information on art topics and artists. Specialized terms are defined, and entries offer further reading suggestions.

Database

Architecture Database (British Architectural Library, Royal Institute of British Architects)
Entries include articles, reviews, obituaries, and biographies from 400 periodicals as well as monographs, conference proceedings, exhibition catalogs, and technical literature.

Web Site

Cyburbia: Architecture Resource Directory:
http://cyburbia.ap.buffalo.edu/pairc/
architecture_resource_directory.html
Contains a directory of Internet resources relevant to planning, architecture, urbanism, and growth.

Communications

Print Resources

Block, Eleanor S., and James K. Bracken.
Communication and the Mass Media: A Guide to Reference Literature. Englewood, CO: Libraries Unlimited, 1991.
Detailed descriptions of reference sources in the communications and media field. Organized by type of source.

Index to Journals in Communication Studies through 1995. Ed. Ronald J. Matlon. Annandale, VA: National Communication Association, 1997.
Provides the tables of contents for twenty-four journals in the field. Also includes an author index and a keyword index.

Web Site

ComWeb Megasearch: http://cios.org/ www/comweb.htm
Search engine offers full-text search (only by keyword) of 20,000 Web pages from communications, journalism, speech, and rhetoric-related sites.

Drama

Print Resources

Cambridge Guide to the Theatre. Ed. Martin Banham. New York: Cambridge UP, 1995.
Covers the history and practice of worldwide theater. Thousands of entries are listed alphabetically.

Critical Survey of Drama. Ed. Frank N. Magill. Rev. ed. 7 vols. Pasadena: Salem, 1994.
Essays on drama topics organized by author and genre. Final volume is a cumulative index.

Drama Criticism. Ed. Lawrence Trudeau. 9 vols. Detroit: Gale, 1991–.
Designed specifically for the beginning student or the average theatergoer. Provides critical essays on authors and their works.

Database

International Index to the Performing Arts (Bell & Howell)
Sources covering a wide range of topics within performing arts.

Web Site

Theater Resources Index: http://wwar.com/ theater/perform.html
Information about artists, events, and academic drama departments.

Film

Print Resources

International Dictionary of Films and Filmmakers. Ed. Samantha Cook. 5 vols. Detroit: St. James, 1994.
Separate volumes for films and filmmakers, actors and actresses, and writers, producers, and artists. Provides a summary, a list of film credits, and suggestions for further reading.

Katz, Ephraim. *The Film Encyclopedia.* 4th ed. New York: Harper, 2001.
Includes nearly 8,000 entries on film topics, with biographical information on actors, directors, producers, screenwriters and cinematographers. Provides definitions of industry terminology.

New York Times Film Reviews. Time-Life Books. New York: Garland, 1913–.
Over 100,000 reviews of motion pictures. Organized by the date the review appeared in the *New York Times.* Provides a name index for searching author, director, producer, composer, etc.

Database

International Film Archive (International Federation of Film Archives, available through SilverPlatter)
An index of the International Federation of Film Archives. Also includes a list of members and a bibliography of publications.

Web Sites

American Film Institute Search: http://www .afionline.org/links/
American Film Institute's home site describes the AFI's founding as a nonprofit organization and its mission in preserving film heritage. Lists links to AFI's history of awards, events, and projects.

The Cinema Connection: http://online .socialchange.net.au/tcc/
Classic films throughout cinematic history and art/cult classics.

ScreenSite: http://www.tcf.ua.edu/ ScreenSite/contents.htm
Provides educators and students with resources to facilitate the study of film and television.

Foreign Languages and Literatures

Print Resource

Campbell, George L. *Concise Compendium of the World's Languages.* New York: Routledge, 1995.
Lists and provides nontechnical descriptions of over 100 international languages.

Web Sites

ERIC Clearinghouse on Languages and Linguistics: http://www.cal.org/ericcll/
Information on current developments in research, instructional methods and materials, program design and evaluation, teacher training, and assessment practices in language and cultural education.

WWW Foreign Language Resources:
http://www.itp.berkeley.edu/~thorne/
HumanResources.html
Foreign language sites intended for native English speakers, listed in alphabetical order from Arabic to Yiddish.

History

Print Resources

Cambridge Ancient History. **Ed. Averil Cameron and Peter Garnsey. 14 vols. Cambridge: Cambridge UP, 1998.**
Articles by historians on chronologically arranged topics covering only ancient history.

Documents of American History. **Ed. Henry Steele Commager and Milton Cantor. 10th ed. Englewood Cliffs: Prentice, 1988.**
Compiles primary resources from American history, including letters, speeches, memoirs, poetry, newspaper articles, sermons, and more.

Encyclopedia of American History. **Ed. Richard B. Morris and Jeffrey B. Morris. 7th ed. New York: Harper, 1996.**
Entries are arranged in chronological order and by subject, with a separate section of biographies and a basic chronology of American history.

Encyclopedia of World History. **Ed. Patrick K. O'Brien. New York: George Philip, 2000.**
Over 6,500 articles on all areas of world history, arranged alphabetically. Includes a general chronology of people, dates, and events spanning 17,000 years.

Slavens, Thomas P. *Sources of Information for Historical Research.* **New York: Neal-Schuman, 1994.**
Bibliographic information for all types of reference sources such as online databases.

Databases

America: History and Life **(ABC-Clio)**
A bibliographic reference to American and Canadian history.

Historical Abstracts **(ABC-Clio)**
Over 500,000 entries on the history of the world, excluding Canada and the United States. Lists sources from 2,000 journals worldwide.

Web Sites

Argos Directory of Ancient and Medieval History and Culture: http://argos.evansville.edu/
Peer-reviewed, limited-area search engine covers the ancient and medieval worlds. Argos is designed to provide specific and academically viable results for teachers, students, and scholars.

Gateway to World History: http://www
.hartford-hwp.com/gateway/index.html
Main links to search utilities for history resources, academic departments and university home pages, and world history associations.

Horus Links: http://www.ucr.edu/h-gig/
horuslinks.html
Focuses on areas of history; histories of specific countries, times, and places; online services about history; and links collections.

WWW Virtual Library: History: http://www
.ukans.edu/history/VL/
The central catalog of the main network provides direct links to other network sites through its index. Select from main categories and by countries and regions.

Law

Print Resources

Burnham, William. *Introduction to the Law and Legal System of the United States.* **St. Paul: West, 1995.**
Specifically aimed at those who have not completed law school. Provides an overview of primary topics and methodology in American law. Appendix includes an extensive list of notable cases.

Great American Court Cases. **Ed. Mark Mikula and L. Mpho Mabunda. 4 vols. Detroit: Gale, 1999.**
Describes and analyzes over 800 notable court cases, most of which were heard by the Supreme Court. Provides an overview of each case, a discussion of its importance, and excerpts from judges' opinions.

Database

Index to Legal Periodicals and Books **(Wilson, available through OCLC FirstSearch and SilverPlatter)**
Includes references to journals, yearbooks, reviews, and government publications. Most are from North America and the United Kingdom.

Web Sites

CataLaw: http://www.catalaw.com/
Lists all major worldwide catalogs of law and government on the Internet. Site can be searched by legal topics and regional (including international) law as well as for extra information such as legal directories and law societies.

Internet Legal Resource Guide: http://www
.ilrg.com/
This categorized index of over 4,000 international sites is quality controlled to include only the most substantive legal resources.

Literature

Print Resources

The Bloomsbury Guide to Women's Literature. **Ed. Claire Buck. New York: Bloomsbury, 1992.**
Essays provide a geographical and historical overview of women's literature. Reference section includes alphabetical entries for works, authors, and terms. Some entries include bibliographic information.

Contemporary Literary Criticism. **Ed. Sharon R. Gunton. Detroit: Gale, 1973–.**
Criticism and general information on authors of all genres of writing. Each entry includes passages from and reviews of author's work.

Dictionary of Literary Biography. **Detroit: Gale, 1978–.**
Covers an enormous range of authors, periods, genres, cultures, and nationalities. Provides personal information, a list of publications, and critical reviews.

Nineteenth Century Literary Criticism. **Detroit: Gale, 1981–.**
Excerpts from criticism on all genres of creative writing. Covers authors who died between 1800 and 1899.

Twentieth Century Literary Criticism. **Detroit: Gale, 1978–.**
Excerpts from criticism on all genres of creative writing. Covers authors who died between 1900 and 1960.

Databases

Contemporary Authors **(Gale)**
Biographical and bibliographical references for over 90,000 authors. Covers fiction, nonfiction, poetry, journalism, drama, movies, television, and more.

MLA International Bibliography **(MLA, available through OCLC FirstSearch)**
A bibliography of sources in the fields of literature, language, linguistics, and folklore.

Women Writers Online **(Brown University Women Writers Project)**
Full-text editions of works by over 100 English and American women writers. Focuses on authors from 1500 to 1830.

World Authors **(Wilson, available through SilverPlatter)**
Information on over 10,000 authors from a variety of cultures and across genres.

Web Sites

The English Server: **http://eserver.org**
A niche for literature not necessarily found on the more commercial sites. Offers 42 collections on diverse topics such as design, race, contemporary art, and more. Hypertext, audio, and video recordings are also available.

Internet Public Library Online Literary Criticism Collection: **http://www.ipl.org/ref/litcrit/**
Substantive literary research and criticism; solely dedicated to critical and biographical sites about authors and their works.

LitLinks: **http://www.bedfordstmartins.com/litlinks/**
Organized alphabetically by author within five genres with annotated links.

Voice of the Shuttle: **http://vos.ucsb.edu/**
Humanities Web page directs you to extensive sets of literature links organized by period, nation, subculture, and genre. Includes highlights pages of noteworthy sites.

Music

Print Resources

The Guinness Encyclopedia of Popular Music. **Ed. Colin Larkin. 6 vols. New York: Stockton, 1995.**
Articles on titles, composers, musicians, record labels, and more. Includes discographies where appropriate.

Music Article Guide. **Philadelphia: Information Services, 1986–.**
Annotated guide to articles in over 250 American music periodicals. Designed for school and college music educators.

The New Grove Dictionary of Music and Musicians. **Ed. Stanley Sadie. 29 vols. New York: Grove's Dictionaries, 2001.**
Articles on musicians and works. Entries for musicians include bibliographies and works. Expansive geographical and historical coverage.

Databases

MusicLiterature **(RILM, available through OCLC FirstSearch)**
Indexes sources from over 500 scholarly journals, including articles, books, bibliographies, catalogs, conference proceedings, discographies, and more.

The New Grove Dictionary of Music and Musicians **(MacMillan, information available at http://www.macmillan-reference.co.uk/GroveMusic/)**
Electronic version of the print dictionary. Entries for musicians include bibliographies and works.

Web Sites

UCC Resources for Study and Research in Music: **http://www.ucc.ie/ucc/depts/music/online/**
Music links organized by period, traditional and popular, and genre and thematic categories.

Worldwide Internet Music Resources: http://
www.music.indiana.edu/music_resources/
Indiana University School of Music site offers useful
links to students looking for material with an academic approach.

Philosophy

Print Resources

Bynagle, Hans E. *Philosophy: A Guide to the
Reference Literature.* 2nd ed. Englewood, CO:
Libraries Unlimited, 1997.
Intended for professionals, teachers, students, and
librarians.

Cambridge Dictionary of Philosophy. Ed. Robert
Audi. 2nd ed. Cambridge: Cambridge UP, 1999.
Over 4,000 entries on philosophers and philosophical
terminology. Detailed overviews of the subfields of
philosophy.

Encyclopedia of Classical Philosophy. Ed. Donald J. Zeyl. Westport, CT: Greenwood, 1997.
Covers Greek and Roman philosophy and philosophers
from the sixth century B.C. to the sixth century A.D.

The Philosopher's Index. Bowling Green, OH:
Philosopher's Information Center, 1978–.
Indexes over 400 journals and books in the field from
1940 to the present. Organized by subject and author
headings.

Database

The Philosopher's Index (available through
SilverPlatter)
An index and bibliography of philosophy books and
journals.

Web Sites

Noesis: Philosophical Research Online:
http://noesis.evansville.edu/
Provides access to both scholarly research and a forum
for scholars to publish research. Includes several online journals and encyclopedias.

Philosophy in Cyberspace: http://
www-personal.monash.edu.au/~dey/phil/
Divided into five main categories: branches of philosophy, text-related information (such as journals and
libraries), organizations, forums, and miscellaneous
topics.

Religion

Print Resources

Dictionary of Religions. Ed. John R. Hinnells.
New York: Penguin, 1995.
An alphabetical listing of topics and issues concerning
worldwide religions. Includes a bibliography and index.

The Encyclopedia of Religion. Ed. Mircea
Eliade. 16 vols. New York: Macmillan, 1987.
An expansive encyclopedia of articles on international religions. Covers historical religious issues as
well as contemporary topics. Entries listed alphabetically.

World Religions. New York: Macmillan, 1998.
Covers religious ideas and the practice of religion
worldwide. Provides definitions for important terms.

Database

ATLA Religion (American Theological Library
Association, available through OCLC
FirstSearch)
An index of publications that spans all religions but
emphasizes western religions.

Web Site

Rutgers University Virtual Religion Index:
http://religion.rutgers.edu/vri/index.html
This site's list of categorical links is diverse and coherent in its divisions, and the index is efficiently designed to analyze and highlight important content of
sites to speed research.

Writing

Print Resources

Encyclopedia of Rhetoric and Composition. Ed.
Theresa Enos. New York: Garland, 1996.
Over 450 entries on major people, concepts, and
applications.

An Introduction to Composition Studies. Ed.
Erika Lindemann and Gary Tate. New York:
Oxford UP, 1991.
A general introduction to the composition field.

Database

ERIC (available through OCLC FirstSearch)
Includes over 900,000 annotated references from
*Resources in Education and Current Index to Journals
in Education.*

Web Sites

Research Links in Rhetoric and Composition:
http://instruction.ferris.edu/taylorj/rhetcomp
.htm
Links to journals, Web guides, bibliographies, and
university-maintained sites dedicated to rhetorical
study.

Writing@CSU Links: http://writing.colostate
.edu/resources/
Collection of links to Internet-based writing resources. Includes references for writing across the curriculum as well as topic search sites and tools such as
grammar guides, glossaries, and composition tips.

SOCIAL SCIENCES

General

Print Resources

Social Sciences Citation Index. **Philadelphia: Institute for Scientific Information, 1973–.**
Helps determine the largest, most popular, and most used journals in the field.

Social Sciences Index. **New York: Wilson, 1974–.**
Covers English-language periodicals. Range of fields includes anthropology, criminal justice, economics, law, political science, psychology, women's studies, and more.

Databases

Social Sciences Abstracts **(Wilson, available through OCLC FirstSearch and SilverPlatter)**
Abstracts of articles concerning the social sciences. Includes articles, interviews, biographies, and book reviews.

Social Sciences Citation Index **(Web of Science — Institute for Scientific Information)**
Includes references, bibliographic information, some author abstracts, and links to full-text sources.

Social Sciences Index **(Wilson, available through SilverPlatter)**
Designed for easy use by students, teachers, and researchers.

Web Sites

Research Resources in Social Science: **http://www.researchresources.net/**
General resources on social sciences. Best suited as a starting point for investigation.

Social Science Internet Gateway: **http://sosig.ac.uk/welcome.html**
Browse or search the database of online resources selected and described by subject experts, or use the Social Science Search Engine. Designed for researchers and practitioners of the social sciences, business, or the law.

Anthropology

Print Resources

Abstracts in Anthropology. **Ed. Roger W. Moeller and Jay F. Custer. Westport, CT: Greenwood, 1970–.**
Entries include bibliographic information and abstracts. Articles on a range of current and significant anthropology topics.

Encyclopedia of Social and Cultural Anthropology. **Ed. Alan Barnard and Jonathan Spencer. New York: Routledge, 1996.**
Designed for use by students and teachers. Includes a glossary of terms and suggestions for further reading.

Encyclopedia of World Cultures. **Ed. David Levinson. 10 vols. Boston: G.K. Hall, 1991–.**
Intended for a general audience. The volumes are organized alphabetically by geographic area. Also has a glossary of technical terms.

Web Sites

Academic Info's Anthropology Directory: **http://www.academicinfo.net/anth.html**
Social and cultural anthropology, physical and biological anthropology, and links to general organizations, educational resources, and directories on the Web.

Anthro.net: **http://www.anthro.net/**
Choose from 53 anthropology-related topics to reach specific bibliographic references and links to Internet resources.

Anthropology Resources on the Internet: **http://home.worldnet.fr/~clist/Anthro/index.html**
Collection of links to university departments, anthropological institutions, and resources subdivided by specific focus or branch of study.

Economics

Print Resources

Index of Economic Articles. **Nashville: American Economic Association, 1886–.**
Provides both subject and author indexes.

Journal of Economic Literature. **Nashville: American Economic Association, 1886–.**
Articles and book reviews on economic topics. Each article has a bibliography.

Databases

ABI/Inform **(Bell & Howell, available through OCLC FirstSearch)**
This database indexes articles from professional publications, scholarly journals, and trade magazines around the world.

EconLit **(American Economic Association, available through OCLC FirstSearch and SilverPlatter)**
Citations for over 400,000 dissertations and articles from 1969 to the present.

Web Sites

ECONLinks: **http://www.ncat.edu/~simkinss/econlinks.html**
Developed to provide students with easy access to basic economic and financial information available on the Web.

EconoLink: http://www.progress.org/
econolink/
User-friendly site lets you select from categories: best
sites for content, research, and innovation; best sites
for journalists, activists, and students; and other economics sites.

Education

Print Resources

Berry, Dorothea. *A Bibliographic Guide to
Educational Research.* 3rd ed. Metuchen, NJ:
Scarecrow, 1990.
An annotated bibliography of sources in the field of
education. Title and subject indexes.

Encyclopedia of Educational Research. Ed.
Marvin Alkin. 6th ed. 4 vols. New York:
Macmillan, 1992.
A list of articles on educational research, each with a
substantial list of references.

The Encyclopedia of Higher Education. Ed.
Burton R. Clark and Guy Neave. 4 vols.
Oxford: Pergamon, 1992.
A collection of analytical articles on topics in higher
education. Articles are arranged by subject and orga-
nized alphabetically.

Unger, Harlow G. *Encyclopedia of American
Education.* New York: Facts on File, 1996.
Designed for students and all members of the education community. Covers all areas of American education.

Databases

Education Abstracts (Wilson, available
through OCLC FirstSearch and SilverPlatter)
Covers all education levels from preschool through
college and a wide range of education issues.

Education Full Text (Wilson, available through
SilverPlatter)
Lists sources from 1983 to the present and includes
abstracts and full text from August 1994 on.

Education Index (Wilson, available through
OCLC FirstSearch and SilverPlatter)
Indexes over 450 current periodicals and yearbooks
for all levels of education. Topics include critical thinking, teaching methods, curriculum, and legal issues in
education.

ERIC (available through OCLC FirstSearch,
Cambridge Scientific Abstracts, and
SilverPlatter)
Includes more than 900,000 annotated references
from *Resources in Education and Current Index to
Journals in Education.*

Web Sites

Education Index: http://www.educationindex
.com/
Annotated guide provides not only lists of links but
summaries of each site. Directory includes topics from
pre-K through college as well as continuing education
and careers.

Education World: http://www.education-
world.com/
Updated daily, this site focuses on current issues in the
education field, including technology in the classroom, relevant legislative action, and interviews with
educators.

EducatorsNet: http://www.educationsearch
.com/
Focuses on primary- and secondary-level public school
concerns, such as safety, testing and standards, reform, policy, education and politics, and community
involvement.

Geography

Print Resources

*Companion Encyclopedia of Geography:
The Environment and Humankind.* Ed. Ian
Douglas, Richard Huggett, and Mike
Robinson. New York: Routledge, 1996.
Articles on geography issues arranged under larger
subject headings. Each entry provides a bibliography
and suggestions for further reading.

World Geography. Ed. Ray Sumner. 8 vols.
Pasadena: Salem, 2001.
Provides general information about nations, physical
geography, natural resources, human geography, and
economic geography for each region.

Database

GEOGRAPHY (Elsevier, available through
SilverPlatter)
An international compilation of journals, books, reports, and theses. Entries have both bibliographic information and abstracts.

Web Sites

GEOSource: http://www.library.uu.nl/
geosource/
Contains links to Web pages with information in car-
tography, environmental science and policy, human
geography, physical geography, and planning science.

*Social Science Internet Gateway Geography
Directory:* http://sosig.ac.uk/geography/
Information is divided by resource type: papers and
reports, bibliographic databases, data sources, governmental bodies, news, organizations, journals, and
research projects/centers.

Government

Print Resources

Derbyshire, J. Denis, and Ian Derbyshire. *Encyclopedia of World Political Systems.* 2 vols. Armonk, NY: Sharpe, 2000.
Historical information on and explanation of features of governments around the world. Organized geographically and alphabetically. Provides suggestions for further reading and a cumulative index.

Encyclopedia of American Government. 4 vols. Englewood Cliffs: Salem, 1998.
A list of alphabetical articles on all aspects of the U.S. government.

Encyclopedia of the American Constitution. Ed. Leonard W. Levy and Kenneth L. Karst. 2nd ed. New York: Macmillan, 2000.
Alphabetical listing of articles related specifically to the Constitution. Covers related court cases.

Databases

Congressional Universe (Lexis-Nexis)
Congressional publications, records of congressional hearings, information on committees and members and on specific bills and laws.

GPO Monthly Catalog (U.S. Government Printing Office, available through OCLC FirstSearch and SilverPlatter)
Sources include government-issued reports, studies, fact sheets, maps, handbooks, and more. Also provides records of congressional hearings on bills and laws.

PAIS International (OCLC Public Affairs Information Service, available through OCLC FirstSearch, Cambridge Scientific Abstracts, and SilverPlatter)
More than 400,000 entries including books, periodicals, reports, and government publications.

Web Sites

FedStats: http://www.fedstats.gov/search .html
This site provides easy access to the statistics and information produced by seventy U.S. federal government agencies.

FedWorld: http://www.fedworld.gov/
A program of the U.S. Department of Commerce, this site disseminates information made available by the federal government.

GOVBOT: http://ciir2.cs.umass.edu/Govbot/
A compilation of over 1.5 million Web pages from U.S. government and military sites.

Journalism

Print Resources

Biographical Dictionary of American Journalism. Ed. Joseph P. McKerns. New York: Greenwood, 1989.
Biographical information on nearly 500 persons important to American journalism.

Cates, Jo A. *Journalism: A Guide to Reference Literature.* 2nd ed. Englewood, CO: Libraries Unlimited, 1997.
Annotated descriptions of over 700 reference sources for journalism.

Ellmore, R. Terry. *NTC's Mass Media Dictionary.* Lincolnwood, IL: NTC, 1991.
An alphabetical list of over 20,000 definitions of important terms for television, radio, newspapers, film, and magazines.

Database

Gale Database of Publications and Broadcast Media (Gale Group)
Current information on newspapers, periodicals, radio and television stations, and cable TV companies.

Web Sites

Columbia Journalism Review Resource Guides: http://www.cjr.org/resources/
Consists of reports written exclusively by the *Columbia Journalism Review* or by the *CJR* in conjunction with other groups.

Journalism Access: http://www.mindy .mcadams.com/jaccess/
Access to online newspapers, university journalism departments, organizations, resource lists, and a link to materials on free speech, freedom of the press, and active roles of citizens.

Journalism Resources: http://bailiwick.lib .uiowa.edu/journalism/
Contains links to news archives, information sources, indexes, media law resources, journalism magazines, and teaching.

Political Science

Print Resources

A Bibliography of Contents: Political Science and Government. Santa Barbara: ABC-CLIO, 1975–.
Indexes current articles from periodicals in political science and related disciplines.

International Political Science Abstracts. Paris: International Political Science Organization, 1951–.
Includes bibliographic information and abstracts on journal articles in the field.

A New Handbook of Political Science. Ed. Robert E. Goodin and Hans-Dieter Klingemann. Oxford: Oxford UP, 1996.
Essays that provide an overview of the foundations, history, and current issues of political science. Organized by subdivisions within political science.

Databases

International Political Science Abstracts (International Political Science Association, available through SilverPlatter)
Indexes and abstracts articles from over 800 journals and yearbooks.

Political Science and Government Abstracts (Cambridge Scientific Abstracts)
Abstracts political science-related sources from 1975 to the present.

Web Sites

Political Information: http://www.politicalinformation.com/
Search policy and political sites, browse links to the latest political news, and skim the latest political headlines.

Political Science Resources on the Web: http://www.lib.umich.edu/libhome/Documents.center/polisci.html
A wide variety of materials, including document archives, information resources, statistics, news, court decisions, and more.

Politics.com: http://www.politics.com/
Contains links to the latest polls, nationwide election news, candidate information, media bites, political columns/editorials, and political humor.

Psychology

Print Resources

Biographical Dictionary of Psychology. Ed. Noel Sheehy, Anthony J. Chapman, and Wendy Conroy. New York: Routledge, 1997.
Biographical information on over 700 notable figures in the field of psychology.

Encyclopedia of Psychology. Ed. Alan E. Kazdin. 8 vols. Oxford: Oxford UP, 2000.
Over 1,500 articles on psychological concepts, events, figures, and methods.

Handbook of Child Psychology. Ed. William Damon. 5th ed. 4 vols. New York: Wiley, 1998.
Entries are organized under larger topical headings. Covers wide array of issues and topic in child psychology.

Reed, Jeffery G., and Pam M. Baxter. *Library Use: A Handbook for Psychology.* 2nd ed. Washington: APA, 1992.
Explains how to conduct library research specific to psychology.

Stratton, Peter, and Nicky Hayes. *A Student's Dictionary of Psychology.* 2nd ed. New York: Routledge, 1993.
Alphabetical list of definitions of psychology terminology. Intended specifically for students encountering psychology for the first time.

Databases

PsycARTICLES (American Psychological Association)
Provides full text of 42 journals published by the APA.

PsycINFO (APA, available through OCLC FirstSearch, Cambridge Scientific Abstracts, and SilverPlatter)
Offers references to professional and academic literature in psychology and related disciplines.

Web Sites

Encyclopedia of Psychology: http://www.psychology.org/
Information is classified by category: paradigms and theory, biological factors, environmental factors, people and history, publications, organizations, and career information.

Psychology Online Resource Central: http://www.psych-central.com/
Includes links to graduate schools, licensure, online research resources, conventions, and career planning.

Psych Web: http://www.psywww.com/
Links to scholarly resources, self-help resources, online brochures, careers and academic departments, and an APA style guide.

Social Work

Print Resources

Encyclopedia of Social Work. Ed. Richard L. Edwards and June Gary Hopps. 19th ed. Washington: National Association of Social Workers, 1995.
Alphabetical list of articles on topics in social work and related disciplines.

Ginsberg, Leon. *Social Work Almanac.* 2nd ed. Washington: National Association of Social Workers, 1995.
Facts and statistics on population, children, crime, education, health and mortality, mental health, and the social work profession.

Databases

Social Services Abstracts (Cambridge Scientific Abstracts)
Over 78,000 bibliographic references on current research in the discipline.

Social Work Abstracts Plus **(National Associa-tion of Social Workers, available through SilverPlatter)**
Contains over 35,000 records from social work jour-nals and related fields from 1977 to the present. Includes search aids such as finding word variants.

Web Site

Grassroots: Social Science Search: **http://www.andrews.edu/SOWK/grassroots.htm**
Information on field work, research, values, and ethics as well as on cultural and ethnic diversity, popu-lations at risk, social welfare policy and service, and social and economic justice.

Sociology

Print Resources

Bart, Pauline, and Linda Frankel. *The Student Sociologist's Handbook.* **4th ed. New York: Random, 1986.**
An overview of sociological foundations and method-ologies intended specifically for the sociology stu-dent. Includes sections on periodicals and reference sources.

A Dictionary of Sociology. **Ed. Gordon Marshall. Oxford: Oxford UP, 1998.**
Provides over 2,500 substantial definitions of sociol-ogy terms, methods, and brief biographies of key figures.

Johnson, Allan G. *The Blackwell Dictionary of Sociology.* **Cambridge, MA: Blackwell, 1995.**
Articles on a wide array of topics in sociology and related fields. A separate section of biographies of key figures.

World of Sociology. **Ed. Joseph M. Palmisano. Detroit: Gale, 2001.**
Concise explanations of 1,000 sociological topics, the-ories, concepts, and organizations. Arranged alpha-betically.

Databases

Criminal Justice Abstracts **(Sage, available through SilverPlatter)**
A list of sources from international journals, books, dissertations, reports, and unpublished papers.

Sociological Abstracts **(Cambridge Scientific Abstracts, available through SilverPlatter)**
Indexes information from over 2,600 journals as well as books, conferences, and dissertations.

Web Sites

Sociology Weblinks: **http://www.usi.edu/libarts/socio/sd_wblnk.htm**
Information is indexed by resource type: sociology megasites, sociological theory and works, research and careers in sociology, and journals.

The SocioWeb: **http://www.socioweb.com/~markbl/socioweb/**
An independent guide that categorizes information by type: commercial sites, theory, surveys/statistics, university department, writings, journals, and topical research.

Technical Communication

Print Resources

Eisenberg, Anne. *Effective Technical Commu-nication.* **2nd ed. New York: McGraw, 1992.**
An overview of the background, techniques, and applications of technical communication.

Encyclopedia of Technology and Applied Sci-ences. **11 vols. New York: Marshall Cavendish, 2000.**
Articles are arranged alphabetically and written for those without a strong background knowledge.

Web Site

Open Directory's Technical Writing Page: **http://dmoz.org/Arts/Writers_Resources/Non-Fiction/Technical_Writing/**
Information divided into businesses, organizations, and software categories as well as an annotated list of links to technical writing sites and resources.

Women's Studies

Print Resources

Andermahr, Sonya, Terry Lovell, and Carol Wolkowitz. *A Concise Glossary of Feminist Theory.* **New York: St. Martin's, 1997.**
Explanations for concepts of feminist theory.

Brownmiller, Sara, and Ruth Dickstein. *An Index to Women's Studies Anthologies.* **New York: G.K. Hall, 1994.**
Indexes over 500 anthologies across disciplines to identify articles related to women's studies.

A Reader's Guide to Women's Studies. **Ed. Eleanor B. Amico. Chicago: Fitz Dearborn, 1998.**
Brief descriptions of books on over 500 topics and people in women's studies.

Women's Studies Encyclopedia. **Ed. Helen Tierney. 2nd ed. 2 vols. Westport, CT: Greenwood, 1999.**
Alphabetically organized articles on a wide array of women's studies issues, people, and events. Focuses mostly on the United States.

Databases

***Contemporary Women's Issues* (Responsive Database Services, available through OCLC FirstSearch)**
Indexes books, journals, newsletters, research reports, and fact sheets. Provides information on women from over 150 countries.

***Women's Resources International* (National Information Services Corporation, available through BiblioLine)**
Includes bibliographic references for books, essays, and journal articles. Focuses on topics such as women's studies and feminist criticism and theory.

Web Sites

***Reading Room: Women's Studies Database:* http://www.inform.umd.edu/EdRes/Topic/ WomensStudies/ReadingRoom/**
A virtual reading room, this site includes a database of selected readings written by or about prominent women and indexes materials according to fiction, nonfiction, history, book reviews, poetry, and academic papers and articles.

***Women's Studies/Women's Issues Resource Sites:* http://research.umbc.edu/~korenman/ wmst/links.html**
An annotated list of sites that contain resources and information about women's issues.

NATURAL SCIENCES

General

Print Resources

***The Dictionary of Science.* Ed. Peter Lafferty and Julian Rowe. New York: Simon, 1993.**
Designed for both academic and general readers.

***Notable Scientists from 1900 to the Present.* Ed. Brigham Narins. 5 vols. Detroit: Gale, 2001.**
Biographical information on 1,600 scientists from all scientific disciplines. Offers selected works by each scientist and suggestions for further reading.

***Science and Technology Almanac.* Ed. William Allstetter. Phoenix: Oryx, 1999.**
Reports of notable news stories in each discipline as well as facts, figures, and statistics. Also includes sections on people, history, and countries.

***Scientific American Desk Reference.* New York: Wiley, 1999.**
Each chapter includes an overview, chronology, glossary, biographies, further reading suggestions, and topical articles for a range of disciplines.

Databases

***Complete Cambridge Sciences Collection* (Cambridge Scientific Abstracts)**
Covers full range of sciences and allows you to narrow your search to include databases for specific scientific disciplines.

***Science Citation Index* (Web of Science — Institute for Scientific Information)**
Indexes over 5,700 journals that span over 150 scientific disciplines.

***ScienceDirect* (Elsevier)**
Full-text articles from journals published by Elsevier Science and abstracts from major scientific journals.

Web Sites

***InvisibleWeb.com: Sciences:* http://www .invisibleweb.com**
Choose from 10 subcategories: life, earth, and social sciences; astronomy; chemistry; engineering; mathematics; physics; research and innovations; and publications.

***SciCentral:* http://www.scicentral.com/**
The latest research news in an extensive list of areas of scientific study, subcategorized as biological, health, physical and chemical, earth and space, engineering sciences, and analytical tools.

***Scientific American's Editors' Selections:* http://www.sciam.com/bookmarks/editselect .html**
A compilation by the editors at *Scientific American* of the more interesting, informative, and entertaining sites on the Web.

***SciSeek:* http://www.sciseek.com/**
Includes more atypical topics, such as cryptozoology and astroarcheology, in addition to biology, health sciences, etc.

Agricultural Sciences

Print Resources

***Biological and Agricultural Index.* New York: Wilson, 1914–.**
Indexes over 200 English-language periodicals in the field. Provides a separate listing of citations for book reviews.

***Encyclopedia of Agricultural Science.* Ed. Charles J. Arntzen and Allen M. Ritter. 4 vols. San Diego: Academic, 1994.**
Intended for both general and academic audiences, with thorough articles on a range of agricultural topics.

Databases

***AGRICOLA* (National Agricultural Library of the U.S. Department of Agriculture, available through OCLC FirstSearch and SilverPlatter)**
Bibliographic citations for journal articles, monographs, patents, technical reports, and more. Includes worldwide coverage of agriculture issues.

Biological and Agricultural Index (Wilson, available through OCLC FirstSearch and SilverPlatter)
Citations from a wide range of popular and professional journals. Also includes forestry and ecology.

Web Sites

AgriSurf: http://www.agrisurf.com/
Over 17,500 sites are organized into 34 main categories such as agritourism, aquaculture, feedlots, soil, organic farming, and education programs. Many sites are commercial or business related.

Internet Resources in Agriculture: http://www.nal.usda.gov/acq/intscsel.htm
Comprehensive topical index to resources selected by the U.S. Department of Agriculture's National Agricultural Library.

Astronomy

Print Resources

Astronomy and Astrophysics Abstracts. New York: Springer, 1969–.
Abstracts from journals, books, conferences, and more.

The Astronomy and Astrophysics Encyclopedia. Ed. Stephen P. Maran. New York: Van Nostrand Reinhold, 1992.
Approximately 400 articles on topics covering all areas in astronomy. Intended for a general audience.

Encyclopedia of the Solar System. Ed. Paul R. Weissman, Lucy-Ann McFadden, and Torrence V. Johnson. San Diego: Academic, 1999.
Information on all aspects of the solar system, with entries organized around the physical arrangement of the solar system.

Moore, Patrick. *Atlas of the Universe.* Cambridge: Cambridge UP, 1998.
Informative articles about the planets, sun, stars, and more. Numerous illustrations, photographs, and charts.

Database

SPIN (American Institute of Physics, available through AIP Online Information Service)
Indexes and abstracts current research and publications from major American and Russian journals. Focuses on astronomy and physics.

Web Sites

AstronomicaLinks: http://members.xoom .com/rjtiess/links.htm
Links subjects include articles, news, astronomers and astrophysicists, and terminology. Many of the links are to sites supported by academic institutions or NASA.

AstroWeb: http://www.stsci.edu/astroweb/ astronomy.html
An extensive index for space-related Web sites, offering nearly 3,000 resources pooled by individuals at seven educational institutions.

Athletics and Sports Sciences

Print Resources

Encyclopedia of Sports Science. Ed. John Zumerchik. 2 vols. New York: Macmillan, 1997.
A general reference source of articles on subjects in the sports sciences.

Oxford Handbook of Sports Medicine. Ed. Eugene Sherry and Stephen F. Wilson. Oxford: Oxford UP, 1998.
Articles and information in sports sciences and the treatment of sports-related injuries. Offers background and fundamentals of sports medicine.

Physical Education Index. Cape Girardeau, MO: Ben Oak, 1976–.
A subject index of domestic and foreign articles in fields such as sports medicine, physical education, physical therapy, and health.

Database

SPORTDiscus (Sport Information Resource Centre, available through OVID)
A database of mostly periodical articles. Includes sources from 1949 to the present, some with abstracts.

Web Sites

Scholarly Sports Sites: http://www.ucalgary .ca/library/ssportsite/
This subject directory brings together Web sites of interest to the serious sports researcher, kinesiology librarian, sport information specialist, and college student or faculty.

WWW Virtual Library Physiology and Biophysics Directory: http://physiology.med .cornell.edu/WWWVL/PhysioWeb.html
This site provides links to a wide range of interests, techniques, and publications relevant to contemporary physiology and biophysics as well as physiology and biophysics servers.

Biology

Print Resources

Becher, Anne. *Biodiversity: A Reference Handbook.* Santa Barbara: ABC-CLIO, 1998.
Explores issues surrounding biological diversity. Offers a chronology and biographies of important people in the field.

Biological Abstracts. Philadelphia: BIOSIS, 1926–.
Abstracts of articles from journals in the field. Includes author, organism, and subject indices.

Hine, Robert. *The Facts on File Dictionary of Biology.* 3rd ed. New York: Checkmark, 1999.
Almost 3,000 entries for frequently used terminology in the biological sciences.

Information Sources in the Life Sciences. Ed. H.V. Wyatt. 4th ed. London: Bowker-Saur, 1997.
Chapters cover types of reference works and specific life science disciplines. Detailed information on wide variety of sources.

Oxford Dictionary of Biology. 4th ed. Oxford: Oxford UP, 2000.
Definitions for key terms, biographies for biologists, and chronologies of important discoveries.

Databases

Biological Abstracts (BIOSIS, available through OVID)
References to biological research findings and clinical studies. Most of the citations include abstracts.

Biological and Agricultural Index (Wilson, available through OCLC FirstSearch and SilverPlatter)
Citations from a wide range of popular and professional journals. Also includes forestry and ecology.

BIOSIS (BIOSIS, available through OCLC FirstSearch)
Entries include sources from both popular and scholarly publications.

Web Sites

Biological Web Sites: http://www.geocities.com/Colosseum/Arena/7982/1.html
An alphabetical and topical list of biology-related sites on the Internet. Rates sites on ease of use, learning potential, interactive value, and text/image ratio.

BioNetbook: http://www.pasteur.fr/recherche/BNB/bnb-en.html
Search by topics in a classified listing, do a word search, combine word and topic searches, or search the site directory.

Chemistry

Print Resources

Chemical Titles. Columbus, OH: Amer. Chemical Soc., 1989–.
Entries are organized by keyword and are also in bibliographic form by topic.

Maizell, Robert E. *How to Find Chemical Information.* 3rd ed. New York: Wiley, 1998.
An extensive annotated list of chemistry sources, with entries organized by source type.

World of Chemistry. Ed. Robyn V. Young. Detroit: Gale, 2000.
Over 1,000 entries providing information on general terms, concepts, and applications of chemistry. Biographical entries for notable figures.

Database

Chemical Abstracts Student Edition (Chemical Abstracts Service, available through OCLC FirstSearch)
Indexes over 250 periodicals and over 200,000 dissertations.

Web Site

Academic Info's Chemistry Directory: http://academicinfo.net/chem.html
Geared toward college students and recent college graduates, offering annotated links to topical sites.

Ecology and Environmental Science

Print Resources

The Dictionary of Ecology and Environmental Science. Ed. Henry W. Art. New York: Holt, 1993.
Provides numerous cross-references, illustrations, charts, and diagrams for more thorough explanations.

Encyclopedia of Environmental Issues. Ed. Craig W. Allin. 3 vols. Pasadena: Salem, 2000.
Alphabetically arranged articles on a wide range of environmental issues.

Encyclopedia of Environmental Science. Ed. David E. Alexander and Rhodes W. Fairbridge. Boston: Kluwer, 1999.
Over 300 entries ranging from brief definitions of terms and concepts to longer articles on major topics within environmental science.

Databases

ECODISC (Elsevier, available through SilverPlatter)
Includes worldwide research on subjects within ecology and the ecosystem.

Envirofacts (U.S. Environmental Protection Agency)
Allows users access to databases maintained by the Environmental Protection Agency.

Environmental Sciences and Pollution Management (Cambridge Scientific Abstracts)
Entries focus on topics such as air quality, types of pollution, energy resources, hazardous waste, and water resource issues.

Web Sites

The Ecology WWW Page: http://pbil.univ-lyon1
.fr/Ecology/Ecology-WWW.html
A huge list of links connected to the study of ecology.

The EnviroLink Library: http://library
.envirolink.org/
A comprehensive resource for individuals and organizations interested in social and environmental change.

*The Need to Know Library — Ecology and
Environment Page:* http://www.peak.org/
~mageet/tkm/ecolenv.htm
Lists of useful publications, government organizations, and natural resources agencies.

WWW Virtual Library: Environment:
http://earthsystems.org/Environment.shtml
Offers subject headings linking to an index of related
Web pages in addition to a larger list of other environmental Web resources.

Food Sciences and Nutrition

Print Resources

Ensminger, Audrey H., et al. *Concise Encyclopedia of Foods & Nutrition.* 2nd ed. London:
CRC, 1995.
Aimed at a general consumer audience.

Food Science and Technology Abstracts. Reading, UK: International Food Information Service, 1928–.
Covers articles on food sciences, processes, and products. Indexes journals as well as books, patents, conference proceedings, and more.

Frank, Robyn C., and Holly Berry Irving. *The
Directory of Food and Nutrition Information.*
2nd ed. Phoenix: Oryx, 1992.
Includes information on professional and academic organizations along with bibliographic information and descriptions of journals, indexes, books, databases, and other sources.

Databases

Food Science and Technology Abstracts (International Food Information Service, available
through SilverPlatter)
A comprehensive database of sources in the food technology, food science, and human nutrition fields from books, journals, reports, theses, conferences, and more.

FOREGE Current Food Legislation (Leatherhead Food RA, available through SilverPlatter)
Focuses on worldwide legislation of food additives and food standards. Translates complex legal documents into a concise, easy-to-read format.

Web Site

HealthLinks: http://healthlinks.washington.edu/
Site has a monthly feature news story and provides links to medical journals and to reference, educational, and other health-related sites.

Geology

Print Resources

A Dictionary of Earth Sciences. Ed. Ailsa Allaby
and Michael Allaby. 2nd ed. Oxford: Oxford
UP, 1999.
Over 6,000 definitions of terminology and concepts in geology and related fields.

The Facts on File Dictionary of Earth Science.
Ed. John O.E. Clark and Stella Stiegeler. New
York: Checkmark, 2000.
Offers over 3,000 clear and concise explanations of frequently used terminology in earth science.

Geology. Ed. James A. Woodhead. 2 vols.
Pasadena: Salem, 1999.
Over 80 articles, each of which includes an overview of the subject, definitions of relevant terms, a bibliography, and cross-references.

Databases

GEOBASE (Elsevier, available through OCLC
FirstSearch and SilverPlatter)
Over 600,000 entries with abstracts of books, journals, monographs, reports, and more.

GeoRef (American Geological Institute, available through OCLC FirstSearch and Cambridge
Scientific Abstracts)
Over 2 million references to articles, maps, books, conference papers, and theses.

Web Sites

AGIWEB: http://www.agiweb.org/
The American Geological Institute's home page has links to affiliated sites, such as their magazine *Geo-
Times,* their data repository, and information about careers in the geosciences.

Geology.com: http://geology.com/
Contains a list of geology links organized by topic. Also includes links to an illustrated dictionary of geological terminology, geology journals, and professional organizations.

Mathematics

Print Resources

The Facts on File Dictionary of Mathematics.
Ed. John Daintith and John Clark. 3rd ed. New
York: Facts on File, 1999.

Entries span all branches of mathematics and often utilize illustrations and charts.

Peeva, K., et al. *Elsevier's Dictionary of Mathematics.* **New York: Elsevier, 2000.**
A comprehensive compilation of mathematical terminology with over 11,000 definitions.

Weisstein, Eric W. *CRC Concise Encyclopedia of Mathematics.* **New York: CRC, 1999.**
Mathematical definitions, formulas, figures, and references. Aimed at a general audience.

Database

MathSciNet **(American Mathematical Society, also available through SilverPlatter as MathSci Database)**
Combines two print publications (*Math Reviews* and *Current Mathematical Publications*) for reviews of mathematical research and current bibliographic records.

Web Sites

Mathematical Atlas: **http://www.math-atlas.org/**
Offers the ability to search within the index and a beginner's guide to math subject areas.

MathSearch: **http://www.maths.usyd.edu.au:8000/MathSearch.html**
A search engine for math-related topics by phrase.

Medicine and Health Sciences

Print Resources

Best of Health: Demographics of Health Care Consumers. **Ithaca: New Strategist, 1998.**
Explanations and statistics concerning issues in the health care system.

Compact American Medical Dictionary. **Boston: Houghton, 1998.**
A dictionary for the general reader that provides over 10,000 definitions for all types of medical terms.

Information Sources in the Medical Sciences. **Ed. L.T. Morton and Shane Godbolt. 4th ed. London: Bowker-Saur, 1992.**
Descriptions of print, journal, and online sources in all medical fields. Entries are organized by either type of source or branch of medicine.

Miller-Keane Encyclopedia and Dictionary of Medicine, Nursing, and Allied Health. **6th ed. Philadelphia: Saunders, 1997.**
Entries explain terms, concepts, and practical applications in medicine, nursing, and related fields.

World of Health. **Ed. Brigham Narins. Detroit: Gale, 2000.**
Entries cover a range of issues, principles, and recent developments in the medical sciences and related fields.

Databases

Health and Wellness Information or HealthInfo **(Gale Group, also available through OCLC FirstSearch)**
Draws on over 500 sources to provide records from periodicals, reference books, newsletters, and pamphlets.

MDXHealth **(Medical Data Exchange, available through OCLC FirstSearch)**
Consumer site lists records from magazines, medical journals, medical schools, hospital publications, and bulletins.

MEDLINE **(National Library of Medicine, available through OCLC FirstSearch and Cambridge Scientific Abstracts)**
A general medical database that includes sources in the dentistry and nursing fields.

Web Sites

HealthLinks: **http://healthlinks.washington.edu/**
Site has a monthly feature news story and provides links to medical journals and to reference, educational, and other health-related sites.

WWW Virtual Library of Medicine: **http://www.ohsu.edu/cliniweb/wwwvl/**
Access to government organizations, academic departments, online journals, and independent links. Includes both professional and general-interest sites.

Natural Resources

Print Resources

Dunster, Julian, and Katherine Dunster. *Dictionary of Natural Resources Management.* **Vancouver: UBC, 1996.**
Many entries use cross-referencing or illustrations for more thorough explanation.

Environmental Periodicals Bibliography. **Santa Barbara: Environmental Studies Inst., 1971–.**
Bibliographic information for sources, organized alphabetically by subject.

Database

Envirofacts **(U.S. Environmental Protection Agency)**
Allows users access to databases maintained by the Environmental Protection Agency.

Web Site

Natural Resources Research Information Pages: http://www4.ncsu.edu/~leung/nrrips.html
Organized into subject headings such as government agencies, institutions and organizations, and outdoor recreation research.

Nursing

Print Resources

Miller-Keane Encyclopedia and Dictionary of Medicine, Nursing, and Allied Health. 6th ed. Philadelphia: Saunders, 1997.
Entries explain terms, concepts, and practical applications in medicine, nursing, and related fields.

Mosby's Medical, Nursing, and Allied Health Dictionary. Ed. Kenneth N. Anderson. 5th ed. St. Louis: Mosby, 1998.
A comprehensive source for procedures, drugs, disorders, etc.

Database

British Nursing Index (Bournemouth University, available through SilverPlatter)
References to all major British nursing publications.

Web Sites

Nursing Websearch: http://www.nursingwebsearch.com/
A nursing search engine as well as annotated links organized by subject heading, including education, legal/ethical, and registered-nurse home pages.

Thornbury Nursing Research Engine: http://www.nursing-portal.com/nre.html
Links to other quality nursing sites. Includes a category search and chatrooms.

Physics

Print Resources

The Facts on File Dictionary of Physics. Ed. John Daintith and John Clark. 3rd ed. New York: Checkmark, 1999.
Includes over 2,400 definitions of terminology in the field. Provides appendices about elements, physical quantities, and conversion factors.

McGraw-Hill Dictionary of Physics. Ed. Sybil P. Parker. New York: McGraw, 1994.
General reference source for vocabulary in physics and related fields.

Physics Abstracts. Avenel, NJ: Institution of Electrical Engineers, 1898–.
Abstracts of articles in physics and related fields organized by topic.

Databases

Inspec (Institution of Electrical Engineers, available through OCLC FirstSearch and SilverPlatter)
Includes physics as well as electrical engineering, computers, and information technology sources. Covers mostly articles from journals but also important books, dissertations, and conference proceedings.

SPIN (American Institute of Physics)
Indexes and abstracts current research and publications from major American and Russian journals. Focuses on physics and astronomy.

Web Sites

The Internet Pilot to Physics: http://physicsweb.org/TIPTOP/
Services include an index, online discussion, selected online resources, and a virtual laboratory.

The Physics Encyclopedia: http://members.tripod.com/~IgorIvanov/physics/
A list of links to Web sites, institutions, journals, and online courses on various physics topics organized by subject.

Physics E-Source: http://www.dctech.com/physics/
This site offers a physics-based Internet search engine, monthly feature articles, and an extensive directory of other useful sites.

Physiology

Print Resources

Encyclopedia of Human Biology. Ed. Renato Dulbecco. 2nd ed. 9 vols. San Diego: Academic, 1997.
Each entry provides a comprehensive overview of the subject. Intended for a wide range of readers.

Netter, Frank H. *Atlas of Human Anatomy.* 2nd ed. East Hanover, NJ: Novartis, 1997.
Over 4,000 illustrations of the human body, each thoroughly labeled.

Shaw, Diane L. *Glossary of Anatomy and Physiology.* Springhouse, PA: Springhouse, 1992.
Brief definitions of thousands of terms.

Web Site

Yahoo's Physiology Directory: http://dir.yahoo.com/Health/Medicine/Physiology/
Site has a list of annotated direct links and a directory of links organized by subject heading.

Zoology

Print Resources

Animal Behavior Abstracts. Bethesda, MD: Cambridge Scientific Abstracts, 1973–.
Articles and sources from over 5,000 journals in the field. Entries include bibliographic information and abstracts.

Beacham's Guide to International Endangered Species. Ed. Walton Beacham and Kirk H. Beetz. 3 vols. Osprey, FL: Beacham, 1998.
Basic information on endangered species. Organized alphabetically by species.

International Wildlife Encyclopedia. Ed. Maurice Burton and Robert Burton. 25 vols. New York: Marshall Cavendish, 1991.
General information on animals. Final volume provides both general and systematic indices based on phylum, class, order, and family.

Databases

Animal Behavior Abstracts (Cambridge Scientific Abstracts)
Covers all major zoological journals. Includes both field and laboratory research.

Zoological Record Plus (BIOSIS, available through Cambridge Scientific Abstracts)
Provides an easy search of over 4,500 publications as well as books, reviews, and meetings. Covers a range of zoological topics from biochemistry to veterinary medicine.

Web Site

Internet Resource Guide for Zoology: http://www.biosis.org.uk/zrdocs/zoolinfo/zoolinfo.htm
Links organized by either subject or animal group. Also offers a search function, a list of conferences, and reference information.

ENGINEERING AND COMPUTER SCIENCE

Print Resources

Applied Science and Technology Index. New York: Wilson, 1958–.
Published annually, this work indexes over 350 English-language periodicals. Covers all engineering disciplines.

Chemical Engineering and Biotechnology Abstracts. Cambridge: Royal Society of Chemistry, 1971–.
Covers a full range of theoretical and practical topics in chemical engineering.

The Computer Science and Engineering Handbook. Ed. Allen B. Tucker Jr. Boca Raton, FL: CRC, 1997.
Information on 10 subfields of computer science and engineering. Intended for an audience of engineers and other professionals.

Coulson, J.M., et al. *Chemical Engineering.* 4th ed. 2 vols. Oxford: Butterworth-Heinemann, 1996.
Articles on physical operations used in chemical and allied industries, with each chapter covering a type of operation.

Dictionary of Computer Science, Engineering and Technology. Ed. Phillip A. Laplante. Boca Raton, FL: CRC, 2001.
Alphabetical compilation of over 7,500 terms covering major topics in computer science.

Dubbel Handbook of Mechanical Engineering. Ed. B.J. Davies. London: Springer-Verlag, 1994.
Chapters organized by topic. Numerous illustrations and figures to make definitions more accessible and thorough.

Electrical and Electronic Abstracts. Piscataway, NJ: INSPEC, 1989–.
Abstracts of articles on electrical engineering and electronics found in journals, books, reports, dissertations, and more.

Encyclopedia of Computer Science. Ed. Anthony Ralston, Edwin D. Reilly, and David Hemmendinger. 4th ed. New York: Grove's Dictionaries, 2000.
Over 600 articles on the history of computer science, recent developments in the field, notable figures, and more.

Information Sources in Engineering. Ed. K.W. Mildren and P.J. Hicks. 3rd ed. London: Bowker-Saur, 1996.
Descriptions of sources by specialized fields in engineering.

Mechanical Engineers' Handbook. Ed. Myer Kutz. 2nd ed. New York: Wiley, 1998.
Comprehensive volume on all aspects of mechanical engineering, with over 70 chapters organized by topic. Includes an index.

Perry's Chemical Engineers' Handbook. Ed. Robert H. Perry, Don W. Green, and James O. Maloney. 7th ed. New York: McGraw, 1997.
Information on chemical engineering including new developments, equipment, procedures, principles, calculation methods, and more.

Scott, John S. *The Dictionary of Civil Engineering.* 4th ed. New York: Van Nostrand Reinhold, 1993.
Terms and concepts in civil engineering and related fields.

Standard Handbook for Electrical Engineers.
Ed. Donald Fink and H. Wayne Beaty. 14th ed.
New York: McGraw, 2000.
Articles oriented toward practical applications of electrical engineering.

Webster, L.F. *The Wiley Dictionary of Civil
Engineering and Construction.* New York:
Wiley, 1997.
Over 30,000 descriptions and definitions of concepts,
terms, names, tools, and techniques in civil engineering and related technical fields.

Databases

Applied Science and Technology Abstracts
(Wilson, available through OCLC FirstSearch)
Sources include interviews, conferences, exhibitions,
new product reviews, technically valuable editorials,
letters, tables, charts, and more.

ASCE Civil Engineering Database
(http://www.pubs.asce.org/cedbsrch.html)
Bibliographic access to journals, conferences, books,
standards, manuals, and more.

Bioengineering Abstracts (Cambridge Scientific Abstracts)
Focuses on the medical and biological applications of
engineering. Sources come from journals, conference
proceedings, and Engineering Information's comprehensive database.

*Chemical Engineering and Biotechnology
Abstracts* (Deutsche Gesellschaft für Chemisches Apparatewesen, available through
Dialog@Carl)
Covers over 500 journals in addition to books, technical reports, and conference information.

Computer and Information Systems Abstracts
(Cambridge Scientific Abstracts)
A current index of sources pertaining to computer
research and applications.

Computer Information and Technology Collection (Cambridge Scientific Abstracts)
Updated monthly, this database includes the latest
theoretical research on and practical applications of
computers.

IEEE Xplore (Institute of Electrical and Electronics Engineers)
Includes IEEE transactions, journals, magazines, and
conference proceedings as well as IEEE standards.

Inspec (Institution of Electrical Engineers,
available through OCLC FirstSearch and
SilverPlatter)
Includes electrical engineering, computers, and information technology sources. Covers mostly articles
from journals but also books, dissertations, and conference proceedings.

Internet and Personal Computing Abstracts
(Information Today, available through Cambridge Scientific Abstracts)
Over 180,000 records of sources pertaining to personal computing as well as computers in business,
industry, and education.

Mechanical Engineering Abstracts (Cambridge
Scientific Abstracts)
Citations of journals, articles, and conference papers.
Aimed specifically at specialists and engineers.

Web Sites

*Academic Info's Mechanical Engineering
Directory:* http://www.academicinfo.net/
engringme.html
Includes a reference desk where basic information
and national standards may be found.

Civil Engineering Professions: iCivilEngineer:
http://www.icivilengineer.com/
Offers special features such as the academic department index, conference calendar, engineering news,
and best job search sites.

Open Directory's Electrical Engineering Directory: http://dmoz.org/Science/Technology/
Electrical_Engineering/
Provides links to over 200 electrical engineering sites
and offers additional subject headings under which
more information may be located.

Research Index Computer Science Directory:
http://citeseer.nj.nec.com/directory.html
Topics include numerous annotated links to papers
and presentations.

BUSINESS AND INFORMATION SYSTEMS

Print Resources

The Advertising Business. Ed. John Philip
Jones. Thousand Oaks: Sage, 1999.
Essays are organized into chapters covering operations, creativity, media planning, and integrated communications.

Business Periodicals Index. New York: Wilson,
1958–.
Indexes articles in English-language business journals
and periodicals. Includes a section for book reviews.

Encyclopedia of Business. Ed. Jane A. Malonis.
2nd ed. 2 vols. Detroit: Gale, 2000.
Over 700 essays on all aspects of business.

Encyclopedia of Business Information Sources.
Ed. James Woy. 15th ed. Detroit: Gale, 2001.
An annual guide to bibliographic information on over
1,000 business subjects and issues.

Finance Literature Index. Ed. Jean Louis Heck. 4th ed. New York: McGraw, 1994.
Bibliographic citations for articles about finance in over 50 leading journals.

Harry, Mike. *Information Systems in Business.* London: Pitman, 1994.
Background concepts, business organization, and development methodology for information systems.

International Financial Statistics Yearbook. Washington: International Monetary Fund, 2000.
A comprehensive collection of data on economic issues worldwide. Individual sections on each country provide thorough economic information.

Mahony, Stephen. *The Financial Times A-Z of International Finance.* London: Pitman, 1997.
Brief summaries of terms and concepts in international finance.

Mercer, David. *Marketing: The Encyclopedic Dictionary.* Oxford: Blackwell, 1999.
Brief definitions for basic marketing terms and longer entries for important marketing topics.

O'Brien, James A. *Management Information Systems.* Boston: Irwin, 1993.
Chapters cover foundation concepts, development, technology, applications, and management of information systems.

Databases

Banking Information Source (Bell & Howell)
Sources related to the financial services industry. Bibliographic information and abstracts from publications, theses, and newsletters.

Business and Industry (Responsive Database Services, available through OCLC FirstSearch)
Facts, figures, and key events for public and private businesses and industries. Covers trade magazines, the business press, and newsletters.

Consumers Index (Pierian, available through OCLC FirstSearch)
Information on products, services, and facilities, with a specific emphasis on consumerism and consumer protection.

FINDEX (Cambridge Scientific Abstracts)
A guide to publicly available market and business research. Approximately 33,000 records updated quarterly.

Gale Business Resources (Gale Group)
Detailed reports on over 1,000 U.S. and global industries include full-text essays and articles, rankings, statistical analyses, and more.

Wilson Business Abstracts (Wilson, available through OCLC FirstSearch)
Indexes and abstracts leading business magazines. Articles have citations and abstracts, while book reviews have only citations.

Web Sites

Association for Information Systems: http://www.aisnet.org/
Includes current news, information on conferences, and research reports.

BusinessWeb: http://www.businesswebsource.com/
Offers links and resources organized by type of industry. Search entire site or specific industry.

User's Guide to Research Assistant

HyperFolio for The Bedford Researcher

Prepared by Tari Fanderclai

About *Research Assistant: HyperFolio for The Bedford Researcher*

Research Assistant: HyperFolio for The Bedford Researcher gives researchers a convenient way to collect and organize all of their sources in a single place. *Research Assistant* is a software application that acts as a dynamic filing cabinet to help you manage the process of collecting electronic sources. You can select sources from anywhere on the Web or on your desktop and drag and drop them into a research collection. *Research Assistant* works equally well with texts, images, video files, and audio files. Once sources are collected, additional tools help you to document, evaluate, annotate, and organize sources. You can even create multimedia presentations or export work to share it with others.

Research Assistant: HyperFolio for The Bedford Researcher and the Research Writing Process

Research Assistant: HyperFolio for The Bedford Researcher was designed for students in college English courses that focus on research or include source-based writing. The typical research writing process actually is composed of a series of smaller processes, which sometimes overlap in time. Each of these smaller processes is covered in detail in *The Bedford Researcher*. (References below are to parts of the main text, not to this user's guide.)

Joining the Conversation—identifying a subject to write about and refining it into a workable research topic or question (see Part One)

Collecting Information—searching for sources, locating and collecting useful information, and managing the search process (see Part Two)

Working with Sources—critically evaluating your sources, determining their usefulness to your project, and sorting through to find the ones you will want to use in your final document (see Part Three)

Writing Your Document—organizing sources and other materials into a rough outline and then drafting, revising, editing, and designing the document (see Part Four)

Documenting Sources—citing the sources you use in your final project and creating a list of works cited, according to a standard documentation style (see Part Five)

Research Assistant helps you primarily during the middle of the process, when you are collecting, evaluating, planning, and organizing your materials. A special tool has also been developed to help you document your sources using the MLA, APA, or *Chicago* documentation style.

Each of the following sections in this user's guide focuses on activities related to working with information: collecting sources, taking notes about them (to record publication information, critical evaluations, and general information), and organizing them in preparation for creating the final document. There is also a section on the special tool for documenting sources and generating a draft bibliography. And because research is often shared either with other students or with instructors, a section near the end of this guide covers exporting your work and making it available to others.

Help and Support

This user's guide covers everything you'll need to use basic *Research Assistant* functions to assist you with collecting material for your research writing projects. Your instructor may have more suggestions about how to make the best use of *Research Assistant* for your specific assignments.

More detailed information about the many functions of *Research Assistant* can be found in the built-in help files: click the **Help** icon on the far right of the menu bar. In the help browser, select the **Contents** tab in order to use the help system as a user guide, choosing topics from the table of contents. Select the **Index** tab for an index to the topics covered in the help system. Or click the **Search** tab in order to search the help topics for the term or topic you're interested in.

For help sheets on advanced functions, guidance on incorporating the program into college research assignments, and general information, please visit the supporting Web site at **http://www .bedfordstmartins.com/researchassistant**.

If you have questions about installing the program that are not covered by the following instructions, please read the "readme" file included on the disk. For further technical assistance, please contact our technical support team at 1-800-936-6899 or techsupport@bfwpub.com.

And for more help with conducting research and writing research project documents, please visit the *Bedford Researcher* Web site (**http://www .bedfordresearcher.com**).

Installing *Research Assistant: HyperFolio for The Bedford Researcher*

System Requirements

WINDOWS

- Intel Pentium or compatible processor
- Windows 95 (SP1 or OSR2 recommended), Windows 98/SE/Me, Windows NT4 SP3 or later, Windows 2000, Windows XP
- Internet Explorer 4.0 or later
- Internet connection (optional)
- 10MB of available RAM
- 15MB of available disk space
- Color monitor (256 colors at 800 × 600 pixels or better recommended)
- Mouse

MACINTOSH

- PowerPC 7100 or newer
- Mac OS 8.1 or higher
- QuickTime 3
- Internet Explorer 4.0 or later
- Internet connection (optional)
- 16MB available RAM
- 4MB available disk space
- Color monitor (256 colors at 800 × 600 pixels or better recommended)
- Mouse

Note on Web Browsers

To use *Research Assistant: HyperFolio for The Bedford Researcher*, you need to install Internet Explorer. However, Internet Explorer does not need to be your default Web browser, nor do you need to use Internet Explorer while using *Research Assistant*.

Research Assistant was designed to be compatible with both Internet Explorer 4.x and Netscape 4.x browsers. You can also use it with any other browser that supports Spyglass SDI specifications, as well as with any application that supports OLE (Object Linking and Embedding) drag-and-drop or cut-and-paste operations.

Installation

WINDOWS

1. Close any applications that you have open on your computer.

2. Place the *Research Assistant* CD in your CD-ROM drive. Within a few seconds, the CD should automatically launch the installer.

3. If the installer does not start automatically, you will need to find and run the setup file:

    a. Double-click the **My Computer** icon on your desktop and navigate to your CD-ROM drive.

    b. Double-click the file **setup.exe**. The *Research Assistant* installer will start.

4. Once the installer has started, simply follow the prompts, clicking the **Next** button after you finish each panel. You will be able to select the destination folder and the name of the program group where the *Research Assistant* shortcut will be placed. Setup will also create a desktop shortcut you may use to launch *Research Assistant*. The installer will take only a few minutes to run.

Setup creates two subfolders in the Windows **My Documents** folder: **RAHF Assets** is used as a default storage location for Media Items that you collect; **RAHF Documents** is used as a default storage location for *Research Assistant* documents (Worksheets, Collections, and Templates). You may later change the location of these folders using the Preferences dialog box.

MACINTOSH

1. Close any applications that you have open on your computer.

2. Place the *Research Assistant* CD in your CD-ROM drive. Within a few seconds, the CD should automatically launch the installer.

3. If the installer does not start automatically, you will need to find and run the setup file:

    a. Double-click the disk icon that appears on your desktop.

    b. Double-click the file **RAHFInst**. The *Research Assistant: HyperFolio* installer will start.

4. Once the installer has started, simply follow the prompts, clicking the **Next** button after you finish each panel. You will be able to select the destination folder and the name of the program group where the *Research Assistant: HyperFolio* shortcut will be placed. Setup will

also create a desktop shortcut you may use to launch *Research Assistant*. The installer will take only a few minutes to run.

When it is first launched, *Research Assistant* will create two subfolders in the **My Documents** folder: **RAHF Assets** is used as a default storage location for Media Items that you collect; **RAHF Documents** is used as a default storage location for *Research Assistant* documents (Worksheets, Collections, and Templates). You can later change the location of these folders using the Preferences dialog box.

Collecting Sources: Collections and Media Items

You'll begin collecting sources as soon as you know your research topic. Once you've explored some of the sources and refined the focus of your research question, you'll probably need to collect further sources. The process for collecting sources with *Research Assistant: HyperFolio for The Bedford Researcher* at any stage of your work is the same.

Research Assistant will help you assemble sources in a centralized location and keep track of the sources you find. You won't have long lists of electronic bookmarks, dozens of word-processing files, and piles of paper notes and note cards to sort through; instead you'll have one fully documented Collection.

Each research source you find and put into *Research Assistant* is called a **Media Item**. Media Items can be text, images, audio and video files, and even links. A group of Media Items that is stored together in *Research Assistant* is called a **Collection**. Each Media Item is associated with a **Note Card** on which you can store bibliographic information, annotations, and your evaluation of the source.

Build a complete and thoroughly documented Collection to ensure that you have all of the information you need about the sources you find. Each time you find a good source for your topic, add it to your Collection, even if you aren't certain you'll need it. That way, you won't have to retrace your steps later if you decide you do need a source after all.

Starting *Research Assistant: HyperFolio for The Bedford Researcher*

Research Assistant: HyperFolio for The Bedford Researcher opens automatically when you launch your Web browser, or you can open it from your **Start** menu. (See page 415 for information on modifying *Research Assistant* startup options.)

When *Research Assistant* opens, the **Collection Icon** appears in the lower right corner of your screen. You can drag the Collection Icon to any location on your desktop.

Collecting Text from Web Pages

1. Find a Web page that contains useful information for your research project.

2. In your Web browser, highlight a selection of text that you want to save from a page.

3. Drag the selection to the Collection Icon and drop it there. An icon for the collected Media Item will appear in the Collection pane of the *Research Assistant* window.

4. A Note Card for the collected Media Item (in this case, the Media Item is the text selection) will open, prompting you to fill in bibliographic and other information about the source. You should fill in the Note Card for each Media Item as you collect it, eliminating the extra step of returning to the source later to look up the needed information. See page 408 for details on filling in your Note Cards.

5. As soon as you have collected your first source, you should name and save your Collection! See page 407 for instructions on saving a Collection.

Collecting Other Kinds of Media Items

Here are some more Media Items that you may want to collect.

WEB LINKS (URLs)

You can collect URLs for Web pages and other kinds of files as links that are placed in your Collection.

1. Select a link from a Web page, or select a URL from any text source, including the address or location bar in your Web browser.

    If the URL you want to collect is a link on a Web page, select the link by clicking the link and holding down the mouse button. Then you can drag the link to the Collection icon.

    If the URL you want to collect is in a text document and is not a link, select the URL by highlighting it. Be careful to highlight only the URL and not any surrounding text. If you select text around the URL, you will collect the highlighted material as text rather than as a link.

2. Drag the link or URL to the Collection icon and drop it there. *Research Assistant* will create a link icon in your Collection for the Media Item, and it will open a Note Card for you to record information about the source.

IMAGES

You can collect images from Web pages, from your desktop, or from any other applications that support the drag-and-drop function.

1. Select the image you want to collect.

    To select an image, click the image or the file icon for the image and hold down the mouse button. Then you can drag the image.

2. Drag the image to the Collection icon and drop it there. *Research Assistant* will add the image to your Collection and open a Note Card for you to fill in.

AUDIO AND VIDEO FILES

You can collect links to audio and video files in the same way you collect other Web links. You can also collect an audio or video file by dropping the file itself on the Collection icon.

CONTENT FROM PRINTED SOURCES

If you use your text editor or word-processing program to compile your notes from your printed sources, you can add these sources to your Collection.

You can open a file of your notes, select a section of the text, and drag it to the Collection icon. When you fill out your Note Card, do so with the publishing information for the printed source from which you took those notes.

You can also add a complete file of your notes to the Collection by simply dragging the icon for the file to the Collection icon. If you plan to collect your notes as complete files, you should create a separate notes file for each of your printed sources, because each Note Card for a collected Media Item can hold Publishing Info for just one source. If you put more than one source in a single collected Media Item, you will not be able to enter accurate Publishing Info on that item's Note Card. You might lose the information in such a case, and of course it will not be available to *Research Assistant* when you generate your bibliography from your Collection or Worksheet.

Saving a Collection

Once you've placed the first Media Item in a Collection, you should name and save your Collection.

If you are using *Research Assistant* on a computer in your classroom or lab, be sure that you do not save your *Research Assistant* files to a folder located on the computer you're using. Ask your instructor for help if you aren't sure where to save these *Research Assistant* files you create.

1. In your *Research Assistant* window, select **Save Collection** from the **File** menu or click the blue disk icon on the Collection toolbar. The **Save** dialog box will open.

2. In the **Save in** field, your **RAHF Documents** folder is selected. If you need to save your *Research Assistant* files in a different location, navigate to that location.

    Your **RAHF Documents** folder is located inside your **My Documents** folder and is a good place to store Collections, Worksheets, and other documents you create with *Research Assistant*.

    If you need to save your *Research Assistant* Collections, Worksheets, and other documents in a different location, create a folder for all of those documents. You will find it very useful to have all of them located in the same place.

3. In the **File name** field, type a name for your Collection.

4. Leave the **Save as type** field set to **RAHF Collections (*.hfc)**.

5. Click the **Save** button to save your Collection.

6. Save your Collection frequently as you work, either by selecting **Save Collection** from the **File** menu or by clicking the blue disk icon.

Working with an Existing Collection

There are a number of operations you may want to perform on a Collection you've already created.

OPENING EXISTING COLLECTIONS

1. Click the blue file folder icon on the Collection toolbar. The **Open** dialog box will appear.

2. In the Open dialog box, double-click the name of the Collection you wish to open. (If you have saved your Collection in a location other than the default **RAHF Documents** folder, you will need to navigate to that location in the **Look in** field at the top of the Open dialog box.)

OPENING MULTIPLE COLLECTIONS

It is sometimes useful to open several Collections at once; for example, you may be building a Worksheet in which you want to include Media Items from more than one Collection. Simply open each Collection as described in the preceding two steps.

The status bar in the lower left corner of your *Research Assistant* window tells you how many Collections you currently have open.

The Collection selector, located just below the icons for opening and saving existing Collections,

allows you to move between open Collections. Click the bar containing the name of the currently active Collection and you'll get a pull-down menu from which you can select a different Collection.

CLOSING A COLLECTION

1. Make sure that the Collection you want to close is the active Collection, the one named in the Collection selector bar.

2. Click the heavy black **X** to the right of the Collection selector.

If you've made changes to the Collection, you will be prompted to save them before the Collection closes. If you've made no changes, the Collection will simply be closed.

Adding Media Items to Existing Collections

Open the Collection and begin collecting more Media Items. The new Media Items will be placed in the open Collection.

If you have multiple Collections open, Media Items you collect will be placed in the active Collection—the Collection whose name appears in the Collections selector and whose contents appear in the Collection panel of the *Research Assistant* window. Use the Collection selector as described in the preceding steps to select the appropriate Collection.

Moving or Copying a Media Item from One Collection to Another

1. Open the two Collections you want to move or copy Media Items between.

2. Using the Collection selector as described in the preceding steps to move between the two Collections, find the Media Item you want to move or copy, and select it by clicking its name.

3. Right-click on the Media Item you selected. A popup menu will appear.

4. From the popup menu, select **Copy** if you want to copy the item to another Collection, or select **Cut** if you want to remove the item from this Collection and place it in a different Collection.

5. Select the Collection to which you want to copy or move the Media Item.

6. Place your cursor anywhere in the Collection panel and right-click. A popup menu will appear.

7. From the popup menu, select **Paste**, and the Media Item you cut or copied from the other Collection will be added to the currently selected Collection.

Using the Media Items in a Collection

VIEWING A MEDIA ITEM IN A COLLECTION

In the Collection panel of your *Research Assistant* window, double-click the icon for the Media Item you want to view. A viewer window containing the Media Item will open.

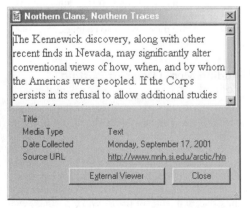

The viewer varies slightly for each type of Media Item; for example, sometimes you'll have an **External Browser** button rather than the **External Viewer** button in the example shown here.

Click the **External Viewer** or **External Browser** button to open the collected Media Item in another application; Web pages, for example, will be displayed in a browser window, while text will be displayed in your text editor or word-

processing program. If you wish to open more than one of your collected Media Items at the same time, you'll need to open them in external viewers.

Click the **Source URL** if you want to go to the original source of the Media Item.

Click the **Close** button to close the viewer.

OPENING THE NOTE CARD FOR A MEDIA ITEM IN A COLLECTION

Right-click on the icon for a Media Item in a Collection and select **Note Card** from the popup menu. The Note Card will open.

You can add, change, or delete information in any panel of the Note Card.

DELETING A MEDIA ITEM FROM A COLLECTION

Right-click on the icon for the Media Item you want to delete from your Collection and select **Delete** from the popup menu.

Research Assistant does not ask whether you're sure you want to delete a Media Item from your Collection. As soon as you select **Delete**, the item is deleted! Be careful to select the correct Media Item when deleting.

Taking Notes about Sources: The Note Card

When you're collecting sources for a research project, it's important to record information about the source when you collect it. Although you may not take all of your notes about the source right away, you should record the publishing information for the source so that you don't have to hunt for it later. You should also record enough information about the contents of a source to help you later when you're organizing your sources and deciding which ones to reread.

Each Media Item that you collect generates a Note Card. The Note Card is a convenient place for you to record publishing information and initial notes about a source. When you drop a Media Item on the Collection Icon, *Research Assistant: Hyper-Folio for The Bedford Researcher* opens the Note Card for that Media Item, and you should fill in as much of the Note Card as you can right away. (You can also edit the Note Card later if you need to.)

Note Cards have three panels: General, Publishing Info, and Evaluation. Click the tabs in the upper-left corner of the Note Card to move from one panel to another.

Filling in the General Panel

1. The Note Card will have a **Media Item Name** filled in. That's the name the item will have in

your collection. If the default name doesn't help you remember what the item is, give it a new name.

2. The Note Card will also have a **URL** filled in. This is the URL pointing to the original source, so don't change it!

3. The **Keywords** field allows you to enter keywords you can use if you want to search collections for items addressing particular topics. For information on keywords and searching, see the *Research Assistant* help feature, or go to the *Research Assistant* Web site.

4. In the **Notes** box, make some notes that will help you remember what the article is about. Because you can export a Note Card to a file and then print it, you can take all of your notes for a source in this box.

Your Note Card will now look something like this:

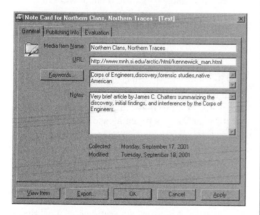

5. Click the **Apply** button to save the information you just entered.

Filling in the Publishing Info Panel

If you want *Research Assistant* to help you draft your bibliography, you must fill out the Publishing Info panel for each of your sources!

1. Click the selector at the right side of the **Source Type** box.

2. From the pull-down menu, select the type that best describes the source of the Media Item you just collected. You'll now see a number of fields to fill in.

3. Select the **Documentation Style**—MLA, APA, or *Chicago* style—that you'll use for your paper.

If the documentation style for your assignment is not listed, select the style that is closest to the one you need. Consult your instructor if you are not sure what to select. You can select any style for now, as the fields you need to fill in are the same for each one.

Be sure to select the same Documentation Style for all of the items in your Collection so that later, when you generate your bibliography, all of the items will be in the correct format!

4. Fill in the fields with the publishing information for this source.

Some sources, such as Web sites, do not always give all of the information requested by this form. Fill in all available information. When you are preparing your bibliography, you can consult your documentation style guide or your instructor for advice on what to do about the missing information.

If your source has multiple authors, click the small button to the right of the **Author** line. A form will open with multiple author lines so that you can record all of the authors.

Your Note Card window should now look something like this:

5. Click the **Apply** button to save the information you just entered.

Filling in the Evaluation Panel

It's critical to your research that you evaluate your sources carefully, considering whether the information is trustworthy and valuable. For example, what are the author's credentials? What might the author's biases be? Are the points in the source supported with evidence? How timely is the source? The Evaluation panel is a place to record your judgments of each source according to several important criteria. Later, when you're deciding which of your sources to use in your project document, you'll be able to review your evaluations to see which sources you consider the best.

Research Assistant can even provide you with a ranked list of your sources. You can find more information about ranking sources in the *Research Assistant* help feature, or on the *Research Assistant* Web site at **http://www.bedfordstmartins.com/researchassistant**.

1. Use the slider bars to rank your source according to the criteria listed.

    If you do not know what a particular ranking criterion means, click the **Information** icon to the right of the slider for that criterion. A popup window explaining the criterion will appear.

2. You can also write notes about your evaluation in the **Evaluation Notes** box near the bottom of the panel.

    Your Note Card window should now look something like this:

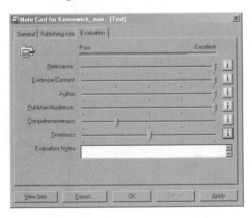

3. Click the **Apply** button to save the information you just entered.

4. Click the **OK** button to close your Note Card.

Opening and Editing an Existing Note Card

You can open a Note Card for an existing Media Item by right-clicking on the Media Item's name and selecting **Note Card** from the popup menu. You can edit a Note Card at any time.

Printing a Note Card

You might want a printed version of a Note Card, particularly if you've taken many of your notes for a Media Item on its Note Card. Although you can't print a Note Card directly, you can export the Note Card's contents to an HTML file, which you can open in your Web browser and print.

1. Open the Note Card you wish to print.

2. Click the **Export** button at the bottom of the Note Card. The **Export** dialog box will open.

3. In the Export dialog box, you can accept the defaults, or you can change the name and location of the file you're exporting.

4. Click the **Save** button.

5. You can now open the file in your Web browser and print it.

Working with Sources: Worksheets

Once you've gathered and taken notes on your sources, it's time to organize them in ways that will help you to begin your draft. Worksheets can help you as you sift through your sources to discover which will be useful in your project document and how you will use them.

A Worksheet allows you to organize a Collection of sources in a format that will help you with your writing. On your Worksheet, you could list the points you want to make in your document and organize your sources beneath each point. You could create lists of pros and cons and the sources that could inform your discussion of each. You could create an outline, a timeline, or any other presentation of the source materials from your Collection. You might create several Worksheets for a single project so that you can view your sources in a variety of ways. For some projects, your Worksheets may be more than a prewriting tool; they may comprise part of or even the entire final product.

Creating a New Worksheet

1. From the **File** menu, select **New** and then **Worksheet**, or click the green **New Worksheet** icon above the Worksheet panel. The **New Worksheet** dialog box will open.

2. On the right side of the New Worksheet dialog box, under **Create New**, select **Worksheet**.

3. In the white panel of the New Worksheet dialog box, select the **Blank Worksheet**, or see page 412 for information on using one of the templates.

4. Click the **OK** button, and a new Worksheet will open in the right panel of the *Research Assistant* window.

5. On the left side of the *Research Assistant* window, open the Collection or Collections from which you will select content for your Worksheet.

6. If you plan to print your Worksheet, you can design it with the page outlines in view. From the **File** menu, select **Page Setup** and choose your paper size. Then, from the **View** menu, select **Page Breaks**.

You're now ready to begin adding content to your Worksheet. Sometimes you'll add your sources first so that you can move them around the Worksheet and consider how they relate to one another. At other times, you'll begin by placing text boxes and other annotations of your own on the Worksheet, so that you can group your sources under headings that you create.

Adding Sources to Your Worksheet

1. Select a Media Item from a Collection, drag its icon to the Worksheet panel, and drop it there.
    Media Items are copied to Worksheets from Collections, rather than moved, so that if you place a Media Item from a Collection in a Worksheet, it is also still available in the Collection.

2. Drag the Media Item around the Worksheet until you have placed the item where you want it (you can move it at any time).

3. Save your Worksheet before you continue! See below for information about saving your Worksheet.

4. Continue adding Media Items from your Collection to your Worksheet, arranging them in the order you want them to appear.

Here's a section of a Worksheet that a writer has just begun:

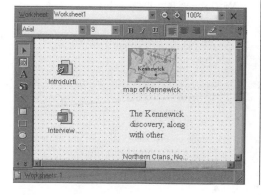

Adding Text and Annotations to Your Worksheet

The Worksheet toolbar, to the left of the Worksheet panel, provides a number of drawing and annotating tools.

For example, you can add text boxes to your Worksheet:

1. Click the **Text** button—the one with the capital A—on the Worksheet toolbar.

2. In the Worksheet space, click and drag the cursor with your mouse in order to draw a box.

3. Click inside the box and type your text there.

4. You can now drag your text box to any location on your Worksheet.

You can also use the drawing tools to add lines, arrows, circles, and boxes to your Worksheet. Click the icon for the drawing tool you wish to use and draw on your Worksheet using your mouse.

Here's a section of our sample Worksheet after the writer has added text and annotations:

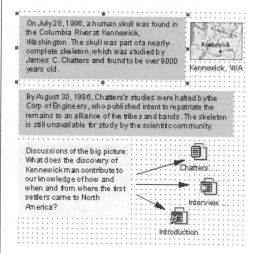

For more ways to enhance your Worksheet, see the *Research Assistant* help feature, or visit the *Research Assistant* Web site at **http://www.bedfordstmartins.com/researchassistant**.

Saving Your Worksheet

Save your Worksheet as soon as you've made the first addition to it, and save it frequently as you work on it.

If you are using *Research Assistant* on a computer in your classroom or lab, be sure that you do not save your *Research Assistant* files to a folder located on the computer you're using. Ask your instructor for help if you aren't sure where to save these *Research Assistant* files you create.

1. From the **File** menu, select **Save Worksheet,** or click the green disk icon above the Worksheet panel.

2. In the **Save in** field, your **RAHF Documents** folder is selected. If you need to save your *Research Assistant* files in another location, navigate to that location.

    Your **RAHF Documents** folder is located inside your **My Documents** folder and is a good place to store Collections, Worksheets, and other documents you create with *Research Assistant.*

    If you need to save your *Research Assistant* Collections, Worksheets, and other documents to a different location, create a folder for all of those documents. You will find it helpful to have all of them located in the same place.

3. In the **File name** field, type a name for your Worksheet.

4. Leave the **Save as type** field set to **RAHF Worksheets (*.hfw).**

5. Click the **Save** button to save your Worksheet.

6. Save your Worksheet frequently as you work, either by selecting **Save** from the **File** menu or by clicking the green disk icon.

Working with Existing Worksheets

OPENING AN EXISTING WORKSHEET

1. Click the green file folder icon on the Worksheet side of the toolbar. The **Open** dialog box will appear.

2. In the Open dialog box, double-click the name of the Worksheet you wish to open. (If you have saved your Worksheet in a location other than the default **RAHF Documents** folder, you will need to navigate to that location in the **Look in** field at the top of the Open dialog box.)

    You can now edit your Worksheet.

OPENING MULTIPLE WORKSHEETS

It is sometimes useful to open several Worksheets at once; for example, you might want to search several Worksheets for particular kinds of Media Items. Simply open each Worksheet as described in the preceding steps.

    The status bar at the bottom of the Worksheet panel of your *Research*

Assistant window tells you how many Worksheets you currently have open.

    Just below the icons for opening and saving existing Worksheets is the **Worksheet selector.** Click the bar containing the name of the currently active Worksheet and you'll get a pull-down menu from which you can select a different Worksheet.

CLOSING A WORKSHEET

1. Make sure that the Worksheet you want to close is the active Worksheet, the one you can see in the Worksheet panel of your *Research Assistant* window.

2. Click the heavy black **X** to the right of the Worksheet selector.

    If you have made changes to the Worksheet, you will be prompted to save them before the Worksheet closes. If you have made no changes, the Worksheet will simply be closed.

Viewing Individual Media Items in Your Worksheets

To view the contents of a Media Item in your Worksheet, double-click its icon.

    To view or edit the Note Card for a Media Item in your Worksheet, right-click on the icon for the Media Item and select **Note Card** from the popup menu.

Using Built-in Worksheets to Work through the Research Writing Process

Research Assistant: HyperFolio for The Bedford Researcher comes with several built-in, preformatted Worksheets designed to help you with specific parts of the research writing process. These Worksheets help you to organize your sources in predetermined ways, which in turn can help you discover new ways of looking at them and new ideas to use in your paper.

    Each of these built-in Worksheets is provided as a **Worksheet Template.** When you use a Worksheet Template to create a new Worksheet, you will have all of the formatting and information on the original Worksheet Template, but you will be able to add your own content.

    Here are the Worksheet Templates included on the *Research Assistant: HyperFolio for The Bedford Researcher* CD:

WHEN COLLECTING SOURCES

• The **Launch Pad** template contains links to search engines, directories, and other resources that can help you get started with your research. You can add your own notes and resources to the Worksheet.

- The **Search Library Catalogs**, **Search Databases**, and **Search the Web** templates help you conduct and keep track of searches as you explore your topic and collect information.

- The **Keywords and Searches** template helps you keep track of the searches you've conducted by recording the resources you've searched and the keywords used in each search.

- The **Exploring a Topic** template helps you identify who is interested in a topic and how they are affected by it.

- The **Similarities and Differences**, **Identifying Conversations**, and **Evaluating Conversations** templates can help you identify and choose a conversation that is most appropriate for your research writing situation.

WHEN WORKING WITH SOURCES

- The **Primary and Secondary Sources** template helps you identify primary sources (original works of art or literature or evidence provided directly by an observer of an event) and related secondary sources (sources that comment on or interpret primary sources).

- The **Grouping Your Sources** template helps you place your sources in related groups.

- The **Clustering** template provides you with a format for grouping your sources and using lines, circles, and other visual cues to indicate how they are related to one another.

- The **Timeline** template provides you with a format for creating a timeline and organizing your sources according to it.

- The **Positions on an Issue** template helps you identify the various positions on an issue and organize your sources according to those positions.

- The **Evidence for and against a Position** template helps you sort through the arguments for and against a particular position, identifying the strong and weak evidence in your sources for each side.

WHEN PREPARING TO WRITE YOUR DOCUMENT

- The **Causes Leading to a Single Effect** template helps you trace the multiple causes that lead to a single effect and organize your sources according to that causal explanation.

- The **Effects Brought about by a Single Cause** template helps you trace the multiple

effects brought about by a single initial cause and organize your sources according to that causal explanation.

- The **Developing an Argument** and **Reasons Supporting an Argument** templates help you define and develop an argument.

- The **Outline and Bibliography Builder** template assists you with building an outline and organizing your sources according to that outline. Once you've completed your outline Worksheet, you can generate a draft of your bibliography from the Worksheet (see page 414 for instructions).

Here's how to create a new Worksheet using a Worksheet Template:

1. From the **File** menu, select **New** and then **Worksheet**, or click the green **New Worksheet** icon above the Worksheet panel. The **New Worksheet** dialog box will open.

2. On the right side of the New Worksheet dialog box, under **Create New**, select **Worksheet**.

3. In the left panel of the New Worksheet dialog box, select the icon for the template you wish to use.

4. Click the **OK** button, and the Worksheet template will open in the Worksheet panel of the *Research Assistant* window.

5. Use this Worksheet as you would a Worksheet that you created yourself, adding your own sources, text, and other annotations and saving it as you would any other Worksheet.

Your instructor might provide you with templates tailored for particular assignments. If so, place the template file your instructor gives you in your **RAHF Documents** folder, which is located inside your **My Documents** folder. The next time you create a new Worksheet, the template your instructor gave you will be one of your options.

Printing a Worksheet

You can print an image of your Worksheet. You can also print individual texts and images from the Worksheet on separate pages, and you can print a separate list of URLs for all of the Media Items in the Worksheet.

1. If you have not already set up your paper size and margins, do so before printing.

- From the **File** menu, select **Page Setup**. The **Page Setup** dialog box will open.

- Select your paper size and orientation and change the margins if you need to.

- Click the **OK** button.

2. If you did not design your Worksheet with page breaks in view, view them now and make sure your Worksheet is within the borders of the pages.

   - From the **View** menu, select **Page Breaks**.

   - Make the necessary edits to your Worksheet layout.

3. From the **File** menu, select **Print Worksheet**, or click the **Print** icon on the *Research Assistant* toolbar. The **Print** dialog box will open.

4. In the **Select Printer** field, choose the printer to use.

5. Under **Page Range**, choose whether to print all pages, a selection of pages, or only the page you are currently viewing. (If your Worksheet is only one page long, some Page Range selections will be unavailable, as they will not apply.)

6. Indicate the **Number of Copies** to print.

7. If you need to change the orientation from Portrait to Landscape, click the **Layout** tab to do so.

8. Click the **Print** button, and the **Printing Options** dialog box will appear.

9. The **Printing Options** box contains a checklist of Worksheet contents that you can print. You can select any or all of them. By default, all options are checked, but printing all of the available materials from a Worksheet — even a small Worksheet — uses a great deal of paper. Be sure to deselect (uncheck) the print options for materials you don't need!

   - Check **Worksheet Image** to print the Worksheet itself.

   - Check **Text Contents** to print the contents of each text item from the Worksheet on separate pages.

   - Check **Images** to print copies of image items from the Worksheet on separate pages.

   - Check **Table of Links** to print a list of the URLs of all Media Items on a single page.

   - Check **Background** to print the Worksheet's background image on a separate page.

10. Click the **OK** button, and the Worksheet materials you have selected will be sent to the printer you chose.

Drafting a List of Works Cited: The Bibliography Generator

If you have filled out the Publishing Info panels in all of your Note Cards, *Research Assistant: Hyper-Folio for The Bedford Researcher* can use the information you provided to create a draft of a bibliography or works cited page. You can generate a bibliography draft from either a Collection or a Worksheet.

The bibliography that *Research Assistant* generates will be a head start on the bibliography or citations page for your project document. But it will not be perfect, and you will need to open it in your word-processing program and revise it before including it in your final document.

Here's how to generate your bibliography:

1. Make sure that the Media Items for all of the sources you need are included in a single Collection or Worksheet. If you need to, you can create a new Collection or Worksheet and copy to it the Media Items for the sources you'll use. Then you can generate your bibliography from that Collection or Worksheet.

2. Open the Collection or Worksheet that you will use to generate your bibliography.

3. From the **Tools** menu, select **Generate Collection Bibliography** or **Generate Worksheet Bibliography** according to whether you are using a Collection or a Worksheet to generate your bibliography. The **Export Bibliography** dialog box will open.

4. If the **Save in** field is not set to save to the folder where you are keeping your *Research Assistant* documents, navigate to the folder you want to use.

5. Type a name for your bibliography in the **File name** field.

6. Leave the **Save as type** field set to **Rich Text Format (*.rtf)**. (Rich Text Format files can be opened in any word-processing program.)

7. Click the **Save** button to save your bibliography.

8. You can now go to the folder where you saved your bibliography (if you are using the default folders, your file will be in your **RAHF Documents** folder, inside your **My Documents** folder). Double-click the icon for the file you just saved. The file will open in your word-processing program or your text editor, where you can edit it.

Sharing Your Work

After you've collected your sources and used one or more Worksheets to help you sift through and organize them, you're ready to begin the drafting process. At this point, you may want to share some of your work with classmates and your instructor in order to get feedback. You may also want to work with some of your materials in different formats.

One way to share your work or view it in a different format is to print it. You can export the contents of your Note Cards to files that you can print (see page 410). You can also print Worksheets as well as individual Media Items and other components of those Worksheets (see page 413).

There are two more ways to export and share information from *Research Assistant* files. You can export your Worksheets and Collections as Web pages (HTML files), and with some exceptions, you can email Collections and Worksheets.

EXPORTING COLLECTIONS AS WEB PAGES
(HTML FILES)

1. From the **File** menu, select **Export** and then **Active Collection**. The **Export Active Collection As** dialog box will open.

2. Set the **Save in** selection to the folder where you want to save your HTML file.

3. In the **File name** field, type a file name *with no spaces in it* for your Web page.

    URLs (Web addresses for Web pages) cannot have spaces in them, so you should use file names with no spaces in them for your Web pages.

4. Leave the selection in the **Save as type** field set to **Web Pages**.

5. Click the **Save** button.

6. You can now open your Web page file in your Web browser to view it. You can use a Web page editor to edit it, and you can place it in your Web directory for others to use.

The Web page that you generate from your Collection may have a few problems; for example, if any links point to files on your local machine, others who use your Web page will not be able to use those links. You can copy those local files to your Web directory and use your Web editor to change those links so that they point to the new file locations. Or you can use your Web editor to remove links that point to local files.

EXPORTING WORKSHEETS AS WEB PAGES
(HTML FILES)

1. From the **File** menu, select **Export** and then **Active Worksheet**. The **Export Active Worksheet As** dialog box will open.

2. In the **Save in** field, navigate to the folder where you want to save your Worksheet Web page.

3. In the **File name** field, enter a name *with no spaces in it* for your Worksheet Web page file.

    URLs (Web addresses for Web pages) cannot have spaces in them, so you should use file names with no spaces in them for your Web pages.

4. Leave the **Save as type** selection set to **Web Pages**.

5. Click the **Save** button to save your Worksheet Web page.

6. In the folder where you saved your Web page, you will also find a folder with the same name as your Web page file. In that folder are the assets—the text and Media Items—associated with your Worksheet. In order to share your Worksheet with others, copy both that folder and your Web page file to your Web directory. Be sure to put the folder and the Web page file in the same directory (folder) within your Web directory.

EMAILING WORKSHEETS

If you read and send email with a MAPI-compliant application, such as Netscape Mail, Outlook, or Outlook Express, you can use the **Send** function of *Research Assistant* to email a Worksheet as an attachment.

1. From the **File** menu, select **Send** to open the **Send Worksheet** dialog box.

2. If you are mailing your Worksheet to a recipient who has *Research Assistant* installed on his or her machine, you can select the **Native worksheet format**. If you are mailing your Worksheet to a recipient who does not have *Research Assistant*, select **Web Archive**.

3. Click **Send**, and your email client will open a message window so that you can write and address the message to accompany your Worksheet.

If an email recipient has trouble viewing your attached Worksheet, try exporting the Worksheet to a Web page format instead. Place the Web page and accompanying assets folder in your Web directory for your intended recipient to view them. Or use your zip application to compress the HTML file and the assets folder and email the archive file as an attachment.

Setting *Research Assistant: HyperFolio for The Bedford Researcher* Preferences

If you have *Research Assistant: HyperFolio for The Bedford Researcher* installed on your own computer, you can customize it by setting preferences. If you are using *Research Assistant* in a lab or classroom, consult your instructor before trying to set any preferences.

Complete information on *Research Assistant* preferences is available through the help feature or on the *Research Assistant* site at **http://www .bedfordstmartins.com/researchassistant**. Below is information on setting the most commonly used *Research Assistant* preferences.

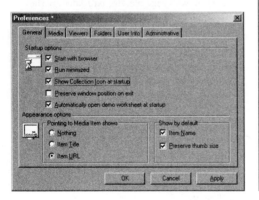

From the **Tools** menu, select **Preferences** to open the **Preferences** dialog box and click the tabs at the top of the Preferences box to select the kind of preferences you want to set.

When first opened, the Preferences window displays the **General** panel.

Use the checklist under **Startup options** to indicate what you want *Research Assistant* to do when it starts. Click unchecked boxes if you want to check them; click checked boxes if you want to uncheck them.

- **Start with browser**: Check this box if you want *Research Assistant* to start automatically when you launch your Web browser.

- **Run minimized**: Check this box if you want *Research Assistant* to minimize itself when you start.

- **Show Collection icon at startup**: Check this box if you want the Collection icon to be displayed on your desktop as soon as you start *Research Assistant*. (If the Collection icon is not displayed at startup, you can display it by selecting **Collection icon** from the *Research Assistant* **View** menu.)

- **Preserve window position on exit**: Check this box if you want *Research Assistant* to remember its position on your desktop when you exit the program and to open in the same location the next time you start the program.

- **Automatically open demo worksheet at startup**: Check this box if you want the *Research Assistant* Quick Start Worksheet to open automatically each time you open *Research Assistant*.

Acknowledgments (continued from p. vi)

Patrick Crossland, "Who's Getting into College?" Reprinted by permission of the author.

The Dewey Decimal Classification, © 1996–2001 OCLC Online Computer Library Center, Incorporated. Used with permission.

Kevin Fahey, "Hero without a Code: Hemingway's Nick Adams." Reprinted by permission of the author.

Gaele Lopez, "What's in It for Me? Voter Apathy among 18- to 24-Year-Olds in America." Reprinted by permission of the author.

Holly Richmond, "The Richmond Family History Web Site." Reprinted by permission of the author.

Maria Sanchez-Traynor, "Teachers at the Intensive English Program Are 'Here to Help.'" Reprinted by permission of the author.

Rianne Uilk, "The Impact of Senate Bill 186." Reprinted by permission of the author.

Figure and Photo Credits

Figure 2.1: Used with the permission of the Colorado State University.

Figure 2.3: Copyright © 2000 Bigchalk.com, Inc. All rights reserved.

Figure 2.4: Copyright © 2001 Altavista Company.

Figure 2.5: Copyright © 1992–2000 by Project Vote Smart. Reprinted by permission.

Figure 2.6: Reproduced with permission of Yahoo! Inc. Copyright © 2000 by Yahoo! Inc. YAHOO! and the YAHOO! logo are trademarks of Yahoo! Inc.

Figure 2.7: Text from Mariët Westermann, *A Worldly Art: The Dutch Republic, 1585–1718.* Copyright © 1996 by Laurence King Publishing, Ltd. Reprinted by permission. Art by Gerard Dou. *Old Woman Reading.* Copyright © Rijksmuseum Amsterdam.

Figure 2.8: British Broadcasting Corporation © 2001.

Figures 4.1a, 4.1b: Copyright © 1992–2001 OCLC. Reprinted with the permission of OCLC Online Computer Library Center, Inc. FirstSearch is a registered trademark of OCLC Online Computer Library Center, Incorporated.

Figure 4.2: Netscape Communicator Browser window © 1999 by Netscape Communications Corporation. Used with permission. Netscape Communications has not authorized, sponsored, endorsed, or approved this publication and is not responsible for its content.

Figure 5.2: Reprinted with the permission of Harvard University.

Figure 5.4: Copyright © 1992–2001 OCLC. Reprinted with the permission of OCLC Online Computer Library Center, Inc. FirstSearch is a registered trademark of OCLC Online Computer Library Center, Incorporated.

Figure 5.5: Copyright © 2000 Bigchalk.com, Inc. All rights reserved. This selection contains an excerpt from Robert Hughes, "Visionary Homebody: The 17th-century Dutch Painter Pieter de Hooch Raised Orderly Domesticity to the Level of Sanctity" from *Time* (February 22, 1999). Copyright © 1999 by Time, Inc. Reprinted by permission.

Figure 5.6: Reprinted with the permission of Google, Inc.

Figure 5.7: ProFusion Web Search Engine screen, **www.profusion.com**. Copyright Intelliseek, Inc. All rights reserved.

Figure 5.8: Copyright © 2000 by AskMe Corporation, Inc. Reprinted by permission.

Figure 5.9: Copyright © 1996–2002 Ask Jeeves, Inc. *Ask Jeeves* is a registered trademark of Ask Jeeves, Inc.

Figure 5.10: Copyright © 2001–2002 The Excite Network, Inc. All rights reserved.

Figure 5.13: Reproduced with permission of Yahoo! Inc. Copyright © 2000 by Yahoo! Inc. YAHOO! and the YAHOO! logo are trademarks of Yahoo! Inc.

Figure 6.2: Boston College Libraries Information System Quest main menu. Reprinted with the permission of the Thomas P. O'Neill Jr. Library, Boston College.

Figure 8.2: Dean Lillard and Jennifer Gerner, excerpt from "Getting to the Ivy League: How Family Composition Affects College Choice" from the *Journal of Higher Education* (November–December 1999). Copyright © 1999 by The Ohio State University Press. All rights reserved.

Figure 15.10: Reprinted with the permission of St. Olaf College, **http://www.stolaf.edu**.

Figures 15.15, 15.17: Used with the permission of the Colorado State University Department of English, **http://writing.colostate.edu**.

Figure 15.21: Netscape Communicator Browser window © 1999 by Netscape Communications Corporation. Used with permission. Netscape Communications has not authorized, sponsored, endorsed, or approved this publication and is not responsible for its content.

Figure 15.22: Reprinted with the permission of the Dell Computer Corporation.

Appendix A

Figure 1: Pieter de Jode after Adriaen vande Venne. *Stages of Life.* Private collection.

Figure 2: Gerard Dou. *Portrait of a Young Woman.* Private collection.

Figure 3: Johannes Verspronck. *Portrait of a Man.* Collection Rijksmuseum Twenthe, Enschede, The Netherlands.

Figure 4: Johannes Verspronck. *Portrait of a Woman.* Collection Rijksmuseum Twenthe, Enschede, The Netherlands.

Figure 5: Gerard Dou. *Old Woman Saying Grace.* Copyright © Bayerische Staatsgemäldesammlungen, Alte Pinakothek, Munich.

Index

Directory of Figures and Tables

Tables

Directory of Charts and Activities